Rediscovering the Bible

LUCAS GROLLENBERG

Rediscovering
the Bible

SCM PRESS LTD

Translated by Richard Rutherford from the Dutch
Nieuwe kijk op het oude boek
published by Elsevier, Amsterdam, The Netherlands
© Elsevier 1968

English translation first published 1969
by Newman Press, New York, under the title
A New Look at an Old Book

This edition © SCM Press 1978

334 01372 0

First British edition published 1978
by SCM Press Ltd
58 Bloomsbury Street, London WC1

Printed in Great Britain
by Richard Clay (The Chaucer Press) Ltd, Bungay, Suffolk

Contents

v

PART II
THE FOUR GOSPELS

Foreword

This book arose out of a series of lectures which I gave to Roman Catholic missionaries in South Africa. They had asked me to fill up certain gaps in their knowledge. In their theological instruction they had been told nothing about the modern historical approach to the Bible which had been commended and enjoined by Pope Pius XII in his Encyclical *Divino Afflante Spiritu* of 1943. In ten lectures, I was to explain the principles of the critical approach and to show how it worked, above all in connection with the four gospels. I accepted the invitation that I could spend most of the time at my disposal on the Old Testament, because I feel that familiarity with the origin and character of Israelite and Jewish literature is by far the best approach to understanding the special nature of the gospels.

Some time after I had given the lectures in various places in South Africa, the text was published in Dutch in a biblical monthly. A publisher then asked to issue them in book form. I revised the lectures for this, but did not expand them into a complete introduction to the Bible. The sub-title, 'An Exploration into Modern Bible Study', explained the character of the book. That was in 1968.

The book seemed to fill a gap. A reprint was needed within a year. Fr Richard Rutherford, an American priest studying with us in Nijmegen, paid a spontaneous tribute of his own. He wanted to make the book available in the USA and enthusiastically took on the laborious task of translating it. I was constantly amazed at his command of Dutch idiom and at the way in which he was able to adapt the illustrations I had used for a different readership. Editions have since appeared in other languages, but Fr Rutherford's still seems to me to be the best translation. I am delighted at the initiative taken by SCM Press to reissue our work.

Readers have sometimes told me that they have found the first chapter rather difficult, that it is too detailed and presupposes too

1

much. They therefore suggested that some readers might prefer to begin at Chapter II. I gladly pass on the suggestion.

1978   LUCAS GROLLENBERG

Part I
The Gospels
in
Preparation

I

The Books of Moses

When our grandparents were young, they could find out very easily whether or not someone was still a believing Christian. They only had to ask this question: "Did Moses write the first five books of the Bible or not?" If the person answered "No!" then there was no doubt about it. He had abandoned his Christian faith.

This may sound like an exaggeration. Yet, fifty years ago it was in fact the case that, in some circles at least, a person's "orthodoxy" was thought to stand or fall with his acceptance or rejection of Moses' authorship. In this chapter we want to describe briefly how this question became so acute and then the reasons why it ceased being an issue as time went on. We offer the following, therefore, as an introduction to the Books of Moses and at the same time as a sketch of the development of modern biblical scholarship.

First, a word about the names of the books. The Jews refer to the first five books of the Bible with the Hebrew word *torah,* which in English is usually translated as "the Law." In the 4th century B.C. the *Torah* already existed as a great Hebrew work. Later, after 250 B.C., it was translated into Greek in Alexandria, Egypt, for the Jews living there who no longer understood the language of their ancestors. It seems that the division into five parts took place at that time, perhaps because longer scrolls were not available. Thus the origin of the name Pentateuch: *pente* meaning "five" and *teuchos,* "scroll" or "volume."

Each of the five parts received its own name which, sometimes Latinized, is still used in our Bibles:

Genesis, "origin," because the first chapters describe the origin of heaven, earth and man as well as the origin of the people of Israel.

5

Exodus, "departure," because it begins with the description of Israel's departure out of Egypt.

Leviticus, the "levitical book," because it is almost completely devoted to prescriptions regarding worship and its ministers, the Levites.

Numbers, because of the census with which it begins.

Deuteronomy, from "the second law" or "repetition of the law," given by Moses just before his death.

I
A CONTINUOUS STORY

A quick glance at the contents of the Pentateuch is sufficient to see that the work professes to be a continuous story. It begins by relating that God created the world and man. Noah, the hero of the Deluge, is joined by an unbroken chain of ancestors with Adam, the first man. Abraham is a direct descendant of Noah, and himself the great-grandfather of the twelve sons of Jacob who, because of Joseph's adventures, end up in Egypt where their descendants attain great numbers. From the tribe of Levi stems Moses who leads his people out of Egypt. By way of Mount Sinai and the oasis, Kadesh, he brings the twelve tribes to the threshold of the Promised Land. There Moses dies on Mount Nebo.

However, the outline on the opposite page shows that the last part of this story, the life of Moses, takes up four of the five books. Further, the second half of Exodus, the whole of Leviticus and the first part of Numbers "take place" at Mount Sinai. Before the end of Numbers the Israelites have already reached the border of the Promised Land, the "fields of Moab" opposite Jericho. Thus it seems that relatively little happens after God's appearance on Sinai. But quite a bit does happen, if you consider the enactment of laws an "event," for Moses' lawmaking activity dominates the rest of the story. Sometimes a specific incident gives rise to these prescriptions, but this is not usually the case. In the rest of Exodus, in Leviticus and in Numbers you frequently come across the introductory phrase "And Yahweh spoke to Moses," followed by a series of laws. In Deuteronomy Moses enacts a large number of laws after first delivering an admonishing sermon; then he continues his exhortations.

CONTENTS OF THE "BOOKS OF MOSES"

(Each line summarizes about five chapters)

The fact that there are more laws than stories in the Pentateuch might perhaps explain why the whole work was called "the Law." But here we must be careful not to deceive ourselves. The Hebrew word *torah* has a much broader meaning than our word "law." Actually it came to mean instruction; it can be an authoritative statement in a doubtful situation, a practical rule of behavior, but also a threat, promise or plea of a prophet. For example, it is used in this way in Isaiah (8, 16. 20; 1, 10 and 2, 3 might also be compared with these). A story, too, may be referred to as *torah*. In the introduction to Psalm 78 the author calls his whole poem on the history of salvation a *torah*. For the Jews, then, the stories of Genesis about creation, the Deluge and the patriarchs as well as those about the plagues in Egypt were just as much *torah* as the laws and prescriptions of Numbers and Leviticus.

It is understandable why Moses came to be regarded as the author of the whole work. Not only is he clearly the central figure from the beginning of Exodus until the end of Deuteronomy, with the laws which he enacted taking up most of the text, but it is also stated explicitly in several places that Moses *wrote down* certain facts or laws. This is already seen in Exodus after the battle with the Amalekites (17, 14), after the sealing of the Covenant (24, 4) and at the new proclamation of the Law after the incident of the golden calf (34, 27-28). Further on, in Numbers, Moses is said to have written down the list of encampments during the journey through the desert (33, 2), and finally, just before his death, Moses wrote out his "song of witness" (Dt. 31, 19. 22).

On the basis of the texts just referred to and many other references besides, the Jews living at the beginning of the Christian era were convinced that Moses had written the whole "Law." This is apparent in many texts of the New Testament. Think only of Jesus' words in the fourth gospel addressed to the Jews about Moses in whom they had placed all their hopes: "If you really believed him you would believe me too, since it was I that he was writing about; but if you refuse to believe what he wrote, how can you believe what I say?" (Jn. 5, 45-47). Moses' authorship of Genesis apparently caused no difficulty, despite the fact that it was a history which he himself had not experienced. For, as we have already said, an unbroken chain of ancestors joined Moses to Adam. Thus he could have learned from tradition everything that had taken place from paradise and the Fall up until his own day.

But no one probably ever questioned the origin of his knowledge about this ancient history. And if anyone ever did, then he would remember that Moses enjoyed a very intimate relationship with God, as a confidant and friend (Ex. 33, 11; Nm. 12, 7-8). Moses could have learned from God himself, then, how he went about creating the world, how he got along with man in paradise, and, finally, what his relation with the patriarchs was like in the period before written history. Therefore we must not be surprised to find that great Jewish writers of the 1st century A.D., such as Philo and Flavius Josephus, were convinced that Moses, the greatest of all the prophets, had written with his own hand even the account of his death at the end of Deuteronomy.

II
THE FIRST DIFFICULTIES (AFTER 1500)

For nearly fifteen centuries Christendom continued to consider Moses as the author of the first five books of the Bible, written at God's command and under his inspiration. Even the most critical scholars of the Middle Ages never thought that it could be otherwise. To do so would have meant that they were interested in the question of authorship. But they were not. They were concerned with the texts of the Bible as a source of data for their reflection about God, man and the world. The whole Bible was for them a "given" in the deepest sense of that word, given by God to them, and the question as to the human way in which the texts came about did not occur to them at all.

In the 16th century it became apparent that profound changes were taking place among the peoples of western Europe. Let it suffice to mention only the Reformation and the Renaissance, two names which describe extremely complex phenomena. Of everything which could be mentioned concerning these two periods, the following seems to be important for our subject. The intellectuals and scholars of this new era are much more interested than those of the Middle Ages in what the individual man experiences, reflects upon, and produces as an expression thereof. They felt a strong relationship with classical antiquity, they admired the beautiful forms in which men of old expressed their ideals, and they tried to approach the literary masterpieces as closely as possible by reading them in the original languages. The invention of printing made this possible for vast numbers.

The urge to end original forms also manifested itself in the area of religious experience; besides the emphasis on personal faith the Reformation is characterized by a large-scale study of original Bible texts, while expressly passing over ecclesiastical traditions and customs of a later period.

These brief observations will be sufficient to illustrate that in the 16th century objections could arise for the first time to the old tradition which considered Moses as the author of the whole Pentateuch, and also that these objections were almost entirely of a literary nature. On the one hand, they could not imagine an author otherwise than a classical writer who, it was taken for granted, observed the laws of style and composition. On the other hand, the Pentateuch was now being read from the Hebrew text, and all kinds of things were observed which until then had remained unrecognizable in the usual Latin translation.

Differences in Style, Contradictions, Etc.

Moses begins with a very systematic description of the creation of heaven and earth and everything on earth, including human beings as man and woman, and ends this section in Genesis 2, 4 with a kind of conclusion. In that same verse he suddenly seems to begin again, supposing that the earth is a desert; then he describes the origin of man in a completely different way from that in the first story and only then do the plants and animals get their turn. This story is written in a different style, and furthermore the proper name of Israel's God, Yahweh, is added to the general word for God used in the first description, *elohim* (a plural form which could also be used for a single deity).

In Genesis 4, 17-18 the descendants of Cain are mentioned. Their names are very similar to those of Kenan's descendants listed in 5, 12-23. In 4, 26 it is related that Adam had a son whom he called Seth and at that time mankind began calling upon God with the name Yahweh. Then suddenly in 5, 1 the history of Adam is resumed.

Further on, in the story of the Deluge, we come across a number of similar repetitions. According to 6, 19 Noah is supposed to take one pair of each type of animal with him in the ark;

according to 7, 2 he is supposed to take seven pairs of the pure animals and only one pair of impure ones. In 7, 7 Noah is already in the ark with his family, but according to 7, 13 he is to enter the ark with his family as if this had not yet taken place.

In the story of Abraham we see chapter 20 begin with the observation: "Abraham left there . . ." while in the preceding verses nothing at all was said about Abraham and his place of residence. The adventures of Sarah which follow are very similar to those already described in 12, 13-20. Her experience here, in chapter 20, is described in greater detail, with more attention being paid to the motives of those involved. Furthermore, God is referred to here with the general name *elohim,* while in chapter 12 he is called Yahweh.

In Exodus the father-in-law of Moses is first called Reuel (2, 18), but further on he bears the name Jethro (3, 1). Then the name Yahweh is revealed to Moses (3, 13ff.), which seems to take place a second time in 6, 2-3 (while the author seems to have forgotten what took place in Gn. 4, 26). After God's apparition on Mount Sinai in chapter 19 we read: "So Moses went down to the people and spoke to them . . ." which is followed immediately by (20, 1): "Then God spoke all these words. He said, 'I am Yahweh your God. . . .'" According to Exodus 33, 7 and other texts as well, the "Tent of Meeting" stood outside the Israelite camp. But elsewhere, for example Numbers 2, 2, the same tent stands in the middle of the camp. In addition to repetitions and inconsistencies in the contents of these texts, scholars of the 16th and 17th centuries also observed many differences in style and diction which made the attribution to one author very improbable.

Did Moses Use Documents?

In 1753 Jean Astruc, a professor of medicine and at the same time court physician of Louis XV, published a book with "conjectures about the documents which Moses seems to have used in writing the book of Genesis." At that time many scholars undertook investigations in broad and diverse fields. The above-mentioned physician went into the problems which had arisen since people began reading the Pentateuch as a literary work. He supposed that Moses had used ancient documents. In one of these God was always referred to with the Hebrew word *elohim* and in

another with the name "Yahweh." Besides these two major documents, Moses also used many fragments of other works and wrote
this all down in four parallel columns, which only later were forged
into the book now known as Genesis.

This opinion found wide acceptance. Other scholars applied it to
the remaining books of the Pentateuch. It was found to be much
more difficult, however, to point out original documents for the
many chapters which did not contain stories, but only laws. For
this reason, in the many studies on the books of Moses which
appeared after Astruc, his "document theory" is expanded,
changed and adapted in many different ways. For the sake of clarity we will pass over here the various suppositions concerning the
origin of the supposed documents. Put very simply, we can say that
about the middle of the 19th century a "four document theory"
was held by many. It suggested that the Pentateuch is the result of
the combination of four documents that were originally independent and separate. Let us describe briefly how scholars conceived
of these four documents.

The Priestly Document

This document began with the description of how God (*elohim*)
created the world in six days and rested on the seventh (Gn. 1,
1—2, 4a). Following immediately was the genealogy linking
Adam with Noah (Gn. 5). After its own version of the Deluge
(elements from 6—8), this document related God's covenant with
Noah (Gn. 9, 1-17). Again in the form of a genealogy it set
forth the history from Sem to Abraham (11, 10-26). Concerning
Israel's patriarchs, Abraham, Isaac, Jacob and Joseph, it contained
mostly chronological indications and genealogies (such as 25,
7-20; 28, 4-9; 46, 8-27) and only a few stories (17 and 23).
In very few words it told of the subjection in Egypt, followed by a
more detailed description of Moses' calling (Ex. 6, 2—7, 7) and
from then on began to use the name Yahweh. This document
described a few of the Egyptian plagues and then dwelled extensively on the celebration of the Passover (12, 1-20. 40-51). It
related something of the manna and the quails from the journey in
the desert (bits of Ex. 16) and especially the countless laws and
prescriptions concerning worship. And so the detailed chapters
25—31 and the almost identical execution of these commands in

35—40 all belong to this document, as well as the entire book of Leviticus. Likewise, large parts of Numbers belong to it—e.g., the censuses (1 and 26), the many laws and prescriptions concerning worship and its ministers (2—6; 15; 17—19, etc.)—sometimes enacted in relation to particular incidents.

Because this document referred to God with the word *elohim* in Genesis—i.e., before the revelation to Moses—it was originally called an "elohistic document." On account of the very definite priestly interest of the author, and to distinguish it from another document likewise called elohistic, scholars quickly began tu call it the "priestly document," abbreviated with a P.

The Yahwistic Document

A second document used the name Yahweh from the very beginning—namely in the story of creation, paradise and the Fall (Gn. 2, 4b—3, 24). The narration of Cain's fratricide followed (4). This text then sketched the increase of corruption (6, 1-8), punished by the Deluge (elements of 7 and 8) and the new eruption of evil (9, 18-27), reaching a climax in the dispersion of the sons of man into many peoples who were no longer able to understand each other's language (elements of 10; 11, 1-9). With the calling of Abraham it begins a series of vivid stories about the patriarch and his descendants, Isaac, Jacob and Joseph (most of Gn. 12—13; 15—16; 18—19; 24, etc.). It also related something of the oppression in Egypt, the birth and calling of Moses (Ex. 3), some of the plagues and some elements of what happened on Mount Sinai and in the desert, including Moses' death. On account of its use of the divine proper name "Yahweh," this document was called the Yahwistic document (J, from the German spelling Jahweh).

The Elohistic Document

Another document contained the stories of a parallel text that usually called God *elohim,* except that it began at a later period—namely, with the story of Abraham (Gn. 20; 21; 22, etc.; it seemed possible, however, that the first lines of this document had been incorporated in Genesis 15, as well as a calling of Abraham). Then followed stories about Jacob (28, 10-22, etc.)

and Joseph (parts of 37; 40, etc), about the exodus from Egypt and about Sinai, which in this document is called Mount Horeb. Also the laws in the so-called "code of the Covenant" (Ex. 20, 22—23, 19) were considered to belong to this document, as well as further elements from the journey through the desert to Moab and the death of Moses. This Elohistic document was abbreviated as E.

Deuteronomy

The fourth document coincided almost completely with the fifth book of the Pentateuch, Deuteronomy. Except for several sections in the last chapters, beginning with 27, which belonged to the other three documents, this book revealed everywhere the same monitory style, more forceful in Moses' speeches before his death than in the "deuteronomic code" (12—26) for which they provide a framework. Some scholars were of the opinion that traces of this document were also to be found elsewhere in the Pentateuch—namely, in the prescriptions of Exodus 12, 24-27 and 13, 3-6. This fourth document was referred to as D.

III

THE FOUNDATION OF THE MODERN VIEW (AFTER 1880)

One of the key words of the 19th century was "evolution," understood as gradual development, growth from simple forms to more complex ones, from lower to higher stages. Scholars perceived such a development in all areas of observable reality, in nature, in human history in all its expressions such as technology, philosophical thought, religion and art—in short, in the entire culture. It is no coincidence that the beginning of that century saw the word "anachronism" being used widely for the first time, especially in conversations and articles on literature and art. This word refers to an incongruity in the proper order of time (from the Greek: *chronos* meaning "time," and *ana,* "back" or "against" in some cases of compound words). To say, for example, that George Washington sent a telegram to the king of England would be speaking anachronously. Maintaining a bodyguard of halberdiers in our day can also be called an anachronism.

In earlier centuries men were guilty of anachronisms without realizing it. To mention just a few well-known examples from the world of art: Breughel commissioned the building of a tower of Babel in late Gothic style, using the technology of his own time, and Michelangelo's painting of the first man was modeled on the most handsomely built man he could find in Rome; Rembrandt clothed his biblical figures in oriental dress as he knew it from the goods which merchant ships sailing from the Orient had brought to Amsterdam, and painted details according to the customs which he observed among the Jews in his own surroundings.

It was inevitable that 19th-century Scripture scholars working on the Pentateuch would observe that the usual attribution of authorship to Moses was a colossal anachronism. Someone who had lived fourteen centuries before Christ had been treated like a classical Greek or Roman author, while in reality, they believed, the art of writing could scarcely have been discovered in Moses' time, and he himself could certainly not have mastered it. This also disposed of the supposition that Moses had used documents in composing his work. The clearly recognizable documents with which the Pentateuch was composed must then have come into being at a much later date and in an order which could easily be determined. For evolution taught that more highly developed forms do, after all, always come forth from lower ones. And that which is thought out and differentiated always comes after that which is natural and spontaneous.

About the middle of the 19th century various attempts were made to give certain parts of the Pentateuch a place in Israel's historical development, which had reached its climax in the theology and cult of Judaism. It was one of 19th-century Germany's most famous Bible scholars, Julius Wellhausen (1844-1918), who put an end to this searching. First, we will describe how this man arrived at the ingenious synthesis which regular publication in books and articles made world-famous after 1878.

The Work of Julius Wellhausen

In the first chapter of one of his books, Wellhausen describes how, as a young theologian, he was attracted by the stories of Saul and David, Elijah and Ahab, and how he was deeply moved by the words of Amos and Isaiah and the other prophets. But in the study of these writings he always felt bothered by a bad conscience, "as if I started with the roof instead of with the foundations; for I did not know the Law, which was said to be the underlying principle and the presupposition of the other Hebrew books." Finally, he decided to struggle through Exodus, Leviticus and Numbers with the help of a bulky commentary. But he waited in vain for the light that the Law was expected to throw on the historical and prophetic books. "On the contrary, the Law marred the delight I found in those books; instead of giving me a better insight into them, it was rather disturbing, like a ghost that makes noise but is not visible or effective."

The young student went through a period of confusion. He was vaguely aware of a gap between the legislation contained in the Pentateuch and the other biblical literature. Where he saw points of contact between the two, he felt unable to opt for the opinion that the Law was older. During the summer of 1867 he happened to learn that a well-known Old Testament scholar had assigned to the Law a place in history after the prophets. "Though hardly knowing any of the arguments in favor of this hypothesis, I was immediately won over to it; Hebrew antiquity could be understood without the *Torah*."

So Wellhausen himself discovered what was already more or less clearly put forward by others. The biblical and traditional presentation of Israel's history involved an enormous anachronism: the attribution to Moses and his time of many institutions and laws that originated and developed in much later periods.

In the following years the energetic scholar accumulated arguments for the theory that the historical sequence of the four documents was J-E-D-P.

The first document was thought to have been composed in the middle of the 9th century, about 850 B.C. The parallel story of E followed roughly a century later, about 750 B.C. These two documents were combined in a new document, J-E, the work of one editor, ca. 650 B.C. Deuteronomy (D), written shortly before its so-called "discovery" under King Josiah in 621, was attached to J-E about 550 B.C.

Finally, the Priestly Document was composed between 500 and 450 B.C. It served as a framework into which the documents J-E-D were fitted about 400 B.C. This is substantially the form of the Pentateuch as we now know it.

The outline below will illustrate how revolutionary this new view was. According to the generally accepted chronology, the exodus from Egypt took place roughly in 1445 B.C., and Joshua conquered the land of Canaan about 1400. He already possessed, according to the biblical tradition, the complete Pentateuch written by Moses (Jos. 1, 7-8, etc.). The new theory placed the oldest elements of the so-called books of Moses in the 9th century, about 550 years after Moses, and also maintained that the Pentateuch received its final form preferably ten centuries after the founder of Israel's religion had appeared on the scene.

OUTLINE OF WELLHAUSEN'S THEORY

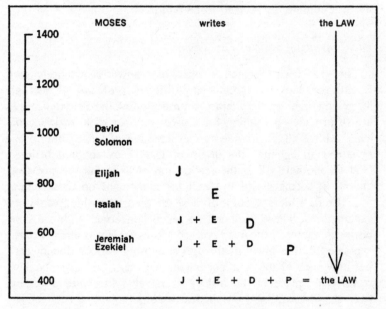

The disturbance which followed in the wake of this new theory has been compared to the revolution which Copernicus had effected several centuries earlier when he showed that the earth was not the center of the universe but simply one of the planets orbiting around the sun. Natural scientists and others interested in astronomy were quickly won over to the new theory, for it offered an explanation of a great many phenomena which until then were not understood. But others had a great deal of difficulty with the theory. For them the old view (a universe with the earth and humanity as its center) was so closely tied up with other convictions so dear to them that they intensely opposed the new insight at first. It took them a long time to see that the essence of the old convictions harmonized quite well with the new theory. Something similar also happened with Wellhausen's thesis. In this case the theory was well received and even enthusiastically accepted by people who in their own thought had already turned away from ecclesiastical orthodoxy and were industriously searching for rational explanations of religious phenomena. The new view encountered severe opposition in traditional Christian milieux where it was seen as undermining the foundations upon which the ecclesiastical community seemed to be built.

The Convincing Basis of This Theory

The new theory seemed to offer, in a powerful synthesis, convincing solutions to a great many different problems. It not only threw new light on the literary composition of the Pentateuch, but it also provided a solution for a great number of historical problems. Above all, it provided an explanation of what hitherto had remained an enigma: the origin of Israel's exceptional belief in God (monotheism, i.e., the recognition of only one, *monos,* God, *theos*). It seems useful to dwell for a moment on these points.

1. From a literary point of view the theory provided some new explanations. These were not so much concerned with the composite character of the five books of Moses (this was already partly explained by the previous theories supposing various documents), but now each of the four documents with its own particular style received its place in the history of Israelite literature as known from the historical and prophetical books.

The stories of J, with their unequaled narrative style (think only of paradise and the Fall; God's visit to Abraham; the destruction of Sodom; Isaac's journey in search of a bride; Joseph recognized by his brothers, etc.), no longer emerged from a remote and misty past in which perhaps the art of writing was yet unknown; rather, the author belonged to the 9th century, a time when Israelite narrative literature was flourishing. He lived in the milieu which produced the unforgettable stories about Saul, Jonathan, David and Absalom (1 and 2 Samuel).

The document E was situated a century later, about 750 B.C. Its narrative style is less direct, less natural; its stories presuppose a deeper reflection on the relations between God and man. Prophetical preaching clearly seemed to have influenced the author's environment. Compare, for example, Genesis 20 (Abraham is called a prophet!) with the corresponding Yahwistic narrative in Genesis 12, 10-20. The narrative in Genesis 22 also shows characteristics of E: Abraham's feelings and his obedience to God are strongly emphasized.

The monitory style of D is very similar to that of Jeremiah. If you read the admonitions of Moses in Deuteronomy 1—11 and then open the book of Jeremiah to chapters 7, 11, 17, 18, 23 or 29, you will find yourself in the same literary climate.

In the same way every reader of the Bible can observe the similarity between the laws and prescriptions concerning worship which belong to the Priestly Document and quite a few texts from the last part of the book of Ezekiel (40—48).

And so it became even clearer that to attribute the entire Pentateuch to Moses was historically impossible: one man would have expressed himself in different literary styles which developed successively only many centuries after him.

2. From an historical point of view many difficulties came to be seen in a new light. For example, in the stories about Samuel, Saul, David and succeeding kings, all kinds of liturgical practices are related which are completely in opposition to the law of Moses. This is understandable if the particular parts of the law only came about long after those kings had lived. There was also the fact, up till then very puzzling, that the name Moses, the man held to be the founder of Israel's legislation, is only mentioned twice in prophetic texts dating from before the exile. This too becomes more understandable when the tradition that Moses was the lawgiver *par excellence* is seen to have exercised its greatest influence during and after the exile.

3. From a philosophical point of view finally, the new theory offered a satisfactory solution to the question of Israel's unique monotheism. The idea of God found in J, the oldest document, was evidently very primitive indeed: Yahweh molds man out of clay; he walks in the garden; he closes the door of Noah's ark; he sits at Abraham's table, etc. In the document E, a century younger, we see a more spiritual and well-considered conception of

God: God himself no longer appears visibly among men, but he appears to Abimelech in a dream just as to Jacob, Laban and Joseph. The document D offers a further phase in the development, with its purely ethical image of a God who must be loved by man with his whole soul and all his power. At the end of this development is the God of P, completely separated from this world, who effects the work of creation by speaking a single word and who can be worshiped only by means of a carefully elaborated ceremonial.

Besides a rather materialistic idea of God, the oldest documents also show traces of very primitive forms of religion—e.g., remnants of fetishism (cf. the anointing of a holy stone in Genesis 28, 18). There Yahwism is still a monolatry—i.e., the cult of one God without excluding the existence of other divinities. Monotheism in the strictest sense is found first in P—i.e., in the last period, at the very end of the evolution.

The more problems of a different nature are solved by one hypothesis, the more convincing the hypothesis is. Even a highly simplified presentation of the new theory regarding the Pentateuch like the one above makes it clear why it immediately attracted so many supporters. You must keep in mind, however, that our ascribing this to Wellhausen alone is a simplification. In fact, different scholars in various countries were carrying on investigations in this same direction. However, Julius Wellhausen possessed, in addition to all his other gifts, the talent of exposing an insight in a clear and convincing way. Besides, he was also engaged outside the boundaries of his own country; his theory received wide circulation in the English-speaking world through his article "Israel" in the *Encyclopaedia Britannica*. And we should not forget that in those days the idea of evolution had a magic attraction: when a phenomenon could be shown to be the result of some very long and gradual process, it was considered to have been explained satisfactorily and no one asked any further questions as to its origin. In our case, the new theory seemed to give a satisfactory explanation for the remarkable phenomenon of Israel's religion. For the future it would be no longer necessary to have recourse to "supernatural" miracles and revelations.

Opposition from the Churches

Only on rare occasions did the proponents of the new theory express this so clearly. Traditional Christians, however, read it all the more clearly between the lines of their publications. They looked upon Wellhausen and his supporters first and foremost as cunning enemies of their deepest certainties. An example can perhaps best clarify how they received the new theory.

Christians had always read the marvelous and profound stories about Abraham (Gn. 12—25) as a history written by Moses. Only a few centuries separated this privileged man of God from his ancestors, in whom the history of salvation had had its beginning. By means of tradition, written or passed on by word of mouth, Moses could have been well informed about the principal events of Abraham's life. Furthermore, he could consult the Lord as often as he wanted in the Tent of Meeting. This immediate inspiration was a guarantee of the historical exactness of the history which Moses had written.

According to the new theory, these chapters about Abraham were like a patchwork quilt put together centuries later by anonymous authors. Thus chapter 16, describing the birth of Ishmael, was atrributed to the so-called Yahwist, a Judean author of the 9th century. However, several verses (3 and 15-16) were added later by a redactor, who borrowed these from the Priestly Document written after the exile. Chapter 17, with the story about God's covenant with Abraham and the circumcision of the male members of his family, was written entirely by the author of P. The story of God's visit to the patriarch and the destruction of Sodom and Gomorrah which followed, in chapters 18 and 19, was again the work of the 9th-century Yahwist. Beginning with chapter 20 the reader encounters still another anonymous writer, the Elohist. The story about the tomb near Hebron, chapter 23, again stemmed from the Priestly Document, and thus from the period of the exile or even later. But the marriage of Isaac, in chapter 24, was again the work of the Yahwist. *In this way the faithful reader of the Bible lost all the certainty which Moses' authorship had guaranteed him.*

Wellhausen had also drawn expressly historical conclusions: the stories about Abraham, Isaac, Jacob and Joseph did not contain any reliable historical data concerning those persons. In his opinion, they could be called "historical" only insofar as they faithfully reflect the ideas which the Israelites of the 8th and 9th centuries had concerning their ancestors. The theory did not deny that an historical person called Moses ever existed, but held that nothing about him could be known with certainty. The ten commandments, related by E and D as revealed by God to Moses, were, according to the theory, no more than a summary of the ethical teaching of the prophets. No wonder that the exceptionally influential German scholar was considered by some very orthodox Christians as the antichrist himself. All of this seems to illustrate sufficiently what we said at the beginning of our exposition about the method our grandparents used to test a person's faith.

Also, Roman Catholics who were involved in Scripture studies generally opposed the new theory. Only a few expressed an appreciation of it. One of these was Father Lagrange, the French Dominican who in 1890 founded the now famous *Ecole Biblique* in Jerusalem. During the International Scientific Congress of Catholics held at Fribourg, Switzerland, in 1897, he criticized a purely negative approach to the theory and pointed out the serious dangers tied up with such an approach. It would unnecessarily estrange many intellectuals from the Church—unnecessarily, inasmuch as what people called an "age-old tradition" with reference to the question about Moses' authorship was so only to an extent. Insofar as the tradition presented Moses as the founder of the Yahwistic religion, historically it stood on very firm ground. What had been handed down concerning Moses' authorship, Lagrange considered to belong to the literary order, a relatively late tradition and not authoritative. Then he indicated a way in which faithful Catholics could accept important elements of the new theory.

Unfortunately, this proposition encountered very strong opposition from Catholic specialists and non-specialists alike. Suddenly, on June 27, 1906, the bitter disputes which the Fribourg discourse and also Lagrange's further publications on "the historical method" had provoked were silenced. On that day the Pontifical Biblical Commission, established four years previously, issued a decree which might be summarized as follows: The arguments brought forward by critics are not sufficient to disprove the age-old tradition which regards Moses as the author of the Pentateuch. It is possible that he made use of oral and written sources and that he entrusted the actual task of writing to secretaries; also, minor changes, additions and inspired glosses may have crept into the text during the long centuries of its transmission, but the substance of the work goes back to Moses himself.

During the following decade the ecclesiastical authorities watched over Catholic biblical publications. Whenever a scholar published something in which he attempted to incorporate some elements of the new theory in his exegesis, he was promptly called to order.

IV
RADICAL RENEWAL

"For fifty years the Churches will refute my theory, only then to accept it into the Creed with more or less subtle arguments." Wellhausen wrote these words in 1883.

In fact, in 1951 there appeared a French translation of Genesis, preceded by an introduction to the Pentateuch. In it the contents were divided among the four sources, referred to as J, E, D and P, and situated in Israel's history much the same way as Wellhausen had suggested. The author of this essay was the Dominican Roland de Vaux, successor to Fr. Lagrange as director of the *Ecole Biblique*. In the front of the book all the ordinary ecclesiastical approbations were to be found. With this development, Wellhausen's prediction seemed to be gloriously fulfilled!

However, things were not quite that simple. Wellhausen could not have foreseen the events which contributed to a profound change of attitude. One of them was World War I (1914-1918). Indeed, one can observe a very definite difference in approach and tone between the publications dating from before those four horrible years and the studies which appeared afterward. In 1912 one of the leading figures in German biblical scholarship wrote concerning Wellhausen's system, already considered classical: "The main lines are so well established that further research can at most change details of minor importance." In the 1920's, however, a well-known scholar proclaimed that "of the building which Wellhausen and his school had constructed, not a stone is left upon a stone." Another German scholar, who in 1912 was a faithful supporter of the entire classical system, judging from the handbook which he published at that time, boldly wrote in 1926: "The four source documents are a phantom," a figment of the imagination. In 1925 an Englishman, summarizing the situation in Old Testament studies, used the following image: "Everywhere uncertainties abound, and like the dove after the Deluge, we seem to find no solid ground anywhere to the sole of our foot."

Indeed, World War I had been a terrible shock. Books on modern history treat its far-reaching consequences in all areas (e.g., World War II). In relation to our subject, it seems useful to point out the deep disillusionment which the war caused. As we said, many had begun to think in terms of evolution, of the progress of mankind. Man was irreversibly on the road to a better and higher life. Then suddenly it became apparent that mankind was capable of stubbornly prolonging a war which quickly was seen to be senseless, in which more than three million people murdered each other, while the lives of countless others became a burden due to suffering beyond measure. The word "evolution" as an expression of an optimistic view of life disappeared from everyday conversations, and when referring to the past, the concept was used much more cautiously.

Yet, World War I was not the actual cause of the uncertainty surrounding the Pentateuch. Even before the war, factors were at work which eventually had to have their influence on the established insights, and afterward still others arose. To illustrate the present approach, we will treat a few of these factors. Let us begin with a negative one.

The Method in a Blind Alley

The four documents had been chiefly distinguished on the basis of literary peculiarities: differences in the use of language, style, etc. In our simplified presentation of the theory, we could not of course give sufficient attention to two things. First, for many texts, pericopes and verses it remained unclear to which document they were to be attributed and whether or not they could be the work of one of the "redactors" who had forged the documents together. Secondly, the method of splitting up the sources made it theoretically possible to go on distinguishing original documents *ad infinitum*. And this is just what happened. When, for example, in the second verse of a chapter the term "he said" was used and in the fourth verse "he spoke," and when the expression "they quarreled" of the third verse was alternated with "they wrangled" in the sixth verse, the diligent pupil of the Wellhausen school suspected a fusion of two different versions of the same story. Then he tried to reconstruct the original "documents" and even to detect the words inserted by the supposed "redactor" who had combined the sources to make one story. Even the public was initiated into this method. One could buy translations of the Pentateuch in which each pericope and even each verse was marked as belonging to document J ^{1}, J ^{2}, J ^{3} or E ^{2}, E ^{3}, etc.—and then, of course, all different redactors: R ^{1} or REJ ^{1}, etc. This present book would be too expensive if we printed a page of one of the so-called "rainbow bibles": each phrase belonging to a different "document" was printed against a background of a different color, so that in fact on many pages of the Pentateuch nearly all the colors of the rainbow were to be seen as in a mosaic.

It is easy to understand that young theologians returning from the trenches after World War I did not feel attracted to this stuffy kind of scriptural study, clearly the work of "ivory tower scholars" and completely out of touch with real life. They were troubled, first of all, by their own desperate situation for which they sought support in the Bible, and, secondly, by the mystery surrounding the real life of the authors of the Bible whom they could not at all imagine to be "ivory tower scholars" who weaved documents together.

The Discovery of the Ancient East

While Wellhausen and his students were splitting up sources at their desks and basing their judgments on all kinds of suppositions (e.g., that in Moses' time the art of writing was not generally known, or that laws in which reason dominates had to be more recent than those in which feeling still had the upper hand, and the like), elsewhere men were busy investigating the flood of recently excavated texts, trying to get acquainted with the real life of the ancient East.

As early as 1822 Champollion had found the key to the hieroglyphic script of ancient Egypt, and from 1848 onward, scholars were certain that their deciphering of the cuneiform texts was proceeding in the right direction. But it was only during the first decades of the 20th century that the specialists in this field were able to publish coherent surveys of the history, culture and religion of the ancient civilizations of the Near East. Wellhausen possessed a knowledge of the pre-Islamic Arab world which far surpassed that of his contemporaries. Remarkably enough he did not, insofar as we know, delve into the newly discovered texts from the great cultures which preceded and surrounded Israel. At any rate he did not allow his views on Israel's religious history to be influenced by them.

Yet, with these discoveries it became progressively clearer that some of his presuppositions could no longer be maintained. First of all, it became evident that a very expansive written literature existed long before Moses appeared on the scene, as well as many collections of laws. By means of comparison it was seen that certain biblical laws, which Wellhausen had situated in the last stage of Israel's evolution on the basis of their form and content, could in reality be very much older.

Interest in "Social" Phenomena

Another factor played a role in Europe's cultural history. The second half of the 19th century saw the rise of sociology, the science of life in community, which since the beginning of this century has begun to play an even greater role. In many areas, thought and scientific research centered more and more upon the group as a living unity rather than upon the individual. This is especially true for the "history of religions," which is concerned with the social expressions of religion in all kinds of communities. Research in this field revealed, among other things, that the purest insights and forms did not always come at the end of an evolution. In the history of literature, old sagas, folk songs, epics, etc., were studied as expressions of the soul or spirit of the community rather than as creations of individuals.

Of course, all of this also had its influence on biblical scholarship. Scholars no longer limited their work on the Pentateuch to the determination and analysis of supposed documents, subdocuments and redactional operations. They now tried to penetrate into the living world that must lie behind the texts—or, better still, of which the texts were the written deposits. Here is just one example: It had already been observed that a kind of law book had been incorporated in Exodus 20, 22—23, 33. Instead of only determining that it belonged to E and thus was written about 750, scholars recognized that this collection of laws must be from an earlier date. They tried then to get an idea of the society in which this law book arose and came to be observed. In other words, they went in search of the text's "Sitz im Leben" (the German technical term for "situation in life"). In the same way, other large literary units were studied, such as Leviticus 17—26, the so-called Law of Holiness, as well as shorter ones, like the ten commandments. An attempt was made to discover the underlying form of the two versions of the Decalogue and to determine its original place. The narrative sections of the Pentateuch were treated in the same way. As early as 1901 Hermann Gunkel ushered in a new phase in the study of Genesis by characterizing the stories about the patriarchs as "sagas" and studying them in comparison with similar literature of other peoples.

Cult and Tradition

In the years before 1929, some scholars had already supposed that worship had been the original "Sitz im Leben" of many of the texts gathered together in the Pentateuch. From 1929 on, the discoveries at Ras Shamra, the ancient Ugarit on the Syrian coast, brilliantly confirmed their suppositions. There a great many texts, all of them older than 1200 B.C., and surprisingly close to some songs and stories of the Old Testament in language, style and form, were found in temple buildings. Thus they were evidently preserved and used in close association with worship.

In fact, in ancient Israel it was the priests who gave instruction, *torah,* and made decisions regarding worship and social life. Accordingly, Israel's "law" was born in the sanctuaries and there it grew into the codes which were finally collected in the Pentateuch.

But in addition to sacrifices and songs of praise, Yahweh was honored in these same sanctuaries through commemoration of the great benefits which he had shown to Israel. The original and very close relation between cult and the "history of salvation" is still to be seen in texts like Deuteronomy 26, 1-11, a liturgical directive for the offering of first-fruits. When the priest has set the basket of fruit upon the altar, the believer was to make the following pronouncement: "My father was a wandering Aramaean. *He* went down into Egypt...few in numbers; but there he became a nation, great, mighty and strong. The Egyptians ill-treated *us*.... But *we* called on *Yahweh*.... Yahweh heard our voice...and Yahweh brought us out of Egypt.... He brought us here and gave us this land.... *Here* then *I* bring the first-fruits of the produce of the soil that *you, Yahweh,* have given me." The italics help us to see to what a large extent such a liturgical action involved the Israelite personally in the great historical events that marked the origin of his people. Observations like this gave rise to the supposition that such texts were not so much summaries of the story which the Pentateuch (as well as Joshua) relates, but rather lay at its roots. The historical themes continually being referred to in worship—namely those of the patriarchs (the "wandering Aramaeans"), the oppression in Egypt, the liberation out of slavery and the entrance into the Promised Land—might have been elaborated in the course of centuries by means of all kinds of narrations and combined with other themes, like the revelation of God and the Covenant on Mount Sinai and the journey through the desert.

In connection with this, the certainty grew that the origin of the Pentateuch stories went much further back in history than the supporters of the classical system could suspect. In their day they had aroused so much opposition partly because of their complete skepticism with regard to what the "documents" said about Israel's oldest history. In the light of the new facts and hypotheses such skepticism no longer seemed to be justifiable. No longer was it a question of a brainchild of four (or more) "authors" of the 9th century and later, but of the heritage, already centuries old, of a community which from its very beginning had sung and celebrated "the great deeds of God."

The Challenge of the Nazis

Still another factor contributed to a drastic change of the "climate" in which Old Testament studies were being carried on. Before 1914 scientific investigation of the Bible was for the most part historically orientated. It was actually a sector of the history of religions. The Old Testament was studied as a document reflecting the religion and culture of Israel. Essentially this approach did not differ from, for example, the study of early Persian documents, seen as historical witnesses of the religion of the ancient Persians. As we have noted, new impulses were given to the study of the Old Testament at the turn of the century (e.g., through the above-mentioned investigations of Gunkel), directed mostly toward literary forms, and through the nascent interest in the continually growing archeological material from the world encircling old Israel. But even here the study remained primarily historical, a part of the history of religions. If the many Christians involved in the work were scarcely aware of this, it was perhaps because of the fact that in other fields of theology as well, historical investigation demanded almost all the attention at that time.

World War I destroyed very many things held as self-evident, including the opinion just mentioned. In the turbulent years after the war, expressions of unrest were heard from German Old Testament scholars who felt it to be an illusion to treat that part of the Bible "objectively," with the cool gaze of an outsider who is not at all involved in it. Still hesitating, one such scholar wrote in 1921: "Should not our work on the Old Testament develop into an authentic theology that is speaking (*logos*) about the living God (*theos*) worshiped in our churches as the Father of Jesus Christ?"

In the 1930's we see this striving for a more theological approach becoming increasingly stronger. In the inextricable mass of stimulating factors, the pressure of National Socialism is clearly to be distinguished. If this new view of life forced the German Churches to reflect upon their Christian faith, it drew attention especially to the Old Testament. For, according to the theorists of the new movement, this book in particular was to be abolished as a "Religionsbuch," being a product of the Jewish spirit which was considered inferior in all respects.

It was painful that their principal arguments had been prepared by investigators of the Old Testament themselves. As we said, they had treated that book for several generations as the witness of an historically determined religion. The discovery of the Babylonian culture, in so many ways much higher, brought out the limitations of Israel all the more clearly. One of the founders of this science of Assyrian-Babylonian philology and literature, Friedrich Delitzsch, had expressed with continually growing sharpness his disdain for the Old Testament. Finally, in his book *Die Grosse Täuschung* (1921)—i.e., the great delusion or great deception—he maintained that the Christian Church and the Christian family would be a whole lot better off if that Jewish book were abolished. He called it an "unbroken conglomeration of contradictory reports and whole stories of non-historical, purely fabricated sagas and fables; in short, a book filled with conscious and unconscious deceptions, in part self-deception; a very dangerous book, to be used only with the greatest care." With disdain he described, for example, the attitude of the Jews who did not make use of Cyrus' permission to return to their homeland and to rebuild the temple of their god in 538 B.C., and who remained in the "accursed" Babylon because there they could get rich more easily. "Already in those days," he wrote, "the people served their national god Jaho [as Delitzsch spelled Yahweh] only as a means and an instrument for purely secular purposes—namely, the preservation of the Jewish race, the strengthening of Jewish nationalism and the achievement of the very worldly promise proclaimed by the prophets: that Israel would become the greatest and most powerful people on earth and that it would draw all the wealth of the other nations to itself." Delitzsch was willing to concede that here and there, especially in some Psalms, there are statements which can serve as an expression of the "Christian feeling," but he said that these came in by chance and furthermore are much too scarce to justify using the whole Old Testament in the Christian life. He believed that Goethe was correct in stating that "Judaism belongs to the pagan religions." But he added that it was a particularly repulsive kind of pagan religion. Ancient Babylonian paganism stood much higher, and so did ancient German paganism. "It would be much more advisable," he wrote as a Christian to Christians, "for us to fall back from time to time into the deep reflections which our German spiritual heroes expressed about God and the hereafter and immortality, and which Wilhelm Schwaner so excellently sought out and collected in his German Bible (4th edition, 1918)." Delitzsch intended to shake the German nation out of its somnambulism and to arouse it to the recognition that, of all the current questions, that of the Jews deserved the most serious consideration. "To contribute to the correct appraisal of it on the grounds of the history of Israel, I have written this book."

The most influential Christian theologian of the beginning of this century, Adolf von Harnack, published in 1920 a study on the early Christian heretic Marcion. In it he wrote: "The rejection of the Old Testament in the 2nd century [by Marcion] was a mistake which the Church rightly opposed; that it was maintained in the 16th century was the unavoidable lot of the Reformation; but for Protestantism to hold onto it after the 19th century as a canonical book is the result of a religious and ecclesiastical paralysis. To clean house and to honor the truth completely in our confession and education is the great deed which now—perhaps already too late—is demanded of Protestantism."

The 79-year-old writer of these lines, full of self-assurance, did not suspect that a reversal was approaching which he himself would still partially experience, to his great distress. In the person of Karl Barth, Protestantism did precisely the opposite of what von Harnack had proposed and demanded. Even a brief sketch of the reversal which this Swiss theologian brought about in Protestant thought would bring us here too far afield. Let us mention only that Barth, who from 1921 taught at Göttingen, and afterward at Münster and Bonn, was one of the first to detect the dangers of National Socialism for the Christian faith. He was one of the few who also had the courage to oppose it openly. For this reason he was removed as professor in Bonn in 1934. In that same year a student and comrade-in-arms of Karl Barth published a book which bore the very clear title *The Old Testament as Witness of Christ*. This title was at the same time a thesis and a program. According to the author, Wilhelm Vischer, the Christian Church stands or falls with the recognition of the unity of the two Testaments. A Church which subordinates the value of the Old Testament witness to that of the New ceases to be "Christian." For what the apostles proclaimed was correct—namely that Jesus of Nazareth is the Christ, the Messiah of the Old Testament. Whoever believes this in common with the whole early Church must say: Even when one studies the Old Testament with modern scientific methods, it points everywhere to Christ who is the very meaning which God intended for it. In the German theological world, Vischer's book was like an alarm. Because the question concerning the value and meaning of the Old Testament became involved in the struggle which in the final analysis revolved around the very existence of the Christian Churches, earlier attempts at a more theological approach to Old Testament study were highly stimulated.

It is no coincidence then that the leading figures in this science after World War II were certainly convinced that belief in Christ is a necessary condition for a correct interpretation. One of their number explained at a congress in 1956: "It is an encouraging sign of the growing clarity of our exegetical situation that even investigators who otherwise walk very different paths are in agreement in recognizing that this presupposition of all theological investigation is part and parcel of the faith." He added that in 1928, at a similar congress in Bonn, he experienced how reference to this fundamental point struck against a wall of almost complete lack of understanding.

V
THE PRESENT SITUATION

After this rapid survey, though admittedly rather arbitrary, we are nevertheless now in a better position to understand something of the remarkable fact, mentioned above following Wellhausen's "prophecy" (cf. p. 23), that the Catholic introduction to the Pentateuch of 1951 maintained the J-E-D-P outline with ecclesiastical approval. Father Roland de Vaux, an author highly esteemed by all his fellow scholars, could hardly use these four letters in 1951 in the same way as Wellhausen did. What he in fact did intend was apparently acceptable to the orthodox faithful, even without his Church "accepting it into the Creed with more or less subtle arguments." Here we have two points which call for further attention.

Mirror of Many Centuries

De Vaux indeed used the four classical letters, and most scholars follow him in this. They concede that this classification of the great variety of material brought together in the Pentateuch has not yet been replaced by a better one. But they avoid the term "documents" and speak rather of "traditions," of "currents of thought," and sometimes also of "schools." Each of the four groups of texts, they say, had its own history, in the form of a tradition often centuries long, first oral, later also written, in which the material acquired the traits of the mileux and the circumstances in which it was passed on. It is supposed that it was the sanctuaries of ancient Israel in particular where the oldest traditions received their form. It was there surely that the great things which God had done were recalled in rites and stories, and together with them the epic of their ancestors. They were living traditions; in other words, each generation passed them on in the light of its own experiences. This holds true for customs and laws just as much as for stories, precisely because the priests in the spirit of the tradition had to issue directives for behavior in new situations.

According to most scholars, the material brought together in J was handed down in the territory of the tribe Judah, perhaps in connection with the principal sanctuary of Hebron. It is there that a number of the J stories take place and the Yahwistic version of the Joseph story grants the patriarch Judah an attractive role. The setting down in writing of those traditions, by one person or a "school," must have taken place during the reign of Solomon or shortly afterward.

The traditions set down in E seemed to have lived among the tribes in central Palestine, the territory of Ephraim, perhaps in sanctuaries like Bethel and Shechem. These seem to have been written down later than those of J. They lead one to suspect the influence of prophets like Elijah. As a help to remember these opinions, the letter J can also refer to Judah and E can signify Ephraim.

It was also from the northern kingdom, which since the separation under Jeroboam led its own life, that the core of the Deuteronomic law book had its origin. It is generally accepted that after the destruction of that kingdom in 721 faithful worshipers of Yahweh fled to Judah and there cultivated a number of their own traditions. Finally, the P-traditions, with their special interest in the furnishings and functioning of the sanctuary, in sacrifices and feasts and everything belonging to the liturgy, probably stem from the priestly circles of Jerusalem. During the exile and especially in the following centuries, they must have taken great pains to put those traditions in writing.

All of this will perhaps be more meaningful by sketching it on the same outline which served to illustrate Wellhausen's thesis. On the revised version, printed on the next page, we have made the four letters a bit longer. This is to show that the process of writing down the traditions could have taken many years. Furthermore, Moses is inserted lower on the outline. He is no longer situated before 1400, but at the end of the 13th century B.C. Above him, however, we have brought in several additional centu-

OUTLINE OF THE THEORY ACCORDING TO DE VAUX

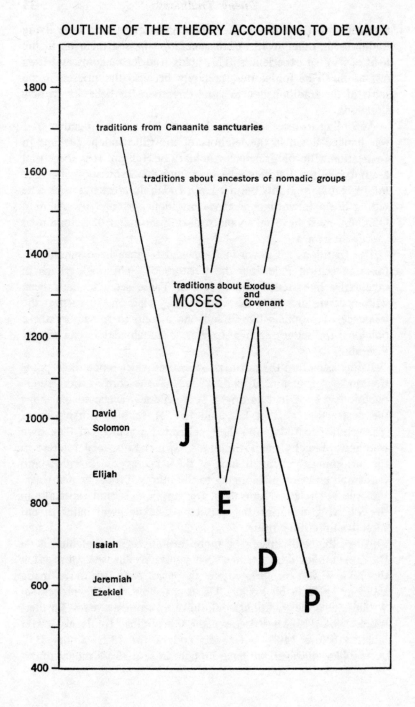

ries. Some of the lines are to begin there, in order to show (very schematically, of course) that the traditions have a history of many centuries. Some of them may go back to the time before Moses, and thus to the ancestors of Israel, and in some few cases perhaps back even before them to traditions already existing in Canaanitic sanctuaries.

The fact that the main lines come together in Moses illustrates the modern conviction that this man, Israel's leader at the time of the exodus from Egypt, was the actual founder of its existence as a people. The fact that many different traditions agree so well on the fundamental facts and experiences of God to which they witness can only be explained by their common origin. Moses most probably did know how to write and perhaps could even use more than one form of writing (hieroglyphic and cuneiform writing), but we do not know whether he himself left any written documents for his people, and there is no text in the Pentateuch which we can attribute directly in its present form to Moses. One can of course deplore this gap in our knowledge. Yet, it seems that we should rather be thankful for this certainty: what Moses began has remained alive down through the centuries. Alive—in other words, it gathered other elements to itself, developed, and adapted itself to changing circumstances; in short, it lived on in the historical existence of the people of God. And this is reflected in many of its facets in the Pentateuch, from the very beginning until the 5th century B.C.

The Attitude of the Churches

With a variation of Pilate's question, the reader may perhaps sigh and ask, "Is this view now the true one? Who will guarantee me that in 50 years it won't again be completely different?" From everything we have seen above, it must be quite clear that no one can ever guarantee this. On the contrary, in 50 years new developments will certainly have taken place and there will be new points of view. But this perspective does not in any way detract from the "truth" of the present view. Indeed, it is based on the various insights which have been arrived at in the last 100 years in particular, and after much more difficulty and strife than can be described in this historical sketch.

No reasonable person can simply disregard these achievements and continue to maintain, "I will go on believing that Moses himself wrote the entire Pentateuch." Now, one may observe that Catholic authorities did just this in the decree of the Pontifical Biblical Commission referred to above. Quite true. But that was in 1906. At that time a few very gifted persons could see that many of Wellhausen's insights, especially in the area of literature and history, could very well be included in an orthodox view of the Bible. But they were indeed few, such as Lagrange. For the great majority the developments before and after 1914-1918 described above were necessary to arrive at such an insight.

This is equally true for a number of Protestant Churches of a more orthodox orientation. Obviously by different means than through papal decrees, Moses' authorship was strongly maintained. One of the results of that continual opposition in the Churches was to be seen in the formation of priests and ministers. What they heard in classes on the "introduction to the Pentateuch" was not much more than a discussion on, and especially a polemic against, the four-document theory. Again and again it was proved that Moses himself could very well have written such and such a text. Because of this, very little time remained to treat the actual value of the Pentateuch for a life of faith.

Precisely because of the stricter organization of the Roman Catholic Church, the changed attitude came to light there, too, in a clearer and more authoritative way than in other Christian communities. In 1943 Pius XII issued an encyclical letter on biblical studies which is referred to, using its first three words, as *Divino Afflante Spiritu*—that is, "under the inspiration of the divine Spirit." This encyclical pressingly encouraged the use of modern critical methods in the study of Holy Scripture and urged that no new data be left unused in order to arrive at the original intentions of scriptural texts. Later generations may very well consider this encyclical as the most important official act of Pius XII's reign. If Scripture may be approached "historically," and if that method may also be applied to old traditions about its origin (e.g., Moses wrote the Pentateuch), then this opens new possibilities in other areas as well. Traditions and practices formerly thought to be eternally valid may appear less absolute and therefore subject to change. There is no reason why this cannot be extended to many of the differences separating the Churches. Might *Divino Afflante Spiritu* not have prepared the way for John XXIII who himself was an historian? Everyone knew that this encyclical on the Bible was for a great part written by Professor Bea. Was it a coincidence that precisely this man appeared as the great champion of the unity of Christians?

The Situation of the Bible Reader

With all of this, reading the Bible has not become any easier. This is true, first of all, for Bible history. Formerly this seemed to be crystal clear, from the creation of the world in 3761 B.C. via the biographies of Abraham, Isaac, Jacob, Joseph and his brothers and the more detailed one of Moses up until his death in 1405 B.C. In reality, however, the actual course of history was quite different, an infinitely more complex process, of which only a few lines are in some way clear. What can be said at the present time concerning "Bible history" and how one can "relate" it will be treated later. First the reader will have to undergo still further "disillusionment" on this point.

Furthermore, something similar can take place with each chapter and with each individual text. The modern exegete will refer to the oldest core of the text, to the forms which it received in the course of tradition, to the work of those who put it in writing, and finally how it was included in the larger context of the definitive book of the Bible. Let us illustrate this concisely with two examples, a story and a liturgical law.

In the unequaled chapter 22 of Genesis which relates Abraham's sacrifice, scholars recognize as the primitive core a story which we call "aetiological." Just as among other peoples, there existed also in Israel the practice of illustrating an old custom or usage with a story (*logos*) about its ground or origin (*aetios*), which often had as its point of departure a related name or term. The core of Genesis 22 is thought to have been such a story which explained the name of a particular holy place with the words: "God will provide" (cf. verses 8 and 14). During the process of tradition the name of that sanctuary was lost; it can no longer be discerned in the text as we have it today. However, the story had still another function. In the nations surrounding Israel there existed the barbarian though heroic custom that in times of great distress the leading figures (in particular) sacrificed their first-born sons. Such a dreadful deed was obviously intended to force the national divinity to intervene. Partly because of this, such a custom was abhorred in Israel from the very beginning. They were conscious there that everything is from Yahweh, and thus also that everything brought forth from the earth, animals and men belonged to him. But the oldest law laid down expressly that the first-born of men must be "redeemed" (e.g., Ex. 34, 20). Nevertheless, the rite of the surrounding peoples continued to exercise a great attractive force on Israel precisely because of its implication that "nothing was too good for the divinity." Think only of the suggestion which, according to the prophet Micah, the people proposed in a penitential mood: "Must I give my first-born for what I have done wrong, the fruit of my body for my own sin?" (Mic. 6, 7) The prophet answered this suggestion with the famous words concerning justice and humility, specifying these as being the only things which Israel's God desired of his people (cf. p. 197). In other places that same answer was given by relating the "God will provide" story of Abraham, the founding ancestor of Israel. The "sons" of Abraham must indeed be prepared to give up everything, even their most precious possessions, but God does not demand human sacrifice. He himself provided a ram in place of the first-born son. When the theme of the "son of the promise" was brought into the Abraham cycle, the story received a new depth. In ordering the sacrifice of Isaac, God seemed to withdraw all his promises. In his unequaled manner the elohistic narrator brings his reader face to face with unconditional obedience. Finally the story was given its present place in the Genesis narrative, thus becoming the high point of Abraham's life: after withstanding this test, his preparation to be "father of all believers" was completed. All that remained was to buy a tomb for his wife Sarah, his first possession in the land promised to him (Gn. 23), and to help his son find a bride (Gn. 24). Then he could die in peace (Gn. 25). As we now have it in Genesis, the story is therefore not so much a photo recording one moment in history, but rather a painting which is the work of countless believers. Without a doubt its appealing power must at least be partially attributed to this fact.

Modern studies on the history of the Passover lead us to suspect what a long and complicated history preceded the narration of Exodus 12, as we now have it, about the paschal lamb and the unleavened bread. From its nomadic past Israel held on to a very primitive rite: in the spring at the full moon a young animal was sacrificed in order to ensure fertility and well-being for the flock. In addition the entrances to the tents were marked with the blood of the animal to ward off evil spirits. When Israel became an agricultural people in Canaan, it celebrated there the first harvest of the year, the barley harvest, by offering the first baskets to Yahweh and by eating only from the new harvest, without anything from the old, for seven days—thus without yeast. Both feasts quickly received their authentic Israelitic form: they became commemorations of Yahweh's historical benefit, the exodus out of Egypt. But an analysis of the various legislative and historical texts which have reference to these two feasts shows that they were celebrated separately for centuries—the paschal feast in clan or family, and the presentation of first-fruits, of course, in a sanctuary. The centralization of the entire cult in the temple at Jerusalem stimulated the bringing together of these two spring festivals at the end of the 7th century (cf. pp. 98f.). Only after the exile did they definitively become one feast. The "priestly" texts in the Exodus narration (Ex. 12, 1-20. 43-50) reflect this situation. In this example we also see how it was a matter of course for biblical writers to anchor later developments in an historical beginning. We will say more about this in the following chapter.

II

New Points of View

One could sum up the development of modern biblical science in one sentence: Men went behind the texts of Scripture in search of the people who expressed themselves in it. In the previous chapter we described in broad lines the beginning of the expedition into the real, colorful life which lies crystallized, as it were, in the Bible texts. Before turning to the next part of the Bible, it seems useful to us to consider a bit more closely some of the newly discovered areas.

I
ISRAEL IN ITS MILIEU

Perhaps I can best begin here with a personal recollection. As a student I was once working through an anthology of Egyptian texts. One of the pieces was a fragment of a letter written by a government official of the time of Ramses II or thereabout—at any rate before 1200 B.C. Rather sarcastically he wrote to another government functionary about his journey through the territory of Palestine and Syria. The countryside there differs drastically from that of Egypt, as it stretches southward from Cairo. It consists of the banks of the Nile, two narrow strips of land on both sides of that majestic river. This ribbon-like country owes its fertility to the annual flooding of the Nile, for it seldom rains there and every day the burning sun draws its course from east to west across Egypt. To the symmetrical character of this countryside we may surely attribute the exceptional clarity and composition which strikes us so forcefully in ancient Egyptian art. We can also understand, then, that the man who had to travel through mountainous Syria felt very uneasy most of the time. He never got a clear view of things; he only saw a small part of the twisted path that wound its way along walls of rock and ravines. Around every bend some new danger could be lurking. This particular official wrote: "You tremble all over; your hair stands on end." The following group of letters must mean: "And your soul lies in your hand." This made me think of a sentence in my Latin breviary: *Anima mea in manibus meis semper*—i.e., "My soul is continually in my hands," a translation of Psalm 119, 109. It is a very biblical expression which also appears in other places; to lay his soul in the palm of his hand would mean to take his life into his hands, to risk his life (cf. 1 Sam. 19, 5; 28, 21; Job 13, 14). Thus the old Egyptian expressed hmself very biblically. But he wrote his letter about the same time as we now place Moses, and at any rate long before any written form of the Old Testament existed. Therefore, that man didn't express himself biblically; rather, it is just the other way around: the Bible expresses itself in the manner of the East.

In this way I shared personally in the surprising discoveries which Scripture scholars made as a group at the beginning of this century. At that time the work of deciphering had progressed to such an extent, as we have seen, that scholars could publish coherent descriptions of life and religion in Mesopotamia and Egypt, as well as anthologies of the many texts they had used. The number and variety of those texts has grown continually since then, more languages have been deciphered, and the history of more ancient cities and peoples have been laid open. Moreover, the anthologies have become more substantial. At the present time, in a good book store that handles modern-language translations of ancient oriental texts, anyone can buy imposing works that in one way or another are related to or are of interest for the Old Testament. Besides historical texts, you will find there myths about creation and primitive times, stories about heroes, sagas, songs of praise and prayers, love songs, proverbs teaching worldy wisdom, philosophical reflections, prophecies and oracles, liturgical prescriptions, law books of all kinds, letters, etc., that have been translated from the languages used in Egypt and Mesopotamia, Asia Minor, Syria, Palestine and neighboring countries. With the help of such anthologies, every Bible reader can "make discoveries" like the one just mentioned.

Possibility of Comparison

Two consequences of this disclosure of the ancient Near East are important for our subject. First, it became clear that Israel appeared only relatively late on the ancient world scene. That was indeed quite a new insight. Until then it was believed that the Bible was the world's oldest book. According to the opinion then in vogue, Moses had written the Pentateuch more than 14 centuries before Christ, many centuries before the oldest known historian. Moreover, he went further back in history than any other, for he narrated the very beginning of all history.

From the outline on the following page it is easy to see that great cultures were dying out or had already disappeared when Israel appeared on the scene as a nation. But we are concerned here with another consequence, the importance of which cannot be underestimated. Acquaintance with that world made it possible to compare Israel's culture and religion with those of preceding and neighboring nations. As a result, the awe-inspiring opportunity was given to us to see what was proper to Israel, to see what distinguished this people from those others. I sometimes use the following example to illustrate how one can see what is proper to a given phenomenon only when it is possible to compare it with similar phenomena. Suppose that on some island in the middle of the ocean there is only one doctor. For the population he is an exceptional person and they think the world of him: "The doctor taps your chest; he puts little tubes in his ears and thus listens to the noises which the sickness makes in your body. Sometimes he puts a needle into your arm and then the pain disappears; he also gives you little sweets and somehow you recover very quickly." Now suppose that suddenly four more doctors appear on that island. They, too, use stethoscopes, give injections, distribute medicine, etc. At first this might cause some confusion. Yet the population would quickly discover the actual reason why they thought so much of the first doctor. They would realize that it was not the instruments or the therapy which he applied, but the manner in which he used them: his personal care for each patient and the constant dedication with which he undertook each examination.

Christendom experienced something similar in its view of the Bible. To put it briefly: Until recently Christians considered every-

ISRAEL IN THE ANCIENT EAST
Some names from her prehistory

	EGYPT	MESOPOTAMIA		
3000	First EGYPTIAN dynasties ("Old Kingdom") Hieroglyphics developed	SUMERIAN culture in Mesopotamia Cuneiform writing developed		3000
	the pyramids Khufu (Cheops) Khafre (Chephren) Menkaure (Mycerinus)	city-states temple towers		
2500	"Ptah-hotep"	dynasties of Ur and Lagash		2500
	"Meri-ka-Re"	Sargon I of Akkad Naram-Sin		
2000	("Middle Kingdom") Amen-em-het I – III	third dynasty of Ur		2000
	Sesostris I – III	ASSYRIANS		
		Shamshi-Adad I	BABYLONIANS Hammurabi	
	the "Hyksos"	HITTITES		
	("New Kingdom")	Labarnas Mursilis		
1500	Amenophis I – III Thutmose I – III			1500
	Akhnaton "Amarna period"	Shuppiluliuma		
			Ashur-uballit	
	Ramses II Merneptah	Muwatallis	Shalmaneser I	
	Ramses III			
	Ramses IV-IX ("period of decline")	**ISRAEL**	Nebuchadnezzar I Tiglath-pileser I	
1000	Shishak	DAVID SOLOMON split		1000
	("Late Period")	"JUDAH" and "ISRAEL" Isaiah	Shalmaneser III	
	Psammetichus		Ashurbanipal	
	Necho	Jeremiah	Nabopolassar Nebuchadnezzar	
500				500

thing they read in that holy book as "revealed" and thus incapable of being compared with other things. All kinds of institutions, like sacrifice, the temple and prophecy—all seemed to be given exclusively to Israel and especially ordained for that nation as a preparation for Christ. Then suddenly, in that same ancient world, nations were uncovered with similar institutions and customs which were apparently common to all. At first that discovery was a source of unrest. Was there nothing unique about Israel? And what then is left of "revelation"?

As early as 1902 Friedrich Delitzsch delivered his famous speech "Babel und Bibel" which set off a violent struggle, even outside Germany. He "proved" that the Old Testament was a late and inferior "hand-me-down" of the so much higher Babylonian religion, and that ancient Babylon might be a better source than the Bible to furnish elements for a modern rational religion which could satisfy the intellect as well as the heart. The norms which Delitzsch applied to his comparison were so much a part of his own time and milieu that his speech was quickly relegated to the shelves of curiosity shops. But some of his professional colleagues succumbed to the exaggeration of "pan-Babylonianism"—i.e., that everything in the Bible, up to and including the Christ story, would have had its origin in some ancient Babylonian epic!

As early as the 1920's the "Babel und Bibel" polemic belonged forever to the past. As a positive result, however, texts being discovered in ever greater numbers were used more and more in the study of the Bible, not only in clarifying countless details in the Hebrew and Aramaic texts, but also in specifying more precisely what in fact was unique about Israel's religious experience.

Ancient Eastern Piety

May I first try to give a rough sketch of the piety which Israel encountered in its world. The ancients, Babylonians as well as Egyptians, were not aware of the concept of "nature," nor did they have a notion of "natural laws" as we understand them. The powers active in nature were for them personal in a certain sense and thus just as unpredictable and arbitrary as a human being. When a drought of long duration was followed by heavy rainfall, they didn't explain it as a result of an interaction between high and low pressure areas, as we do, but they would say, for example:

"The bull of heaven has scorched the earth's soil with his singeing breath and now the rain god is driving him away," and in the dark clouds they saw his extended wings. They besought the often savagely flooding Tigris to be calm. Some of the Pharaohs solemnly threw a letter into the Nile each year asking the Nile god to be so kind as to flood the banks of the river again. Thus men of antiquity stood in the middle of countless personal powers and felt that they were involved in their relations.

In that world there was no place for atheism. In a certain sense the difference between faith and disbelief was unknown there, for every person was involved with the gods. If I remember correctly, the index of a modern study on the Babylonian pantheon contains the names of 3,300 gods. I'll mention only a few important ones. "Heaven" was *Anu*. The name of the god *Enlil* meant "firmament." There was also a god *Sin*, the moon, and *Shamash*, the sun. The daughter of *Sin, Ishtar*, is the planet Venus; as morning star she is the goddess of war; as evening star, the goddess of love. *Hadad* is the storm. The god of the city Babylon was called *Marduk*, and to the extent that the city grew in importance, he received a higher place among the gods. His son was *Nabu*—i.e., herald; he was the planet Mercury, who announced the sunrise.

In the flat country of Mesopotamia, each large city had its temple tower which functioned as a "holy mountain." It consisted of three, five or seven terraces, decreasing in size, and was considered to be a connection between heaven and earth, a meeting place for gods and men. At the foot there were one or more temples, while elsewhere in the city more temples were to be found. In the Babylon which Nebuchadnezzar had completely rebuilt, archeologists found 53 large temples, 955 smaller chapels and 384 street altars. From the inscriptions and texts it is clear that there were innumerable priests of different classes and kinds, oracle-speakers, exorcists and very intricate liturgical ceremonies. Everyday life was governed by a number of prescriptions in order to avoid actions which could arouse the anger of a god, and also to perform those things which would promote the good will of other gods.

There was also a close connection between the great religious festivals and the rhythm of nature. Thus at the beginning of each year, in the spring, the fertility of the soil resulting from the rainfall and spring sun would be celebrated with stories about the gods ("myths") and all kinds of ceremonies ("rites"). Put in another way, the story of the revival of the god (myth) was performed with actions and song (rite). Thus the humiliation of *Marduk,* his suffering and death, and his descent into the underworld seem to have been celebrated in Babylon during an annual feast lasting twelve days. In it he conquered the powers of chaos and death, and when he again ascended his royal throne, he contracted a sacred marriage with his goddess, which was enacted by king and queen, priest and priestess; this divine marriage was to effect what it symbolized: the fertility of everything that lived in the land. It is clear that something like this could only take place among people for whom there was no difference between a symbol and the reality symbolized. When someone wrote the name of an enemy on a potsherd and then broke it into pieces, he was convinced that he struck the enemy himself.

During a recent visit to the Near East, I experienced this very thing myself. One day I asked a Bedouin from the desert if my companion—a draftsman—might make a sketch of him. Even the very suggestion frightened the man so much that he protested violently. This was a serious matter for him, for that charcoal sketch would render him vulnerable; it would give the artist power over his very person. On a frieze of an Egyptian temple I once saw a series of animals pictured. Among gazelles, antelopes and other known animals of the desert, I also saw mythological animals with four feet and a bird's head and the like, which can only exist in one's imagination or in a dream. But for the ancient Egyptian they could be just as real as "real" animals. For the man of antiquity, to be "real" meant to "do something," and a thing was "real" insofar as it had some effect. Thus some monster which appeared to him in a dream was just as real for him as the cow in its pasture; it made him really afraid. To get a feeling for their religious experience, one would have to pour over such data for a long time. This highly symbolic way of thinking will come up again later on when we discuss biblical patterns of thought and expression.

The Uniqueness of Israel

With its experience of a mystery lying behind and in all existing things as one personal power transcending and controlling them all, Israel stood completely alone in this religious world. This power was referred to with a word containing four consonants: Y H W H. In this word the Israelites heard a verb form in the third person: "he is." Thus both sides of their experience were given expression. First of all, he is not something determined; he is unlimited and no one image or concept could describe him. At the same time he "is" in a very dynamic sense of the word "to be": he is involved in everything, he is everywhere actively present and he shall continue to be so forever. Thus Israel believed itself related to a god who was exalted infinitely far above man, completely different from man, inexpressible and unapproachable, but who, *at the same time,* is exceedingly near and involved in everything that happens in nature, in history and in the life of every man. We will frequently come back to this point. Here we mention only some expressions of that faith which a foreign visitor to Israel couldn't fail to notice. Israel was the only nation whose god did not have a goddess at his side. This was connected with the fact that they held their god to be above all processes of nature. The word "goddess" did not even exist in their language.

Also closely connected with their experience of God was something which elsewhere in the Eastern world was unthinkable and incapable of being understood: they worshiped their god without any reference to an image of him. To others, symbol and reality were hardly distinguishable, and influencing a person was thought possible by exercising influence upon an image of him. However, to Israel an image of Yahweh would be contrary to the belief in his complete transcendence above all possible influences. Thus, within the circle of Yahweh-worshipers, all kinds of practices like fortune telling or consulting spirits and the dead were also forbidden. For they confessed that no supernatural powers exist—demons, spirits or gods—which can work independently of Yahweh and influence men without his knowing it. There is but one free power, one reality supreme over all, reigning with sovereign dominion over everything in nature and in history and deserving the name "power." He is at work in all that happens—rain and drought, victory as well as defeat—and whatever he intends through various events, he announces to Israel in completely understandable terms by means of his "mouthpieces," the prophets. One might read the striking confession of this faith in Deuteronomy 18, 9-15.

Still another point is related to all of this. Israel seems to have been the only one of all those nations—some of which were more highly cultured—that had a concept of what we call "history." The other peoples could scarcely recognize any connection in the events which they experienced. The annual cycle of nature repeated itself endlessly and time seemed more to be a circle than a straight line. Besides, everything that happened seemed in part at least to come forth from the arbitrariness and capriciousness of their countless gods. Israel believed itself spoken to in its history by that one divine power; it traced its origin back to an historical deed of his. The vicissitudes of life which it had undergone in its long history were seen to be a part of the relation, the dialogue, which Yahweh had begun with his people at the time of the exodus out of Egypt. In this way it could see a line running through historical events, a dynamic process which would obviously result in the fulfillment of history itself.

One may observe: This is all well and good, but are you sure that it isn't a construction of later times? Did ancient Israel actually stand so alone in that world, or do we read this into the Old Testament? Was Israel itself conscious of its uniqueness? Furthermore, the comparison doesn't seem completely honest. Perhaps the Old Testament preserved only the best of Israel's utterances as a kind of officially approved anthology. Is it then fair to compare the explicit religiosity in it with that of texts which every now and then have turned up in the ruins of Mesopotamia and Egypt and in which every Tom, Dick and Harry expressed his feelings quite freely?

These are very difficult questions. Non-biblical religious texts are now so many in number that they certainly give us a correct picture in broad lines of the dominating religiosity. With regard to the main characteristics of Israel's faith referred to above, we must indeed say that in a certain sense we can now see them more clearly than was possible for the historical Israelites. For a pure form of the "religion of Israel" never existed. Rather, we should speak of a process of fermenting which before Christ actually never came to a full stop. This can be illustrated as follows.

Yahweh Remained a Wanderer's God

"My father was a wandering Aramaean. . . ." Thus began the confession of the Israelite according to Deuteronomy 26 which he was to pronounce when the first-fruits of his field were offered, as we saw above. In that text (cf. p. 28), he expressed something which Israel considered characteristic of itself: from the life of a wanderer it had changed to an established existence. To put it technically: from "nomads" the Israelites became a "sedentary" people—i.e., they settled in one place.

According to the modern "history of religions" school, two very different experiences of reality were connected with these ways of life, and thus two very different religious attitudes. For the kind of nomads who lived as sheep herders and the like (Israel's ancestors were just this kind of nomads), daily reality was determined for the most part by the pasture lands. When a familiar territory had to be abandoned because of incessant drought or some danger to the tribe, this meant setting out for unknown parts, an adventure which meant risking the very existence of the tribe. The signal to set out, according to specialists in the study of religions, was given by the tribal chief under the inspiration of its god. This inspiration he experienced as a command and a promise: "Depart from here, to a new territory, that I will show you." This god then was thought to be a leader and to make the journey together with his worshipers, ever present, protecting and caring for them. All that he demanded was obedience and trust. It goes without saying that they couldn't conceive of any other gods. He was not tied down to any particular place or territory; he didn't live in a temple and he was not worshiped in the form of a particular ritual which demanded specialized ministers. When an animal of the flock was slaughtered to eat its meat, this obviously "holy" action was experienced then as a celebration to the community together with the real "shepherd" of the group, the divinity, to whom also the animals belonged.

Among sedentary peoples it was completely different. For them their established residence was always the same; their ancestors had lived there, and there, too, their children would be buried. Their existence depended on the annually revitalized fertility. Behind and in that order of the seasons and of their own limited world, they saw the world of their gods. These, too, were sedentary. They lived in temples and they were worshiped in detailed rituals performed by specialized personel. The characteristics of the ancient oriental piety sketched above were those of sedentary religions. Men and gods formed an equal part of the cosmic order, which was maintained by means of the rites. In this regard the gods needed men just as much as men needed them.

In explaining Israel's indisputably unique character, the following assumption has been made. While other sedentary cultures had almost completely forgotten their original nomadic heritage, a conscious awareness of it continued to live on in Israel. Thus the god of Israel retained a number of the characteristics, as it were, of the nomadic god. During its troubled history, Israel lived in a constant tension according to this view. The two experiences were incapable of perfect harmony with each other. It was only natural that settling in Canaan led to a religious experience common to "sedentary" peoples. But the "nomadic" origin of Israel's religion was evidently strong enough to maintain its influence.

In this connection exegetes often refer to the sealing of the Covenant at Shechem, which is recalled in the last chapter of the book of Joshua. It is believed that Joshua acted here on behalf of the group, which under the leadership of Moses had come out of Egypt and had come to know Yahweh through the exodus and its experiences in the desert. It was in central Palestine that this Yahweh group was then making the change to a sedentary way of life. Other nomadic tribes, too, each worshiping the "god of its founding father" in its own way, were involved in that same process. At Shechem Joshua, it is thought, proposed that these tribes join "him and his house" (Jos. 24, 15) and from then on recognize Yahweh as their God, which meant of course their only god; as nomads they could not do otherwise. In this way "the God of Abraham" and Yahweh, "he who led us out of Egypt," are thought to have become one and the same. Thus this "us" came to include a greater number of tribes.

The pact made at Shechem may have been intended to strengthen the new tribes against the Canaanites, a sedentary people from of old. But soon Israel became just as sedentary. From the united tribes David made an authentic oriental state. He conquered the ancient city of Jerusalem and there took for himself the place of the Canaanite monarch. Furthermore, he annexed large areas with their "pagan" population to the old area of the tribal federation. With the help of Canaanite architects Solomon built a temple for Yahweh, exactly in the manner of the other peoples.

The prophet Nathan opposed, on behalf of Yahweh, the building of the temple (2 Sam. 7, 5-7), and that protest will be heard repeatedly in the course of history in many different ways. For the wanderer's god, Yahweh, could not be made completely subservient to the hard and fast ordinances of a sedentary religion. The acceptance of all kinds of Canaanitic forms did, however, considerably enrich the old faith. Formerly they had considered the interest of the "shepherd god" to be limited to a group of wandering worshipers; now functions were attributed to him which for the Canaanites belonged to El and Elyon, the "Most High" of the divine world. Thus Yahweh became the creator of heaven and earth, the supreme ruler of the entire cosmos and all powers at work in it. In adopting the Canaanite ritual surrounding the king, Israel took on a new form for its future expectations; divine functions which were attributed to the earthly king were "translated" into Messianic expectations, which have become so characteristic of Israel.

But even as king of the universe, Yahweh remained primarily the god of wanderers. This seems to be the main reason why the faith of Israel did not perish at the time of its destruction as a sedentary people. In the last analysis, Yahweh was not tied down to his land and his temple. That's why the priest Ezekiel could envision the divine throne as a mysterious moving chariot. After the destruction of the temple, Yahweh could leave his "house" and go to the exiles in far-off Babylon, and from there he could lead them back again as the shepherd of his flock (cf. Is. 40, 11).

The reader is perhaps surprised at the facility with which we spoke about Israel's origin in the above sketch. What is the basis for the supposition that only one group led by Moses came out of Egypt and that the federation of the twelve tribes came about only later? After all, the book of Genesis relates in detail how Jacob and his sons went down to Egypt. Exodus describes how Moses led all their descendants through the Red Sea to Mount Sinai, while the first chapter of Numbers states very precisely how many men over nineteen years of age belonged to each tribe. Altogether there were 603,550, not counting the 23,000 descendants of Levi older than one month. Now the previous chapter made it clear that quite a few later developments were worked into the continuous story of the Pentateuch, which proposes to be a factual report. But does this insight go so far as to allow one to meddle with the historical correctness of such fundamental reports as that of the twelve tribes in Egypt?

To answer this question properly, we must delve into the various ways in which biblical people spoke about the past, and this is very closely connected with their way of sensing things and of thinking and expressing themselves, which in some respects differs quite a bit from what we modern Western men are used to.

II
THE LITERARY NATURE OF THE BIBLE

When we speak with someone about one of the innumerable objects around us, there can be no misunderstanding about the term used. A table is not a chair and a motorcycle is not a train. But it is quite another thing when we want to share with someone what we feel, think, mean or believe. In that case we use words which don't always precisely call up for the other person exactly what they mean for us. We realize that we must know him for some time and enjoy a certain familiarity with him before we can be sure that he will not misunderstand our words. To the extent that we begin to communicate more deeply, the limitations of that awe-inspiring phenomenon which we call "speaking" also become more apparent: man can never perfectly express in words that which moves him most deeply. Something so uniquely his own always remains, which he cannot even share with his most beloved. He is always "the other."

In conversation with a foreigner, mutual understanding is doubly difficult because of the difference in language. This is especially true when his language derived from and is used in another part of the world, in another climate, in another culture. Then vast differences in the way we sense things, absorb them and express ourselves will hinder our communication.

The chance of misunderstanding is even greater still when that foreigner belongs to the past, with the result that his words reach us only by way of a document. What he intended to say stands recorded there, crystallized, in specific sentences and words. All the other means which he used at that time to try to express what moved him—the tone of his voice, his gestures, the further explanation and his attitude known from a longer acquaintance—all of this is forever lost. All that is left is a dead text.

Such is the case with the Bible. Those whose words we have in that book (or rather, that library of documents) spoke different languages and lived in regions of the world with a completely different climate from ours and another culture—and all of this in a past which daily becomes more remote. An historical approach which attempts above all to determine what the biblical writers meant will therefore have to pay attention to—let us say—their "psychology." It goes without saying that the study of the languages which they used (Hebrew, Aramaic and "biblical Greek") is in the strict sense the gateway to an investigation into the ways in which they sensed things, thought and expressed themselves. We would like to devote the following paragraphs to this last point, with special attention being paid to manners of expression that are related to the much discussed question of the historical fidelity of biblical stories.

Hebrew versus Greek Thought

It seems a general law that peculiarities are only observed in an environment which doesn't have them. We saw already that the special character of Israel's religion really only became clear when that of its predecessors and neighbors came to light. But this law also applies to the Bible as a whole. That book clearly has its own character which strikes one as soon as it is compared with other books. In earlier centuries this was also seen, but this was, it seems, self-evident. The Bible was seen principally as God's word, as inspired by the Holy Spirit, and thus in a certain sense having its origin more from God than from man. No wonder that it differed from all other books.

In our day we try to clarify the character proper to the Bible by comparing the ways of thinking and manners of expression of biblical writers with others with whom we modern Western men are more familiar. In recent years this has often been done by contrasting "Hebrew" (or Semitic) with "Greek" thought. The way in which the differences between these two ways of thinking are characterized for the most part can in fact contribute to a better understanding of what is meant in scriptural texts. But this can also give rise to misunderstanding. Therefore, we will begin with a short sketch of the usual description and then add several observations of our own.

What we are concerned with here are two different experiences of reality. The *Greek* stands in the world observing and judging. He sees that he is surrounded by "things" which he can distinguish from each other. For example, if he is struck by the phenomenon of the world of birds, with so many sorts and varieties, he can set aside the differences among them, like color, size and shape. Those are secondary for him. What is common to all birds is the "essence" of bird. That is the unique something which corresponds in his mind with the concept of bird. Even if all birds should become extinct, in his mind he could still reflect upon that unique something, that "essence." Thus the mind becomes a mirror of the essence of things and their order, since for the Greek the world is *cosmos*—i.e., order, harmony. Consequently, he also strives for an ordered mind, for sharp distinctions, clear concepts and evident proportions. The words "logic" and "logical," so familiar to us, come from the Greek word *logos* and the verb *legein*. With these terms the Greeks thought simultaneously of gathering, choosing, counting, summing up, naming, speaking, explaining and reasoning. For them the word was at the service of man's intellect. In a statement, story or treatise, one tries to express as clearly as possible what he sees in his mind. That is the essential connection of things; that is the truth. By means of the extremely refined instrument of language he reveals that truth so that it can also be seen by another.

Thus we can understand the connection between the great and masterly accomplishments of the Greeks: rhetoric, mathematics and the plastic arts. Clarity, order and harmony were their primary concern.

For this reason the Greek has a dislike for things which happen unexpectedly. These disturb the order of things and the harmony in the human community. They are connected with matter, material things, all those secondary things which the mind must set aside if it wishes to touch upon the essence of things. To the extent that the material world escapes his ordering activity, the Greek would prefer to be redeemed from it. Freed of matter, he would like to be taken up, undisturbed, into the completely satisfying contemplation of the eternal realities, of "the" truth, "the" good and "the" beautiful. However, his body binds him to what happens in time, that measuring stick of changing things. But in the vicissitudes of life couldn't there also be some established order which continually returns? A Greek sage is supposed to have said that the famous Trojan War is just as much future as past, inasmuch as the same course of things will repeat itself, continually.

The *Hebrew* experiences reality in a very different way. In every fiber of his body he senses an involvement with his environment. He cannot create that distance between himself and things which is necessary to compare them, to distinguish their essence from secondary factors and to form the purest possible idea of that essence. For him it is not a question of what they are in themselves, but what they mean to him, what they do to him and what he must do with them. The world of things and men is not a mirror of eternal realities, but an environment in which he is placed to fulfill a task, to answer a call. He is always on the road toward that "fulfillment" of his life, which cannot consist in understanding and observing, but in activity and personal involvement. This he experiences together with others, and with them he forms a group of which he considers himself to be a living part, a kind of organ.

Language for a Hebrew is not an instrument to express as purely as possible what he sees, but to involve the other in what moves him. His word *dabar,* meaning "word," is concerned with action, with a feeling which forces itself outside of him. There it goes on to effect something in another person immediately present, and, further, in the group and in the world. *Dabar* is at once the spoken word, the undertaking and the event. Thus his language does not have the refinement which is necessary to express concepts and insights as precisely as possible. Instead of carefully constructed complex sentences, he uses short declarative sentences joined by "and," and for the most part beginning with a verb, a fact which implies action. Often he says the same thing in two sentences with different words, as if knocking twice on the door he wants to open, for he is not so much concerned with communicating insight as with causing something to happen. In all his literature, hardly one logically constructed argument can be found, hardly one ordered treatise. If he wishes to treat some question (and for him that can only be a question concerning man, his task and goal, his relation to God), then he introduces a specific person who has experienced some adventure with his fellow men and with God. Wherever the material for the story may come from, whether from memory or from the imagination, the story is "true" insofar as it really moves the listener or reader to action.

For the Hebrew, unexpected events are not an unpleasant disturbance of the order of things. On the contrary, God reveals himself through such events, and this can only mean that God communicates what he is planning to do or what he wishes to be done. Such an event is a call to those who experience it. Since those people live but once, events cannot repeat themselves, for reality is continuity, history, an adventure ever moving forward and never to be turned back, having its climax in God.

Life's real values, then, cannot be contained in terms of seeing, insight, knowledge and observation, but in terms of listening, deciding and obeying. A man is not first and foremost a species of the genus "animal" who is gifted (secondarily) with reason, but one spoken to by God and therefore a bearer of responsibility.

To complete this sketch of the contrast, a few words of commentary seem desirable. First of all, we must keep in mind that some of the peculiarities which are attributed to that "Hebrew" thought were common to the milieu in which Israel had its origin. The term "Semitic" is used broadly enough to characterize that whole world. In that way the ancient Egyptians fall under the term as well as the Canaanites, though these were influenced by other cultures not strictly Semitic. There, too, people were accustomed to think dynamically; there, too, human speech was experienced as a transferring of activity or motion; there, too, things were not distinguished according to essence and secondary characteristics, and people were not interested in what things are, but in what they do and mean. It was in such thought patterns, common to the Semitic world, that Israel expressed its faith in God. This then determined its own experience of reality and went on more and more to characterize it.

That "more and more" does not indicate a rectilinear process, as we have already pointed out. It does indicate a troubled history in which many influences have left their mark. Hebrew thought was no exception. The Assyrians, who in the 8th century destroyed the northern kingdom, as well as the Babylonians, who in 587 brought about the end of surviving Judah, were closely related to Israel with regard to race, language and culture. It was a different story with the Persians who, after conquering Babylon in 538, ruled the whole Middle East for several centuries. The "way of thinking" of these Aryans differed drastically in some respects from Semitic thought. Now it was the Persians who exercised leadership in organizing the remaining Judeans in what from that time on can be called Judaism. The great men who gave shape to the community in Palestine, Nehemiah and Esdras, held high offices in the Persian court. Even the religious life of Jewish settlements far away from Palestine, such as the one on the island of Elephantine in the Nile (near present-day Aswan), was directed by Persian officials. After an unquestionably strong influence from this sector, Alexander the Great entered the scene. He died in 323 B.C., and in his wake followed the Hellenization of the entire cultured world. More and more Jews in that world came to speak Greek as their mother tongue. All of this had to have its influence on their thought. Even a cursory glance at the 1,200 years which lie between the oldest text of the Bible and the most recent one urges caution, then, in defining a particular way of thinking which all biblical writers would have in common.

One should be equally careful in using the concept "Greek thought." It is sometimes presented in such a way that every Greek would seem to have been a pupil of Plato. But his greatest and most influential disciple, Aristotle, thought quite differently from his master on important points. And in the centuries after them, philosophical schools sprung up which had still different ideas from those two great masters.

Furthermore, a comparison with the Bible would be of value when contrasted with the whole of Greek literature and not primarily with philosophical works, for the Bible reflects the entire literature of the believing community and not only that of select thinkers.

Textbook versus Literature

This brings us to another contrast. Let us temporarily propose it as follows: the Bible as textbook versus the Bible as "literary work."

All books can be roughly divided into two groups. To one group belong all books which offer information, whatever the subject may be; to the other group belong the works in which writers attempt to express their personal experiences. In an informative book the personal feeling of the author plays no role. Whether it is a book on biology, the population explosion, space or any other clearly defined subject, the personal experience of the author remains outside the reader's range of sight and judgment. Whether he is old or young, moody or even-tempered, embittered or content, has nothing at all to do with it—not even the degree to which he is interested in his subject. All that the reader expects of such an informative book is that the subject be handled as clearly as possible on the basis of equally reliable data. The author's success depends upon the extent to which he gathers data and critically sifts it, reasons clearly and possesses the gift of communicating his knowledge.

Books of the second kind fall for the most part under literary works. Novels and poetry involve a deep expression of one's own experience. Authors of the so-called historical novels are also aware of this in their descriptions of personalities out of the past. In her *Zelfportret als Legkaart* (Self-Portrait as Jigsaw Puzzle), published in Amsterdam in 1961, Hella Haasse wrote the following on this point: "I see how in the course of years I have portrayed the same thing in different disguises, compelled to write by the need, always the same, of freedom. The mask and the decor weren't important; for whatever I wrote, *it was about myself.*" (The italics are ours.) She continues: "A writer who thinks that he can let go of himself and, independent of himself, create other people, other things in another time, another environment, another order, is a victim of self-deception." A little further on she quotes an Englishman, Raymond Williams, who made the following observation: "Even at the simplest levels of literature, a writer is hardly likely to concern himself with a story or a character unless these have some meaning to him and seem important in his general experience of life. We do not pick our favorite stories, of any kind, any more than we pick our favorite historical personages or our preoccupying abstractions, by chance. We pick them beause they represent aspects of experience which, however submerged the connection, are relevant to our own experience" (*Drama from Ibsen to Eliot,* p. 19).

If we now consider the Bible in terms of that global division of books into informative and literary, then, again very globally, we can say that at the present time the Bible is counted among the second rather than the first. This statement implies that formerly it was counted among the informative works. This can be illustrated as follows:

For many centuries Western Christendom also looked upon the Bible as a book containing "truths of the faith." The expression "to believe someone on his word" means in our languages "to accept that he speaks the truth." And the truth consists in this: that things which one has not seen or experienced himself really are or happened just as the other person says. When one accepts this, then he is said to "believe" his informant. Therefore, believing in a religious sense has often been defined in that manner: Christian faith was the acceptance on God's authority that certain things which one cannot himself see or experience really are just as he says; thus they are "the truth." The Bible therefore contains truths which one believes, truths of the faith or revealed truths. These are seen as a kind of completion or superstructure for the many truths which man can arrive at on his own, verify and prove, whether simply by observation or reflection, or partially by means of scientific research.

Needless to say, there are also countless practical admonitions in the Bible which are illustrated by examples from human life. Thus it has always been clear to its faithful readers that man will reach or miss his final goal according to the extent to which he is prepared to help his fellow man (Mt. 25, 34-46). Even the deepest knowledge of divine truths and clearest insight into the world of the invisible will be completely worthless when one is wanting in that everyday charity which is honest, compassionate and patient (cf. 1 Cor. 13, 1-7).

Nevertheless the Western Church maintained a great interest in what we call the intellectual element in the faith. The ecclesiastical authority was also a "teaching authority" which saw to it that the truths of the faith were expressed as purely as possible and sometimes took strict measures to protect the community of the faithful from the influence of false teachings. The Church found revealed truths in two sources, the Bible and tradition.

In the 16th century the Reformers came out against an exaggerated emphasis on the intellectual side. For them biblical faith meant above all a surrender of the heart, a turning to God of the whole person. They also protested against ecclesiastical tradition as a source of truth. For them, the Bible alone could be the norm for the faithful Christian who, enlightened by the Holy Spirit, was considered capable of learning divine truth from the Bible himself, without the help of others. Consequently, during the theological disputes between the Roman Church and the Protestant Churches, both sides continued to use the Bible as an "informative" book that contained truths.

Still another factor played a role here. After the Middle Ages, Christians gradually lost their feeling for the symbolic value or meaning of scriptural stories. Put in another way, their concept of "truth" was severely restricted in its scope. A story was considered true only when it was a faithful account of something which actually happened in the past. More or less consciously, people reasoned as follows: an historical report has greater value to the extent that it more objectively mirrors the facts; now the Bible, being God's word, is our most valuable book, and thus its stories must be the most objective accounts possible. Or perhaps the approach was rather a negative one: the Bible cannot contain any fictitious stories, sagas, legends and the like—in short, not one single story about the past which is the product of one's "subjective" imagination—for God is absolute truth. It is blasphemy to imply in any way that there could be human "concoctions" in the book which he underwrites.

Until recently this was the general view of Christians, both Catholic and Protestant. They were not aware that in so doing they imposed their own norms on the Bible and thus treated that book, if we may use the comparison, much like the peoples they were colonizing, imposing on them the standards of their own culture. It is not a coincidence that precisely in a period of opposition to colonialization the proper character of the Bible could again become visible. A much more thorough treatment of the question would be necessary to describe all the factors which led to this development. Let it suffice to mention here only the historical approach, the beginnings of which we sketched in the first chapter. In any case the result is that today the Bible is considered more to be a literary work than belonging to the group of informative books. It certainly does contain information, but such information is subordinated to or is at the service of the experience of reality which biblical men were trying to express.

Perhaps one of the reasons why the contrast described above between Hebrew and Greek thought has become so popular is that,

in its own way, it says the same thing: the Bible is not so much
"Greek"—i.e., communicating objective truth—as "Hebrew—i.e.,
a witness to an experience. However this may be, the modern
approach is evidently confusing for many of the faithful. They
question to what extent the Bible is still "true." This is especially
troublesome when it's a question of the narrative parts of Scripture. Therefore in the following paragraphs we would like to discuss some of the ways of thinking which have influenced the biblical representations of the past.

III
BIBLICAL "HISTORIOGRAPHY"

More than half of the Old Testament consists of stories. This is
also true for the New Testament, for the four gospels and the book
of Acts make up 60% of the whole work. The following chapters
will enable us to get better acquainted with the enormous variety
of that material. There are stories which were first passed on by
word of mouth for many generations before they were written
down. Others were the work of only one man, the author himself.
Sometimes he simply records what he himself had seen and heard,
while in other cases he simply draws on his imagination. There are
but two extreme possibilities. Most Bible stories fall somewhere in
between.

The rest of this chapter will be devoted to several peculiarities
of biblical storytelling, which are connected with what we referred
to above as Hebrew thought. We will begin with the simplest.

Nations and Tribes Pictured as Persons

We read in Genesis 10 that Ham had several sons, among them
Egypt and Canaan. A bit further on Canaan is said to have
brought forth Sidon, his first-born. Everyone knows that Egypt and
Canaan are nations and Sidon a city. How do we explain the
peculiarity that nations and cities are represented as persons, as
father and son?

Sometimes we, too, speak of countries as if they were people.
We say, for example, that England has taken this or that initiative
or that France is for or against something. When England's

national soccer team wins, we say that England won. Thus we use the word "England" in different senses. It can refer to the island in the Atlantic, but also to the people who live there, the English nation; at the same time it can mean the person or team, as in our example, who represents that nation. There is a connection between those various meanings of the word which we don't distinguish very clearly when we speak globally or poetically, but which can be very precisely distinguished from each other in our mind.

Now we have seen that the Semitic mind sees things more in terms of a whole than in terms of parts. He is not so much inclined to make distinctions and to analyze things. More easily than we, then, he will consider a nation and the peoples who live there as one, and he will identify a representative of that people with the whole.

Furthermore, we have already seen that Israel came forth from nomadic tribes which settled in Canaan. Now a tribe was made up of a group of families who took it for granted that they all stemmed from one and the same ancestor. The unity of the tribe was based upon that conviction of being related by blood. When a number of tribes formed a larger union, then the ancestors were made blood relatives. In many instances we should really say the "supposed" ancestors. Striking examples of this can be found in the world of the Arabian tribes. A tribe which had withdrawn from a larger federation was called, for example, "the Separated." Soon thereafter they would refer to their ancestor as a certain "Separation." If later on another group, called the "Unified," joined up with them, then "Separation" was said to have a son whose name was "Union."

This can throw some light on the way, so strange to us, in which ancient Israel spoke about the lands and nations in the surrounding world and also about its own past.

When David had organized the tribes into a kingdom and made tributaries of a number of surrounding nations, completely new horizons opened up for the Israelites. Through the presence of merchants and envoys their contacts reached still further. Thus they discovered the enormous diversity of peoples in the wide world. They put some order in that multiplicity by dividing the then known world population into three groups. The group in the East, in and around Mesopotamia, they called Sem. They thus referred to a people belonging to that group—e.g., the Assyrians—as a "son of Sem." Further away still, but in the same direction, lay the country of Elam with its inhabitants, the Elamites. Thus Sem also had a "son" called Elam. Where we would say that those two nations belonged to one group, in Israel they would consider them as "sons" of that group, which then would be called the "father."

The peoples to the northwest and west, in Asia Minor and on the Greek islands, including Cyprus and Crete, they called Japhet. The smaller groups were again referred to in like manner. One of those "sons" was called Javan or Ion, the Ionians of our history books.

The group southwest of Israel they called Ham, and its divisions were again called "sons." Thus Egypt (*Misraim*), the actual Egypt on the Nile, was a "son" of Ham, as likewise was Ethiopia further south (*Cush*).

Where did Canaan belong? The name meant "purple snail," for the whole coastal region was characterized by the snails which washed ashore in great numbers and which had been used to make purple dye as long as people could remember. Thus the name Canaan also meant "purple country." In Greek that snail and purple are called *phoinix;* thus the Greeks named the area *Phoinikia,* our Phoenicia. Now the Israelites knew that Canaan had been under Egyptian influence for many centuries; culturally as well as politically it was, so to speak, a part of Egypt. Therefore they said: "Canaan is a son of Ham," or "Ham is the father of Canaan" (Gen. 10, 6).

That country of Canaan was also divided into parts, the cities with their territories. On that purple coast lay one of these, Sidon, for a long time one of the most important cities of Canaan. That situation is expressed as we saw above: "Canaan became the father of Sidon, his first-born. . . ." (Gn. 10, 15).

This way of describing in terms of blood relationship the relations between peoples which formed a specific group, and between a certain country and its parts, Israel also used in describing its own past. We have already mentioned the Covenant at Shechem which united several tribes in the faith of the Yahweh worshipers who had come out of Egypt. For some reason, presumably astrological (twelve signs of the Zodiac) they evidently attached a certain value to the number twelve. The whole group was called Israel. Each tribe also had a name of its own, this being derived from an ancestor or from the territory it inhabited or from some special activity. Thus Naphtali was the name of a region, just like Ephraim. According to some scholars, Judah, too, was originally the name of the mountain region south of Jerusalem. If Issachar really means "wage earner," it might have been a name used in mockery for one of the tribes of Israel because many of its members had gone into the service of city monarchs. Therefore, those twelve tribes of Israel could be referred to as the "twelve sons of Israel." Jacob was an ancestor of one of the leading tribes in the federation, a concrete historical person. When this man was identified with the supposed founding father Israel, the notion of Jacob and his twelve sons took shape.

A Mr. Canaan therefore never existed whose oldest son was named Sidon who in his turn could call the gray-haired Ham "grandpa." What actually existed was the varied population of the "purple country" that was called Canaan after the snail. And so the people there were known as the "sons of Canaan." This isn't really so strange. When Martin Luther King won the Nobel Peace Prize, it's not too difficult to imagine the mayor of Atlanta, in a very rhetorical speech in his honor, singing the praises of "this son of the deep South." Today, however, no one would go on to tell a story about a supposed marriage between a Miss Georgia and Mr. Deep South. But this is just what the Israelites did. They were accustomed to describe the situation and nature of a sector of the population as well as their relationship with them in a story about that one person, the supposed ancestor.

Names Characterizing Origin and Lot

In stories of that kind they liked to start from the sound or possible meaning of the name. We have already observed that in the ancient East the name of a person or thing was considered to belong to his essence. His name was the expression of his character, a mirror reflecting his vicissitudes, and thus in a certain sense the person himself. Sometimes a story characterizing the nature, origin or vocation of a person or thing will end with the words, "And so he was called. . . ." In most cases the process was reversed. Because some person, place or thing from the past bore a certain name, a story was told which revealed the connection between that name and the character and lot of the person or thing referred to.

This is certainly the case with the name Jacob. Long before Israel existed, this name was already known and probably meant at that time: "May he [God] protect." In the language of the Israelites the name Jacob, pronounced *ya'aköb,* was identical with the third person singular of a verb which was derived from the noun *'aketb,* heel. This verb form meant: "He lies in wait for one's heel, he is cunning, he deceives."

To understand the story about Jacob and Esau, one must know something about the latter. That old hunter had been identified with the (supposed) ancestor of Edom, the country and people southwest of the Dead Sea. Their mountain region was called Seir. Both names, Edom and Seir, resemble words in the everyday speech of the Israelites. The first looked like *edom* and *admoni,* "red, reddish," and the second resembled *se'ar,* "hair."

When the story originated, during or shortly after the reign of David, Edom was subject to Israel. Now it was believed that in their nomadic days the Edomites had belonged to the same group as the ancestors of the Israelites, but that they took up a sedentary way of life and were organized into a kingdom before Israel. Edom was thus an older "brother" of Israel and yet subject to him. How were they to explain this situation?

The story of Rebekah and her twins provides the answer (Gn. 25, 19-34). She carries these two children in her womb. Esau —that is, Edom—appears first: "The first to be born was red, and as though he were completely wrapped in a hairy cloak. . . ." The second twin was born "with his hand grasping Esau's heel. . . ." The names appear in other details as well—for example, the red color of the soup which Esau desires to eat (25, 30) and in the story where Jacob "deceives" his older brother and thus lives up to his name (27, 36).

That Edom's subjection to Israel under the great King David was really a part of Yahweh's plan is expressed in a typically biblical way in Genesis 25, 23 by means of a divine revelation to the pregnant Rebekah:

> There are two nations in your womb,
> your issue will be two rival peoples.
> One nation shall have the mastery of the other,
> and the elder shall serve the younger.

Another example: North of Edom and likewise on the other side of the Jordan valley and the Dead Sea lived two nations which were also related to Israel, Ammon and Moab. An Israelite heard a familiar word in each of those names: in the first word *'amm,* indicating a blood relative or an ancestor, and in the second *ab,* the normal word for father, while the *m* can mean "from" or "out of." These data give us a hint as to the origin and meaning of the story about Lot and his daughters which the modern reader finds so strange, if not repulsive (Gn. 19, 30-38). In the early period of the kings Israel didn't think too highly of these two related nations east of the cursed Salt Sea, which later came to be called the Dead Sea. They expressed this by relating the origin of those nations in a particular manner. They made them the descendants of Lot, who is presented as Abraham's nephew. Lot flees with his two daughters from Sodom where their husbands were killed. In a cave, somewhere east of the Dead Sea, they arrange to get their father drunk, and each has a child by him. That's why one is called "son of my blood relative" or "related by blood" (Ammon) and the other is called "from father" (Moab).

For the first readers this story was much more fascinating than it can possibly be for us (and less offensive). Two nations which they despised (cf., e.g., Dt. 23, 4) are put in their place here, and as "radically" as possible, even irrevocably. For they did so on the basis of their names, and thus of their very being. Now, no translation can directly bring out this precise quality of the story. The "play on words" (for the Israelites, more than just "playing") must be tediously explained to other readers. They must rely on footnotes to see that the climax is really already being prepared by the emphasis of "from father" (*me'ab*) in verses 33, 34 and 36.

Furthermore, the incest of the two women is usually related without any trace of disapproval. That evil was in fact forbidden in Israel. But the first readers saw this more as a social longing for survival than as selfish passion in the daughters of Lot, who wanted to secure the continuance of their father's line at all cost. This end also justified the means of incest in the readers' eyes. Tamar was driven by this same urge, further on in Genesis. We will return to this shortly.

After absorbing and having reflected upon all these examples, one may ask: Canaan, together with Egypt, Ethiopia and other lands, formed the group Ham. "He" was a "son" of Ham just as

Assyria and Elam were "sons" of Sem. Now if those three groups, Sem, Ham and Japhet, together formed all of humanity, and if the Hebrew word for men and humanity is *adam*, why didn't they say, "Adam had three sons, Sem, Ham and Japhet"?

We answer that at one time it may very well have been expressed in that way in Israel. But this was no longer possible after the ancient story of the flood had been taken over from Mesopotamia and was given a place among the "origin stories." The hero of that story, who in Israel received the name Noah, was the only survivor, and he alone could be the "father" of the three "sons." Except for Ham, these three remain rather vague in the story. The Yahwistic version relates that Noah began to till the soil after the Deluge. He lived up to his name (cf. 5, 29) by being the first one to plant a vineyard. Thus it was his privilege to harvest from the cursed earth the precious blood of the grape which more than any other drink gladdens the hearts of men (cf. Ps. 104, 15). Noah got drunk on it and in an intoxicated fit undressed himself. Ham saw it, and the text seems to say that he took pleasure in it. Perhaps more was said in an older version of the story, for Noah became very angry when he heard "what his youngest son had done to him." However this may be, it is remarkable that he then curses not Ham, but Canaan, the son of Ham. He shall be suppressed by his brothers and be their "meanest slave" (Gn. 9, 20-27).

Here, too, we are confronted with a story characterizing the situation and nature of a particular group of the population by relating something of its beginnings—that is to say, something about its founding father. This story differs from those others in that it doesn't start with or make an allusion to the meaning of the name Canaan.

Characteristic of the sons of Canaan in the eyes of the Israelites was their sexual degeneration. In our sketch of ancient oriental piety, we already made mention of the way in which the earth's fertility was celebrated in the form of divine marriages performed ritually. In Canaan the worshipers of the Baals and the Astartes were actively involved in these rites: each temple had its male and female prostitutes for the purpose. In the rough story of Genesis 38 this is mentioned in passing. It concerns Tamar, who, like the daughters of Lot, did not eschew any means to have children for her deceased husband. By disguising herself as a prostitute she managed to become pregnant by her father-in-law Judah. In this way she earned the honor of being included in the genealogy of King David and thus of Christ. Now, in verses 21 and 22 the Hebrew text has the word "sacred [prostitute]"—i.e., a woman attached to a sanctuary who performs religious prostitution. If the Israelites showed little opposition to the incest in the cases mentioned, so much more did they abominate the sexual character of the Canaanitic religion. It could only be detestable in Yahweh's eyes. In the fact that they brought about the disappearance of the Canaanites as an independent group, partly by enslaving it and by absorbing it into their own nation, the Israelites saw the hand of Yahweh. He had punished Canaan for its immorality. In the typically biblical manner already mentioned in the case of Israel and Edom, they let this course of events be announced centuries earlier by a powerful word, this time not directly from Yahweh, but pronounced by Noah: future servitude was announced to the supposed ancestor as a punishment for his immoral behavior.

In the story it is Ham who commits the sexual sin against Noah. Many scholars suppose that in an older version of the story, Canaan himself was listed with Sem and Japhet and not Ham. That is perhaps possible. For the ancient writer and his readers however, it didn't make any difference if a son was cursed for what he himself had done or for what his father had done. Also in this regard, their way of thinking was different from ours.

Related Ways of Seeing and Presenting Things

We saw that the Hebrew looks at things more as a whole than in component parts. And those entities for him are not "static" things—i.e., determined and strictly outlined—but rather sources of power. He experiences them as something "dynamic." Thus his clan or tribe is a living entity whose power of inspiration is also at work in him. When David sends word to his priests to announce to the elders of his tribe, "You are my own flesh and blood," he intends more than we do when we use similar imagery (2 Sam. 19, 13). That consciousness of an exceedingly profound solidarity contributed not only to the custom which we pointed out above—i.e., referring to a group of people as one person—but also to other ways of seeing things common to the Bible which are very closely connected with that custom. They are so closely connected that they frequently coincide and are very difficult to distinguish. This will be apparent from several examples, an arbitrary selection from the Bible's abundance.

After Jericho fell to the Israelites, they attacked the city Ai. This venture was a failure. No one knew that one of the Israelites had stolen part of the booty from Jericho, which had been dedicated in its entirety to Yahweh. When they realized that "something was rotten" among the people, they cast lots. The guilty one was revealed—Achan. Then we are told (in the Hebrew text) that he was burned and stoned—Achan himself, and also "his sons and daughters, his oxen and donkeys and sheep, his tent and everything that belonged to him" (Jos. 7, 25-26).

Apparently Achan formed a unity with his family and possessions—in short, everything which bore his name—and that personal entity is again so bound up with Israel that his sin injured the whole people. This example can clarify two things somewhat: first, the ease with which a group acts as one person, refers to itself as "I" and is spoken to as "you," and second, the facility with which a person is identified with that which bears his name or mark, with that which he brings about—in short, with everything that is experienced as a kind of extension of his personality.

In the book of Numbers, for example, one reads the story of Israel's march through the territory of Edom (20, 14-21). Moses sends messengers to announce to the king of the Edomites: (translated literally) "Thus speaks your brother Israel, 'You know all the misery that has befallen us; how our fathers went down to Egypt. . . . Let us pass through your country.' But Edom said to him, 'You shall not pass through me, otherwise I will advance against you with the sword.' Then the sons of Israel said to him, 'We will go up along the highway, and if I and my livestock drink of your water, I will pay for it. . . .' "

Besides the remarkable shifting back and forth from singular to plural, there is also a fusion of concepts which we would clearly distinguish: Edom is at once the king, the people and the territory.

In 1 Samuel the Philistines didn't know what to do with the ark of God which they had captured from the Israelites. Everywhere it comes, God strikes the people with all kinds of plagues—thus the panic on the part of the inhabitants of Ekron when the ark was sent there. "Then the Ekronites cried, 'They have brought the ark of the God of Israel to bring death to me and my people!' Then they summoned all the Philistine chiefs and said, 'Send the ark of the God of Israel away; let it go back to its sanctuary; otherwise it will bring death on me and my people.' " (5, 10-11).

A modern reader might think that the author allows the king of Ekron to speak here on behalf of his people. But he doesn't mention the king. For him and his first readers that wasn't necessary either, for where we strictly distinguish—here is the king and there the people whom he represents—the biblical people saw them as one entity. The king pleading the cause of his people *is* that people.

The person who *is* the group in this way can be the founding father of a tribe—and then either an actual father, such as Achan (if his sons and daughters were allowed to live, Achan would not have been removed), or a fictitious father, such as Canaan (he was cursed because of the sexual sins of his group, the sons of Canaan). The story allows such sins to be committed by his father, Ham, with whom Canaan in his turn is one. But that person can also be the actual leader of the group, like the king of the Edomites and like Moses who addresses Edom as his brother Israel.

The story about the ark among the Philistines offers still another example related to the previous one. We would say concerning the Ark of the Covenant that this object was not God himself but a symbol of his presence, that it represented him among his people. The storyteller doesn't make this distinction. When the ark is brought into the Israelite camp, he describes the Philistines as saying, "God has come into camp!" After the ark had been the source of so many plagues on the Philistines and was sent back to what was obviously an Israelite city, Beth-shemesh, the inhabitants were witnesses of Yahweh's fear-inspiring presence. They did their best to be rid of the ark. The narrator continues: "The men of Beth-shemesh then said, 'Who can stand his ground before Yahweh, this holy God; to whom shall we let him go up, away from us?' " In Hebrew the word for ark is masculine. Grammatically, then, both Yahweh and the ark can be the subject of the verb (1 Sam. 4, 7; 6, 20). When someone sends a messenger, he is not strictly distinguished from the one on whose behalf he comes. That's why Joseph's brothers speak to the man sent in pursuit of them as if he were Joseph himself. He goes along with their suggestion and then says: "Very well then, it shall be as you say. The one on whom it [the cup] is found shall become my slave," meaning of course that he would become Joseph's slave (Gn. 44, 10; cf. v. 17).

A messenger from God is also often spoken of as if he were God himself. On her flight from Sarai (Sarah), Hagar meets such a messenger in the desert; in our translations he is usually called an "angel." After her talk with this "angel of Yahweh," the story goes on to speak about "Yahweh who had spoken to her" (Gn. 16, 13). Similar instances can also be found in Judges at the calling of Gideon (6, 11-14) and where Samson's birth is foretold (13, 2-23).

Several messengers of God seem to appear in Genesis 18, the story of God's visit to Abraham. Here, too, the shifting from singular to plural is remarkable. Abraham sees three men approaching and says: "My Lord, I beg you, if I find favor with you, kindly do not pass your servant by ["you" being singular]. A little water shall be brought; you [plural] shall wash your feet and lie down under the tree. . . ." (Gn. 18, 3-4): Yahweh and his messengers are one.

Sometimes a person is called to act as messenger or angel of Yahweh. Such a man is then referred to as a "prophet." Further on we will speak in greater detail about this function. Here let it suffice to mention that alternation between the first and third persons is often seen in prophetic discourses. The prophet often changes from speaking about Yahweh to speaking on behalf of Yahweh, or better, in the person of Yahweh. Of the many examples we could have chosen, one illustrates the preceding point and also provides a transition to the one that follows. It is the following passage from Deuteronomy (29, 1-5):

Moses called the whole of Israel together and said to them: "You have seen all that Yahweh did before your eyes in the land of Egypt, to Pharaoh, to his servants and to his whole land, the great ordeals your own eyes witnessed, the signs and those great wonders. But until today Yahweh has given you no heart to understand, no eyes to see, no ears to hear. For forty years I led you in the wilderness; the clothes on your back did not wear out and your [singular] sandals did not wear off your [singular] feet. You had no bread to eat, you drank no wine, no strong drink, learning thus that *I*, Yahweh, am your God.

The nation here is at the same time one and many, and Moses changes unobserved from his own I to the "I" of Yahweh.

Principle and Beginning

The text just quoted is the beginning of a speech to the Israelites which the book of Deuteronomy puts on the lips of Moses before the people marched into the Promised Land. It is now certain that this sermon was composed some six centuries after Moses, probably in connection with a ceremony celebrating the renewal of the Covenant. As you read further, observe the term "today." You will also notice, then, that the speech in its entirety (chapters 29 and 30) unmistakably supposes the fact of the Babylonian exile which began with the first deportation in 597 B.C.

Moses is presented here as saying something which was formulated only centuries after him. To our way of thinking, that is "reading something back into the distant past." This is done frequently in the Bible; therefore we will try to get an idea of the way of thinking which lies at the base of it.

We saw that a person is present in that which proceeds from him. The founding father of a tribe continues to be present in his tribe, and the personality of the one sending is at work in his messenger. Moses was held to have been the mediator when the Covenant was made between Yahweh and his people. A primitive story described how he, at the foot of Sinai, after the theophany and formal proclamation of the conditions of the Covenant, sprinkled both partners with the blood of the sacrificed animals: the altar, symbol of Yahweh and thus Yahweh himself, and the people who were present. While so doing he said, "This is the blood of the Covenant that Yahweh has made with you, containing all these rules" (Ex. 24, 8).

Modern Western men would now say that Moses laid at that time the foundation of Israel's existence as the people of the Covenant. At that particular moment in history he fulfilled that exceedingly important task. Thereafter he disappeared forever from the

scene. From then on what he had established went its own way
through the centuries. But the Israelites apparently didn't look at it
in this way. For them Moses remained in a certain sense just as
alive as the Covenant of which he had been the mediator. No new
measures could be taken regarding Israel's conduct before Yahweh
without reference to Moses.

Therefore we can understand how in the 6th century it was still
taken for granted that "Moses" should address the Judeans, the
remnant of Israel, at some celebration commemorating the
Covenant.

Thus, too, even later, until the beginning of the 4th century, all
kinds of new stipulations were proclaimed by "Moses." We will
give one example. Jews who lived for from Palestine, in the Diaspora or the Dispersion, had to make long journeys through
"unclean" lands in order to be able to celebrate the Passover in
Jerusalem. Sometimes they arrived too late to fulfill all the pre-
scribed purification rites on time. In that case the temple authorities allowed them to celebrate the Passover in the second month
instead of the first. This stipulation was incorporated in the book
of Numbers: when still at Mount Sinai Moses was told of these
people's difficulty, and he consulted Yahweh on the question. Then
he formulated the new regulation in his name (9, 3-13).

The notion of "reading back into the past" is of course an idea
of modern men who draw a sharp line between now and then. Evidently biblical people saw rather the connection between past and
present, and they felt themselves very much involved in the
past—obviously not the past seen as the indefinite time which preceded the "now," but the "creative moments" of their own past.
Put in another way, they experienced a bond with the persons and
events which were of "fundamental importance" in laying the
foundation of that which to a great extent defined their own lives.

Now and then I hazard the following formulation: biblical
people didn't make as precise a distinction as we do between "principle" and "beginning." If at a given time something became a
principle of thought and conduct, then they put this in words by
saying that it was revealed or defined "in the beginning." This formulation, too, is but an approach, an attempt to point out what
might lie behind the ways in which things are represented in so
many biblical stories. Of course the clearest examples are found in
the Pentateuch. It was in that work, after all, that Israel gave liter-

ary form to its principles, and indeed in the context of a grand story about "the beginning"—its own beginning and that of all existing things.

Moses' era was not the only "creative" or "fundamental" moment of Israel's past. At a given point Abraham, too, came to be seen as one of those "beginnings"—namely, when he became the ancestor of all Israel and, in a later stage, also "the father of believers." Several insights and customs were given their "foundation" in his life. The rite of circumcision as a sign of the Covenant is a good example.

As far as we know at present, circumcision was in use among the Canaanites and the other nations surrounding ancient Israel, with the exception of the Philistines. They came from a different cultural background, the area Caphtor, as the Bible calls their place of origin, probably Crete or perhaps the coastal region of Asia Minor. Not being circumcised, they attracted attention in Palestine. You will recall from 1 and 2 Samuel how the name "uncircumcised" was applied with contempt to them (e.g., 1 Sam. 14, 6; 17, 26). The price which David had to pay for the hand of Saul's daughter is a striking example—"a hundred foreskins of the Philistines!" (1 Sam. 18, 25).

The primitive rite of circumcision in vogue among many peoples of different continents was a part of the initiation to marriage and, with this, incorporation into the tribe. It concerned the mystery of life and thus was pregnant with religious meaning everywhere. In Israel it signified and effected incorporation into the people of Yahweh. But as long as the rite was practiced by surrounding nations, the Israelites could not be very consciously aware of its special meaning.

For the Judeans who were deported to Babylon in 597 and 587, this was suddenly changed, since the Babylonians did not practice circumcision. In this new situation, being circumcised suddenly became a distinguishing mark, a sign that one belonged to Yahweh, and thus a "sign of the Covenant." Circumcision retained this meaning, even in the post-exilic community at Jerusalem. The practice became even stronger when the rite fell more and more into disuse among the non-Jewish groups in Palestine. Now the story of Genesis 17 was edited during or shortly after the exile: God imposed circumcision as a sign of the Covenant on Abram who henceforth became Abraham.

Abraham was, so to speak, the absolute beginning of Israel as the people of the Covenant. But he was called to this role out of a world which had its own "beginning." After the Deluge was incorporated into Israel's treasury of stories, Noah became such a "beginning." He was the "father" of humanity at the time of its new beginning. Earlier in this chapter we saw that the discovery of wine was attributed to him, a reference to the sound of his name: "source of consolation." But prescriptions which the Jews considered to be valid for all of humanity they described as being proclaimed by God to Noah—e.g., the command not to eat meat with blood in it (Gn. 9, 4).

The world which perished in the Deluge also had a beginning, the absolute beginning of everything which we call the "creation." With this we arrive at the famous first three chapters of the Bible. After what has preceded, the reader will expect that in these stories Israel gave expression to all kinds of "principles" which in its particular experience were thought to be "fundamental." Thus they are so heavily laden with meaning that the scope of this work will not even permit us to treat them summarily.

However, I would like to mention expressly one very important consequence of the approach sketched in these pages. If one looks for a report of historical facts or a commemoration thereof in the first three chapters of Genesis, then he has misjudged the nature of those stories. The stories about Adam and Eve in paradise are considered by most scholars to stem from the 9th or 8th century B.C., the work of a Yahwistic writer. In his circles it was the custom, as we have seen, to describe the character and situation of groups of people (Edomites, Moabites and their own nation) in the form of a story about a supposed ancestor, an "origin story." It is safe to assume that the author of Genesis 2 and 3 used this same form to characterize the nature and situation of "man"—in Hebrew, *adam*.

Put in a modern way, we would say that he expressed in that story his vision of "the phenomenon of man." Even a superficial reading of these two chapters leaves one with the impression that the writer must have been a great religious thinker and a great poet. We shall never completely sound the depths of his story.

The first chapter of Genesis was written several centuries after chapters 2 and 3. That narration of the creation of the world in six days after which God rested on the seventh received its final form in priestly circles during the exile or shortly thereafter. Later on we shall see the reasons why precisely at that time the sabbath took on an extremely fundamental meaning for the Jews. And they wanted that meaning to have its expression in the creation story, which is actually a solemn poetic confession of faith. This was done by making the "foundation" of the week the root of all reality: God himself observed six days of work and rested on the sabbath "in the beginning" when he called forth the world from nothing.

The reader who would look for information about the actual course of events in it would likewise be doing this magnificent chapter a great injustice. Now and then I have met people who insist on that approach at all cost. As a last hope I have given them an answer which because of its absurd point of departure should hit home. Suppose that modern science would one day prove that the universe came about in six days. Even then we may not say, "See, the Bible was right after all!" but only, "What a remarkable coincidence that this should be in the Bible in precisely the same way!"

Now that we, in connection with this "principle and beginning" theory, have landed on the question of historical information, we must devote a few words to it with regard to the stories about the patriarchs and the cycle about the exodus out of Egypt and the journey through the desert. There the situation is different. Most scholars are of the opinion that historical individuals did exist answering to the names of Abraham, Isaac and Jacob. They hasten to add that nothing further can be said with certainty about the lives of these figures. R. de Vaux, whom we referred to above, is one of the most respected scholars in the area of Israel's ancient history. He recently closed a lecture on this question for an American audience with the words: "We shall never be able to write an historical biography of Abraham, Isaac and Jacob, or even something that would resemble a history of the period of the patriarchs. The elements necessary for that will always be lacking to us, and those which we do possess, in the Bible and outside it, allow us to see that the origin and formation of the people of Israel were extremely complex." After everything we said to illustrate the ways of thinking treated above, the reader will no longer be shocked at this authoritative statement. He will also already have come to the conclusion that, for similar reasons, almost nothing can be said with certainty about the person and

work of Moses, even though four of the five books are about him.
I like to compare Moses to a mountain looming up in the mist. Its
outline can be made out vaguely, enough to know that it is really
there and that it must be immense, but its details can't be distinguished. What really took place in that decisive period, perhaps
even more than in the era of the patriarchs, lies so deeply buried
under everything which later was related to it that there is hardly
anything left to be seen of it. Expressed in the words of our
approach, this "beginning" was buried under the "principles." Yet
the biblical way of seeing and presenting things sketched in this
paragraph is not the only one in which historical events hide from
us precisely where they have a fundamental meaning. There was
also another factor involved here which we will try to describe.

Miracles and Predictions

In literature every story has its "hero," even though he may be a
coward; plays, novels and films generally center around one leading character. The Bible doesn't leave any doubt concerning who
its leading character, the hero of its story, is. That is God. From
the first page to the last he plays the leading role as the text
describes his relations with mankind whom he created, leads,
judges and pardons.

In determining this we are very close to the "secret" which makes
the Bible what it is for countless people: *the* book. For this reason
I hesitate to say anything about the biblical descriptions of God's
"activity." Yet a modern introduction to the Bible would be
incomplete if this point, however delicate it may be, were left
out—especially since at the present time discussions about the
faith are mostly concerned with notions about God.

Let us begin with the two seemingly opposite "poles" in Israel's
consciousness of God which we have already seen in connection
with the name Yahweh. God is completely different from whatever
we imagine him to be, and there is nothing which can be compared
with him or which could be an expression of him, contain or grasp
him. At the same time he is unimaginably close, at work in all
things and personally involved in everything that happens in the
world, nature and history, and in the life of every man. This is
sometimes condensed in two technical terms: "transcendence," the
property of surpassing, rising above all things, and "immanence,"

that of being intimately present in all things. And then Israel is described as being unique because of its simultaneous recognition of both properties in the mystery of God.

We hinted above at what might have been the origin and first growth of this exceptional consciousness of God (pp. 50f.). Certainly at the time of the kings and prophets it achieved a high level of maturity. This is apparent from the way in which it is given expression, and in the growing treasury of stories. The certitude that God rises infinitely above everything which exists or is thinkable found expression, for example, in stories about apparitions of God. Anyone who caught a glimpse of him said with the parents of Samson, "We are certain to die, because we have seen God" (Jgs. 13, 22), or with the prophet Isaiah, "What a wretched state I am in! I am lost . . . for my eyes have looked at the King, Yahweh Sabaoth!" (Is. 6, 5). The revelation of God's presence is so overwhelming that no man can survive it, particularly a man who, as Isaiah intended to denote in the above words, is "sinful"—i.e., one who habitually neglects God's reality by proudly going his own way. But the prophet knows at the same time that the infinitely exalted God is very close to his people and has bound himself "with heart and soul" to Israel. Therefore he is not afraid to compare that same transcendent God with a farmer who looks after his vineyard with the utmost care, hopes for good fruit, and is utterly disappointed when there is nothing but sour grapes to be harvested (Is. 5, 1-7).

God is described just as humanly in all sorts of stories. He takes some clay, molds an *adam* from it and then breathes life into it. With his own hand he closes the door of the ark behind Noah, and a little further on he walks with Abraham. His relation with Moses is one of friendship; they talk together "face to face," as Exodus 33, 11 tells us. But then immediately, in another story, a kind of correction is made from the other pole. Moses wanted to see God's glory. He had to wait in a cave until God's glory had passed, and then he would be allowed to glance at his back. God himself told him the reason: "My face is not to be seen" (33, 23).

Now the spiritual climate of our times has made us especially sensitive to this last aspect of Israel's experience—namely that God is totally different, that he is absolutely transcendent. For us it is almost self-evident that no event, no person, nothing at all can be an *unmistakable* witness to God's presence. In other words, nothing and no one can provide *irrefutable* proof for the existence or activity of God. These can be seen only "with the eyes of faith." For the man who looks for proofs, God is totally absent. When Israel witnesses to God's "immanence," then it does so therefore on the basis of its *faith*. It experiences in faith that its privileged leaders and the nation as a whole are in continual conversation with Yahweh. In the light of faith it recognizes God's hand in all the vicissitudes of life and his claim on them. Many biblical stories witness to what we may very well call a "vision of faith." When they present God as speaking or acting, they don't intend this to be a commentary in the modern sense; they aren't describing something which each and every onlooker can ascertain. They simply portray a "dimension" which only the *faithful* could see.

We shall begin with an example which shows how a prophet defines that "dimension" in an event. In Isaiah's time—roughly 740 B.C.—Assyria with its ever growing power and urge to conquer set its sights on Syria and Palestine. If we had sufficient historical data at our disposal, we could describe in detail why King Tiglath-pileser wanted to conquer that coastal region, the plans he had made for the conquest, and how he organized his campaigns and strategic victories. We could "explain" the entire affair, therefore, in human terms. In principle that was also possible for Isaiah and his contemporaries. Yet this prophet proclaimed that it was Yahweh who called the Assyrian armies to Palestine in order to chastise his people. He had taken the initiative for that campaign (cf. Is. 5, 26; 7, 18; also cf. below, pp. 191f.).

In and behind a visible event, understandable in itself, Isaiah saw the hand of Yahweh directed toward his people. Or to put it in more general terms, it was because of its personal relation to Yahweh that Israel could see a message in certain events, a personal gesture of its God. We say expressly: because of that relation. Thus that meaning cannot be seen by outsiders.

Every reader can fill this in from his own experience. Think of two people in love, where the relationship is very mature and exclusive. Not only does everything take on a different light for them, but they discover, too, that certain gestures can be pregnant with meaning, with deeply personal messages, which no onlooker could even suspect, let alone see and understand.

The comparison with our subject is of course inadequate. For Israel is not an individual but a *group,* and its partner in the relation is not a man but *God*. As a result of the former, that "message-bearing" meaning of certain events had to be put in words and developed in a story so that all *together* could understand it, meditate on it, sing of it and pass it on to the newcomers, the succeeding generation. As a result of the latter, the event had to be clearly pictured as an *action of Yahweh,* as transcending all human possibilities.

Now, the endless variety of ways in which this is done in Israel's biblical stories falls into two major groups: miracles and fulfilled predictions. The Pentateuch offers examples of both. Nearly all exegetes of Exodus are convinced that the story of the "ten plagues" with which God struck Egypt is in no way intended to be a factual commentary. In the text itself the "plagues" are more often called "signs" and "wonders," and also "judgments" (cf. 7, 8—11, 10). Precise analysis shows it to have grown out of several traditions, with each one telling about a couple of plagues. But these, too, had grown up around an old kernel, the precise content of which can no longer be determined with certainty. The Dutch scholar G. Te Stroete wrote in his commentary on Exodus (1966) concerning this story: "It is exceedingly artistic and is really a kind of epic which, during a long and complicated history of growth, has developed into its present form and length. A sort of cumulative process took place which for that matter continued in post-biblical times. Rabbis know of 50 and later as many as 250 plagues!" A bit further on he speaks about Israel's need to confess and define Yahweh's greatness and his exaltation above the "gods" of the nations; in the service of the true God, it believed itself to be exalted far above politically stronger Egypt, and it especially believed that its God was stronger and more powerful than Pharaoh who claimed divine honor: "All of this took shape in the expansion of the story of the plagues, *which we must therefore read first of all, in the light of Israel's faith,* as a popular miracle story with a strongly legendary strain. We must be quick to add that *the stories in which they confessed Yahweh's greatness and his power over the cosmos* were not just thrown together haphazardly. The storytellers or authors were evidently acquainted with Egypt and with certain natural phenomena which sometimes happened there."

In relation to our question, one should read this with the emphasis on the phrases which we italicized. They also hold true for the story of the passage through the Red Sea, or perhaps the Reed Sea. It is generally assumed that the prose narration (13, 17—14, 31) and the victory song (15, 1-19), equally impressive at each reading, are two versions which evolved from the primitive cry of jubilation (15, 21) concluding the whole song:

> Sing to the Lord, for he is gloriously triumphant;
> horse and chariot he has cast into the sea.

The whole song, too, is the end result of a coalescence of several traditions, each one portraying God's saving intervention as strikingly as possible in its own way. In answer to the question as to the "historicity" of the events pictured here, Te Stroete points to the epic character of the stories and their religious intention. "They bear witness to the faith of Israel in Yahweh's power, in his exaltation above Pharaoh's horses and wagons. Yahweh fights for Israel and saves it from certain destruction. The epic-religious character of the story doesn't detract from the fact that we are dealing here with history. Regarding the precise course of the historical events, we are groping in the dark. Neither the place nor the nature of the miracle can be precisely defined. One may perhaps put it like this: in some way or other (J doesn't have an actual passage through the sea) a number of Egyptians (perhaps only a few) died by drowning when they wanted to pursue a group of fleeing Hebrews. The Hebrews, possibly much later, saw this event as the work of Yahweh their God. This insight, based on faith in the salvific and historical dimension in what happened, inspired the shaping of the story about it, as we now find it in the Bible."

These were two extreme examples which we chose and explained, especially in view of the question of "Bible history." They should not be isolated. Everywhere else in the Pentateuch where God is described as saying or doing something, there, too, we have an expression of that "vision of faith" just referred to. There, too, it is a question of bearing witness to a dimension of what happens, which only could be seen by those enjoying the personal relation with God in the Covenant and which could not be ascertained by outsiders.

What we referred to above as "fulfilled predictions" is an allusion to a biblical way of looking at things which seems to be closely related to the one just treated. The belief that Yahweh was at work in a particular event or course of events was given expression by relating that he had announced it long before and that in those events his plans were being carried out. Two examples from the Pentateuch we have already mentioned in another context. Yahweh favored David's subjection of Israel's older "brother," the tribe of the Edomites. They testified to this belief in the story of the pregnant mother of the tribe, Rebekah, who centuries before had received the prediction of the lot of her twins (cf. p. 66). That Israel finally ousted completely the perverse population of Canaan was the work of Yahweh, who punished them in that way for their religious fornication. Thus he fulfilled the word which he spoke through Noah after the Deluge (cf. pp. 68f.). It can perhaps be said that Israel could express the concept of "history" (for which it had no proper term) in the following way: the fulfillment again and again of Yahweh's words.

Conclusions

As an illustration of the biblical ways of seeing and presenting things, which we have described briefly in the preceding paragraphs, we gave only examples from the Pentateuch. We did this, first of all, for the purpose of elucidating the previous chapter, and also because the following chapters, when treating the narrative books of the Bible, will offer several other striking examples.

Once again let me emphasize that, in describing the peculiarities of the biblical ways of presenting the past, we always took as the norm our own Western manners, almost without realizing it. Knowledge of the past means for us knowledge of what happened then, and we value this knowledge more highly to the extent that it is more precise and more "objective"; we are willing to grant a certain value to colored and partial descriptions of the past, as well as those partly derived from the imagination, as propaganda or psychological and artistic works, but then we wouldn't call them "real history." We can scarcely imagine that an explanation of what we consider "real history" may very well have been completely incomprehensible to the biblical historians. Perhaps only the most open among them would have had sufficient contact with the speaker to be able to ask the perplexing question: "What can possibly be the use of knowing precisely what happened then?"

Just like their first readers they were practical-minded. As we saw in our sketch of Hebrew thought, they didn't ask what something *is,* but what it *does.* Also, where it concerned things from the past, they didn't ask what things *were like then,* but what they *accomplish now* when they are told. The "truth" of a story was defined according to the degree in which it meant something to them. Less capable of making abstractions than we Greco-Western men, they could only communicate the deep realities of their existence to each other in images, in figurative language and in stories.

Thus it was not important for them whether the meaningful story stemmed from reliable recollections or from the believing imagination. That's why the authors of great historical works sometimes put stories of a different nature and origin one after the other, in an order which was undoubtedly the result of much consideration, but never with warnings like: "Take care, reader; by way of clarification I am now turning from a very old and authentic document to a story I recently heard or which I have thought up myself." They couldn't write such a warning or footnote because the implied distinction in "historicity" lay completely outside their range of vision.

For us modern Christians this will remain a difficult point for the time being. I write this from experience. I don't know how many times I've heard, after a careful explanation of a fragment of the Bible, the disappointing remark from someone in the audience, "If I understand you correctly, it is only a story. . . ." The fact that Bible history has been passed on during the past two or three centuries without paying much attention to its nuances has made it apparently difficult for us to get used to the thought that the Bible belongs to "literature." After seeing *Who's Afraid of Virginia Woolf,* no one would say, "That didn't really happen; it is *only* a play," or after reading *Dr. Zhivago,* that it is *only* a novel. For everybody assumes that these genres communicate not facts but an experience of reality.

For the biblical people this reality is their personal relation with the living God, infinitely exalted and ever near, a never-ceasing appeal for their heart. That is the experience which they attempt to express and to communicate. Thus, the unique character of the Bible lies not in the fact that it shouldn't be called "literature," but that this literature can be tasted only by readers whose own experience of reality is related to that of biblical people. The Bible was written by believers for believers. It is our hope that this will become clearer in the course of the succeeding chapters.

III

History as Preaching

After the Pentateuch we meet in our Bible the four books entitled Joshua, Judges, Samuel and Kings. In this chapter we will see that together with Deuteronomy they originally formed one great historical work. But the position of the small book of Ruth between Judges and Samuel gives rise to the question of the sequence of the books of Scripture. In connection with other questions as well, it therefore seems useful to begin this chapter with several remarks about the way the books of the Bible are ordered.

I

A Word about the Canon

The Greek word *kanōn*—actually meaning (straight) rod, ruler, guideline and the like—came to be used by the Christians in referring to Holy Scripture as the guide and rule of their life and thought. Later they began to apply it more specifically to the list of books which belonged to Scripture. When doubts arose in the early Church on this matter, the question asked was whether or not a given book was "canonical." In other words, it was a question of its "canonicity."

From the outline on the following page one can see that in the Old Testament we distinguish between the Hebrew canon and the Greek canon. The left column shows the sequence and division of the books in the Hebrew Bible. Its first and most important part is "the Law" with its five books; then "the Prophets" follow. Notice that those eight books are divided into the four "early" and four "later" prophets. In the third part, "the Writings," the Psalms occupy the first place among the three great poetical books. There-

THE OLD TESTAMENT

The Hebrew Canon	Additions in the Greek Canon
THE LAW *Genesis* *Exodus* *Leviticus* *Numbers* *Deuteronomy*	
THE PROPHETS EARLY: *Joshua* *Judges* *Samuel* *Kings* LATER: Isaiah Jeremiah Ezekiel The Twelve	 Baruch
THE WRITINGS Psalms Proverbs Job THE "FIVE ROLLS": Song of Songs *Ruth* Lamentations Ecclesiastes *Esther* Daniel *Ezra-Nehemiah* *Chronicles*	 Jesus Ben Sirach Wisdom of Solomon *Tobit* *Judith* *1 Maccabees* *2 Maccabees*

upon follows a group of five smaller works. Daniel stands alone, and after Ezra-Nehemiah the list concludes with Chronicles.

This division of the sacred books into three groups was current among the Jews at the time of our Lord. According to the evangelist Luke, he spoke to his disciples about the fulfillment of " . . . everything written about me in the Law of Moses, in the Prophets and in the Psalms. . . ." (24, 44). "The Psalms" here obviously refers to the whole third group, "the Writings," of which they formed the first and most important part. But this division was in vogue even before Christ. The book which the wise Jesus Ben Sirach wrote about 190 B.C. at Jerusalem (Ecclesiasticus) was translated about 60 years later in Egypt by his grandson. He begins his Foreword as follows:

Many and wonderful are the gifts we have been granted by means of the Law and the Prophets and *the others that followed them,* an education in wisdom on which Israel is indeed to be complimented. But it is not enough merely for those who read the scriptures to be learned in them; students should also be able to be of use to people outside by what they say and write. So it was that my grandfather Jesus, having devoted himself more and more to reading the Law and the Prophets and *the other volumes of the fathers* and having gained ability enough in these matters, was brought to the point of himself writing down some of the things that have a bearing on education in wisdom, in order that those studiously inclined and with obligations in these matters might make all the more progress in living according to the Law.

You are therefore asked to read this book with good will and attention and to show indulgence in those places where, notwithstanding our efforts at interpretation, we may seem to have failed to give an adequate rendering of this or that expression; the fact is that you cannot find an equivalent for things originally written in Hebrew when you come to translate them into another language; what is more, you will find on examination that the Law itself, the Prophets and *the other books* differ considerably in translation from what appears in the original text.

After some remarks about himself and the pains he had taken, the translator concludes his Foreword about those for whom he had done the work, namely "those who, domiciled abroad, wish to study how to fit themselves and their manners for living according to the Law."

It is clear that for both grandfather and grandson "the Law" was canonical in every respect, the holy book *par excellence,* and the rule of life. "The Prophets" also seem to be a clearly defined entity. But, as our italics emphasize, different words are used all three times when referring to the third group. The number of books in this group did indeed continue to fluctuate. Well into the first century of the Christian era certain edifying books were treated as sacred in some circles and rejected in others. It was not until after the destruction of Jerusalem by the Romans in 70 A.D. that the heavily stricken Jews of Palestine felt compelled to reorganize themselves. To achieve this goal, their principles of thought and life had to be determined as precisely as possible. At that time, it seems, in the town of Jabneh, also called Jamnia, the extent of the third group was established once for all.

In that way the Hebrew canon with its 24 books, as shown in our left-hand column, was established. The Jews liked to speculate on numbers. Because the story of Ruth was sometimes included in the book of Judges and the Lamentations joined with the work of their supposed author, Jeremiah, the total number of "books" was then 22, the same number as there are letters in the Hebrew alphabet. This was sometimes the occasion of profound statements on the perfection of biblical revelation.

Modern Jews prefer to call their Bible the "Tenak." This word is formed like our word NATO, which is composed of the first letters of North Atlantic Treaty Organization. In Hebrew the three parts of the canon are Torah (the Law), Nebiim (the Prophets) and Ketubim (the Writings). Because TNK cannot be pronounced, vowels are inserted—hence, TaNaK or TeNaK (with the k being pronounced softly). Christians who, in their discussions with Jews, accommodate themselves to this usage and prefer to speak of the "Tenak" rather than "the Old Testament" should bear in mind that for the early Church, and thus for the writers of the New Testament, Holy Scripture contained more than the Tenak. The following will clarify this somewhat.

In Alexandria and its environs, the most important center of Greek-speaking Jews, these three groups of biblical books were successively translated into Greek. The first, of course, was "the Law"—most probably as early as the 3rd century B.C. Then came "the Prophets" and finally a number of books from the third group. As we were able to conclude from the Foreword of Ben Sirach's grandson, the number of these books fluctuated there as well. The work of the wise Jesus Ben Sirach of Jerusalem quickly received a place in that number together with other translations of edifying books published in Palestine or elsewhere, whether in classical Hebrew or in Aramaic, the ordinary everyday language of the Jews. But there were also pious Jews in Egypt who made a contribution—likewise intended to "edify" the faithful—to sacred literature.

We do not know whether the Jews of the Greek-speaking world ever established a determined canon. It is certain, however, that the first Christians regarded the Bible in its Greek form and extent as their Holy Scriptures. Early Christian theologians and the leaders of Churches were now and then involved in disputes concerning the number of books to be recognized. By 400 A.D., agreement on this point had pretty well been reached. In the right-hand column of our outline the books are listed which the Church accepted as canonical in addition to the 24 books of the Hebrew canon. There are seven. Several additional parts are included in the translations of Esther and Daniel.

Because of those disputes these seven books came to be called "deuterocanonical." The Greek word *deuteros* means "second"; these books were accepted as definitively canonical on a second ballot, so to speak, but the name itself had its origin only in the 16th century. You won't find them in most Protestant Bibles. The Reformers of the 16th century, who in everything wanted to go back to the original forms, were of the opinion that the Hebrew Bible was closer to this ideal than the Greek. Thus they accepted the canon which the rabbis of Palestine had established after the year 70. In their first Bible translations they often put the deuterocanonical books in an appendix at the end, sometimes printed in less elegant type in order to better emphasize the difference between these "apocryphal" books, as they called them, and the actual books of Scripture.

In our outline of the canon we have italicized a number of
names of scriptural books. These contain primarily stories; there
are also some laws, as in the Pentateuch, but here the laws always
appear within the context of a story. At a very early stage the
Christians combined these narrative books into one group, and the
practice has continued down to our own day. In most Bibles they
are called "the historical books." Until recently the so-called
"Bible history of the Old Testament" was based on these books
and taught to children and adults alike in every way possible.
Whatever the method, they all had one thing in common: each
story, without distinction, was considered to be a faithful account
of past events and retold as such with most of its details. Bible history then was a continual narration of events from the creation of
the world in six days down to and including the war of the Maccabees. Sometimes biographical details were borrowed from the
prophetic books, and the years of the Babylonian captivity were
filled in, above all, by means of stories found in Daniel (chapters
1—6 and 13—14). What happened after the time of the Maccabees—i.e., after 130 B.C.—was described from data derived from
Greek and Roman historical works dealing with that period,
especially the Greek works of Flavius Josephus who died about
100 A.D.

After our sketch of the ways in which biblical people conceive
and present things, it is not necessary to demonstrate that such a
presentation of Bible history is no longer justifiable in the present
stage of biblical scholarship and thus no longer permissible. How
then are we supposed to present the historical facts? Let's hold off
on this question for the time being. First we want to see what the
modern approach means for our understanding of the four "historical books" following the Pentateuch, significantly called "the earlier prophets" by the Jews. After a short summary of the contents
of each book, including the traditional opinion concerning the
person of the author, we will treat the new theories about their
origin. Afterward we will illustrate the rich variety of traditions
incorporated in the four books by means of seven examples.

II

JOSHUA, JUDGES, SAMUEL AND KINGS

The Book of Joshua

This book tells the story of the hero whose name it bears from the moment he succeeded Moses as leader of Israel, in the first chapter, until his death in the last (24). Within this framework the facts are recounted in a strictly logical sequence. From the camp at Shittim, opposite Jericho, Joshua sends spies over the Jordan to scout this most important city guarding the entrance to the Promised Land (2). The Israelites cross the Jordan; its waters stand still, and Joshua erects twelve stones at Gilgal as a memorial of the crossing (3—4). Upon their arrival on holy ground the Israelites are circumcised and celebrate the Passover (5). After the miraculous collapse of the walls of Jericho (6), the second most important city, Ai, barring access to the central hills, is attacked and, after an unsuccessful attempt on account of Achan's sin (7), finally taken. The Covenant is reaffirmed, between Mount Gerizim and Mount Ebal (8). After the treaty with Gibeon and three other cities in the center of the country (9), Joshua first defeats the kings of the southern part with the spectacular help of Yahweh (10), and then those of the north (11). Here the report gives a full list of their names (12). The land is then divided among the tribes (13—19). Joshua designates the "cities of refuge" (20) and the levitical cities (21). The tribes from across the Jordan return to their homes (22). Joshua gives a farewell address (23) and then another one at Shechem, followed by a renewal of the Covenant, whereupon he dies and is buried (24).

It is easy to understand why Jewish tradition considered Joshua himself to be the author of this survey report with its impressive series of heroic deeds in which he played the main part. Ancient Christian commentators took over this opinion. Later Catholic scholars attributed only some parts of the book to Joshua, proposing others as its principal authors—e.g., the priest Phinehas (22, 13, etc.) and even Samuel or an anonymous contemporary of his. However this may be, the book had to have been written before David captured Jerusalem (cf. 15, 63).

The Book of Judges

The beginning of this book depicts the situation of the tribes after Joshua's death. Yahweh punishes them for their infidelity by sending enemy invasions. When the Israelites cry for help, he sends a liberator in the person of a "judge" (1—3, 6). The greatest part of the book (3, 7—16, 31) relates six stories about such heroes: Othniel, Ehud, Deborah and Barak, Gideon, Jephthah and Samson. Scattered between these stories are short passages mentioning still other judges: Shamgar (3, 31), Tola, Jair (10, 1-5), Ibzan, Elon and Abdon (12, 8-15). The final section adds two stories (17—19 and 19—21) which also took place during the period of the judges, when ". . . there was no king in Israel and every man did as he pleased" (17, 6; cf. 19, 26-30).

Faithful to the tradition, many Christians continued until the first decades of this century to regard Samuel as the author of this book. However, some of them preferred an author from the first years of the monarchy (cf. 1, 21).

The Books of Samuel

The first of the two parts, a division which the first Greek translators made, begins with the birth and calling of Samuel, the war with the Philistines, their capture of the Ark of the Covenant and their decisive defeat during Samuel's years as prophet (1 Sam. 1—7). The following chapters deal with Saul and his exploits. After an expedition against the Amalekites, this first king of the Jews is rejected (1 Sam. 8—15). Then follow the unforgettable stories of David's rise to power, beginning with his anointing at Bethlehem, until Saul's death on the battlefield (1 Sam. 16—31). After the murder of Saul's son Ishbaal (or Ishbosheth), David extends his reign over all the tribes and defeats the Philistines once and for all. He makes Jerusalem his capital and receives from Nathan a divine promise concerning his dynasty. After that a list of his campaigns and ministers is given (2 Sam. 1—8). The next chapters relate a coherent and striking account of the difficulties in the royal family (2 Sam. 9—20). In a sort of appendix two stories about "plagues" form the framework for two lists of Davidic heroes and their deeds; these in turn provide the framework for the central part of this appendix, which consists of two psalms, the second being entitled "The Last Words of David" (2 Sam. 21—24).

An old Jewish tradition ascribed the authorship of the book to Samuel, but this seems impossible (cf. 1 Sam. 25, 1). For this reason most Christians attributed the book to an anonymous author who is thought to have lived shortly before the division of Solomon's kingdom, about 930 B.C.

The Books of Kings

After relating the story of Solomon's anointing and his father's death (1 Kgs. 1—2), the first part goes on to describe the reign of Solomon himself (1 Kgs. 3—11). Then follows the story of the division of the realm (1 Kgs. 12—13). The remainder of the book is devoted to the reigns of Jeroboam, Rehoboam and all their successors in Israel and Judah. The story of each reign is introduced and concluded by stereotyped phrases. The year of accession to the throne of a king in the one realm is always determined in terms of the other's year of reign. Sometimes the descriptions are very short, giving only a few deeds or facts, but at the end one finds an evaluation of the reign, and always from the same religious point of view. Here and there longer stories are to be found among the stereotyped formulae—e.g., those about Elijah (1 Kgs. 17—2 Kgs. 1) and Elisha (2 Kgs. 2—13).

The last fact recorded in this book (2 Kgs. 25, 27-30) is the release of the Judean king Jehoiachin after 37 years of imprisonment in Babylon and the favors bestowed on him by the new ruler Evil-merodach at the time of his ascension in 561 B.C. The book thus could not have been completed before that year. Many Christian scholars accepted the Jewish tradition which held the prophet Jeremiah to be the author.

III
SEVERAL BOOKS OR ONE?

From this cursory description of the contents of these four books, it is evident that they form an uninterrupted whole. Judges begins where Joshua ends; Samuel begins with the story of its hero who is still a "judge"; in that capacity he anoints the first two kings who then dominate the rest of the book; finally, the opening chapters of Kings seem to be the continuation of 2 Samuel 9—20. However, it took some time for modern Scripture scholars to make use of this clear piece of data in their explanations.

Older Theories

You will recall that Wellhausen and his disciples were especially adept at analyzing literary peculiarities in a text—hence their supposition that such a text had been composed from the various "documents." When they determined that J, E, D and P were the sources of the Pentateuch, the next step was obvious: to explain the composition of the book of Joshua with the aid of that same hypothesis, for further analysis made it clear that that obviously logical whole was a series of many and very diverse fragments. Many of them revealed characteristics of one of the four Pentateuch sources. The conclusion seemed unavoidable, and all the more so because writers like J and E certainly didn't stop writing at the death of Moses on the threshold of the Promised Land. They had undoubtedly also related the climax toward which the whole history of the patriarchs, the exodus and the journey through the desert had been building: the acquisition of Canaan. Therefore, the book of Joshua, being the final episode of that history, must also have had its origin in the fusion of those four sources and consequently should be regarded as the conclusion of the Pentateuch—hence the term Hexateuch (*hex* in Greek meaning "six") in Old Testament discussions.

Nevertheless, many texts were still unruly and couldn't be classified among the sources of the four document theory. Scholars who had already gone further and explained the other three books as well (Judges, Samuel and Kings) with the help of that theory found even less support. The only point which eventually enjoyed general acceptance was the recognition of a number of passages in all four books bearing the characteristics of D—that is, they showed agreement in style and thought with Deuteronomy.

New Hypothesis: ONE Historical Work

This last piece of data, combined with that of the uninterrupted contents, led to the hypothesis of a "deuteronomic history," proposed in 1934 by the German Martin Noth. He suggested that the four books together with Deuteronomy originally formed one large work, composed by *one* author. This man first placed the law book, which now forms the central part of Deuteronomy (Dt. 12—26), within a framework consisting mainly of speeches of Moses. The work then continued with the story of Israel's history from the entrance into Canaan under Joshua up to and including the deportation of Judah to Babylon. The author found his material in the countless written and oral traditions available to him. Then he put the selected material in chronological order and, according to his purposes, he either made a more or less thorough revision or incorporated it just as he found it. Especially at moments which he regarded as historical turning points, he added reflections of his own. These he sometimes put into the mouth of a main character (e.g., Joshua in Jos. 23; Samuel in 1 Sam. 12; Solomon in his prayer of 1 Kgs. 8) or incorporated them in some other way (e.g., Jos. 12; Jgs. 2, 11-16; 2 Kgs. 17). According to Noth, this man was a Judean and wasn't among those who in 587 were deported to Babylon. He therefore wrote his work in Palestine after the fall of Jerusalem and obviously under the influence of that disaster which seemed to be the well-deserved end of Israel's privileged relationship with Yahweh in the Covenant.

This hypothesis found immediate and very favorable acceptance. At one and the same time it offered an explanation for the fact of the uninterrupted contents and D's influence which was often clearly visible as well as for the incongruities which previously had led one to think in terms of a fusion of several "documents." According to Noth, these literary differences reflect the wide variety of the traditions which the one author allowed to retain their own character.

But there was also criticism. The hypothesis did not yet explain everything, and suggestions making it more precise were quick to come. Many scholars preferred a group of authors, and thus not one "deuteronomist," but several writers who were animated by the same spirit and had learned to express themselves in the same manner. In this form the hypothesis was accepted by Roland de Vaux in the popular *Jerusalem Bible,* where he opts for the supposition that there must have been at least two editions of the large work. The books of Kings are cited as the clearest example, with one edition coming just after the reform under Josiah (621 B.C.), and the other during the exile (before 538). He speaks of the authors as "a school . . . of devout men profoundly influenced by the outlook of Deuteronomy. . . ."

What Animated the "Deuteronomic School"?

If it is true that we understand a book properly only when we are familiar with the intentions of the author, then intelligent reading of the books of Deuteronomy up to and including Kings supposes some knowledge of the spirit that animated the above-mentioned "school." Within the scope of this work we can only indicate the most important points.

1. These men were inspired primarily by the conviction that Yahweh willed to be worshiped *only in the temple of Jerusalem and nowhere else*. They believed that he had made his will, this demand, abundantly clear in historical events. The destruction of the northern kingdom by Assyria in 721 was just such an event. On that occasion the greatest part (about five-sixths) of those people of the Covenant inhabiting the largest, most fertile part of the Promised Land and bearing the name of the sacred tribal federation of old, "Israel," was swept off the stage of history. They had evidently failed in their service of Yahweh (cf. 2 Kgs. 17).

Some years later, in 701, still another very significant event took place. At that time the Assyrians attacked the southern kingdom, Judah, and destroyed everything in sight. But against the capital, Jerusalem, they were powerless. Two slightly differing accounts relate how they had to break off their siege (2 Kgs. 18, 17—19, 9a plus 19, 36-37 and 19, 9b-35). In addition we are now in possession of a non-biblical text, the account of the Assyrian king, Sennacherib himself. In saving only Jerusalem and in such a spectacular way, Yahweh clearly showed his preference for that city, while he made his aversion for the local sanctuaries equally clear by allowing all of them to be destroyed together with the surrounding cities and villages.

The deuteronomists' religious outlook will mean a bit more to us when we examine the origin of their abhorrence of the local shrines. Solomon's temple had been built to house the Ark of the Covenant, that sacred symbol of the Yahweh-pact uniting the twelve tribes. However, the cult in the royal temple did not put an end to worship in the innumerable "high places"—i.e., the local sanctuaries which the Israelites had for the most part taken over from the former inhabitants. When Jeroboam founded the northern kingdom, he chose two such places as national sanctuaries (Bethel and Dan), but like Solomon he did not prohibit other local cultic celebrations. Soon, however, these appeared to be a source of danger for the purity of the Yahwistic faith. Those who worshiped there intended, of course, to worship Israel's God. Yet they found themselves unable to avoid ancient forms of Baalism, a fertility cult in which the divine is practically identified with natural phenomena. The rites naturally led to distinguishing between male and female principles in the world of the gods and consequently to sexual excesses (cf. pp. 68f.). An equally serious consequence of this Baal cult was the gradual deterioration of the sense of social norms which belief in Yahweh included.

Some religious circles in the northern kingdom, Israel, tried to preserve the pure Yahwistic faith. During the last decades of that kingdom, and certainly after 734, when it was clear to every serious observer that the end of Israel was unavoidably approaching, many members of those Yahwistic groups undoubtedly immigrated to Judah. They brought their religious traditions with them and were a frequent "shot in the arm" for religious groups in Jerusalem. The severe measures taken by King Hezekiah (about 716-687) against the "high places" and all impure forms of worship (described in 2 Kgs. 18, 3-5) were certainly inspired and supported by these circles. It was probably under their influence that the law book of Deuteronomy (12—26) had its origin, composed from all sorts of traditional material. It begins with the law commanding one temple and place of worship (chapter 12). This law obviously replaces the prescription of the older "Book of the Covenant" which permits the erection of an altar "in every place in which I have my name remembered. . . ." (Ex. 20, 24). Or rather, the new legislation determines that Jerusalem will be that place with the exclusion of all others. That Deuteronomy does not mention the city of Jerusalem by name is partially due to the supposition that Moses *himself* is speaking to Israel *before* the entrance into the Promised Land.

This law book, forgotten during the reign of Hezekiah's successors, Manasseh and Amon, was reinstated in a place of honor after its rediscovery in the 18th year of the reign of Josiah (640-609). Since the power of the Assyrians was reduced (especially in the

last years of Ashur-bani-pal, 668-621) and for all practical purposes no longer felt in Palestine, King Josiah could plan a thorough national renewal. Seemingly it would have taken very little
effort to reconquer the territory which had belonged to the northern kingdom and restore David's empire in all its vastness. But for
the true believer, such a restoration could in the final analysis only
be the work of Yahweh, his response to his people who were firmly
determined to live in absolute fidelity to him. That response took
form in the proclamation of the law book and the unanimous
acceptance of it under King Josiah. Actually we could call the king
and all those who let themselves be guided by the spirit of Deuteronomy by the name "deuteronomists." But in fact we use this
name only for those who were involved in producing the particular
historical work we are now treating.

2. Something further was coupled with the concentration of
cult in the temple at Jerusalem. This exclusiveness was meant to
express as well as foster the attachment of the whole nation to
Yahweh alone. But that loyalty of all toward this one Lord and
God should appear just as much in their mutual relations—i.e., in
the fact that they were to be *one family, one brotherhood.* Hence,
besides a complete attachment to Yahweh ("You shall love
Yahweh your God with all your heart, with all your soul, and with
all your strength"), Deuteronomy strives in many ways to implant
a loving attention for each fellow Israelite, especially those lacking
wealth and power.

3. Finally there is the belief that God would punish infidelity.
The calamity which in 721 destroyed the greatest part of God's
people and the devastating campaigns of the Assyrians in Judah
(in 701) were interpreted as punishments for the decay of the
pure cult of Yahweh and the subsequent social injustices. The proponents of the reform which Josiah put through insisted on the
unbreakable bond between the welfare of the nation and the purity
of religion. This connection did not seem to be based on an imper-
sonal fatalism. It had its roots in the person of the living God who
directs all that happens and *punishes those who forget him whereas
he showers with blessings those who live according to his will.*
This is one of the special themes of the deuteronomic history,
already to be seen in the sermons of Moses (1—11; 27—31)
which form the framework for the law book.

All of this will perhaps be an incentive to read some of Deuter-

onomy—even the legislative part (12—26)—to become familiar
with the spirit of the history as a whole. The first chapter deals with
the theme of the one temple. This theme is taken up again later in
many variations or simply resounds like an echo. It also contains a
striking example of one of the practical consequences of centralization. Slaughtering an animal was always felt to be an act with religious meaning, a kind of "sacrifice." Thus it was preferably carried
out in a "sacred" place, in a sanctuary. By ordering that all
sacrifices be performed in Jerusalem, Deuteronomy had to declare
the slaughter of animals a "profane" action which could be carried
out anywhere in the country. This is the meaning of 12, 13-15.

One should also pay attention to the prescriptions intended to
foster humanity and brotherhood—e.g., in chapter 16. The theme of
"blessings and curses" is eloquently developed in chapters 28—30.

Two Editions

We saw that, according to R. de Vaux, a *first edition* of the
historical work appeared during the years of the Yahwistic revival
led by King Josiah, soon after 621. With this supposition in
mind, its general intention may be seen in the light of the following
observations.

Everywhere in the world strong nationalistic trends tend to
revive glorious memories of the past. The leaders know that such a
revival ordinarily enhances the readiness of the people to engage in
the common cause. But for Yahweh's people such a national goal
could not be separated from the religious one, because this nation
knew no other history than that of Yahweh's intervention, God's
active relationship with his people. And the hope for a better
future for the nation could only be the hope for better relations
between Yahweh and the people.

Thus we can understand why the supporters of the deuteronomic reform intended their great historical work to be a kind of
elaboration of the principles set down in the legislation of Deuteronomy 12—26. As everywhere else, these spiritual leaders wished
to revive the national past. Yet as leaders of God's people they
made a deliberate choice from the traditional material available to
them and put it in a form which made it serve their religious purpose—propaganda for a pure Yahwistic attitude—according to the
threefold conviction described above. To mention but one exam-

ple: they made use of all sorts of different traditions and texts in order to paint a picture of the conquest of Canaan (Joshua), which de Vaux rightly calls "an idealized and simplified picture of a complex history." The penetration of the Israelites into Palestine was in reality a prolonged process. But in Josiah's time, when the people expected both the reconquest of the lost territories in the north and the return of their deported inhabitants, it seemed useful to show how that first conquest had obviously been the work of Yahweh and executed by his faithful servant Joshua. Nor did it seem useless to put into the mouth of Joshua (chapter 23) a speech that King Josiah himself could have delivered.

The *final edition* of this great historical work was published during the exile, after 561. Now that it no longer had the function of putting the choice to the people—fidelity or infidelity, blessing or curse—it could serve as a kind of examination of conscience. Truly, the calamity of 587 had been a just punishment. The deuteronomic history could be read in the spirit expressed in Psalm 51, 4-5: ". . . that you may be found just in your judgment." Should the destruction of Jerusalem and its temple be regarded as the end of the Covenant and as the definitive break between Yahweh and his people? No! From sacred history one could learn that the merciful God is always disposed to make a new start when a repentant heart turns to him in prayer. This message, implicit here and there already in the first edition (cf. Jgs. 10, 10-16; 1 Sam. 7, 6; 12, 22; 1 Kgs. 8, 33), was explicitly expressed in the final edition by means of certain additions (e.g., Dt. 4, 25-31; 30, 1-10; 1 Kgs. 8, 46-51). It also concludes on a hopeful note: Judah's King Jehoiachin is favored by the ruler of Babylon. The believing reader could see in this the very first beginnings of a new future.

IV
SEVEN EXAMPLES

The variety of traditions incorporated in the deuteronomic history is astonishing. Each story, even each concise remark, has its own character and its own pre-history. In order to give the reader some idea of this richness, we have chosen seven examples, the number seven being the biblical symbol of fullness.

1. *The Song of Deborah (Judges 5)*

This famous battle hymn is one of the oldest pieces in the Bible. It was most certainly composed while the poet was still under the influence of the impression left by the battle it celebrated. Historians place the song in the second half of the 12th century B.C., about 1125. Although it resembles an impressionistic painting more than a serious description, the song provides important data concerning the situation and the mutual relations of the Israelitic tribes during that period as well as their common faith in Yahweh. The preceding report (chapter 4), differing somewhat from this hymn, is of a later date.

Thus, here we owe to the deuteronomists the transmission of a text composed five centuries earlier and not having lost any of its original splendor (though some details have suffered in the transmission).

2. *The Samson Cycle (Judges 13—16)*

About 1190 B.C., one of the "Sea Peoples," the Philistines, settled on the coastal plain. They tried to get possession of the fertile hill country which lay between the plain and the highlands of Judah. The Judean tribes also had their eye on that land—hence the continual guerrilla wars waged between the groups. As you may well remember from the days of the German invasions of neighboring countries (e.g., Holland, May 10-14, 1940) and the subsequent years of stubborn resistance to the occupation forces, such a situation provides fertile soil for two kinds of literature. The first recounts heroic deeds performed by "our men" at the expense of the "enemy." Such deeds become more impressive in the telling when the struggle continues for a long time, partly to give courage to the narrator and to his listeners. The second type attributes various exploits done by several men to one principal figure.

In this way the Samson stories bear witness to nearly a century of tension between the Israelites and the Philistines. Here it is impossible to treat the details—e.g., the play on words. They can, of course, only fulfill their striking function when the text is read in Hebrew. At any rate the Samson stories must have impressed those who first heard and read them and even made them "die" laughing. Now, no story has only one meaning. It is the very nature of stories that they can have more than one meaning at the same time, depending partly on the susceptibility of the readers. The deuteronomists clearly indicated what for them was the principal meaning of the Samson stories and why they incorporated them in their work along with stories about other "judges." This they did in a sort of introduction (2, 11-16). This passage should be read together with 10, 6-16, which is even more clearly a sermon in story form intended for their own generation.

3. The Rise of David (1 Samuel 16—31)

These stories are remarkably different from those just mentioned. David was a well-known and highly admired personality, and there were many stories in circulation concerning the adventures which brought him to the throne. The deuteronomists evidently found various collections of such stories. In one of them David was called to Saul's court as a minstrel who also carried the arms of his master on the battlefield. In another series he was an unknown shepherd boy who brought food to his three brothers serving in Saul's army. It seems that the authors found the story of David's anointing by Samuel in a prophetic tradition, unknown to the other story tellers, in which he had seven brothers. Though it is not impossible that heroic deeds of other figures were attributed to David (in 2 Sam. 21, 19 the killing of Goliath is attributed to Elhanan), these stories are very close to the deeds as they were related among the people. The deuteronomists made their choice without being too concerned about inconsistencies or repetitions—as, for example, in the case of the two versions of the story relating David's generosity to Saul (1 Sam. 24 and 26).

4. The Annals of the Court (2 Samuel 9—20 and 1 Kings 1—2)

Most critics agree that these chapters form a literary whole and were written by an eyewitness, probably a member of the court, during the first half of Solomon's reign (about 950 B.C.). It is generally looked upon as a masterpiece combining historical accuracy with an expert analysis of characters, and all of this in prose of superb simplicity. None of the neighboring civilizations produced anything comparable to this work. The deuteronomists took it over without changing anything; thanks to them it has been preserved for posterity.

5. The Dates of the Kings (1 Kings 14, 20; 15, 1. 9-10, etc.)

Those who think that real history is only to be found where dates are recorded will certainly be in their glory here. Dates are given at the beginning and sometimes also at the end of each reign described in the books of Kings. The deuteronomists undoubtedly derived these from official annals or royal archives. Some of the numbers given have suffered somewhat in the course of textual transmission—hence the uncertainty in some cases, as, for example, that of Hezekiah.

It is superfluous to say that these dates are relative. The absolute chronology for this period is based on Assyrian sources. Assyrian historians noted not only military campaigns to the west, in which kings of Judah and/or Israel were sometimes involved (the first case being the battle of Qarqar in 853 B.C. in which Shalmaneser III fought against a coalition including Ahab of Israel), but also eclipses of the sun and moon, thus enabling modern astronomers to provide absolute dates.

6. The Stories of Elijah and Elisha (1 Kings 17—2 Kings 13)

Here we are dealing with the kind of story comparable to the legends of our saints. It should be remembered that one becomes "legendary" only when he has made an exceptionally deep impression on his contemporaries. Though it is possible that the stories about Elisha may have influenced those about Elijah and vice versa, they give us a valuable insight into the personalities and activities of both prophets, as well as into the milieu which they impressed so profoundly.

7. The "Man of God" from Judah (1 Kings 13)

In deuteronomic circles the schism effected by Jeroboam was considered the "primeval sin" of the northern kingdom. By allowing Yahweh to be worshiped elsewhere than in Jerusalem, occasions were created for the idolatry which finally brought Yahweh to totally destroy the kingdom. After reporting this calamity, they added a long reflection on this point (2 Kgs. 17). Likewise, immediately after the tradition which tells how Jeroboam founded his kingdom and established the royal sanctuary at Bethel (1 Kgs. 12), they insert without any warning a didactic story, most probably derived primarily from the imagination (chapter 13). The attentive reader will notice the exact prophecy in verse 2 (cf. 2 Kgs. 23, 15-16), the strange miraculous elements, the opposition between the *nabi*—i.e., (false) prophet from (cursed) Bethel— and the "true" man of God from (elected) Judah.

V
Concluding Observations

By investigating the deuteronomic history more deeply, we are struck by the attitude of the authors toward their material. They are at once *respectful* and *free*. It is clear that they often left unaltered the traditions which they found and selected for their history. But in ordering that material and in adding connecting links, they left their practical goal be the sole guide: to contribute to the religious insight of their readers and thus to strengthen them in their dedication to Yahweh.

In the following chapters we will see that these two attitudes— respect and liberty—toward the traditions to be passed on are characteristic of most of the people who contributed to the formation of the biblical books. This is not only true of the narrative books of the Old Testament. In discussing the gospels, our familiarity with that attitude of biblical writers will be a great help to our understanding.

I'm sure the reader will have observed that the deuteronomists describe those six centuries of Israel's history in the Promised Land according to the outlook and way of presentation which we tried to indicate schematically in the preceding chapter. In their work there are striking examples of "reading back into the past." We have already mentioned their presentation of the quick conquest of all of Canaan under Joshua (pp. 99f.) and his farewell address in deuteronomic style (Jos. 23). In that same style the authors allow Samuel to give a summary of their vision on the period of the judges (1 Sam. 12). Likewise they put their religious outlook concerning the temple at Jerusalem in the words of Solomon's prayer on the occasion of its dedication (1 Kgs. 8), and those who put out the final edition allowed Solomon in that same prayer to add something about the situation of the exile, which would not become a reality until some four centuries later.

Their judgment of the kings of Israel and Judah on the basis of the deuteronomic law concerning the *one* temple also stems from that outlook. All the kings of Israel were accused of "continuing to walk the path of Jeroboam"—that is, of maintaining worship services in Bethel, Dan and elsewhere, and thus outside the only lawful temple at Jerusalem. The kings of Judah, on the other hand, were all of the family of David, and the "house of Yahweh" was indeed their royal temple. Yet, the authors show positive appreciation for only eight of them, while only two receive praise without reservation. These were the proponents of centralization, Hezekiah and Josiah. The appreciation of the other six was tempered by the spiteful remark that they allowed worship in the high places of the land to continue. Most of the kings were condemned, then, because of transgressing a law which, as we saw above, came into existence only long after them, in the course of the 7th century.

Hence we draw the following conclusion: the contents of the books of Joshua to Kings cannot be presented as "history" in the usual sense of the word. The two principal reasons are now clear: the enormous variety of the material incorporated into them, and the nature of their outlook and ways of presentation already present in the narrative material and applied as well by the deuteronomic editors.

Therefore, what can actually be related as history? Relatively little. The actual course of events remains obscure in many points. Scholars can say very little with certainty concerning the way the Israelitic tribes settled Canaan and their earliest history there. This is also true of the institution and early development of the monarchy, and to a certain extent even for David and Solomon. We moderns would very much like to know about such important things as the expansion and consolidation of David's political power, the administration and economy of his kingdom, the density of the population and its distribution in the land, the nature of David's foreign relations, the further development of all these things under Solomon, and so on. To a great extent such information was not contained in the documentation available to the deuteronomists, and it was certainly of no interest to these men themselves. Since we know a bit more from non-biblical sources about the period of the kings, the restriction of their interest has become even clearer. We would like to illustrate this with a few examples.

On a temple wall in Karnak, in Upper Egypt, a list has been found listing Palestinian and Syrian cities which Pharaoh Sheshonk I (about 945-924 B.C.) claims to have conquered. Concerning his campaign the deuteronomists only mention that King Rehoboam of Judah bought off the destruction of his capital with treasures from the temple and the golden shields which hung there. The deed involved the temple and has as a consequence the altering of a certain custom. It wasn't because of the military campaign that the deuteronomists incorporated something of this piece of historical data, but because of the repercussion it had on the temple (1 Kgs. 14, 25-28).

As is clear from Assyrian and other non-biblical documents, supplemented by archeological data from excavations in Tirzah and Samaria, Omri was one of the greatest kings of Israel. Our history devotes only six verses to his brilliant reign (about 874-853), four of which are stereotyped. There are thus really only two. They relate only that he gave up Tirzah as capital and moved to the newly-built Samaria. The reader had to know this to understand the stories about Elijah which follow (1 Kgs. 16, 23-28).

Omri's son Ahab comes off a little better, but not because of any interest in his person. By chance he is the one who plays the role of Elijah's counterpart in the stories about the prophet which were incorporated because of the prophet, not because of the king. Thanks to Assyrian annals, we know that Ahab together with eleven other princes took part in the battle of Qarqar against the Assyrian king Shalmaneser III in 853 B.C. and that Ahab's contingent numbered 1,000 soldiers and 2,000 chariots. What in our opinion is a highly important historical fact, the deuteronomists pass over in silence. For them it apparently belonged to "the rest of the history of Ahab," which the reader, if he was interested, had to look up for himself "in the Book of the Annals of the Kings of Israel" (1 Kgs. 22, 39).

The further we progress in the period of the kings, the more does historical data become available from non-biblical documents. In the light of these, we see all the more clearly how exclusively the interest of the deuteronomists was directed to their religious preaching, and thus how restricted it was from a modern historical point of view. These data, of course, also offer a welcome supplement to the reliable material which they do in fact give. But we still maintain that "relatively little" can be said with certainty concerning the actual course of events, especially in the first part of the period described in the books of Joshua to Kings. Lest this conclusion leave the reader with a rather negative impression, we would like to conclude with a striking fact.

We spoke of the "relatively little" that is historically certain. That was intended by way of comparison with the many things which the deuteronomists do relate. But that "little" is really "quite a lot" when compared with what we know of the history of the surrounding peoples, which is practically nothing. This fact means quite a bit when you think that nations like Ammon, Moab and Edom differ very little outwardly from Israel and Judah. They spoke and wrote the same language. With them, too, the tribal organization developed into a monarchy. They had to endure the same invasions from the world powers, Assyria and Babylon. All of them were swept off the stage of history, leaving scarcely any traces behind. One who wishes to write a history of Moab, for example, will encounter this hard fact. The names of a few kings of Moab have been preserved in long forgotten and only recently excavated Assyrian documents. Further, there is the stone monument of King Mesha, found quite by chance, which anyone who knows biblical Hebrew can read rather easily. As for "cultural monuments," there are a few potsherds and foundations of walls—and that is all. Whatever else is known about the history of Moab is found in the Bible. It stems from the memories of the only people in those parts which was not wiped off the face of the earth in the flood of invasions. In the following chapters it will become clearer that the remnant of Israel continued to exist solely on account of its unique faith, in which it continually clung to Yahweh. This was the only god who was not a part of nature and not irrevocably tied down to one country, city or temple, but who in the depth of his heart remained a "wanderer's god." With their history the industrious deuteronomists have made an invaluable contribution to the preservation of that faith and thus to the preservation of the memories which, in the case of other nations, were lost forever, together with their national existence.

IV
The Narrative "Writings"

On the outline of the canon (p. 86) we italicized the names of the books which have served as a basis for traditional bible history. In the third group, "the Writings," there are four; four more found only in the Greek canon are also to be included. Furthermore, the book of Jonah belongs to this group although it has been placed among the twelve minor prophets. The narrative part of Daniel should really be treated here as well, but we shall leave it for later.

Since all these works were written after the exile and each in its own way reflects something of Jewish piety in that period, we will begin with some reflections on this point.

I
JEWISH LIFE AFTER THE EXILE

The Situation of the Jews

For the Judeans of the period of the later kings, the temple at Jerusalem was Yahweh's residence in the midst of his people, in the land that he had given them according to his promise. Next to his "house" on Mount Zion stood the "house" of the king, offspring of the dynasty of David, to whom Yahweh had promised a never-ending reign in the famous prophecy of 2 Samuel 7. Jerusalem, the temple and the king were witnesses, so to speak, of the reality of the Covenant, visible expressions of God's benevolence toward his people.

We must keep all of this in mind if we want to feel something of what the captivity, the shameful execution of Davidic kings, the two deportations and the destruction of Jerusalem and its temple meant for the Judeans. They could scarcely interpret these calamities otherwise than as the last gesture of Yahweh, who in this way abrogated the relationship with his people. All the visible signs of his favor he took away. The Covenant relationship was obviously broken.

However, there were others more privileged who were granted a deeper look into Yahweh's heart. From this they knew that no human infidelity could conquer his desire for community and his will to continually begin anew. In Palestine, as we have seen, the final editors of the deuteronomic history enjoyed this vision. However hesitatingly, they pointed out the future possibilities open to those who would turn to Yahweh with a contrite heart. In far away Babylon it was the priest-prophet Ezekiel who received the last exiles. He taught those whose roots had been cut that their lot now depended not only on their own personal decision but also on how they could worship together in that unclean pagan land, far from the only place where Yahweh accepted sacrifice. Thus they became familiar with forms of worship not strictly connected with the temple service. Old customs like circumcision and abstaining from certain foods took on a new meaning and became signs distinguishing those who wanted to belong to the community of Israel's God. Also, the very primitive institution of the sabbath received a new content: during the sacred gatherings on that day, listening to the words of the prophets of old and to ancient texts about the Covenant as well as preaching and singing God's praises took the place of the sacrificial rites. Those who participated in these weekly gatherings therefore experienced something of God's presence in their midst. He himself became a sort of "sanctuary" for them (Ezek. 11, 16).

In this way faith in Yahweh was kept alive, and with it came trust in a new future. When the Persians appeared on the distant horizon about 550 B.C., the spirit of Yahweh moved one of the exiles to greet the Persian monarch Cyrus with hymns full of hope as the one sent by Yahweh to lead his people back and restore Jerusalem in grandeur.

And, indeed, immediately after his conquest of Babylon in 539 B.C., Cyrus ordered the Judeans to rebuild the temple of their God in Jerusalem with his support. In the following years several groups of Judeans undertook the long and wearisome journey to their devastated fatherland. There they formed what we usually call the "post-exilic community." The first to arrive laid the foundations for the new temple without delay. Yet it was not until 515 B.C. that the building was completed. The activities of Ezra and Nehemiah belong to the important events of the following century. Both leaders made indispensable contributions to the organization of the Judeans, or "Jews," into a real "theocratic" community— that is, a community ruled (Greek: *krateo* is "rule" or "hold sway") by the will of God (*theos*). This will had found its expression in the "Law of Moses" or the "Law of God" whose representative in the government of the community was the high priest. The secular governor, appointed by the Persian king, had to respect the constitution of this "holy nation and kingdom of priests."

Carefully isolated from the surrounding pagan world and gathered around the temple as the only real center of its life, this community avoided the political vicissitudes of the other nations. In so doing, it also remained outside "history." Therefore, it is no coincidence that the historian looking for facts and events can scarcely say anything about the history of the Jews from Ezra and Nehemiah until the Maccabean revolt, a period of almost two and a half centuries (from about 400 until 167 B.C.).

But if the writing of a book destined to be incorporated in the Bible and read until the end of human history can be called a *fact*, then that long period of apparent silence is full of highly important facts. A number of Old Testament books were completed in their present form during those centuries; the others were written in their entirety in that period. Thus the post-exilic community brought forth the "Scriptures" which were to play such an essential role in Jesus' thought and actions and to become one of the fundamental supports of the young Church.

Furthermore, that Jewish community in and around Jerusalem was the hub of the so-called Diaspora (Greek for "dispersion")—that is, all those Jewish communities formed since the 6th century B.C. outside Palestine. Their number grew continually, first in Egypt and Mesopotamia, and later in Syria and Greece and on the coast of North Africa. According to calculations, all these Jews together numbered some four and a half million at the beginning of the Christian era and constituted some 8% of the population of the Roman Empire. Everywhere they continued to practice their faith in the way that Ezekiel had proposed for the exiles in Babylon. But for them God's word began more and more to take on permanent forms in the "Scriptures," which eventually were read in a Greek translation throughout the Diaspora. Likewise, there were the frequent and often intense contacts with the community at Jerusalem. Later on we shall see that without this facet of post-exilic Judaism, expansion of the Church would have been unthinkable. Now, with an eye to the following section, we must say a few words about two groups in Palestine, one outside and the other within the Jewish community.

The Samaritans

The capital of the northern kingdom was called Samaria. This name is also used for the whole surrounding region. After their devastating conquest of Samaria in 721 and the deportation of the leading classes, the Assyrians brought in national groups from other parts of their world kingdom. Reference to this can be found in the story of 2 Kings 17, 24-28 which, though a simplified presentation of things, at any rate bears witness to the presence of Yahweh worshipers in Samaria. These no doubt stemmed for the most part from those left behind at the deportation. Despite these data and the additional details in verses 29-34a, there is very little known about the history of these Samaritans. When they asked the returning Judeans to be allowed to help rebuild the temple, their request was refused by Zerubbabel and his supporters, probably because they were suspicious of the religious practices and morals of these people who had been living among pagans. The Judean leaders were highly concerned that their new start be without blemish. At a later period these Yahweh worshipers evidently became very influential in Samaria, for they were eventually able to build their own temple for Yahweh on Mount Gerizim, every bit as imposing as Shechem at its foot. Curiously enough, we don't know when or under what circumstances they accepted the Law of Moses (the Pentateuch) as their only "bible." But as time passed they became more and more estranged from the Jews.

Seen from the Jews' point of view, the Samaritans were a schismatic sect, the late and rotten fruit of Jeroboam's "schism." They were worse than the pagans who had never known Yahweh. About 200 B.C. the wise Jesus Ben Sirach of Jerusalem sketched this situation briefly, making no bones about how the Jews felt. This writer despised the Samaritans and their blasphemous cult on Mount Shechem even more than the Edomites and Philistines, those classical enemies of Israel:

> There are two nations that my soul detests;
> the third is not a nation at all:
> the inhabitants of Mount Seir and the Philistines,
> and the stupid people living at Shechem.
> (Ecclesiasticus 50, 25-28)

The reader of the New Testament knows, of course, that in Jesus' day the relationship was no better. He will recall texts like John 4, 9 and especially 8, 48: "Are we not right in saying that you are a Samaritan and possessed by a devil?"

The Levites

The early history of the tribe of Levi is very obscure. We cannot make use of the data provided by several chapters in the Pentateuch (e.g., Numbers 1; 4; 18; 26, etc.), for these descriptions are based on the principle of "reading back into the past" which we discussed earlier (p. 74). Some scholars suppose that at the beginning of the period of the judges a certain tribe, Levi, formed a small minority living somewhere in the territory of Judah. Its members seem to have specialized in cultic functions and to have spread over the territories of the other tribes as professional priests serving the numerous local sanctuaries. As a result of the centralizing reforms (by which worship was made lawful only in Jerusalem: cf. pp. 96ff.), those high places near the cities and villages lost their regular visitors, and the priests attached to them, "the sons of Levi," lost their income. As the reader will have noticed, in the situation supposed by the book of Deuteronomy, the Levites are recommended to the charity of the Israelites along with orphans, widows, foreigners and other indigent people (cf., for example, Dt. 16, 11). The local Levites were excluded from the privileges enjoyed by the priests serving the temple of Jerusalem (2 Kgs. 23, 8-9). During the exile, Ezekiel stated that the priests of the "high places" had promoted the infidelity of Israel. In his sketch of the future temple, he therefore gives them only minor functions, the priestly work proper being reserved to the descendants of the orthodox priestly class of Jerusalem (Ezek. 44, 10-14). Now we understand why only very few Levites wished to accompany Ezra at the time of the return from Babylon to Jerusalem (only 38 Levites: cf. Ezra 8, 15-19). However, in the course of the 5th and 4th centuries B.C., the Levites grew steadily in number and influence, and about 300 B.C. they dominated the daily liturgy in the temple and especially the temple music.

II
THE WORK OF THE "CHRONICLER"

According to an almost generally accepted opinion, the books of Chronicles and Ezra-Nehemiah originally formed one large historical work attributed to the "Chronicler."

This opinion is based on the fact not only that the first verses of Ezra repeat literally the last verses of Chronicles, but also that these books show close affinity in language, style, use of sources, religious convictions and so on.

Since the second part of the larger whole (Ezra-Nehemiah) was accepted earlier as a canonical book, it probably came to be separated from the first part (Chronicles). The reason may be that Ezra-Nehemiah described events (the return from Babylon and the restoration of the Jewish community) not dealt with in any other book. Chronicles, on the other hand, seemed to repeat much of what was already to be found in Samuel and Kings—hence its later incorporation in the canon, where it occupies the last place, after Ezra-Nehemiah. The books of Chronicles could also be considered as providing a sort of supplement to the stories of Samuel and Kings, for they related things which the authors of those books had apparently left out—hence the Greek name *Paralipomenon* ("that which was omitted"). St. Jerome preferred the title "Chronicon" as the best rendering of the Hebrew title, as did Luther who reintroduced this name in the West.

Author(s), Date and Intention

Some modern Scripture scholars who use the term "Chronicler" are of the opinion that it stands for several persons, either two writers with clearly distinct points of view (e.g., regarding the priestly legislation of the Pentateuch) or one principal author and several later ones who made additions in the same spirit.

Whether by one or more authors, the work must have been written in the course of the 4th century B.C., probably about 300. The "Chronicler" belonged to a group of Levites and was particularly involved in everything concerning the liturgy.

The Levites considered the community of the Jews, and only that community (not that of the Samaritans), to be the true continuation of that people chosen by God so many centuries before to be his people. The Jewish community was the realization on earth of God's kingdom, the true "theocracy," prepared by Yahweh in the preceeding centuries. The Chronicler wrote his work in order to *give expression to this faith* and at the same time to *strengthen it* among the members of the community. Although he knew the Pentateuch and the deuteronomic history and recognized them as canonical, he drew up a "levitical vision of sacred history" starting with Adam and ending with the measures taken by Ezra and Nehemiah. His purpose was to form the Jewish community into a real "people of God."

Let us now take a closer look at how historiography was put to the service of preaching and how the past was recalled with an eye to the spiritual needs of the community. We will treat the two parts of that larger whole one after the other.

The Books of Chronicles

A glance at the main divisions of Chronicles may clarify the author's intention:

> 9 chapters with genealogies from *Adam* to *David*
> 20 chapters on *David*
> 9 chapters on *Solomon*
> 27 chapters on the *Davidic kings of Judah*

David, Solomon and their successors in Jerusalem "sit on the throne of Yahweh"—that is to say, the kingdom of Judah is the true theocracy. The Chronicler depicts David and Solomon as interested exclusively in the cult and temple. He leaves the kings of the northern kingdom Israel out of the picture—from the very beginning they separated themselves from the history of God's people.

It is impossible to give here a complete answer to the difficult question of *the sources* from which the Chronicler drew his material. The reader of his works will notice that the author quotes all sorts of books. He speaks of "words, prophecies, visions, books, meditations" (the latter in Hebrew is *midrash:* searching, study, meditation), attributed to prophets such as Samuel, Nathan and Gad for the time of David (1 Chr. 29, 29), to Nathan, Ahijah and Iddo for that of Solomon (2 Chr. 9, 29), and to others for the time of the other kings (cf. 2 Chr. 12, 15; 13, 22; 20, 34; 26, 22, etc.). He also cites repeatedly a "book of the kings of [Israel and] Judah," as well as a *"midrash* on the book of the kings" (2 Chr. 24, 27).

On the other hand he never explicitly quotes the canonical books of Samuel and Kings. Yet it is certain that the texts of these books were available to him, either in the form they now have in our Bible or in a more expanded form. It may well be that his *"midrash* on the book of the kings" was that more expanded form of our canonical books and that parts of it were attributed to the prophets whose names appeared in the story.

Another important source was what we might call his "theological imagination" and that of his contemporaries. Several examples can serve to illustrate this "imagination" at work. The author(s) of Chronicles appear to possess, therefore, that same combination of fidelity toward tradition and liberty in re-presenting the past which we have observed among the deuteronomic authors.

The Chronicler at Work

There is no better way to penetrate the mind of the Chronicler than by comparing what he writes about David, Solomon and the kings of Judah with the accounts in Samuel and Kings. By seeing what he omits and what he adds and changes—in short, by observing how he uses his sources—one discovers his intentions and his teaching. The following examples can at the same time help the reader to become more familiar with the biblical manner of re-presenting the past.

In his description of *David*, the Chronicler omits all the military campaigns and wars, the sins and the setbacks that characterized the precarious life of the founder of the dynasty.

That he is idealizing David is clear from the following: According to the books of Samuel, David was first annointed at Hebron only as king of Judah; not until seven years later did the northern tribes recognize his authority. The Chronicler simplifies the story and makes him king over all Israel from the very beginning (1 Chr. 11, 1-3). With the help of "all Israel" he conquers Jerusalem and from that moment on seems to have but one interest: worship. All his activities are devoted to the organization of the cult and the preparations for building the temple.

We recommend that the reader compare in particular 1 Chronicles 21 with the corresponding chapter, 2 Samuel 24. The first difference to be noticed is that Satan replaces Yahweh here as the instigator of the punishable deed (verse 1). There is also the more elaborate description of the angel of Yahweh. Both changes reflect the development which the religious vision of Israel has undergone in the intermediate centuries. Ornan adds to his gifts "the wheat for the oblation," thus obeying the priestly legislation (Num. 15, 3ff.). The "fifty shekels in silver" paid by David are changed into "six hundred shekels of gold" which he gave Ornan for the site. Instead of buying with silver, David *gives* him gold; the amount is multiplied by twelve, apparently because the king is the representative of the twelve tribes of Israel and is always extremely generous when it's a question of the cult (cf. 1 Chr. 29, 1-5). Finally, the Chronicler changed the end of the story as follows:

2 Samuel 24, 24b-25	1 Chronicles 21, 25-27
So David paid fifty shekels in silver for the threshing-floor and oxen.	So David gave Ornan six hundred shekels of gold by weight for the site.
David built an altar to Yahweh there and offered holocausts and communion sacrifices.	David built an altar there to Yahweh and offered holocausts and communion sacrifices.
Then Yahweh took pity on the country and the plague was turned away from Israel.	He called on Yahweh and Yahweh answered him with fire from heaven on the altar of holocaust and ordered the angel to sheathe his sword.

The connection between David's sacrifice and the cessation of the plague is taken for granted in the text of 2 Samuel, yet not expressly mentioned. The Chronicler makes it explicit by introducing fire from heaven and God's command to the angel. Like the multiplication of the price which David pays, this detail serves to emphasize that God himself has approved the place where the temple is going to be built.

Comparing 2 Chronicles 7 with 1 Kings 8, the reader will notice another insertion of "fire from heaven," again with the intention of putting God's election of the temple site in the limelight.

Describing the reign of the *kings of Judah,* the Chronicler cannot avoid mentioning from time to time the northern kingdom. In the case of Rehoboam's successor, for example, he must tell something about that king's war with Jeroboam of Israel. In reading Abijah's speech to the Israelite troops (2 Chr. 13, 4-12) we must keep in mind that the schismatic kingdom founded by Jeroboam still existed for the Chronicler: the Samaritans were for him the continuation and representation of that former Israel which "broke away" from Judah (cf. Is. 7, 17). Abijah's speech is therefore a sort of self-affirmation of the Jewish community before the Samaritan pretensions, not an historical account.

In many other cases the situation of his own epoch influences the Chronicler's description of former relations between Judah and Israel (cf., for example, 2 Chr. 19, 2: "those who hate Yahweh," and Hezekiah's address in 2 Chr. 30, 6-9 and its effect in v. 10). Unfortunately, the great prophet Elijah had lived and worked in Israel. The Chronicler was nevertheless able to make use of him *once,* and then as the author of a letter of warning to King Jehoram of Judah (2 Chr. 21, 12-15).

The depravity of the schismatic northern kingdom, inherited by the Samaritans, was, however, no obstacle to good behavior on the part of individuals. In the time of King Ahaz some Samaritans not only released Jewish prisoners, but ". . . from the booty they clothed all those of them who were naked; they gave them clothing and sandals and provided them with food, drink and shelter. They mounted all those who were infirm on donkeys and took them back to their kinsmen at Jericho" (2 Chr. 28, 15). Thus these good Samaritans were a preview of the man in Jesus' famous parable.

Two Points of Faith

The principal function of the theocratic community is the *worship of Yahweh* through sacrifice and praise. The Levites considered the "sacrifice of praise" to be the heart of the temple worship. Later we shall see that pious Jews saw in the continuous glorification of Yahweh the ultimate purpose of human existence: they abominated death because it would put an end to the daily praise of their God.

This conviction was partly responsible for the Chronicler's portraits of David and Solomon. The beautiful prayer which he puts on David's lips in 1 Chronicles 29 is typical, with its sentence in which he summarizes how Israel experiences the sacrificial service: "All comes from you, from your own hand we have given them to you" (v. 14). From that prayer come the words which the Christians very early joined to the Lord's Prayer: "Yours is the kingdom and the power and the glory" (vv. 11-13).

The description of 2 Chronicles 7, 1-6 is also characteristic. Notice the exclamation: "Praise Yahweh, for he is good, for his love is everlasting," which the Chronicler uses several times to summarize levitical hymns of praise (cf. the refrain in Psalm 136).

In this context we should also mention the "tall tale" that the Chronicler inserts in his description of Jehoshaphat's reign (about 870-848). In the form of a narration he bears witness to the conviction that the strength and salvation of the community depend on prayer and worship. After the striking prayer of the king, as the representative of the people, and the prophet's exhortation, the Judean troops go forth to do battle with the innumerable hosts of three attacking nations. Yet in the foremost ranks of the Judeans march the Levites, in the festal robes of the liturgy. As soon as they catch sight of the enemy, they begin to praise Yahweh in a loud voice. Immediately the hostile armies turn against each other, and all the Jews have to do is gather the spoils from among the dead. This alone takes them three days.

Another religious conviction which was a determining factor in the re-presentation of the past concerns *retribution:* Yahweh rewards good and punishes evil during the lifetime of man. That was especially true for the kings of David's dynasty (for the development of this teaching, see pp. 233-254).

One example: compare the description of Uzziah's reign in 2 Chronicles 26 with the seven verses treating this same king in 2 Kings 15, 1-7. The old text simply states that the king was struck with leprosy and had to live in confinement until his death, while his son Jotham ruled in his place. According to the general view it is said that Yahweh "struck" the king. The Chronicler cannot pass on this information without inventing a sinful act committed by Uzziah which would explain the leprosy as a just punishment. Therefore, he relates how the king became proud, no longer ascribed his successes to Yahweh and then assumed a priestly function. Thus the Uzziah of the Chronicler transgresses a liturgical law not yet known to the historical Uzziah.

Ezra-Nehemiah

When reading the conclusion of the books of Chronicles, keep in mind the succession of the Persian kings and the years of their reigns. After Cyrus came:

> Cambyses—529-522
> Darius I—522-486
> Xerxes (Artaxerxes, Ahasuerus)—486-465
> Artaxerxes I (Arthahsasta)—465-424
> Darius II—424-404
> Artaxerxes II—404-358.

Remember, too, that there was not *one* return of Judeans from Babylon, but that this took place in groups in the course of many years. Furthermore, the restoration at Jerusalem began with the altar of sacrifice and then with the temple; only later were the walls erected.

The Intention

The *first part* begins with the Jewish version of Cyrus' edict ordering the reconstruction of the temple at Jerusalem and permitting the Judeans to return to their homeland. This took place under the leadership of Sheshbazzar. A list of the returning exiles follows in chapter 2. Zerubbabel and Jeshua are mentioned as the first of their leaders, not Sheshbazzar. In chapter 3 these two are in charge of the reconstruction of the altar, the first Feast of Tabernacles and laying the foundation for the temple. Then the author mentions the opposition they had to endure from the former inhabitants. This hostile situation continued until the reign of Darius I.

The topic of "resistance" is apparently an occasion for him to insert here several letters written in Aramaic and dating from a much later period. Samaritans, with the help of their Persian governor, accused the Judeans before King Artaxerxes of rebuilding the walls of Jerusalem. The king's answer then follows.

The Aramaic of the inserted documents may explain why the author now continues his own story in that language (Ezra 4, 24—6, 18): Zerubbabel and Jeshua take up the building of the temple again, supported by Haggai and Zechariah and with a letter from Darius as endorsement. The consecration of the completed temple took place in the sixth year of his reign (i.e., 515 B.C.), after which the author, now writing in Hebrew again, tells of the first Passover in Jerusalem.

The *second part* introduces Ezra to the readers as the son of a priestly family and "a scribe versed in the Law of Moses." The edict which he received from King Artaxerxes, in the seventh year of his reign, is incorporated in its original Aramaic form (7, 12-26). Besides ensuring financial security, it spoke above all about establishing "the Law of your God" in Judah as the officially recognized constitution of the Jewish community. Then the story changes to the first person. Ezra himself tells who accompanied him from Babylon and how everything went during the journey (chapter 8). Then he relates the disconcerting situation awaiting him in Jerusalem: priests and Levites as well as laymen had married women from the pagan population. "I stretched out my hands to Yahweh my God, and said. . . ." With these words begins the long prayer which was intended at the same time to prick the consciences of the listeners (9). Once again in the third person, the story goes on to tell how the priest Ezra succeeded in bringing those who had married pagan women to the conviction that they should dispose of their "foreign wives" (10).

In the *third part* Nehemiah begins to relate how, as the cup-bearer of Artaxerxes, he obtained permission to go to Jerusalem in the twentieth year of the king's reign and to rebuild the temple. Under strong opposition, especially from three figures whom he mentions by name (Sanballat, governor of Samaria, Tobiah the Ammonite, and Geshem the Arab), he succeeds in restoring the walls in fifty-two days. His description of these activities (3-6) is interrupted only to direct the attention of the reader—that is, primarily God, whom he sometimes addresses explicitly—to his social legislation and his own exemplary conduct on that point. In order to get more inhabitants within the city walls, Nehemiah holds a sort of registration based on an old list (chapter 7, almost identical with that of Ezra 2). In the next chapter Nehemiah disappears almost completely. That chapter relates the solemn proclamation of the Law by the priest Ezra. This was an introduction to a festive celebration of the Feast of Tabernacles. Chapter 9 begins with a reference to the dissolution of mixed marriages, and the rest contains only a long prayer of atonement. We come across the name Nehemiah again in chapter 10, among those who solemnly bound themselves to observe a number of religious obligations. Chapter 11 brings us back again to the measures taken by Nehemiah to have one-tenth of the country population living in Jerusalem. After several genealogies of priests and Levites, 12, 27 returns us suddenly to Nehemiah's account of the building of the walls. Here the solemn consecration is related, and the scribe Ezra turns up again at the head of one of the participating choirs (v. 36).

A sort of conclusion (12, 44—13, 3) sketches the cultic community organized under the leadership of Zerubbabel and Nehemiah. An appendix follows with Nehemiah's own description of the measures he took when he returned to Jerusalem a second time—i.e., shortly after his first sojourn there, which ended in the 32nd year of Artaxerxes' reign.

Method

Even such a short summary shows that all kinds of documents were available to the Chronicler for his descriptions: copies of decrees and official correspondence (in Aramaic), lists of immigrants, family trees, and especially Ezra's detailed account and Nehemiah's personal "memoirs." But he used these documents quite independently—for example, by rearranging their parts. The interested reader can form for himself a picture of the modern hypothesis which reconstructs *the account of Ezra* from the following texts read successively: Ezra 7—8; Nehemiah 8; Ezra 9—10 and Nehemiah 9, and *the memoirs of Nehemiah* (Neh. 1—7; 10; 12, 27-43; 13, 4-31).

This reconstruction, which except for minor differences is accepted by many scholars, raises the question why the Chronicler arranged these precious documents in what seems more to be disorder than order. If they are read separately, Nehemiah seems to be a very different kind of man than Ezra. He seems to have come to Jerusalem under different circumstances and with a different intention. Nehemiah wanted first and foremost to protect the city from its neighbors and to organize the Jewish community into an independent entity. Ezra was a priest and, as we saw, a scribe versed in the Law of Moses. He seems to have been very juridical in his thinking, and he strived above all for purity of cult and race. Not without reason did later generations come to call him the "father of Judaism." Perhaps the Chronicler combined his data concerning the activities of both men in order to give a comprehensive picture of the establishment of the new community, the founding of the "theocracy" (cf. above, p. 111).

In any case, that picture, besides being confusing to the modern historian, is also not complete precisely because of the editor's exclusively religious points of view. Like his deuteronomic predecessors, and perhaps even more strongly than they, he let himself be guided by that limited interest in the choice and especially in the treatment of his material. In the three parts of Ezra-Nehemiah summarized above, the reader undoubtedly observed a certain order: a command from the Persian king, the story of its execution, and finally a religious celebration marking its end. Interest in the theocracy dominates the picture. We hear practically nothing about Ezra's political activity. Yet this must have been important—and, in the eyes of the Persians, the only important aspect. Ezra was in their service, and his mission undoubtedly was connected with their endeavors to get a solid hold on Palestine, that important corridor to Egypt. To attain this objective, they somehow had to be assured of order and peace in that country.

The Chronicler leaves that side of Ezra's activities so vague that we don't even know with certainty which Persian king was the author of Ezra's edict. In so doing this biblical author created a problem which is considered the most difficult one in the whole of Old Testament scholarship. Even an introduction of this kind cannot completely pass over it.

Fixing a Date

On the grounds of Ezra's account, the Chronicler relates that Ezra came to Jerusalem in the seventh year of Artaxerxes' reign. If he means Artaxerxes I, then that took place *in 458*. Further on Nehemiah himself writes that he arrived in the 20th year of that reign and remained until the 32nd—i.e., from 445 to 433—and some time later returned a second time to work in Jerusalem. Consequently, most scholars consider it improbable, if not impossible, that Ezra could have come in 458, so long before Nehemiah. The circumstances of that time in Mesopotamia and Syria would scarcely have permitted a journey without an escort (Ezra 8, 22). And were Ezra's reforms in Jerusalem (not yet rebuilt!) so ineffective that Nehemiah could still encounter abuses like the one described in Nehemiah 13? This seems improbable. For these and other reasons many scholars assume that in Ezra's account Artaxerxes II is meant, and that Ezra didn't arrive till *398* with his endorsement to impose the Law—that is, long after Nehemiah's second stay. That the latter is present at Ezra's proclamation of the Law (Neh. 8, 9) and that Ezra participates in the dedication of the walls (Neh. 12, 26) could then be contributions of the Chronicler. It does in fact seem more probable that Ezra's religious reforms could begin only after Nehemiah had provided the Jewish community with a stronger material footing and a more certain chance of survival. But yet the year 398 seems too late to some. A non-biblical document states that in 419 the Persian government issued prescriptions for the Jews in Upper Egypt concerning the celebration of the Passover in accordance with that same "law of God" which Ezra introduced in Jerusalem. It would be strange if that would take place in southern Egypt earlier than in Jerusalem —hence the middle solution, based on a hypothetical slip of the pen. It is proposed that "the 37th year" was the original date in the text (Ezra 7, 7-8) instead of "the seventh year," thus bringing Ezra to Jerusalem *in 428* rather than 458. In this way he could have collaborated with Nehemiah during the latter's second period in office.

We hope that the readers who haven't skipped over this paragraph are not too discouraged by these difficulties. The famous question is still being studied, and it is quite possible that new discoveries will throw more light on the background of Ezra's activities. Despite the difficulties, it cannot be denied that in this part of his work the Chronicler gives us a concrete picture of one of the most important periods in the history of God's people. The persons presented here are much more men of flesh and blood than those in the books of Chronicles. Ezra and Nehemiah—particularly the latter—come to us as real believers who, in the situation presented to them, dedicate themselves totally to what they see as the cause of their God.

III

THE BOOKS OF MACCABEES

In our list of biblical historians the Chronicler is followed by the authors of the two books of Maccabees. To speak of "1 and 2 Maccabees" in one breath can be misleading, for here it is not a question of *one* book that has been split in two because of its length as was the case with the books of Samuel, Kings and Chronicles. In this case "the second book" was not only written by a different *author,* but also in a different *country,* at a different *time,* in a different *language* and a different *style.* All that both books have in common is part of their subject matter.

That subject matter is the struggle of the Maccabees for the preservation of the Jewish faith, in 167 B.C. and the years following. It has been said to have had "worldwide historical consequences," and that is no exaggeration. Without the sharp reaction of the Maccabees, the Jewish community of Palestine would have been absorbed by its "pagan" surroundings to such an extent that it never could have become the point of departure and basis of the movement which we call Christendom.

In subsequent chapters our study of the prophets will provide an occasion to mention earlier periods of crisis when Israel's existence as a nation was a stake. Our discussion of the books of Maccabees calls for a short sketch of this last crisis, prior to the beginning of the Christian era when the Jewish faith encountered an extremely dangerous enemy: the attraction of Hellenism and the power and pretensions of its champions.

The Rise of Hellenism

In 334 B.C. Alexander the Great began his campaign against the Persians with a very explicit ideal. His father, Philip of Macedon, considered himself an offspring of Heracles, and his mother believed that she was a descendant of Achilles. From the time he was thirteen the gifted scion, Alexander, enjoyed the privilege of studying at the feet of Aristotle. That master not only developed his thirst for exact knowledge, but communicated as well a boundless admiration for Greek culture. After the young prince, scarcely 24 years old, had conquered the land of the Pharaohs and there had chosen the site for a completely new harbor city to be named Alexandria after him, he pushed through to the heart of the Persian empire. Then he led his troops further still to the rivers of India. More and more clearly he saw the fulfillment of all his dreams: he would unite all men in *one* world, *one* in language and culture and *one* in their worship of his supernatural person.

But when Alexander was 33, death surprised him in Babylon. His world empire, only scarcely organized, fell apart. A savage struggle arose among the generals, the Diadochi, who "succeeded" to his power. Finally the ingenious Ptolemeus, son of Lagus, was able to attain dominion over Egypt. Another important part of the empire, including Mesopotamia and Syria, fell to Seleucus.

In their territories both rulers promoted with all their power the "Hellenizing" which Alexander had begun so ambitiously. But they fought with each other, too, over the possession of Palestine which was the coastal region joining their lands. That territory remained a cause of tension between the Seleucids, who built their new capital in Syria on the Orontes River and called it Antioch, and the Ptolemies who ruled their kingdom from Alexandria. The latter were able to maintain their control of Palestine throughout the entire 3rd century (301 to 198 B.C.) despite repeated invasions from the north.

At first the change from Persian rule to that of the Ptolemies meant little more for the Jews than a change of tax collectors. The Ptolemies recognized the Jews' "theocratic" form of government. Jerusalem and its surroundings formed in their eyes something like a temple domain. The reigning high priest was responsible for the regular payment of taxes in accord with their assessment of the territory.

The new rulers of Egypt were much more interested in the regions surrounding that rugged, mountainous territory of the Jews, called Judea in Hellenistic Greek. They were especially interested in the coastal plain where the only good north-south connection ran, the plain of Galilee and the great commercial centers in Transjordania, from Petra in the south to the cities of Bashan in the north. There the results of their developmental work were quickly visible. Old cities were completely rebuilt around or near earlier centers according to the latest, expansive planning: streets as straight as an arrow running perpendicular to each other and flanked by colonnades. They were also given new names, mostly after the new Greek rulers, their family and relatives. Thus ancient Acco on the coast was enlarged to become the modern seaport city of Ptolemais, and the former capital of the Ammonites received the name of Philadelphia at its renewal. The buzzing modern life surrounding Judea on all sides could not leave the members of the Jewish community untouched. Their thought and activity were regulated for the most part by their Law. This formed, to use a common term from a later day, a "hedge" around them which protected them from outside influences. But that screen soon proved to be insufficient, especially for those Jews who were of the ruling classes or rich or better educated when they came in contact with the new culture. They had to travel a lot. When they left Judea, they immediately found themselves in Hellenized cities where Greek was spoken, where new buildings were set aside for games and sports in the Greek manner such as theaters, gymnasiums (athletic schools from the Greek *gumnos*, "naked"), baths, and, above all, temples in honor of many different gods. To these belonged also the local Baals of former times and their goddesses, who of course had received Greek names. A Jew who didn't feel at home walking along the colonnades of the spacious squares with their innumerable statues, who couldn't take part in the new forms of human society or hold his own in the conversations of the day on philosophical questions, literature and politics, must have felt very backward, like someone from a very underdeveloped region.

It is understandable that a division soon began to manifest itself within the Jewish community. A strong group of intelligent and influential people thought that Judaism should adapt to the new culture. For their children's sake, too, it would not be fair for the Jews to continue to maintain customs which stemmed from a primitive and barbarian past. In the clear light of Greek reason, after all, it was quite evident that such things as a "holy" seventh day on which all work was forbidden, a careful distinction between "clean" and "unclean" food, and especially something like circumcision—let alone the foolish idea of a god who could not be represented by an idol and who resided in a completely empty temple!—brought back memories of a time long past with its dark world of taboos and magic.

For other Jews these customs and opinions had a divine origin. Indeed, they made the members of that nation a people apart, but this *apartheid* was at the same time the result and sign of their exceptional privilege of being the people of the true God. Israel was his possession in this world, his "inheritance" among the nations. Adaptation to the uniform culture of Hellenism would be nothing less than betrayal of God, their own past and the future of his kingdom.

Opposition between the "progressives" and "conservatives" was growing within the Jewish community when Antiochus the Great captured Palestine from the Ptolemies in 198 B.C. The deciding blow came at the battle of Panion near the mouth of the Jordan, the city later to be called Caesarea Philippi. Antiochus' victory was partly due to the charges of his elephants, the living tanks of those days, which he had imported from India together with their drivers (cf. 1 Macc. 6, 30-46). This monarch, too, recognized the Jewish community as a theocratic state and he gave it all kinds of privileges and even financial support. However, he was unable to realize Alexander's great political ideal of one world empire, for he, too, was to be surprised, this time by the fast growing power of the Romans whom he continued to underestimate for too long. After the famous defeat at Magnesia in 190 B.C., they imposed extremely heavy taxes on him. As a last resort he turned to plundering the treasures of the ancient temples of Mesopotamia. In those days famous temples served the same purpose that great banking houses do for us. He was killed in 187 B.C. during one of these expeditions. His son and successor Seleucus sent his chief minister Heliodorus to take possession of the temple treasury of Jerusalem. A vehement revolt among the people deterred him from going through with it. Later he murdered King Seleucus to take the throne for himself. It was then that Antiochus IV, Seleucus' brother, appeared on the scene.

Jewish Faith under Attack

In the person of this Antiochus, Hellenism declared open war on Judaism. Because of this, Jewish tradition has painted him as a sort of monster, the symbol of the powers opposing God. Since he also figures in the book of Daniel, it seems useful to say a bit more about him.

As a young man Antiochus had been one of the twenty important hostages his father had to give the Romans after the defeat at Magnesia in 190. He was the only one of the twenty not released after three years. Thus the king's son stayed in Rome, where he could move about freely, live a comfortable life and make friends in the highest circles. At the request of his brother Seleucus, he was allowed to return after fourteen years as a hostage, but only in exchange for his brother's son Demetrius. Since Seleucus' hold on the throne was secure, the hostage took his time returning. He profited from the opportunity to visit Athens where he gave his passionate love for Greek culture free rein for a while. This he did lavishly, providing the capital for cultural projects. Thus he promoted with vast sums the further building of the Olympeium, the temple in honor of Zeus Olympius, one of the largest edifices of antiquity.

In 175 B.C. the news reached him at Athens that his brother Seleucus had been murdered by his chief minister and friend Heliodorus. He quickly made preparations to take possession of the throne of the empire with the help of the troops which the king of powerful Pergamum lent him. That empire still embraced a great part of the ancient Eastern world, and despite a century and a half of Hellenization, it still revealed a great diversity of nations and cultures. Antiochus began his rule with the firm resolution to realize the ideal of Alexander in the vast territory over which he ruled. This unity was to be achieved partly by all inhabitants unanimously worshiping Antiochus, their king. The coins which he regularly had minted show very strikingly how he demanded more and more attention for his divinity as time went on. His earliest coins bear a good likeness of him, sometimes with a star on his head, a symbol of his being taken up into the divine. The inscriptions still read simply *King Antiochus.* A few years later *Theos Epiphanes* is added; he is then a "god" in human "appearance." Later still you find the inscription *Nicephorus,* "the victorious one," a title of the supreme god, Zeus; the god's features and beard also became a part of Antiochus' portrait.

The new ruler very quickly encountered the divided community of the Jews. The "progressive" Jason, a brother of the ruling high priest, Onias, offered Antiochus a great sum of money with the request that he be appointed high priest. In return he would take measures to make Jerusalem a real Hellenistic city. Both the money and the cooperation delighted the king immensely, especially in light of his plan to conquer Egypt which had become extremely weak under the last Ptolemies. His first Egyptian campaign was successful, but meanwhile in Jerusalem Jason had been ousted by Menelaus who was even more progressive. Antiochus supported the latter. In 168 he marched south with a still larger army to break the resistance of Alexandria. But then he encountered the power which had also proved too much for his father. At the order of the Senate, a Roman legate haughtily forced him to desist from the campaign. This loss of face certainly contributed to the energy with which Antiochus then put into the Hellenization of Judea. In 167 B.C. he built a fortress in Jerusalem dominating the temple and the city. There he quartered a large garrison. With that power as support, his officials forced through the Hellenization, assisted by progressive Jews. An Athenian specialist in Greek worship directed the religious reforms.

No longer was any Jew allowed to live according to the Law, and sacrifice in the temple was now patterned completely along Greek lines. Above the altar of sacrifice there arose an altar dedicated to Zeus Olympius, and the accompanying idol is said to have had the features of Antiochus himself. In any case sacrifice had to be offered to that Zeus on the 25th of each month, the day celebrated monthly throughout the empire as Antiochus' birthday. Elsewhere in Judea altars were also erected to Greek gods, and the Samaritan temple of Yahweh was dedicated to Zeus Xenius, "the hospitable."

Thus in that part of his kingdom as well, Antiochus tried to realize the ideal of Alexander, without suspecting how deeply the Jewish faith was rooted in the hearts of some of his subjects. For them Antiochus' reforms reached their climax in the desecration of the temple. In their opinion that was an atrocity beyond all thinkable proportions, a "world-shaking" crime in the most literal sense of that word. Immediately afterward they no doubt breathlessly awaited the destroying blow which the world deserved for this brutal neglect of its creator.

The "product of human skill" (Psalm 115; Vulg. 113b) now being worshiped in the temple, Zeus Olympius, was at the same time the supreme god of the Syrians, *Baal Shamem*, which in their language meant "lord of the heavens." That second word could be taken for something completely different from "heaven." It made them think of the stem *sh-m-m* referring both to utter desolation and to its destructive effect on the soul of the onlooker. Furthermore, the Jews did not like to pronounce that first word, Baal. When they had to speak about such a false god, they used a word which means "abomination" or "something detestable." Therefore you can understand the Jewish "translation" of the *Baal Shamem* erected in the temple by Antiochus: "the abomination of desolation," or perhaps more clearly, "the disastrous abomination" (cf. Dan. 9, 27).

At this the reaction of the faithful people immediately burst into flame. The spark was struck in Modin, a village on the northwest ridge of the Judean highlands, where you can look out over the coastal plain to the Mediterranean Sea. From the old Mattathias, a member of a priestly family, the spark leaped to his five sons. Each of them had a nickname. The third son, Judas, was called Maccabaeus. Because he was the leader, this name was later on extended to his brothers, and in a certain sense to the entire resistance movement.

The First Book of Maccabees

The first of the two books devoted to that movement gives an account which approaches historiography in the modern sense. After an historical introduction, the author treats successively the activities of *Judas,* who in 162 finally regained for the Jews the right to live according to their own customs; then those of *Jonathan,* who took over the leadership after Judas' death in 160 and who in 152 succeeded in being appointed high priest by the Seleucid king; and finally the activities of *Simon,* who became leader when Jonathan was imprisoned and executed in 143. A year later Simon obtained exemption from taxation for the Jews. That essentially meant political independence, for the first time since the fall of Jerusalem in 587 B.C.! When Simon was treacherously murdered in 134, his son John Hyrcanus took over the leadership, but the work of this second generation wasn't included in the scope of the book. Therefore, the author concludes his work after mentioning John with a sentence which begins as follows: "The rest of John's acts, the battles he fought and the exploits he performed, the city walls he built, and all his other achievements, are to be found recorded in the annals of his pontificate. . . ."

The reader will undoubtedly recognize here the stereotyped sentence with which the books of Kings conclude each description of a reign (cf. p. 93). The author tried in fact to describe the successful struggle of the Maccabees in the manner of Israel's ancient history books. But in so doing he still remained a man of his time—i.e., the end of the 2nd century before the Christian era. This is evident in his book.

On the one hand the author took the deuteronomic history as his example, for he believed that the God of Israel was really the main character of the piece of history which he wanted to describe. Just as in former times Yahweh raised up the judges and the kings Saul and David to save his people from oppression by foreigners, he now called forth Judas and his brothers. In those former days, according to the Deuteronomists, the Israelites had brought the oppression upon themselves because of their idolatrous ways; now, too, the author saw the threat of Antiochus and his successors as a chastisement for the infidelity of so many Jews.

Even the language in which he wrote revealed his conviction. He didn't choose the everyday language of the Jews, Aramaic, which was also the language of popular writing; nor did he choose Greek, the language of the educated and of higher forms of literature. He chose Hebrew, the language of the Law and the prophets, then used only in the liturgy and theological treatises, much like Latin in the Roman Catholic Church. This fact alone was already a confession of his belief in what his heroes meant for the history of God's relation with his people.

Likewise, his approach and choice of words have the ring of old stories about judges and kings. At high points prose turns to poetry: the main characters express themselves in poems with a liturgical tenor. The godless ways of Antiochus provoke a lamentation from the people (1 Macc. 1, 24-28) and from the author (1, 36-40 and 3, 45) as well as from Mattathias (2, 7-13), who then encourages his sons with a sort of didactic psalm mentioning the salvation of faithful Israelites from Abraham to Daniel (2, 49-64). Finally there is the eulogy on Simon which follows the statement that during his reign Judah "was at peace" (14, 4-15). That expression, which reminds one of the book of Judges, is also used in relation to Judas (7, 50), while after one of his victories Jonathan begins "to judge the people" (9, 73). The author allows "all Israel" to mourn at Judas' death with the opening words of

David's famous dirge for Saul and Jonathan: "What a downfall for the strong man, the man who saved Israel single-handedly" (9, 21; cf. 2 Sam. 1, 27).

The expression "all Israel" is also characteristic of the intention to relate sacred history in the classical manner. The writer almost never refers to the members of the Jewish community with *Joudaioi,* the term most common in those days—i.e., the inhabitants of Judea and thus Jews. However, he does keep this name when citing texts of treaties and the like. He himself chooses to refer to them in his story as "Israel," the ancient, sacred name of the people of Yahweh.

On the one hand, then, the author of 1 Maccabees tried to write sacred history in the manner of the ancient Israelite history books; on the other hand, he was a man of his time. Whereas the old writers spoke of "Yahweh" without fear, our author shares the scrupulousness of his contemporaries in the faith, who never pronounced the holy name and even avoided as much as possible all direct references to God. In 1 Maccabees 1, 64 we read (literally) "It was a dreadful wrath that visited Israel," and in 3, 8 that Judas turned "wrath away from Israel." God is not mentioned here. Every reader understood whose wrath was meant. Often substitutes were used, mostly "heaven." This occurs, for example, when we read of Judas encouraging the little group of resistance fighters in 3, 18-19: "It is easy for a great number to be routed by a few; indeed, in the sight of heaven, deliverance, whether by many or by few, is all one; for victory in war does not depend on the size of the fighting force; it is from heaven that strength comes." It also occurs further on in his proud words: "Better for us to die in battle than to watch the ruin of our nation and our holy place. Whatever be the will of heaven, he will perform it" (3, 59-60). Jesus, too, held to this usage—for example, where he says that "there will be more rejoicing in heaven over one repentant sinner. . . ." (Lk. 15, 7).

The Hellenistic spirit of the times also left its mark on the content and form of the book. In the last sentence of his story about Judas, the author speaks, in the manner of Kings, about "the other deeds of Judas, the battles he fought, the exploits he performed and *all his titles to greatness. . . .*" (9, 22). With these last words the author expresses his admiration for the Maccabean brothers in a way not found in older books of the Bible. His explicit "hero worship" elsewhere in the book also seems to be of Hellenistic inspiration. In the same way he describes with admiration the monument which Simon had built on the family grave at Modin. With its high, decorative colonnade and its splendid sculptures, it was so imposing that it could be seen from the sea, and it was clearly a mausoleum in Greek style.

Although Judas fought for the preservation of Jewish customs and for freedom to live strictly according to the Law, the author does not seem to realize how much his hero acted in the Hellenistic spirit when he enlarged the liturgical calendar, firmly established in the Law, by two annual celebrations: the feast of the dedication of the newly built altar of sacrifice ("Feast of the Dedication," later called "Hanukkah"; cf. 4, 49) and that of the victory over Nicanor ("Day of Nicanor"; cf. 7, 49).

Equally unconcerned, the writer speaks of Judas' alliance with the Romans (8, 17-32) and relates further on (chapter 12) how Jonathan sent envoys to Sparta at its renewal. In his letter the Spartans are called "brothers" of the Jews. He does this on the basis of an old document added to the letter. In it King Areios of Sparta is said to have written to the high priest Onias (about 300 B.C.—i.e., a century and a half earlier) as follows: "It has been discovered in a document concerning the Spartans and Jews that they are brothers, and of the race of Abraham. . . ." The whole procedure is very Hellenistic, although the Jews nevertheless maintain the belief in their special position. Jonathan's letter to the Spartans also bears witness to this. He would like very much to enjoy friendship and alliance "though we have no need of these, having the consolation of the holy books in our possession. . . ." He goes on to say that the Jews certainly remember their brothers the Spartans when offering sacrifices and prayers. This is completely in the spirit of Hellenistic brotherliness. He writes, "We were unwilling to trouble you . . . during these wars. But now, having the support of heaven to help us, we have been delivered from our enemies, and it is they who have been brought low. . . ." (12, 5-15).

Although the author could have experienced only the last years of the more than thirty years which he describes (167-134 B.C.)—and indeed only as a child—quite a lot of reliable, firsthand information was available to him, which he worked into his book with great care. The precise listing of persons, places and dates (according to the Seleucid calendar which began in 312/311 B.C.) may also be attributed to Greek influence absorbed during his formation as writer. He does not relate miracles. But his religious point of view sees God's hand at work in the events which he describes. Partly because of this, he felt personally related to the Maccabees and involved in the cause for which they fought at the price of their own lives, firmly trusting in God.

The Second Book of Maccabees

The second book is almost as long as the first. Yet it treats only a part of the same material. The story begins with the arrival of Heliodorus in Jerusalem to take possession of the temple treasury, under Seleucus IV—thus before 175 B.C.—and ends with Judas' victory over Nicanor in 160 B.C.

The compiler's preface is not found until 2, 19-32 because of the two letters presented as a sort of introduction to the book. In the argument of these letters the Jewish community at Jerusalem encourages the Jews in Egypt to celebrate the feast of the dedication of the temple there as well.

The date of the first letter is given as 124 B.C. It refers to an earlier one sent to Egypt by the Jews of Jerusalem as early as 143 B.C. concerning the Feast of the Dedication, which they call the "Feast of Tabernacles of the month Chislev (December)." Obviously the name comes from the affinity of the new feast with that Feast of Tabernacles which was better known to the Egyptian Jews. Both have the waving of palms and last for eight days (2 Macc. 10, 6). There is no reason to doubt the authenticity of this first document (1, 1-9). The second, longer letter (1, 10—2, 18), on the other hand, is fictitious. It is supposed to have been written by Judas Maccabaeus before the solemn purification of the temple in 164 B.C., and thus before there was even a reason for the feast! By attributing this second letter as well as a large number of legendary stories to Judas, the author no doubt thought that he could arouse his fellow Jews in Egypt to a common celebration of Hanukkah.

After these recommendations, the actual book begins in 2, 19 with a preface by the verbose author himself. He says that his book is a summary of a five-volume work on the Maccabees by a certain Jason of Cyrene. It's unfortunate that this great work has been lost; by comparing the two we could see how the author looked upon his work of making a summary. Did he choose particular sections from Jason's book without changing much in them, or did he rework Jason's entire text into a new version?

However this may be, on the one hand the book offers a number of historical details which 1 Maccabees does not have. Excellent information was obviously available to Jason. On the other hand, it is lacking the sober style maintained by the author of the first book, despite his personal attachment to his heroes. The writer of 2 Maccabees explicitly wants to fascinate, move and instruct his readers. This strikes us as being rather bombastic and far-fetched. Read, for example, his description of the reaction to Heliodorus' plan and what happened to him in the temple (3, 9-40), or the story of the old Eleazar and how the seven brothers together with their mother were martyred (6, 18—7, 42), or how Antiochus met his end (9, 5-29) and how Razis "heroically" committed suicide (14, 37-46). Then you will understand what is meant by the words often used to typify this style of writing: "rhetorical" and "pathetic." We should remember, however, that this style was probably in vogue among the Hellenized Jews as one of the forms used to express the faith which united them.

The book obviously wanted to arouse interest and love among them for the temple at Jerusalem, the middle point of the Jewish faith. This was emphasized by the one who prefaced it with the letters, but it is also quite clear from the author's intention. The first part concludes with the death of the sacrilegious Antiochus and the ceremonies accompanying the new beginning of worship, the "dedication of the temple" (4, 1—10, 8). The second ends with the death of Nicanor, who had threatened to level the temple to the ground and then was struck down by Judas and his men, whose "chief and greatest fear was for the consecrated temple" (15, 18).

Because the author tries with so much awareness to communicate his own involvement to his readers, his book gives a description of the facts and his own elaboration of them as well, thus mirroring his experience of the faith and, of course, that of his milieu, the Egyptian Diaspora. His experience revealed different accents from that of many Jews in Palestine.

One can see immediately that this author isn't scrupulous about using the divine name. He speaks of God in many different ways: almighty God, Lord, the living Lord, the Lord of the heavens, the creator, the king of kings, the all-seeing one, the just judge, etc. Furthermore, he is unprejudiced when witnessing to his belief in a retribution of men's deeds after this life. Later on, in connection with the book of Job, we will treat the pre-history of this belief separately. Here let it suffice to refer to the clear statements concerning the resurrection in the story of the seven martyred brothers (chapter 7) and in that of Razis' suicide (14, 46). The old Eleazar could have pretended to have eaten the meat of pagan sacrifices and thus escape martyrdom. But he says in 6, 26: "Even though for the moment I avoid execution by man, I can never, living or dead, elude the grasp of the Almighty." When one has sinned before his death, it is possible for the living to attain reconciliation for him by their sacrifices and prayers. The author shows Judas and his men acting in accordance with these "holy and devout thoughts" when they find pagan amulets on their dead comrades (12, 38-45).

The Egyptian Jews also believed that the great men who in former times "stood in the breach" for the sinful people through their prayers (just as Moses did according to Psalm 106, 23) now continue to live with God and there pray for their people. This is clear from a dream which Judas had. First he sees the dead high priest Onias with outstretched arms praying for the whole Jewish people, and then he sees the prophet Jeremiah doing the same. Afterward the prophet gives Judas a golden sword with which he is to "strike down enemies" (15, 11-16).

The Maccabees of the first book had placed their trust in the "help of heaven," and to this the author attributed their victory. In various places the author of 2 Maccabees makes this even more explicit by means of heavenly visions and apparitions. Shortly before Antiochus committed his sacrilege against the temple, "all over the city for nearly forty days there were apparitions of horsemen galloping through the air, in cloth of gold, troops of lancers fully armed. . . ." (5, 2-3). Later, five of these shining horsemen rode in the vanguard of the Jewish army in the battle against the general Timotheus, while two of them protected Judas, screening him with their armor (10, 29-30: a visual elaboration of v. 28).

These horsemen were "angels," as is clear from the answer to their prayer before the battle with Lysias. The Jews prayed to God to send a good angel, and then "a rider attired in white appeared at their head brandishing golden accoutrements" (11, 8).

The summary of Jason's book seems to have been very popular among the Jews in the Diaspora, and so also was the Greek translation of 1 Maccabees. Those readers didn't make our distinctions concerning literary character and historical reliability.

The Christians also enjoyed reading these two stories in their Bible. They too were constantly exposed to persecution and martyrdom because of their faith, and they saw in the brave Maccabees, who were so visibly supported by God, an inspiring example.

Without a doubt the first book was very popular among the Hebrew-speaking Jews of Palestine. Yet in the course of time the worn-out copies of it were not replaced, which is unusual for books of such universal interest. Eventually the Hebrew text disappeared entirely from circulation. After Simon had achieved a certain political independence for the Jews in 142 B.C., his son John Hyrcanus and later successors, although they were high priests, began to live more and more as pagan monarchs. Their dynasty, the Hasmonean (named after a supposed ancestor of the Maccabees), became an object of hatred for the faithful Jews and especially for the Pharisees, that group of pious Jews which sprung up when John Hyrcanus was in office. Later, under the Romans, they preferred to forget everything which had to do with that hated dynasty, even its glorious beginning. Thus it is clear why not a word is said in the extensive corpus of rabbinic literature about the Maccabees; not even the name of Judas is mentioned. The Hanukkah feast, however, became so popular that it could no longer be eliminated. But in the ritual of the feast every trace of its Maccabean origin has been eradicated. And so it happened that no one thought the laborious and expensive work of recopying 1 Maccabees worthwhile; thus copies became more and more scarce. The great Scripture scholar St. Jerome (ca. 347-420) was still able to get his hands on one of them. A few centuries later they had all disappeared. Among the thousands of fragments of Hebrew books dating from the beginning of the Christian era which since 1947 have been discovered near the Dead Sea, not one contains a word from 1 Maccabees; even the pious Essenes wanted nothing to do with the godless Hasmoneans.

IV
SEPARATE STORIES

Of the books which we italicized on our outline of the canon, five still remain to be seen. Each one presents *one* story and has its title from the name of the main character. Since the dates of their composition are uncertain, we can better arrange them according to another criterion—namely, the degree of their "canonicity." It is easy to understand that this corresponds to the extent to which their texts have received a fixed form. Ruth and Jonah have an undisputed place in the Hebrew canon, and their texts have no variants. Esther is considerably longer in the Greek canon than in the Hebrew. Judith and Tobit have been preserved only in Greek, in several recensions.

Ruth

"In the days of the judges famine came to the land. . . ." Thus begins the short story of Ruth. Although from the land of the pagan Moabites, this woman was privileged to become the mother of David's grandfather.

It happened this way. Because of that famine a man from Bethlehem, Elimelech ("God is king"), left the territory of Bethlehem with his wife Naomi and his two sons and settled on the other side of the Dead Sea, in the land of Moab. There he died. Each of his sons married a local woman, Orpah and Ruth, but soon afterward followed their father to the grave. Naomi returned to Bethlehem accompanied by Ruth, who did not want to be separated from her. During the harvest Ruth, now a poor widow, walked behind the reapers gleaning grain to obtain something to eat for her mother-in-law and herself. It turned out that the reapers worked for Boaz, a relative of Naomi's deceased husband. At Naomi's suggestion Ruth attracted the attention of their older kinsman in such a way that he would want to make use of his right as *go'el*, "redeemer." He married Ruth, and their oldest son, Obed, fathered Jesse, whose son was David.

This course of events is told with such finesse that at first glance one never thinks to ask what the author had in mind. Just as is true in the modern theater, the decor is limited to what is absolutely necessary. We are not told which road the family chose to go to Moab, nor where they lived there. After the arrival of Naomi and Ruth in Bethlehem, the author relates the only circumstance which is necessary for the story: it was the beginning of the barley harvest. Later he mentions the city gate, because it is there that the negotiations take place, and also the custom of handing one's sandals over to another as a sign that one surrenders his right of ownership to the other. Every detail which could distract our attention from the main characters is carefully avoided. The writer portrays them by what they do and, above all, what they say. Of the eighty verses making up the story (not counting the conclusion, the genealogy of David—4, 18-22), fifty-eight contain direct address. First there is the striking conversation between Naomi and her daughters-in-law, with Ruth declaring that she wants to stay with her. Then there is Naomi's response to the women of Bethlehem, and later on the conversations between Ruth, the reapers and Boaz, Naomi's advice to Ruth, and, finally, the legal transactions at the city gate. The reader is continually fascinated by this narrative style and certainly not less by the noble characters of the central figures who are so deeply and simply devoted to each other. Contrasting minor characters strengthen this impression: opposite Ruth stands Orpah who fails to show the same generosity, and opposite Boaz there is the other man with the right of redemption, who is not willing to jeopardize his own inheritance.

Nevertheless, the modern reader will ask what this story really means. First of all, therefore, he must keep in mind that a biblical story usually has more than one meaning at the same time and that these cannot always be precisely distinguished or categorically defined. This is all the more difficult if the story is intricately woven together and told by a master.

The author probably began with an old piece of data concerning family relations between David's ancestors and the Moabites. A trace of this is still to be found in the historical note in 1 Samuel 22, 3-4; when David was being pursued by Saul and had reason to be afraid for his relatives, he sought shelter for his parents with the king of Moab. It is quite certain that the author wanted to show in his story how Yahweh had arranged for a Moabite woman to be accepted into the family at Bethlehem. Her oldest son would then be a legitimate descendant of that family. With extreme care he tells how this adoption took place on the grounds of two old Israelitic institutions. The first was that of the *go'el,* "redeemer" or "claimant." According to this venerable tradition, a person being victimized could rely on one of his relatives to come to his rescue. It was his duty, for example, to take vengeance in the case of murder. If an Israelite had to sell himself as a slave to be able to discharge his debts, then one of his nearest relatives had to act as "redeemer." The same was true when one had to sell his inheritance to pay his debts. Then the "redeemer" had to buy the thing in question to ensure its remaining in the family (cf. the stipulations of Leviticus 25, 25 and 46-49 and an application of the custom in Jeremiah 32). The other institution which the author shows in operation here was the levirate law (from Latin: *levir,* "brother-in-law"). If a woman survived her husband without having any sons, the brother-in-law was obliged to marry her, and their first-born son would then be the heir of the deceased. Boaz acted in accordance with both these customs. He married Ruth and rescued the land which had belonged to Naomi's husband. The reader must wait until almost the end of the story, however, before being informed of this.

The inclusion of Ruth in David's genealogy therefore took place in accordance with law and justice, but also, and above all, according to the desire of this noble woman herself. While Orpah chose to return to "her people and her god," Ruth expressly desired to be adopted by the people of the Covenant: "Wherever you live, I will live," she says to Naomi. "Your people shall be my people, and your God, my God." And Boaz praised the generosity with which she left her own parents and homeland to go to a people she did not know for the sake of her mother-in-law: "May rich recompense be made to you by Yahweh, the God of Israel, to whom you have come, to find shelter beneath his wings" (1, 16 and 2, 12). Thus, no Israelite had to be ashamed of the foreign blood in King David's veins!

One might wonder in which period of Israel's history this could have been said. People have often pointed out the superior narrative style of the book of Ruth, which is closely related to that of the classical works dating from the early period of the monarchy, such as the court history of David and the story of Joseph in

Egypt. No miracles occur there either, and the mysterious leadership of Yahweh is seen throughout the decisions and deeds of the central figures, whose character is given expression above all in their words. The only difficulty is to see why in that period one would be ashamed of a foreign woman among David's ancestors.

Now, every history of literature has its period of "second bloom," sometimes called a "renaissance," in which gifted writers have made the old classical style completely their own. Certain data from the Hebrew usage in the book of Ruth seem to indicate that it was written in such a period. If this is so, we can trace one of the intentions of the author, and perhaps even the most important one. Let us remember that Nehemiah and Ezra encouraged, despite all their good intentions, a mentality which was ashamed of foreign blood in the family. We already mentioned once that the law book of Deuteronomy excluded from community with Israel both the Ammonites and Moabites (cf. p. 67). Nehemiah applied this stipulation very severely. He himself wrote how he treated Jews who married Moabite and other foreign women: he cursed them, beat them and pulled out their hair (Neh. 13, 1-3 and 23ff.). One might also look up how Ezra convinced all the Jews who had married foreign women to send them and their children away (Ezra 9—10). The author of Ruth may have intended his story as a protest against this discrimination. The seemingly innocent form in which it is cast (perhaps *had* to be cast) is nonetheless striking. The form was innocent because it brought the reader into the atmosphere of the Bible (then only the Pentateuch). He recognized all kinds of figures. Abraham and Isaac also had to leave their homeland because of famine. In the congratulatory words of the people to Boaz and Ruth (4, 11-12), the reader heard echos of Genesis. Just as Yahweh had guided the lives of the patriarchs, from the moment he called Abraham to leave his familiar surroundings and go to a land he didn't know (Ruth also did this—2, 11), so too did he have a hand in the pre-history of David, his Anointed or Messiah. If Yahweh himself had made use of another race in realizing his salvific plan for Israel, and even from the "field of Moab" (the term is used seven times!), and if that Moabite woman was furthermore an example of devotion and fidelity, where do you get the right to treat foreign women the way you do?

Jonah

The author of the short story about Jonah directed a similar reproachful question to his readers. Apparently he had Jews in mind who based their dislike and rejection of non-Jewish groups on scriptural texts. As we will see in the following chapter, all kinds of oracles about foreign peoples were incorporated in the "later prophets." In many of them their complete destruction was announced. Jewish readers looked forward anxiously to the fulfillment of those prophecies. Their community had now suffered long enough under the pressures of foreign rulers. When will Yahweh accomplish their promised destruction? Certainly he could only be interested in his beloved Israel. God's future was only for those who belonged to that people. Praying for the coming of God's kingdom partly included praying fervently for the fulfillment of what he had ordained for the pagans. If that prayer for their downfall was to be honest, then of course it had to be coupled with practical measures to ensure the racial purity of the Jewish community by excluding all foreign elements from it.

This was, in a few words, the mentality against which the author of Jonah seems to be protesting. In his eyes it was based upon an egocentric explanation of certain biblical texts, which left so many other texts out of consideration and thus painted a false picture of God's character. Through the mouth of Jeremiah God certainly indicated his way of proceeding clearly enough: "On occasion I decree for some nation, for some kingdom, that I will tear up, knock down, destroy; but if this nation, against which I have pronounced sentence, abandons its wickedness, I then change my mind about the evil which I had intended to inflict on it" (Jer. 18, 7-8). Jeremiah was appointed as "prophet for the nations," but he first had to make Yahweh's will known to his own people. Again and again he warned and begged the Judeans to make a conversion of heart to Yahweh, for only then would he "change his mind about the evil which he intended to inflict" and not carry it out. But again and again Jeremiah encountered their unwillingness. Their kings led the way in this. Jehoiakim even went so far as to have Jeremiah's warnings and threats read to him and then with his own hand tore the piece read from the scroll and threw it into the furnace. This is the way that beloved chosen people treated the words of its God! They made life miserable for Jeremiah, so that the prophet wanted to escape his thankless task (9, 1; 20, 9). An earlier prophet had also desired to do that—Elijah, who made a day's journey into the desert, sat down under a furze bush and begged his God to take his life (1 Kgs. 19, 4).

Now to the story about Jonah. The author found the name of his hero in 2 Kings 14, 26 where the prophet Jonah, son of Amittai, is mentioned. He lets Yahweh give this Jonah the order to go to Nineveh, the capital of the Assyrians, that nation so detested for its destruction of the kingdom of Israel. Everywhere in that city Jonah is to announce that the evil of its inhabitants had risen to Yahweh. Understandably the prophet wants to escape that precarious order. He takes a boat to far away Tarsis on the other side of the inhabited world, with which the proud ships of Tyre carried on trade. But then Yahweh mobilizes the powers of nature, for they too are subject to him. A storm endangers the ship and he sends a huge fish which deposits his disobedient prophet on land again. After this it is impossible for anyone to doubt that the man who goes to preach is in fact sent by Yahweh and speaks his powerful word. That word to the most evil of all cities is an unconditional decision to destroy it: "Only forty days more and Nineveh is going to be destroyed!" And behold, what Israel has always stubbornly refused to do, the people of Nineveh do without hesitation, its king leading the way. He proclaims a great fast for man and animal, urging everybody to "renounce his evil behavior. . . ." That king speaks as Jeremiah (cf., for example, Jer. 25, 51; 26, 3; 36, 37), and, also in the words of that prophet, he hopes that God "will change his mind" and "renounce his burning wrath." And that in fact happens. God does not carry out his threat.

At this Jonah is furious. The writer reaches a climax in which he lets the prophet express his bitterness in one of the most beautiful of Israel's confessions of faith: "Ah! Yahweh, is not this just as I said would happen. . . . I knew that you were a God of tenderness and compassion, slow to anger, rich in graciousness, relenting from evil!" (Cf. also Ex. 34, 6; Pss. 86, 15 and 103, 8, among others.) The little man Jonah becomes completely grotesque when he goes on to ask in the words of the great Elijah to be allowed to die. Yahweh then shows himself so slow to anger that he can even be patient with this Jonah. He lets a miraculous tree grow up and then wither again to be able to show the egocentric man his divinely tender care for everyone and everything, even for the inhabitants of Nineveh and their pets.

The Jewish reader who so anxiously looked forward to the downfall of the pagan nations could take it from here. If he was at all open-minded, he could recognize himself in Jonah, the chosen Jew, who was so proud of his privilege of being a Hebrew and of worshiping Yahweh, the God of heaven, who made the sea and the land (cf. 9, 1). He could also see himself in Jonah's selfish smallness, which the writer allows to come out so sharply, partly by contrasting it with the sincere piety and unselfishness of the sailors, and especially with the spontaneous repentance on the part of the Ninevites.

This short story also has more than *one* meaning, and no reader will ever exhaust it. One who tries to base his belief on the Bible is struck again and again by that man who wants to flee his God and in the end can still encounter him as his Lord. There is also more than one reason why Jesus and his disciples, judging from various citations and allusions, liked so much to talk about this story. One of them is undoubtedly the Jonah-attitude which they saw in so many Jews. Jesus also depicted that same attitude in stories of his own invention. The older brother of the prodigal son protested bitterly against his father's mercy (Lk. 15, 28) and the workers hired first are angry with their employer because he is good toward those who worked but one hour (Mt. 20, 15).

Esther

At first glance the Hebrew book of Esther is diametrically opposed to what seemed to us to be the primary intention of Ruth and Jonah—so much so, that one wonders how it ever found a place in the Bible.

The Persian king Ahasuerus (i.e., Xerxes, 486-446 B.C.) puts away his wife Vashti and chooses the beautiful Esther to be his queen, without realizing that she is a Jewess. Her stepfather Mordecai, who was able to inform the king through Esther of a dangerous plot, refused as good Jew to kneel before Haman, a favorite of the king. The latter succeeded in obtaining a royal decree ordering the extermination of all Jews in the world empire. The fatal day was to be the 13th of the month Adar. With the help of a coincidence Esther succeeds in getting the first place among the king's favorites for Mordecai instead of Haman, who was then hanged on the gibbet he had prepared for Mordecai. In a new royal decree the roles are reversed: the Jews are allowed to kill all their enemies on the day determined for their own extermination. Besides the ten sons of Haman and several hundred Persians in the capital, the Jews murdered 75,000 others elsewhere in the empire. On the 14th and 15th of Adar they rested, and since then they celebrate those days annually as a joyful feast, Purim, the word being explained at the end of the story as the plural of *pur,* a word that was supposed to mean "lot."

This story is fascinatingly told, and is often exciting, with all kinds of striking details. The central characters clearly oppose each other. The fallen Vashti is succeeded by the exalted Esther, and opposite Haman, the severe hater of the Jews, stands the devoted Mordecai. The king lets himself be influenced, and thus the lot of the Jews can be reversed.

The question whether or not the book belongs in the Bible is an old one. At the end of the first century A.D. when the Hebrew canon was receiving its final form (cf. p. 88), Esther remained an object of discussion for a long time. Some rabbis didn't want it to be recognized as Holy Scripture. Nowhere in the book is God mentioned, nor is he even clearly referred to in a roundabout way. Besides, the book belonged to a feast that could scarcely be called religious. The people did go to the temple to hear the book of Esther read to them, but, as R. de Vaux comments in his book on the institutions of Israel, "except for that reading and the distribution of alms, to which the pious attached a religious meaning, it was a completely profane feast. It was celebrated in pleasure and festive meals, and on that occasion all kinds of liberties were allowed. According to the rabbis one was allowed to drink until he no longer could distinguish between 'accursed be Haman' and 'blessed be Mordecai.' Later there was added the custom of wearing costumes for the occasion, and so the Purim feast became the Jewish *mardi gras.*"

Thus it is understandable, in addition to the discussions of the rabbis, why up until now not one fragment of Esther has been found in the Dead Sea excavations; the book is the only one of the Hebrew Bible that the Essenes apparently did not have in their library. Likewise, in the New Testament not one allusion is to be found.

Yet, further study reveals an authentic biblical witness to Jewish faith in the story. Even though they don't mention him, Esther and Mordecai act from a faithful trust that God will save his people. The fasting of Mordecai and the Jews, of Esther and her servants (4, 1-3. 15-17), was unthinkable for the writer and his readers unless accompanying a very intense prayer. When Mordecai points out to his stepdaughter her duty to take the part of her people before the king, even though this could mean her death, he says: "If you persist in remaining silent at such a time, relief and deliverance will come to the Jews from another place. . . . Who knows? Perhaps you have come to the throne for just such a time as this" (4, 14). The insomnia which is the occasion for Ahasuerus to have the annals read to him is for the author no more a "coincidence" than, for example, the dreams of the cupbearer and baker are in the story of Joseph, also a slave who because of a whole list of "chance circumstances" becomes powerful enough to act as redeemer of his tribe. Israel had learned to know its God as a savior from certain destruction. That was his "essence" in their eyes. They were accustomed to express this belief in stories of salvation, in which they also liked to describe the downfall of their oppressors. And then it depended on the character of the storytellers, their milieu and the "spirit of the times" whether they would let their oppressors perish through a direct miraculous intervention by God or through a seemingly "inner-worldly" course of circumstances and human decisions, for there too he was sovereign! Often they allowed Israel's enemies to endure precisely the same torture they had prepared for Israel. This was also seen to be an expression of divine justice. One might consider the Hebrew story of Esther as a sort of commentary in story form—a visualizing, if you will—of the theme taken up in Proverbs 26, 27, in Job 4, 8 and in prayers like Psalms 7, 16-17; 9, 16 and 35, 8.

Nevertheless the Jews in Egypt felt the need to make the story more expressly religious. Thus they incorporated in their translation several additions which can be found in their original places in the *Jerusalem Bible*. We will mention three of these additions. At the beginning of the story they placed "Mordecai's dream": a year before Vashti fell into disrepute the whole coming drama was revealed to Mordecai in symbols. According to the biblical view of "fulfilled predictions" (cf. p. 82), the translators used this dream to make it quite clear that everything which followed was ordained by God. In addition there are the two moving prayers, one by Mordecai and one by Esther, inserted between 4, 17 and 5, 1. Esther's prayer accompanies her fasting and acts of penance. And finally the translators enriched the book by including between 8, 12 and 8, 13 the second royal decree, favorable to the Jews, as they imagined it to have been. Notice the similarity of style with that of 2 Maccabees.

Where did the author of Esther get his material? He gives a number of details about the capital, Susa, life in the palace and certain governmental customs, which lead one to suspect that he lived in the Persian Diaspora or was acquainted with it. He (or his predecessors at an earlier stage of the story) could have found the raw material in the story of Gautama the magician, well known to readers of Herodotus. Gautama had posed as Smerdis, the brother of the deceased king Cambyses, and was unmasked by a woman introduced into his harem. The people were enraged, and "the massacre of the magicians" followed. This was commemorated annually with festivities. The Jews were themselves certainly the object of such wrathful violence somewhere at some time or other and escaped it in an extraordinary manner. With regard to the Purim feast, the Persian New Year celebration has been suggested as a possible source. Whatever may be the value of these suppositions, the story of Esther is not historical in the modern sense, but fictitious. This is also true for the remarkable detail which the author repeats three times: the Jews slaughtered those who threatened their lives, but "they took no plunder" (9, 10. 15. 17).

Judith

Anyone acquainted with ancient oriental history will be not a little perturbed when he begins reading the book of Judith. Nebuchadnezzar is introduced as "the king of the Assyrians" and his chief general bears the name Holofernes. That's about the same as saying that when Abraham Lincoln was President, his chief general was Charles de Gaulle. In any event, ruling from his capital, the great city of Nineveh, the very proud Nebuchadnezzar wanted to conquer the whole world and force all peoples to worship him as god. With this as his goal Holofernes sets out with an enormous army. No geographer of the biblical lands can trace his route on a map, for between the names of known countries, cities and peoples there are unknown ones, with everything crisscrossed and jumbled. The story goes that Holofernes is nearing Judah. "All Israel" takes up the task of organizing its defense under the leadership of the high priest, who at the same time urges fasting and prayer. When Holofernes hears of this, he summons the generals of Moab and Ammon to question them about Israel. Achior, the leader of the Ammonites, summarizes the history of Israel for him, starting with the patriarchs and working down to the restoration of Jerusalem after the exile. He concludes that if this people remains faithful to its God, it is unconquerable. Enraged at this, the general sends Achior to be left outside the fortress of Bethulia which is near Dothan and dominates the only entrance to Jerusalem. The Israelites obligingly take in the pagan who had explained the meaning of their history so well. Holofernes prepares a siege of the city and cuts off all its water sources. Then Judith, both wise and beautiful, comes on the scene; she has been a widow for more than three years, and despite all her wealth she lives very piously. The decision of the inhabitants to hold out for five days more and then, if no help should come, to surrender the city she condemns as blasphemous, an ultimatum to God. She doesn't say what her own plan is, but she asks their prayers that it succeed. In her inner chamber she utters a fervent prayer of supplication, and then, impressively made-up, she sets out with her servant for the enemy camp. She cleverly plays upon the vanity and passions of Holofernes. When she is alone in the tent with the general, drunk beyond his senses, she cuts off his head with his own sword. With that the struggle is decided. The pagan army is panic-stricken, and the Israelites effortlessly drive them from the country. Achior abandons his pagan religion, lets himself be circumcised, and together with his whole family is taken into the people of Israel. The high priest from Jerusalem comes to praise Judith; she herself intones a victory hymn in the manner of Deborah. She remains the chaste widow as before and dies at the age of 105. All that time, and long after her death, Israel enjoys peace like that in the days of the greatest of judges. One of the old versions of the book goes on to speak about a feast which was to have been inaugurated after the victory over Holofernes, but there is nothing further known about it.

In this story, too, God uses the winning beauty of a Jewish woman to save his people from certain destruction. However, that theme is developed here much more deeply and broadly than in Esther. By calling Nebuchadnezzar king of the Assyrians and by giving him a Persian general, the author makes a symbol of that historical figure: he characterizes all human powers who in foolish self-glorification are blind to the fact that they have received their existence from a creator and can't bear that others recognize this. Judith—i.e., "the Jewess"—also is such a symbol. She stands for the group of people who have been given the insight into that factual situation and who also express and ratify it by making God the foundation of their lives, by conforming in all things to his desires and also by never doubting his help—not even in the worst crises. The meaning of human history is revealed most deeply in the struggle between "Nebuchadnezzar" and "Judith." According to human standards Judith has to lose, but yet she wins.

Thus we might indicate in our own way the writer's intention. He wrote his story in Hebrew, probably in the course of the 2nd century B.C., the time of the Maccabees. "Nebuchadnezzar" had therefore the form of Antiochus IV, and Judith that of the community of the faithful Jews who, thanks to Judas and his companions, could again live according the the Law within the shadow of the new temple. That is why the rich widow of Bethulia strictly observed all laws and pious customs: she fasts and does penance, she carefully carries out all ritual purifications, and she explains to Holofernes that "Israel" is exposed to danger because it has been unfaithful to the commandments of God. The general had already heard from Achior that Israel would be unconquerable if it should observe them strictly again. Achior's explanation (chapter 5) is interwoven with allusions to Holy Scripture, and the same is true of Judith's prayer and her victory hymn (9 and 16). Just like the author of 1 Maccabees, the writer of Judith is completely at home with Scripture. The only difference is that the latter author doesn't give an account of recent events based on precise information. With the help of Israel's sacred books he describes a quasi-historical event, which at the same time portrays the further, final struggle in which God will settle with the powers who tried to upset his plans for salvation.

This is why a search for the remains of the city Bethulia is doomed to failure. Even though the original Hebrew form of the name is no longer clearly recognizable in the Greek spelling ("house of God" or "daughter of the land"?), Bethulia is just as much a symbol as the beautiful widow Judith. The city had to lie near Dothan, for the plain of Megiddo began there, which was to provide the decor for the ultimate struggle, the Armageddon of Revelation (16, 16). This dimension of the book of Judith is difficult to define, but it will become clearer perhaps when we discuss Daniel, written in the same Maccabean circles as Judith.

The Hebrew text of Judith has unfortunately been lost. Luckily, however, the book was so well liked by the Egyptian Jews that different versions of the Greek translation circulated among them. Three of them have come down to us. The Latin translation which St. Jerome made gives a completely different version, perhaps following an Aramaic recension of the original. This version was incorporated in the Latin Bible text in official use in the Roman Catholic Church, the so-called Vulgate, from *editio vulgata,* the "commonly used edition." This is the reason why English translations vary and why the verses are numbered differently.

Tobit

The same holds true, even to a greater extent, for the text of the book of Tobit. The author of this story also wrote in Hebrew, or more probably in Aramaic. This text, too, is lost. The extant versions of the Greek translation exhibit considerable differences, and St. Jerome's Latin edition (based on an Aramaic text?) goes its own way entirely. But in all those versions, including St. Jerome's, the book has preserved its unique character which had made it so beloved by innumerable generations of Jews and Christians and because of which it has probably had more influence than many other parts of the Old Testament.

Tobit lived as an exemplary post-exilic Jew in Galilee when in 734 B.C. he was deported to Nineveh with his tribe Naphtali by the Assyrians. There he continued to live faithfully according to the Law and received a high position at court. In that function he deposited large sums of money with his fellow tribesman Gabael, who lived far away in the Median city Rhages. As a result of his good works, the burial of dead countrymen, Tobit falls into disrepute. Then his highly placed nephew intercedes for him. Again Tobit is the victim of an accident as a result of his piety: bird droppings fall into his eyes and he goes blind. His wife Anna mocks him for his scrupulous fidelity to the Law, after which he pours out his heart to God. At that same moment in the capital of Media, Ecbatana, the Jewish girl Sarah does the very same thing. The demon Asmodeus had now for the seventh time killed her bridegroom during their first night together. God decides to help both suppliants by sending them his angel, called Raphael—i.e., "God heals."

Tobit decides to send his son Tobias to recover the money he had deposited earlier in Rhages. He gives him a series of warnings and lets him set out, under protest from Anna, with his dog and the young Jew Azarias, Raphael in disguise. In the Tigris they catch a fish, the entrails of which Tobias is to save. They may come in handy sometime, his companion tells him. While on their way they lodge at the home of Sarah's parents in Ecbatana, and his companion arranges a marriage between Tobias and the unhappy girl. The demon flees as soon as he smells the heart and liver of the fish, which Tobias had put on the brazier. During the days of the wedding feast Azarias goes to pick up the money in Rhages. Loaded down with gifts and congratulations they return to the anxiously waiting parents in Nineveh, Tobias with his bride and dog and the faithful traveling companion. The gall of the fish cures his father's blindness, Azarias reveals who he is and disappears into his invisible world, and the happy father composes a beautiful hymn of praise for God and the city of Jerusalem. Before his death at the age of 158, he warns his son to leave Nineveh, still to be destroyed according to Jonah's word, and to go to live with his wife's parents in Media. There Tobias lives a long and happy life.

In a capsule version like this, the literary form of a story seems to be somewhere between a fairy tale and an adventure novel. That impression isn't completely incorrect. Research had pointed out some resemblances to the very old and widely spread fairy tale theme of "the grateful dead": a good living merchant buries at his own expense a poor victim of murderous brutality, who later on, disguised as a servant, comes to his aid during the man's first night with his new bride. The woman was possessed by a demon in the form of a snake; coming forth from her mouth it had killed five other bridegrooms before him—hence the possible connection with our story. It is certain that the writer took part of his inspiration from the popular story about Ahikar. This chancellor of the Assyrian king was ousted by his stepson Nadin (also known as Nadab and Nabat) and afterward regained the king's favor; in the context of that adventure he provided many lessons in worldly wisdom. Further on we will meet that "wisdom book" again in another context (cf. p. 216). We mention it here only because the author of Tobit also supposed that it was known to his readers and even made Ahikar the nephew of Tobit in his story. Ahikar helps him in his time of need and also comes to celebrate the happy return of Tobias in Nineveh, accompanied by his stepson.

But most of all the author has his inspiration from two other "sources": his Bible and the religious views of the pious Jew of his day, probably the beginning of the 2nd century B.C., prior to the Maccabean revolt. On the one hand, he had the biblical stories of the patriarchs in mind, and in particular that of the journey of Abraham's servant to look for a bride for Isaac (Gn. 24). In it we hear of God's angel, who accompanies the traveler and who ensures the success of his mission by arranging a chance meeting with the girl destined to be Isaac's wife. Not once but twice we find there the description of how Abraham's servant experiences that miraculous guidance from God: he falls on his knees, worships God and blesses him because he guided him on the right path (Gn. 24, 26-27. 48).

On the other hand, the author was also familiar with the exhortative parts of the Bible—e.g., Proverbs 1—9. A wise man likewise speaks there to "my son" about a journey and a road, the straight path which man must follow in order to ensure the success of the journey of life. It is the path of the "fear of the Lord," of dedication to God, fidelity in marriage, honor for one's parents and honesty toward all men.

The way that ideal was experienced in the Jewish milieu of his day led the author to emphasize certain expressions of it—e.g., giving alms and especially sincere prayer in all circumstances of life. In that way the faithful can learn to see disappointments and setbacks as being part of the loving care with which God guides him on the path of life. The author confesses his unshakable faith in that guidance, therefore, not only in his delightful portrait of the "providential" way everything takes place, but also in his many expressions of praise and thanks which he both simply and pleasantly puts in the mouths of his characters. Tobit is a joyful book.

V

A "MORE HUMAN" BIBLE HISTORY

Traditional "bible history" considered all the books discussed in this chapter to be reliable accounts in the strict sense. Describing the period of the monarchy, for example, it used, besides the books of Samuel and Kings, the "complementary details" of Chronicles which were held to be equally reliable. When speaking about the Assyrian pressure on Israel and Judah, it related what happened to the prophet Jonah on his journey to the capital of Assyria, and likewise how Tobit came there in 734 and from there sent his son to Media. Its treatment of Judas Maccabaeus used without any inhibitions the reports of 2 Maccabees about the heavenly apparitions he received. It goes without saying that this use of the "historical books" is no longer admissible. To put it quite bluntly, the teacher who nowadays relates bible history in that traditional manner should realize that he is telling lies.

One should not conclude, however, that the critical approach to the narrative sections of the Bible leaves us with only a few historical facts and, consequently, with a very meager bible history. Of course, if the story of Jonah is fiction, then that fascinating prophet disappears from the historical scene of the 8th century. But another historical character emerges, namely the man who invented Jonah. We may say, in more general terms, that in the new approach many more interesting people appear on the stage of history than in the traditional one, for those who expressed the faith and piety of their community and influenced their fellow Jews by composing moving stories are not less historical than the kings, the prophets and the conquerors of former times.

Thus a modern bible history will tell more about human beings, men of flesh and blood as we are, and less about miraculous interventions from above. It will relate that King Uzziah contracted leprosy (and try to find out why the Deuteronomist wanted that fact remembered), but not that he was struck with that disease as a punishment for a liturgical transgression. That is an explanation given by the Chronicler, and thus to be brought in where bible history treats the religious views of the 4th century and their forms of expression. It will no longer look for Holofernes' march to Bethulia in the annals of Nebuchadnezzar's reign, but will treat that story together with that of the Maccabees and their supporters, who did not fight for their faith with arms alone. And so on. . . .

But although we have now said something about all the "historical books," we are actually not yet at the point where we can draw definite conclusions about this subject, for we have not yet discussed the prophets. Those historical figures not only helped to determine the actual course of Israel's history, but without their interpretation of events in the light of Israel's faith, an historical work such as that of the Deuteronomists could never have been written. Hence the topic of our next chapter.

V

The Prophets

In the second section of the Hebrew canon (cf. p. 86) the books of Joshua—Kings are followed by the four "later" prophets. They are Isaiah, Jeremiah, Ezekiel and the Twelve. The last mentioned is a collection of twelve texts, each bearing the name of a prophet. To the first three the Christians added the book of Daniel, which the Hebrew canon numbers among "the Writings"—hence the four "major" and twelve "minor" prophets of our Christian Bibles.

If we may be permitted a highly simplified comparison of the modern approach to the prophets with that of earlier ages, we see the following. The old view regarded them primarily as the authors of the books bearing their names and thus as inspired theologians. It paid special attention to those passages where the divinely inspired authors described the coming, the person and the activity of the Messiah. For this reason Christian art has often depicted the prophets with a scroll in their hands or as writing while looking intensely into the far-off future.

In contrast to this view, the modern explanation sees them primarily as speakers, as preachers who were intimately involved in the historical situation in which they found themselves. They were Yahweh's heralds, proclaiming to their contemporaries the role their concrete situation had in his divine plan and what he expected of his people at that particular moment. Thus the new approach undertakes not only the task of explaining the "Messianic predictions" as a part of those proclamations, but also and especially that of showing how and why that preaching has come down to us in the books bearing the names of those prophets. This statement of purpose is likewise an indication of the major divisions of this chapter.

157

I
PROPHETISM IN ISRAEL

We will begin with some remarks about the historical phenomenon of prophecy. It had already taken root several centuries before the appearance of the figures who gave their names to the scriptural books we will be discussing in this chapter. Thus we would first like to sketch this phenomenon in order to better understand the role those great prophetic figures played in the critical situations of Israel's existence.

From "Nabi" to "Classical Prophet"

The story of Saul in search of his father's she-asses provides a good introduction (1 Samuel 9, 1—10, 16). After Samuel anointed him, Saul was promised three "signs" as a proof of his divine appointment. In the story as preserved, only the third "sign" is related as having been fulfilled. Evidently this was considered to be the most important one. Saul indeed meets the company of prophets coming down from the high places with their musical instruments and, just as predicted, "the spirit of God seized on him and he fell into ecstasy in their midst" (10, 10). This last is often translated by "he began to prophesy."

The Hebrew verb, here translated as "prophesy," stems from the noun *nabi,* usually rendered as "prophet." The verb form we are concerned with here means "to act as a *nabi.*" Since in Israel's ancient stories the *nabis* are often depicted as persons falling into ecstasy, with the help of music and dance, some modern translators render the word as "to rage, to rave, or to be in a state of frenzy or delirium." As appears from the story just referred to, that state of frenzy was contagious. We may conclude from the remarks of the bystanders (10, 12) that "nabi-dom" was not esteemed very highly. The son of a well-known and respectable farmer shouldn't associate with the likes of the *nabis!*

The story of 1 Samuel 19, 18-24 confirms that description. In it the contagious nature of that ecstatic state is painted very vividly, as also are its consequences. Saul stripped off his clothes and, like all the agents he had sent, he too "prophesied" in Samuel's presence and "falling down lay there naked all that day and night." It should be noted that Samuel is represented here as the leader of those prophets and as living among them. At this early period (ca. 1000 B.C.) "prophecy" of this kind apparently was officially accepted as a religious phenomenon.

Let us turn now to 1 Kings 22 and 18. Before setting out for battle, the king of Israel consults a group of *nabis*, 400 in number. He and his ally, the king of Judah, sit on their thrones and the 400 "prophesy" before them, while one *nabi* manipulates iron horns and chants appropriate cries, which are then taken up by the others (22, 10-12). Probably their conduct was not much different from that of the 450 *nabis* gathered around the altar of Mount Carmel in chapter 18: "They performed their hobbling dance around the altar.... So they shouted louder and gashed themselves, as their blood flowed down them. Midday passed, and they ranted on until the time the offering was presented."

In the stories about Elijah and Elisha we meet several groups referred to as "sons of the prophets." According to Hebrew idiom one should understand this term as meaning "members of the class or guild of *nabis*." Those stories reveal the presence of such guilds at Gilgal, Bethel and Jericho, and describe their members as eccentrically dressed and living in poverty. Public opinion considered them to be mentally disturbed. When a disciple of Elisha came to the camp of Ramoth-gilead and took the officer Jehu aside for a moment, the latter's companions asked him, "Why did this madman come to you?" (2 Kings 9, 11). The Hebrew expression used here, *meshugga*, "idiot" (still living on in the Dutch words *mesjokke* and *besjokke*), occurs much later too. In the days of Jeremiah (ca. 590 B.C.) we meet it in a similar context— namely, where the priest Zephaniah was ordered to dismiss from the temple every "madman who acts the prophet (*nabi*)" (Jer. 29, 26).

This kind of "prophesying" was not a prerogative of ancient Israel, and archeology has provided us with parallels from neighboring lands. About 1090 B.C. the king of the Phoenician port of Byblos refused admittance to an Egyptian envoy. Suddenly a young courtier fell into a trance, and in this ecstatic state he uttered a message from the god of the city ordering the king to receive the foreigner. Other parallels come from Mari on the Middle Euphrates where in the 18th century B.C. the king received messages from his god through the mediation of similar prophets.

The first kings of Israel, as well as those men who narrated the stories just mentioned, were convinced that Yahweh, Israel's God, could use these peculiar forms of religious experience to make known his will and intentions. We can take it for granted that from the very beginning only certain personalities from the entire group acted in Yahweh's name. Reading 1 Kings 22, for example, we can see that Micaiah, son of Imlah, had a much deeper awareness of Yahweh's unique character and special demands than his 400 colleagues. Likewise, there can be no doubt that in this regard Elijah and Elisha were head and shoulders above the "sons of the prophets" whose leaders they were. Their religious experience was evidently not so dependent on the ecstasy of the group. Yet, when Elisha finally agrees to speak a word from Yahweh in 2 Kings 3, he says, "Now bring me someone who can play the lyre." When the musician begins to pluck his strings, the hand of Yahweh comes upon Elisha (vv. 15-16).

It is only in the course of the 8th century B.C. that we meet the prophetic figures whom Israel immortalized by preserving a number of their sayings in its holy books. (Hence their German name, *Schriftprofeten.*) Without affirming that all of them were absolutely free of psychological abnormalities, we can infer from their words that they did not utter them in a state of frenzy; they were clearly conscious of their continual personal contact with Yahweh. They lived in the awareness that they were called by him to act as his spokesmen. Thus these prophetic figures gave the word *nabi* a new meaning. In times to come it would be an honorable title, attributed in the elohistic tradition to Abraham (Gn. 20, 7) and later still to all the great ancestors of Israel as well (Ps. 105, 15).

"Prophet" thus meant spokesman—"mouthpiece"—of another who for one reason or other cannot speak himself. There is a striking illustration of this in two related passages in the book of Exodus. When Moses objects to his mission because he cannot speak well enough in public, God appoints his brother Aaron to assist him: "He will be your mouthpiece, and you will be as the god inspiring him" (4, 16). Further on this relationship is described as follows: "See, I make you as a god for Pharaoh, and Aaron your brother is to be your prophet" (7, 1). Just as a god makes use of a prophet as his "mouth" to speak to the people, so too must Moses make use of Aaron as his spokesman.

People often interpret the prefix *pro-* in the Greek word *prophētēs* in a temporal sense defining a prophet as one who says beforehand what is going to happen; he fore-tells (predicts) the future. However, it actually meant "on behalf of, in place of." A "prophet" says what another intends to say but for one reason or other does not do so. Hence in the 2nd century B.C. a learned commentator of Aristotle was called the "prophet of Aristotle"— i.e., the interpreter of his intentions, speaking on behalf of the philosopher long dead.

Thus the Alexandrian Jews who translated the Old Testament from the Hebrew rightly chose the word *prophētēs* to render *nabi,* for it was the task of the prophets to speak on behalf of the infinitely exalted and always present God. According to Israel's belief, Yahweh had acquired absolute rights over his people by saving them from Egypt and making them his own property. It was Israel's duty to be faithful and thus witness to God's reality. When this awareness of God's rights weakened, the prophets appeared on the scene. They were made aware of his claim in a deeply personal way—in a concentrated form, so to speak. They felt called, almost forced, to make that claim of the living God heard by the people. In his name they threatened punishment for the stubborn and promised salvation to those who were faithful to Yahweh's word—hence the references to the future in their preaching. They did this not so much from a precise foreknowledge of the concrete things God would bring about in the future, as from their intense awareness of Yahweh's sovereignty over the entire universe. The holy God cannot endure evil, and therefore will make an end of it. Only the man who recognizes him as Lord can exist for him; for this reason too, such a man will go on existing. Their "Messianic predictions" also were founded on this certainty.

In their own minds these prophets-by-calling stood in direct opposition to the prophets-by-profession. The latter *nabis* remained attached to the national religion until the fall of Judah in 587 in order to act as Yahweh's "official" spokesmen. Micah does not mince his words when speaking of these prophets. For him they are leading the people astray. "So long as they have some-

thing to eat they cry 'Peace.' But on anyone who puts nothing into
their mouths they declare war" (Mic. 3, 5). Some years previous
Amos was dispelled from the Israelitic state sanctuary at Bethel.
He was told to go back to his own country, Judah, and earn a
living there prophesying. Proudly Amos answered that he was not
a professional prophet and did not belong to their guilds. Yahweh
had called him personally away from his farm to announce his
judgment in the northern kingdom (Amos 7, 11-17). The *nabis*
announced "peace," *shalōm:* they say that all is well with God's
people, that everything is going fine; salvation alone is to be
expected from Yahweh. The prophet-by-calling had to act as
Israel's conscience, and he knew that Yahweh would give him the
strength to perform that precarious task. After his diatribe against
the professional prophets Micah says of himself, "I am full of
strength [of the breath of Yahweh], of justice and courage to
declare Jacob's crime to his face and Israel's to his" (3, 8).

It is no coincidence that Isaiah and Jeremiah never called
themselves *nabi* in the words attributed immediately to them. In
the paragraph headings of our Bibles the professional prophets are
mostly referred to as "the false prophets." Read the condemna-
tions of these deceivers of the people in Ezekiel 13, for example,
and especially in the book of Jeremiah. Besides the places where
they are mentioned with other leading groups (2, 8; 4, 9; 5, 31; 6,
13), Jeremiah 14, 13-16 and especially 23, 9-40 are devoted
entirely to them. Jeremiah evidently had many clashes with these
liars who proclaimed the vision of their own heart and not a word
from Yahweh's mouth. These were not intimate with Yahweh;
they were not "present at the council of Yahweh" as Jeremiah had
been. Otherwise they would certainly announce something quite
different from *shalōm* to those who stubbornly continue to deny
him by their conduct. For Jeremiah himself this was all quite evident, and it was also to become clear to the Judeans of the exile
and afterward who repentantly came to realize that he and the
others who had called for conversion had indeed spoken on behalf
of Yahweh. But for the prophets' contemporaries the difference
between true and false spokesmen must have been very difficult
indeed. Read Jeremiah 27 and 28 as if you were there yourself.
Jeremiah comes up with a yoke on his neck and speaks the word
of Yahweh, "Bend your necks to the yoke of the king of Baby-

lon." Hananiah took the yoke off his neck and broke it. In front of all the people he said, "Yahweh says this, 'This is how, two years hence, I will break the yoke of Nebuchadnezzar, king of Babylon.'" Who was speaking on behalf of God? Jeremiah predicts in return that Hananiah would be a corpse within a year. According to the concluding sentence, that in fact happened. But what did this "prove"? Didn't his wife say that Hananiah had not been feeling well for some time?

At the Turning Points of History

The appearance of these major prophets is connected with the critical situations which the people of Yahweh were made to undergo after the middle of the 8th century B.C. A good understanding of their preaching demands a certain insight into that troubled history. The outline on the following page can perhaps help to clarify the following description.

The geographical position of Palestine on the main road connecting Mesopotamia and Egypt was a very vulnerable one in the struggle for power between those two great centers. About 1000 B.C. David had been able to establish a state which could profess to be a small world power partly because at that time there were no powers in Mesopotamia or in the Nile valley which could stand in his way. Likewise, the little principalities which came into being at the collapse of his kingdom (Judah, Israel, Ammon, Moab, Edom, the federation of Philistine cities, Damascus, Hamath, etc.) could go on quarreling among themselves for a good hundred years without fear of intervention from outside. That was all changed, however, when in the 9th century Assyria was again on its way to becoming a powerful nation. Danger was looming for the little states in the corridor to Egypt. That situation became very acute after 745 when King Tiglath-pileser III ascended the throne of Assyria. This great monarch began to steer a new political course with regard to conquered areas. Instead of just destroying their cities and imposing taxes on the population, he introduced the system of deportation. The ruling classes, the military and the craftsmen were scattered over the whole Assyrian empire, and colonists from elsewhere settled in their former fatherland. The new monarch's intention was to estab-

THE PROPHETS 'Writing Prophets' in white on black	Date	attacks from EGYPT	The kings of JUDAH and ISRAEL		attacks from MESOPOTAMIA
Nathan Gad			David Solomon	*italics = usurper*	
	950				
Ahijah		Shishak (Sheshonq) →	*(Disruption 931)* Rehoboam	*Jeroboam I*	
Jehu	900		Abijam Asa	Nadab *Baasha*	
Elijah				Elah *Zimri* *Omri*	ASSYRIANS Ashurnasirpal III 883-858
			Jehoshaphat	Ahab	Shalmaneser III 858-824
Elisha	850		Joram Ahaziah *(Athaliah)* Joash	Ahaziah *Joram* *Jehu*	← (battle of Qarqar 854) ← (tribute of Jehu 841)
					Shamshi-adad V 824-810
	800			Joahaz	Adad-nirari III 810-782 ← (tribute 805)
			Amaziah	Joash	(3 weak kings) Shalmaneser IV 781-772
Jonah			Uzziah	*Jeroboam II*	Ashurdan III 771-754
	750			Zechariah	Ashur-nirari 754-746
AMOS HOSEA			Jotham Ahaz	*Shallum Menahem* Pekahiah *Pekah* *Hoshea*	← Tiglath-pileser III 745-727 ← ← Shalmaneser V 727-722
ISAIAH					
MICAH			Hezekiah	deportation without return	Sargon II 721-705
	700	Tirhakah →		←	← Sennacherib 705-681
			Manasseh		*Esarhaddon* 681-669
					Ashurbanipal 669-626
	650				
ZEPHANIAH			Amon Josiah		CHALDAEANS
JEREMIAH Huldah		Necho →			Nabopolassar 625-605 (destroys Nineveh 612)
NAHUM Uriah	600	Hophra (Apries) →	Jehoahaz-Jehoiakim Jehoiachin-Zedekiah	← ←	*Nebuchadnezzar* 604-562
EZEKIEL				deportation to Babylon	*Evil-merodach* 561-560 *Nergal-sharezer* 559-556 Nabonidus 555-538
DEUTERO-ISAIAH	550				PERSIANS
				return	*Cyrus* 550-529 (conquers Babylon 539)
HAGGAI			Sheshbazzar Zerubbabel		Cambyses 529-521 *Darius I* 521-486
ZECHARIAH	500				
			Ezra, Nehemiah		

lish the power of Assyria by completely destroying the national existence of the conquered.

For the first time in its history the people of Yahweh, living in two kingdoms, saw the possibility of complete annihilation looming on the horizon. This obviously would mean that Yahweh would suffer defeat; the god Ashur would prove stronger than he. In 740 Isaiah received his calling, which he described as a vision of Yahweh as the only Lord of the world, as *the* King. Hosea prepared the way for his preaching in the northern kingdom during the critical decades preceding the destruction of 721. Amos appeared on the scene about the same time as Hosea, and a short time later Micah prophesied in Judah.

About 650 B.C. the all-powerful Assyrian armies even penetrated Upper Egypt and destroyed the famous city Thebes (Luxor-Karnak). Shortly afterward, however, their power quickly waned and in the years which followed they even withdrew their occupation forces from Palestine. This was the occasion for the national revival in Judah under King Josiah (ca. 640-609) which we discussed above (cf. pp. 97f.). At the beginning of that period Zephaniah was preaching in Judah. Even before Nahum had sung his harsh poem about the fall of Nineveh (612)—i.e., the end of the archenemy of Yahweh's people—Jeremiah had been called (627) to the heavy task of speaking the word of Yahweh. Those were the disastrous years preceding the destruction of the kingdom of Judah by the new Babylonian empire, for the assumption of power by Mesopotamia was certainly to be felt in Judah, the last milestone on Nebuchadnezzar's route to Egypt. In 598 this king laid siege to Jerusalem because of its disloyalty. It surrendered after three months. Remarkably enough the Babylonian did not destroy it; he deported only King Jehoiachin and a number of representatives of the ruling classes and enthroned Zedekiah as the new king of Judah. Ten years later, in 587, he liquidated rebellious Jerusalem, had the king put to death, and deported all the respected and influential citizens who had not perished.

In Babylon God prepared Ezekiel to guide with his word the precarious situation in which the exiles found themselves. After all, the fall of Jerusalem meant nothing less than the end of Yahweh's kingdom on earth, the end of the Covenant, and Yahweh's definitive break with his people. At the beginning of the preceding chapter we spoke about Ezekiel's task in this completely new situation.

About 550 B.C. a new crisis arose. A prince from the distant region of Anshan established himself as head of the invincible Persian tribes. After conquering the empire of the Medes he attacked the kingdom of Croesus and succeeded in taking his capital at Sardis, in Asia Minor (546). Was the weakened Babylonian empire to be the next to fall to this Cyrus? And were the Judeans to be destroyed with their conquerors? At that time one of the exiles felt compelled to reveal the deeper meaning of Cyrus' activities and thus to bring a message of hope and trust to the repentant people of Judah. This great prophet's name is not mentioned in the Bible. Usually he is called "the second Isaiah" or "Deutero-Isaiah," because his words have been incorporated in the second part of the book of Isaiah (chapters 40-55).

The next crisis came after 538 when the new Persian ruler had granted permission for them to return to the land of their ancestors. The repatriated found themselves among dreary ruins, completely neglected farms and an impoverished population who seemed full of distrust toward the newcomers. God then sent words of encouragement through the mouths of the prophets Haggai and Zechariah. Thanks to their influence, the temple was rebuilt (dedicated in 515 B.C.).

Except for a few works which were more or less prophetic in style, no new prophets appeared, for God's people evidently did not experience any crises in the "quiet" centuries after Nehemiah and Ezra. That period of rest lasted until 167 B.C. when the new culture of Hellenism endangered the Jewish community and the attack of Antiochus IV threatened its existence, as we saw in the introduction to the books of the Maccabees (pp. 125-131). At the highpoint of that crisis the prophetic message came to God's people in the form of a written work, the book of Daniel.

II
THE GENESIS OF THE PROPHETICAL BOOKS

In contrast with many sermons which Christians are used to hearing, the preaching of the prophets consisted mostly of very short sayings. Often their form and content were prepared with extreme care so that they would make an impression on their listeners. Sometimes the prophets give their plastic words even more strength by dramatizing their content in actions. Several examples may illustrate this.

Forms of Preaching

Let us begin with the first verses of the book of Isaiah (1, 2-4). The appeal to heaven and earth, with which the prophet begins, consists of four words, each pair beginning with the same letter. We might render them roughly as follows:

> Hear, Heavens.
> Listen, Land!

"Land" here stands for the earth, of course. The expression "heaven and earth" stands for the universe (cf. Gn. 1).

> Sons I have raised and reared,
> But they, they have rebelled against me!

A Hebrew sentence usually begins with the verb. Here, therefore, the word "sons" must have very special emphasis. The members of Yahweh's people are his sons; this has a deeper meaning than the usual assurance that Israel as a whole is his son (cf. Ex. 4, 22; Hos. 11, 1). Each Israelite shares in this privilege and bears the responsibility for it. Both verbs, "raise" and "rear," can also be used in Hebrew in the sense of causing a nation to flourish and prosper. The verb "to rebel" is also used for a king of a vassal state who refuses to pay tribute and thus rebels against his sovereign (e.g., 2 Kgs. 1, 1; 3, 5; 1 Kgs. 12, 19). It is one of the biblical verbs meaning "to sin."

> The ox knows its owner
> and the ass its master's crib;
> Israel knows nothing,
> my people understands nothing.

Even the dumb animal knows on whom its life depends. Israel has become too dense even for this elementary insight. It may be good to recall that the ox and the ass of our Christmas crib had their origin in this text. Their function is to help the Christian recognize the babe of Christmas as his master.

A sinful nation, a people weighed down with guilt,
a breed of wrong-doers, perverted sons.

This seemingly spontaneous exclamation is in fact composed with
very great care. There is a double climax in the use of the nouns
and adjectives which makes this utterance extremely impressive in
the original Hebrew. We can only try to give some idea of the
meaning by means of the following circumscription. Israel is not
only the nation of God that sins, not only his people that is
weighed down with guilt, not only his intimate family that is made
up of wrong-doers. No, much stronger, the Israelites are the sons
of Yahweh and they cover his country with their shocking perver-
sities. All this is expressed by nine carefully chosen alliterating
words:

> *hoy goy hotē'*
> *'am kebed 'awon*
> *zera' merē'īm*
> *banim mashhītīm*

The last word "sons" closes Yahweh's accusation just as it began.
   Then follows the summary of the prophet, now speaking about
Yahweh in the third person.

They have abandoned Yahweh,
despised the Holy One of Israel!

Considering that the words immediately following, "They have
turned away from him," are almost certainly an addition, the conclusion (verses 2-4) is especially impressive because of the length-
ening of the last line. The expression "Holy One of Israel" was
probably a creation of Isaiah himself. He was certainly aware that,
by molding these two words into a new name, he was giving
expression to the apparent absurdity accepted by all the countless
believers who contributed to the making of the Bible: the holy
God who transcends every thinkable magnitude entered into a
union with an historical people, apparently losing thereby something of his perfect independence (of Israel = belonging to Israel).
And yet he does not lose it. This expression is a kind of forerunner
of the paradox we sing of at Christmas: God is born.

As our second example let us take a look at "the song of the vineyard" in Isaiah 5, 1-7, which has the character of a parable. Perhaps the prophet pronounced this elaborate poem in the temple, in the presence of a large gathering of people from Judah and Jerusalem, and maybe even at the celebration of the Feast of Tabernacles. That feast closed the grape harvest and was always celebrated with exuberant joy. The prophet begins thus:

> Let me sing to my friend
> the song of his love for his vineyard.
> My friend had a vineyard
> on a fertile hillside. . . .

The very first words immediately attracted attention. No one expected something like this from a man who was always hammering at infidelity and crime, who never stopped talking about "the Holy One of Israel." He must certainly have drunk too much wine! Did we understand him correctly? Is he going to sing a love song? He said, "Let me sing to my friend the song of his love. . . ." Does he perhaps have a sweetheart he wants to sing about in the familiar figure of the vineyard? No, it is apparently about a man, his friend, who owns a vineyard and does his utmost to produce an excellent wine. By the sweat of his brow he removed the stones from the plot of ground. He planted the best grape vines he could get, and while they were catching root, he built a tower in the middle of the vineyard and a wall around it. In a corner where there was little ground he carved out a winepress and already saw before his eyes the juice of the ripe, full grapes flowing in it.

But what a disappointment awaited him! When the time for the harvest came, the vines, nurtured with so much care, appeared to bring forth only hard and sour fruit. All of this Isaiah paints in the short space of six lines:

> He dug the soil, cleared it of stones,
> and planted choice vines in it.
> In the middle he built a tower;
> he dug a press there too.
> He expected it to yield grapes,
> but sour grapes were all that it gave.

Then suddenly there is a change of speaker; the friend himself
begins to speak. Already in his question to the inhabitants of Jerusalem and their guests there is a trace of a threatening undertone.
What do they think about this story? Am I to blame for the failure, or is my vineyard at fault? Could I have done more than I
already did? Didn't I have the right to expect the best results at
harvest time?

> And now, inhabitants of Jerusalem
> and men of Judah,
> I ask you to judge
> between my vineyard and me.
> What could I have done for my vineyard
> that I have not done?
> I expected it to yield grapes.
> Why did it yield sour grapes instead?

The people listened breathlessly. This is not just a story about an
ordinary vinegrower! Now the friend begins to tell what he is planning to do with his vineyard. The verses' rhythm changes. Away
with the protecting walls! He will let the vineyard dry up; it will be
trampled underfoot and changed into a desert. And then, with a
single word, it becomes clear to the audience who this friend is:

> Very well, I will tell you
> what I am going to do to my vineyard:
> I will take away its hedge for it to be grazed on,
> and knock down its wall for it to be trampled on.
> I will lay it waste, unpruned, undug,
> overgrown by the briar and the thorn.
> I will command the clouds to rain no rain on it.

This verse reveals the clue. Only God commands the clouds. The
friend is Yahweh! Isaiah goes on to fill in the details. The vineyard
is the house of Israel; the special plants are the men of Judah. The
concluding words were chosen in such a way that they might always have a place in the listeners' memory:

> He expected justice but found bloodshed,
> integrity but only a cry of distress.

The song that began so lovely ends with the harsh cries of the exploited and oppressed. Cries of this kind had once moved Yahweh to save his people from the oppression of Egypt (Ex. 3, 7. 9). Woe to him who misjudges God's ways and annuls the Covenant through oppression of his fellow men!

We do not know whether Isaiah in this beautiful piece of "figurative language" was the first to see an image of God's concern for his people in the vinegrower's care for his plants, or whether he made use of a comparison that was already common. At any rate, from then on those who had heard his song could hardly ever again see someone at work in his vineyard without being reminded of what God had done for them and expected of them.

The prophets give the impression that all kinds of things and actions from daily life became images and signs of that divine reality. Everything they see around them "speaks" to them of it. We would like to give a few examples from the rich world of their figurative language. At the same time, one should remember what we said about "Hebrew thought"—namely, that it does not distinguish as sharply as we do between symbol and reality. Likewise, remember that the name of a person or a thing expresses something of the "essence," with the result that there is often more involved than just a clever play on words. Finally, we must keep in mind that for people like the prophets no chance or neutral things ever happen. When they are struck by the symbolic value of something, then it is Yahweh who lets them see it, and of course he does so for the purpose of incorporating it in their preaching, since his claim on them as his spokesmen is all-demanding.

Amos was once struck by the similarity between the words *kayis,* "summer, summer fruit," and *kes,* "end." That came to him when he saw a basket of ripe summer fruit and Yahweh spoke to him about the approaching end of the house of Israel (Amos 8, 1-2).

In Palestine the first tree to bloom after the winter is the almond. Perhaps that is why it is called *shakēd,* for the participle *shokēd* means "that which is awake." The almond tree, awake so early, spoke to the prophet about his God, who would not delay the execution of what he was to say to his people through Jeremiah (Jer. 1, 11-12).

Since Egypt's might had waned, little Judah had to fear enemy invasions only from the other side, the northern entrance to this narrow country. Jeremiah once saw a kettle hanging above a fire. It was leaning to one side, with the result that its boiling contents came pouring out that side. That was the south side. This especially "spoke" to him about the armies which would come pouring over Judah from the north (Jer. 1, 13-15).

The Babylonian armies came indeed and conquered Jerusalem in 597. The victors deported King Jehoiachin and his court to Babylon together with those who forged weapons as well as technicians who would be needed for defense. But instead of completely destroying the national existence of Judah, they established another offspring of David's stock, Zedekiah, as the king who was to form a new government. Soon God's cards lay quite open for all to see. He had expelled Jehoiachin and his followers from his land and thus excluded them from the Covenant. That Covenant he obviously wanted to continue now with the remaining people under the leadership of a new anointed one, Zedekiah. But for the prophet, it was just the other way around. Two baskets of figs provided him with an image. In one there were first-class figs, and in the other there were rejected ones, too poor to be eaten and only good for the manure pile. You here in Jerusalem are the rotten figs, the rejected ones! Those deported to Babylon are the good figs; Yahweh still has hope for them. Jeremiah relates that God gave him the "vision" of the two baskets. With that he can mean that God gave him the idea when he went to the market one morning and saw a fig vendor sorting his fruit. What he did after that cannot be determined from his text. The only certain thing is that he could *say* to the king and people: the two groups, the exiles in Babylon and those who remained behind, are like two baskets of figs, one filled with good fruit, the other with worthless fruit. Besides putting it into words, the next best thing he could do was to borrow the two baskets from the fruit vendor, take them with him to the temple or palace, and when he had gathered the people around him, to point out: these rotten figs, they are you here, and those good ones, they are Jehoiachin and the others in Babylon.

Jeremiah often heard the people in Jerusalem and especially the leaders talking as if *they* and the king had the lot of Judah in their hands. For the prophet this was not the case at all. The lot of his people was completely in God's hands, "like soft clay in the hand of the potter." Jeremiah frequently saw potters at work in their open shops down by the well. He saw the fast-spinning clump of clay rise and grow in their flexible fingers into the model the artist had in mind. If the potter wasn't satisfied, with both hands he would crush the vessel together again into a formless lump and begin anew (18, 1-6). Here, too, the origin of the comparison or figure is referred to simply as a command from God that had a divine oracle coupled with it.

A bit of household carelessness was probably the occasion for the comparison about Jeremiah's loincloth (13, 1-11). According to the men's styles of those days one could easily determine a Judean's status and class by the quality of his linen loincloth. Jeremiah had once bought a fine new loincloth, but he had put it away in a damp closet or corner. He was not married, the only celibate man in the Bible before Christ (cf. 16, 2; note the "sign value" as well!). When he wanted to put it on one day, he found the loincloth all moldy and no longer wearable. Yes, thus had God once redeemed his people from Egypt to be his status symbol in this world. "For just as a loincloth clings to a man's waist, so I had intended the whole house of Judah to cling to me—it is Yahweh who speaks—to be my people, my glory, my honor and my boast. . . ." But the people did not faithfully fulfill that role. It was too rotten, too corrupt, especially because it no longer recognized Yahweh as its only Lord, but looked for its salvation in the worship of the moon and stars, and in all kinds of practices from Mesopotamia, the land along the Euphrates. The dampness of that country had ruined God's loincloth. Perhaps we should explain that the village of Anathoth where Jeremiah lived drew its water from the well Para. This name sounded almost exactly the same as that of the Euphrates (in Hebrew: p^erat). All of this may perhaps clarify the rather strange story in which Jeremiah buys a loincloth at God's command and then goes to bury it on the bank of the Euphrates, only to dig it up some time later and discover its rottenness.

The next paragraph is likewise characteristic of the prophet's "symbolic thought." Once he heard a group of merrymakers singing, "Fill all the jugs with wine!" The "jugs," of course, were their bellies. Sure, the prophet shouted to them, Yahweh will fill you all with wine, with the wine of his wrath, and then he will smash those jugs one against the other (13, 12-14).

Jeremiah could have simply said this, but he could also have illustrated it with actions, by filling two jugs and smashing them together. He in fact did do something similar on another occasion. Accompanied by several elders of the people and of the priestly class, he bought a jug, went with them outside of the city near the valley of Ben-hinnom, and there smashed the jug before their eyes with the words, "Yahweh Sabaoth says this: I am going to break this people and this city just as one breaks a potter's pot, irreparably" (19, 1-2. 8-11).

A similar "symbolic action" for Jeremiah was to go around with a yoke on his shoulders, as we saw in another context (pp. 162f.). On another occasion he buries foundation stones in the pavement in front of the royal palace in Egypt (43, 8-13), and still later he orders a scroll to be weighed down with a stone and thrown into the Euphrates (51, 59-64).

In contrast with the great variety in the book of Jeremiah, we know but one such action in Isaiah. It is probably due to his character, origin and class that the "illustration" of his preaching was limited to his words. Nevertheless, his disciples later related that he appeared in public for three years without a shirt and went barefoot. This was at the time when the politicians and diplomats of Judah were trying to get military help from Egypt to aid their resistance against the Assyrian domination. Isaiah wanted to make it clear that such reliance on the power of Egypt would be put to shame. Just as I walk around here, "so will the king of Assyria lead away captives from Egypt and exiles from Cush, young and old, naked and barefoot, their buttocks bared, to the shame of Egypt" (Is. 20, 1-5).

The symbolic actions in the book of Ezekiel have a different character still. They seem less spontaneous and more thought-out than those in Jeremiah. Read, for example, how the prophet was to scratch the city Jerusalem on a brick, with its besiegers all around, as a "sign for the house of Israel" (4, 1-3). Then he had to lie down on his side for a long time and eat very little as a sign of Jerusalem's guilt and the famine with which the city would be punished (4, 4-17). He was to do some very remarkable things to portray how a person was to leave a city when being sent into exile. In this way he pointed out the lot awaiting Jerusalem and its king (12, 1-5).

With this kind of dramatization of the message in word and action, we should also include the names which some of the prophets gave their children. These names involved them in the prophets' calling to be "signs and portents in Israel" (Is. 8, 18). Here one should think not only of the value which the name had in the Semitic world, but also that Israelitic names generally referred to community with God and expressed the help which they hoped for and expected from him. Only then will we understand how difficult it must have been for Hosea to give his children names like "Unloved" and "No-People-of-Mine." These names characterized the prophet himself as a proclaimer of doom (Hos. 1, 6-8). The name of the boy with whom Isaiah was to go to meet King Ahaz was likewise pregnant with meaning: *Shear-jashub,* "A-Remnant-Will-Return" (Is. 7, 4). This name meant two things at the same time. It spoke of a *return* to union with Yahweh and all the blessings associated with this. But it also pronounced a judgment— salvation will be given only to a *remnant,* which will survive after the great majority is destroyed.

A second son of Isaiah also received a name which had a double meaning. Even before his birth *Maher-shalal-hash-baz* (Speedy-spoil-quick-booty) was to put into words the assurance that the then two great enemies of Judah would soon fall. The stolen treasures from Damascus and the booty of Samaria would lie at the foot of the king of Assyria even before the boy could say father and mother (Is. 8, 1-4). But the fact that the Assyrians were able to reckon so quickly and thoroughly with their enemies also implied a sharp warning for Judah (8, 5-8).

From the Spoken to the Written Word

If the prophets were primarily preachers and not writers, who then wrote the books attributed to them in the Bible? An attempt to answer this must be seen in the light of the above. In short, the preaching of the prophets was "impressive" in the literal sense of the word. Certainly those who were deeply impressed by a prophetic pronouncement cherished it in their memory, and so much so that they could repeat it verbatim even many years later. Here we should remember that their memories were much better trained than ours. They put much less in writing and read much less than we; furthermore, they were not flooded day and night by waves of words, presented and reproduced mechanically.

Prophetic words were, of course, imprinted deepest in the hearts of those who were most struck by them, in whose souls they resounded. The challenging way the prophets went about preaching probably attracted a circle of like-minded believers, something like a group of disciples, the core of the "remnant" who, unlike the masses, did not reject their message. Once in a statement of Isaiah we find such disciples mentioned. He had urged king and people to place their sole trust in Yahweh, and he branded their uninterrupted diplomatic and military involvements as a lack of trust in God. From their point of view they could only reject this preaching as a kind of treason (Is. 8, 11-15). Thereupon the prophet entrusted his message to several men whom he expressly calls "disciples." They are to be a "seal" on his preaching so that they might form an ever-present indictment of the unfaithful Judeans:

> I bind up this testimony,
> I seal this revelation,
> in the heart of my disciples.

In the case of Jeremiah there is no mention of a group, but we do hear of one man who seems to have fulfilled the whole task of a circle of disciples himself, Baruch. Instead of striving for a high position in the government (for which he no doubt was just as qualified as his brother Seraiah: Jer. 51, 59), Baruch chose to assist the hated prophet as helper and companion. He remained faithful to him in all difficult circumstances and shared his lot when the prophet was taken to Egypt by a party of his fellow citizens.

The scene which Baruch describes in chapter 36 is very important for our question. In 605, an extremely critical year for Judah, after Jeremiah had been forbidden to enter the temple, he dictated to Baruch all the threats he had uttered in the years gone by. Baruch wrote them on a scroll and was to read the text to the people in the temple. When the stubborn king destroyed that scroll piece by piece, Jeremiah dictated the text a second time. Then we read: ". . . at the dictation of Jeremiah he [Baruch] wrote down all the words of the book that Jehoiakim king of Judah had burnt, with many similar words in addition" (Jer. 36, 32).

It should be noted that Jeremiah's statements were apparently very deeply engraved in his memory. Furthermore, we may assume that the intention of the second written version was more far-reaching than the first. Since he was prevented from speaking to the people, he turned to writing the first time as a kind of emergency measure. But on the second occasion setting the text in writing took on the function described in Isaiah 30, 8:

> Now go and inscribe this on a tablet,
> write it in a book,
> that it may serve in the time to come
> as a witness forever.

Finally, in the last lines of his account Baruch seems to be referring to his share in ordering and completing the statements of his master.

For the rest we know very little about those who passed the words of the prophets on to succeeding generations. It is certain that we are for the most part indebted to Baruch for describing the facts of Jeremiah's life incorporated in that book. Likewise, biographical notes in other prophetic books are almost surely the work of such disciples—for example, the first chapter of Hosea and the description of what Amos underwent in Bethel (7, 10-17). When they passed on the words of their masters, the disciples and their successors in the following generations (here we can think of "schools" such as those formed by great artists) combined two qualities which we Westerners find very difficult to unite. They passed on very *faithfully* what they could remember of their statements or what had already become oral or written tradition, but at the same time they felt completely *free* to adapt those words to new situations, either by putting them in a different sequence and thus transferring the emphasis, or by adding words of their own. For them it was always a question of the words of the living God who was also addressing his people in their day. Put in another way, they felt free and even obliged to bring the prophetic statements up to date for their own generation. Further on, as an example of this, we will see how Hosea's words were originally directed to the northern kingdom of Israel, but, after its destruction in 721, were passed on in Judah and show traces of this fact in the form of additions intended for the southern kingdom.

In their transmission, the words of the prophets seldom if ever were ordered in the sequence in which they were uttered. No one had ever taken an interest in that and thus never remembered it. It is usually not clear just which principles were used in ordering them. Why, for example, do Isaiah's disciples put the story of his calling in chapter six and not at the beginning of the book? Another example: in Jeremiah 21, 1—23, 8 a number of statements against the kings of Judah are brought together and put in their chronological order, with one exception—an oracle against the last ruling king, Zedekiah, is given the first place!

The following principle of sequence was once the rule: first came the prophecies of doom for Judah-Jerusalem (A); then the oracles concerning foreign nations followed (B); in the third place there were the promises of salvation for Judah and Jerusalem (C). A glance at the contents of the book of Ezekiel shows that it was composed according to this outline. It was also followed for the book of Jeremiah at a certain stage of its development, for when it was translated into Greek, the oracles against the nations, the present chapters 46—51, still stood after chapter 25—that is, in the middle of the book. It can likewise be seen in the first part of Isaiah (1—35). Its central chapters (13—27) contain the oracles about the foreign nations. But Messianic promises are also found in the first part (1—12), and prophecies of doom in the last. This tells us at least that some collections had already received a fixed form when the A-B-C outline began to be applied.

Especially complicated, of course, is the genesis of "the Twelve," the fourth book listed among the "later prophets." Each of the collections incorporated here has its own history, particularly when it is a question of older personalities. These are indeed found at the beginning, with the result that one gets the idea that they are in chronological order. But other principles likewise played a role. Between Hosea and Amos in the 7th century B.C., we find Joel which stems from the end of the 5th century. Perhaps the redactors saw some meaning in the literal correspondence of the last word of Joel with the first word of Amos. Some scholars think that the twelfth collection was anonymous. To arrive at the number twelve, the word *mal'āki*, "my messenger," from 3, 1 would have then found its way into the title. In that way the prophet Malachi had his origin.

This explanation will have made it quite clear that each prophetic book has its own very complicated pre-history. The discovery of this fact has made every attempt to write a "biography" of a prophet, in which his statements would be chronologically arranged, an impossible undertaking. Even the genesis of the book in which the words of a prophet are collected can only be described in its broad lines. But we have also learned from this that every book contains *both* the preaching of the master (sometimes literally, without one word being changed) *and* that of his disciples in situations of a later date. Familiarity with this phenomenon will be helpful later on when we analyze the four gospels.

How the Book of Isaiah Came into Being

For those who are interested we would like to give a few details concerning the book of Isaiah which took several centuries to grow into its present form. To begin with, everyone can see for himself that chapters 36—39 were derived from 2 Kings 18—19. At one time they formed the conclusion of the book of Isaiah which was evidently considered complete. The reader might compare this with the "historical" chapter concluding the book of Jeremiah; this chapter was derived from 2 Kings 24—25 and clearly added when the completed entity already existed, as we can see from the sentence: "Here end the words of Jeremiah" (51, 64).

It was the German scholar Bernard Duhm, in a commentary of 1892, who put forward the opinion that the section following Isaiah 1—39, namely, chapters 40—55, formed a unit in themselves which was independent of the final section, chapters 56—66. The words of 40—55 were addressed by one and the same prophet to the deported Judeans in Babylon between 550, when Cyrus appeared on the scene, and 539, when he conquered Babylon. The material in 56—66, on the contrary, is certainly not the work of one person; it reflects for the most part the situation of the post-exilic community in Jerusalem.

The first part, chapters 1—39, or rather 1—35, also has three parts. It is generally accepted that the first of these, 1—12, consists almost entirely of words from the great Isaiah himself, with the exception of the conclusion (11, 10—12, 6) which contains exilic and post-exilic additions. Of the oracles against foreign nations (13—27), introduced each time with the technical term *massa,* "oracle," and also "burden" (cf. Jer. 23, 33-40), some are most certainly from Isaiah (e.g., 13; 14, 1-23; 19, 16-25; 21, 1-10). In some other cases doubt exists. The closing chapters 24—27 are not concerned with a particular heathen nation, but describe the judgment of the whole world and the deliverance of God's people. The author who composed this so-called "Apocalypse of Isaiah" from all sorts of traditional material certainly lived after the exile. The third part (28—35) likewise begins with texts considered to be authentically from Isaiah. These are arranged in a series of pronouncements, all of which begin with the word *hoy,* "woe" (28, 1; 29, 1. 15; 30, 1; 33, 1). This section ends with two chapters which undoubtedly are the work of later disciples.

If this last paragraph looks like a telephone book, we hope the reader will forgive us. It is intended as an example of what we said above about the complicated genesis of the prophetic books. Something of this growth process is now clear, thanks to precise historical and literary analysis.

One last observation on this point. We mentioned Bernard Duhm and the year 1892 for the same reason that we treated Julius Wellhausen in Chapter I. Likewise, in the sector of prophetic literature it was the 19th century which launched the "historical approach." Here, too, there was initial opposition from traditionally orientated Christians. In the Roman Catholic Church this again took the form of a decree from the Pontifical Biblical Commission (June 28, 1908). It declared that the modern argumentation was not strong enough to replace the age-old tradition that the great Isaiah had written the whole book with his own hand. In particular it rejected the supposition that it would have been impossible for Isaiah to address the Judeans who 150 years after his death found themselves in the situation of the Babylonian exile as well as the impossibility of his speaking about Cyrus' appearance on the scene. The development which we sketched in connection with the Pentateuch has also taken place in this case since the promulgation of that decree. At the present time, both in Rome and elsewhere, it is more possible to clearly understand that the question of whether a person can project himself into a future situation is *on a very different level* than that of the circumstances in which a particular book came about. The latter can only be answered on the basis of literary and historical data. Just as was true with the Pentateuch and all the differences of opinion about its component parts and details, a certain unanimity has been achieved regarding the way of approaching the prophetic books of Holy Scripture.

III
SOME INDIVIDUAL PROPHETS

Several persons, sometimes dozens, were involved in the composition of nearly all the prophetic books. Except for Baruch, Jeremiah's co-worker, we only know the names of those who stand at the beginning of the books' tradition, the prophets themselves. Their pronouncements were remembered, arranged in a certain sequence and adapted in various ways to new situations by all those anonymous "disciples." At this point we would like to take a closer look at several of those central prophetic figures.

As we have already observed, the way these books were passed on does not allow one to write something about the prophets that could even resemble a "biography." In some cases, however, enough information has filtered through to provide a generally faithful sketch of the prophet's personality, together with the historical situation that determined the content, the major themes, of his preaching as well as the literary form it took. This kind of sketch sometimes makes use of what is often called a "circular argument": from "authentic" words which have been handed down, one establishes the personality of the prophet, and with that one goes on to determine the "authenticity" of still other pronouncements. This method is also used in other areas of historical research—often as the only way to a better insight. The result depends, of course, on the investigator's "prejudices"—i.e., his personal taste and cherished insights. For this reason differences of opinion exist concerning the authenticity of certain texts. This is particularly true for the promises of a prosperous future attributed to pre-exilic prophets. We mention this here partly because in the following paragraphs we will limit ourselves to six personalities from that group.

Hosea

One of the Bible's most striking pronouncements about God's love for man is attributed to Hosea. This is certainly justified, for that subject forms the core of his preaching. What has reached us of that preaching stands at the beginning of the book of the Twelve. Chronologically he is the first of the biblical prophets (*Schriftpropheten*), and, furthermore, he is the only non-Judean among them. From the title of the collection and from the allusions in the fourteen chapters into which it is divided, it appears that Hosea began his preaching in the northern kingdom of Israel during the long and prosperous reign of Jeroboam II (ca. 783-743), probably in the last decade of that reign. He worked also in the turbulent period that followed, supposedly even until the beginning of the Assyrian siege of the capital, Samaria (724).

The Hebrew text of this little book is known as one of the most difficult to understand in the Old Testament. In general, the prophet seems to have expressed himself in very moving statements, sharp and to the point, with all kinds of references which in a short time could no longer be understood completely by those who passed on his words, for they combined them in an order which is far from clear to us; this is especially true for chapters 4—14. This work probably took place in Judah where his disciples sought shelter after the fall of Samaria in 721 B.C. Although the confusing transmission of the text may be partially due to all these circumstances arising from the war, it is certain that Hosea's words were "living" texts for quite a long time and thus were adapted in order to bear a clearer message for God's people—then the remnant Judah—in new situations, among them the Babylonian exile. The Bible reader can see for himself how things have been added for Judah among the words addressed to the northern kingdom of Israel, often called Ephraim and sometimes Jacob—for example, warnings (4, 15), threats (12, 3) and promises (6, 11). On the other hand, Judah is sometimes expressly spoken of as exempt from the lot that Israel deserved (1, 7).

A copyist's sigh, incorporated at the end of the book, shows that the text was already obscure before it was taken into the canon and thus no longer open to change. It can best be rendered in the form of a question: "Who is so wise that he understands all these words; who so intelligent that he grasps their meaning?" From the rough and jerky series of words in 4—14 it becomes clear to the reader in any case that Hosea passionately pleads for the proper attitude that Israel should have toward its God and is harshly critical of the two institutions which should protect and stimulate that attitude: cult and monarchy. But the degenerate rulers brought only anarchy, crime and injustice, and the priests encouraged worship of the native Baals with its repulsive practices. There was no longer any way to recognize Israel for what it should be, the people of Yahweh.

At the beginning of 4—14 the collectors have placed an oracle which well summarizes the essential elements of Hosea's preaching:

> Sons of Israel, listen to the word of Yahweh,
> for Yahweh indicts the inhabitants of the country:
> there is no *fidelity*, no *tenderness*,
> no *knowledge of God* in the country,
> only perjury and lies, slaughter, theft,
> adultery and violence, murder after murder.
> This is the way the country is in mourning,
> and all who live in it pine away,
> even the wild animals and the birds of heaven;
> the fishes of the sea themselves are perishing.

The italicized words point to the attitude which should characterize Israel. "Tenderness" is the rendering of the word *hèsed*, which in our language cannot be translated by one word. Besides "tenderness," translators sometimes use "piety" (in the traditional sense of *pietas* due to God, parents etc.) or "loving kindness." The gospel according to Matthew (9, 13; 12, 7) translates *hèsed* as "mercy" when citing the words of Hosea 6, 6: "What I want is mercy, not sacrifice." In any case it means the loyal, factual recognition of a certain bond with someone. That recognition can express itself in a faithful fulfillment of obligations stemming from the bond as well as in spontaneous signs of one's love.

The *fidelity*, which the prophet puts in the first place, also includes what we call "dependability," that quality which enables a person to entrust another with anything at all. The *knowledge of God* is not only the theoretical knowledge of what Yahweh has done for his people and thus what he expects from them, but also the practical realization of that knowledge. In Israel one knows God only when he recognizes his right to exclusive worship and at the same time recognizes the rights of his fellow men. Therefore, when there is no longer "knowledge of God" in the land, it is a slave to everything which destroys human society: "perjury, lies, murder, theft and adultery." And with that perished likewise the rest of creation which receives its meaning—or, so to speak, the heart of its existence—from God's relationship with man. This effect exceeds the punishment of the Deluge—now even the fishes perish, so great is the corruption of Israel.

Before this central section (4—14) the collectors placed chapters 1—3, evidently because there the deepest roots of what drove Hosea to undertake his preaching are laid bare. The first chapter describes Hosea as receiving the order from God to marry a prostitute. Why? Because by abandoning Yahweh Israel had become a whore. He is to give the three children she bore him names which would successively express God's judgment of his people more and more clearly. The literary form also suggests that the relationship was growing worse with the passing years. If 1, 2-9 is written in verse form, leaving out verse 7 (a promise for Judah), then one can see that the introduction of God's words to the prophet becomes continually shorter:

> Yahweh said to Hosea:
> Go, marry a whore . . . for. . . .
> Then Yahweh said to him:
> Name him Jezreel, for. . . .
> And he said to him:
> Name her Unloved, for. . . .
> And he said:
> Name him No-People-of-Mine, for. . . .

A terrible message lay hidden in the name of the third child which came only after the previous one was weaned—that is, about three years after birth. It is as if Yahweh hesitated to utter that final word, that irrevocable end of everything:

> For you are no longer my people,
> and I no longer I-Am for you!

This is a clear reference to the explanation of his name which Yahweh himself gave to Moses, who was to tell his people, "I-Am has sent me. . . ." (Ex. 3, 14).

Yahweh, too, has now broken the Covenant, but yet his decision is not irrevocable. In chapter 3 Hosea himself tells how he, at God's command, goes in search of his unfaithful wife, buys her back from her new master at a dear price and isolates her for a time from all relations, even with himself. His treatment of that woman portrays what Yahweh was doing with Israel. This is very movingly depicted in the oracles of 2, 4-17, where Yahweh is at the same time accuser, judge and executor of the judgment. When reading this section (in some Bibles 2, 1-12), one should recall the remarks about the Canaanitic worship service (cf. pp. 46f. and 68f.). On Israel's highest hills and near the trees of the most luxuriant valleys there stood temples of the Baals and their spouses. The women of Israel worked there as temple prostitutes and probably wore amulets on their foreheads or between their breasts as a sign of their profession. The prophet sees the hill country of Israel with its idolatrous temples on the heights and in the valleys, and the people who live there, as just such a prostitute. She left her own husband, Yahweh, and has gone chasing after her "lovers," the Baals. She no longer realized that all the precious fruit of the land was received from Yahweh, but looked upon it as gifts from her lovers. That is why Yahweh will no longer continue to clothe her (with fertile trees and rich harvests), as a husband was to clothe his lawful wife, but he would tear away her clothes and put her on display in her nakedness. From the luxuriant land he will make an arid desert.

> She will chase after her lovers and never catch up with them,
> she will search for them and never find them.
> Then she will say, "I will go back to my first husband,
> I was happier then than I am today."

Yahweh puts his loved one in a "desert situation." While enjoying the gifts, she had forgotten the giver. If she is stripped of everything, she will again cling to him alone and thus return to her first love.

We are tempted to think that Hosea experienced in his heart something of the mysterious power of the love that cannot free itself of a loved one despite all her infidelity. Then precisely in that experience something would have been revealed to him of the mystery we call God. But chapters 1—3 are too full of symbolism to be able to support this supposition. It is certain, however, that Hosea was formed in the tradition of the Covenant, which after all had its "home" in his surroundings (Shechem: cf. p. 51). And it is most probable that he was the first one to conceive of the Covenant relationship in terms of the marriage relationship. In that way he "christened," so to speak, an aspect of the Canaanitic cult. Instead of a Baal—i.e., both "lord" and "spouse," who made the earth fertile and involved its inhabitants in that natural process—Israel had a Lord who treated his bride as a human being and demanded of her only what men can give, *hèsed* and everything included in it (2, 21-22 or 18-19):

> I will betroth you to myself forever,
> betroth you with integrity and justice,
> with tenderness and love (*hèsed*);
> I will betroth you to myself with faithfulness,
> and you will come to know Yahweh.

Yet, Hosea's most powerful word seems to be that of 11, 8-9. In chapter 11 Yahweh is not the lover who cannot forget his unfaithful loved one, but the father who does not want to abandon his thankless and recalcitrant son. The text mentions Admah and Zeboiim, two of the five cities whose lack of willingness to repent forced God to "overthrow" them. Better known are those other two which are often mentioned as symbols of iniquity demanding vengeance, Sodom and Gomorrah. Yahweh should actually treat Israel as he did those cities and overthrow it. But then the same thing would happen to his own heart. His mercy burns within him. Where a human father would give his anger free reins at such treatment, Yahweh cannot contain his mercy. He is so different from man:

> Ephraim, how could I part with you?
> Israel, how could I give you up?
> How could I treat you like Admah,
> or deal with you like Zeboiim?
> My heart recoils from it,
> my whole being trembles at the thought.
> I will not give rein to my fierce anger,
> I will not destroy Ephraim again,
> for I am God, not man:
> I am the Holy One in your midst. . . .

Amos

About the same time that Hosea began his work, the Judean Amos was sent to the inhabitants of the prosperous northern kingdom of Israel. This shepherd from Tekoa, a village near Bethlehem, also worked as a fig dresser elsewhere in the land and possibly had learned about the situation in Samaria through his business relations with firms there. The wealthy higher classes were unscrupulously exploiting the poor, while at the same time they hankered after more wealth and prosperity for themselves. And this they did on "religious" grounds. In their pompous feasts at the great national shrines, they often celebrated the old traditions of the "Day of Yahweh," the day on which he would send even greater blessings upon Israel and destroy all its enemies forever. How blind they were to the real state of things! A holy anger seized the man from the country, Amos, who from childhood had been faithful to the Yahwistic traditions about the fundamental rights of God and man and who himself never tolerated any injustice. In the irresistible force with which that anger one day drove him from his rural occupation in order to unleash words of judgment and destruction in the corrupt centers of Israel, Amos recognized Yahweh's command. The piercing roar of a lion, conscious of its own staggering power, often to be heard in the desert of Tekoa—only that imposing sound could give some idea of the way in which the ancient principle of Israel's "election" was being interpreted. As if this special relationship with Yahweh should be nothing more than a guarantee for prosperity and happiness—nota bene—for the "better" classes! For Amos it consisted in the serious task of bearing witness to Yahweh's nature and reality by a society of brotherhood based on law and justice. Precisely because of that election, social injustice in Israel is more of a fault and more liable to punishment than elsewhere. The structure of the long poem with which the collection begins (1, 3—2, 16) already seems to be inspired by this theme. By means of a literary device, similar to the "numerical proverbs," Amos successively names the crimes committed by Damascus, Gaza, Tyre, Edom, Ammon and Moab:

> For the three crimes, the four crimes of Damascus (etc.)
> I have made my decree and will not relent!

Yahweh will punish all those crimes, he says. This Judean sees very clearly, therefore, that Israel's God is the universal defender of justice and humanity. As last on the list of criminal nations, as climax, comes Israel, his chosen people, who is equally guilty of crimes and thus even more liable to punishment. This conclusion must have hit the self-sufficient Israelite audience quite hard, especially in its original form. As it now stands in the collection, this poem seems to have been reworked. The verses about Judah seem to have been added later; this has also been suggested concerning those about Tyre and Edom. Moreover, the addition of further words of Amos seems to detract from the structure of the last part about Israel. But those, too, are very penetrating. If God carries out his judgment, the entire defense apparatus of Israel will collapse. The defenders of the people will scarcely be able to save their own doomed skins:

> See then how I am going to crush you into the ground
> as the threshing-sledge crushes when clogged by straw;
> flight will not save even the swift,
> the strong man will find his strength useless,
> the mighty man will be powerless to save himself.
> The bowman will not stand his ground,
> the fast runner will not escape,
> the horseman will not save himself,
> the bravest warriors will run away naked that day.
> It is Yahweh who speaks.

Following this introduction there are three groups of statements, each beginning with the phrase "listen to this word" (3, 1; 4, 1; 5, 1). The first one begins with a very concise statement of the theme mentioned above. One should note here that "to know someone" in biblical language means that one gives all his attention and care to that other person and, in this giving of the best one has to offer, binds himself intimately to the other.

> You alone, of all the families of the earth,
> have I acknowledged (literally: known);
> therefore it is for all your sins
> that I mean to punish you.

After this series of generally short statements (except for the remnants of a strophic poem: cf. chapter 4, verses 6, 8, 10, 11), the collectors placed another series of three, each beginning with the word "Woe!" (5, 7 in its proper place before verse 10; 5, 18; 6, 1). At the beginning of the second statement in the series there is a sharp word about the "Day of Yahweh" for which they so longed. That day will indeed dawn, says Amos, but then only to pay guilty Israel the wages it deserves. That day will not bring the light of happiness, but the darkness of disaster. Amos illustrates its inevitability as follows:

> . . . as when a man escapes a lion's mouth,
> only to meet a bear;
> he enters his house and puts his hand on the wall,
> only for a snake to bite him.

The core of the last part of the collection (chapters 7—9) is formed by five "visions" which Amos describes in the first person. God lets him see all kinds of symbols of destruction. In the first two visions, Amos pleads with God to spare Israel (7, 1-3. 4-6), but in the third he does so no longer (7, 7-9). In the fourth he simply listens to the judgment (8, 1-3), and in the fifth he even seems to take part in executing it (9, 1-4). The third vision apparently provided the collectors with the occasion to include the story of Amos' activities in Bethel (cf. p. 177), and after the fourth they inserted still another collection of sayings.

Finally, the main theme resounds again in the bewildering question which must have sounded like a blasphemous denial of Israel's central "dogma": Why should Israel mean more to Yahweh than the black Ethiopians? Indeed, he brought Israel out of Egypt, as you say at the beginning of your confession. Yes, but didn't he also lead the Philistines from Caphtor, and the Aramaeans from Kir (9, 7)?

Amos' sense of the justice of Yahweh, for him the God of all peoples, penetrated so deeply that with this question he even dared to call Israel's faith in its divine election into question. He would have ruined the effect it was to have on his audience if he had added what we now have in the text: "Yet I am not going to destroy the house of Jacob completely. . . ." (8b-10). It is understandable, therefore, that some exegetes regard that mitigating statement as an addition of the collectors; the same is true for the promise of salvation which concludes the book (verses 11-15).

Isaiah

Isaiah was a "city man" down to the very marrow of his bones. From his obvious associations with kings and ministers, his feeling for matters of dynasty and politics, his control over his emotional life and his mastery of the language, it has been concluded that he came from the aristocracy of Jerusalem. However this may be, his entire life was shaped by his experience in "the house of Yahweh" on Mount Zion, close to the "house of the king." It was there that the "holiness"—i.e., the all-transcending and unassailable majesty —of the God of Israel made such an overwhelming impression on Isaiah. At the same time the prophet became aware of the paradox that this God wanted to bind himself to the temple of Jerusalem as his only dwelling place on earth. Isaiah put this experience into words in an unequalled passage (chapter 6), and with it he provided us with a high point in the biblical experience of the divine as well as with the key to his whole preaching. In the light of Yahweh's glory, he realized not only his nothingness as a creature, but also and especially his impurity as a sinner, a man living in a corrupt environment. In that "year of King Uzziah's death," Isaiah saw the real king, the immortal Lord of all that happens in history and nature. The goal of his world rule could only be the revelation of his glory in all of earthly reality, just as the Seraphim were granted the privilege of seeing it in anticipation.

From that moment on, Isaiah could not but bear witness to that Yahweh before the inhabitants of Jerusalem and their kings, and attempt to give them some idea of what it meant to have the Holy One in their midst. One of the Seraphim had touched his lips with a burning coal so that he might be able to speak that word of God with pure lips. In the same way a fire would emanate from the God of Zion to purify his people.

Wherever this God turns to man, there he wants to find brotherhood; he hates every form of separation among men. That is why their very injustice is a sin against him: every injustice, oppression, coercion, every shedding of innocent blood and all the wealth and luxury acquired in that way. But the real root of all that selfishness, according to Isaiah, is the attempt of man to make himself

the center of his every thought, desire and activity and to use all
the rest, including his fellow men, for himself. Israel as a nation
did this when it became oblivious of its communion with Yahweh
and in times of danger began to look for help from other nations
and thus (in the ancient world) from their gods.

Shortly after Isaiah's calling, King Ahaz committed this very
crime. In so doing he was the occasion which brought the prophet
to appear in public probably for the first time. It is not without
reason that the book of Isaiah places the report of the prophet's
dramatic meeting with the king (chapter 7) immediately after that
of his calling (6), for this meeting determined his subsequent
preaching. More than others, Ahaz should have realized what
Yahweh's living on Mount Zion meant. From the very beginning
the perpetuation of the Davidic dynasty was connected with Yahweh's dwelling there (2 Sam. 7). Did not the houses of Yahweh
and his anointed on Mount Zion form one architectural unity?
Ahaz did not take this seriously, for when the "house of David"
learned that the armies of Israel and Damascus were marching on
Jerusalem in order to put a king of their own choice on the throne,
". . . the heart of the king and the hearts of the people shuddered
as the trees of the forest shudder in front of the wind" (7, 2). The
prophet assured the king that the plan could not succeed: "It shall
not come true; it shall not be" (7, 7).

But a people, a king, who enjoyed such a relationship with the
Holy One could only go on existing if they entrusted their lot to
him and did not expect salvation from their own human policies.
The prophet expressed this in the famous play on words of 7, 9.
He placed two forms of the stem *amn* (cf. "Amen" of our liturgy!)
opposite each other, "firm, faithful." One might translate it
approximately as follows: "If you do not seek your strength in me,
you will not be strong." *The Jerusalem Bible* renders it very well:
"But if you do not stand by me, you will not stand at all."

Nevertheless, Ahaz thought it safer to call on the Assyrians for
help, asking them to put the two invaders to flight. Thus he did not
seek his strength in God. He did not "believe." In that way he
failed to treat Yahweh as his God and the God of the people he
represented. Therefore the prophet expressly speaks in 7, 13 of
"my God," for Yahweh is no longer the God of Ahaz and his
people.

Then Isaiah announced a destructive invasion by the same

Assyrians from whom Ahaz had hoped for help. Yahweh, the God of that little Mount Zion, would summon their immense armies to Judah as a beekeeper whistles for his bees (7, 18). With the razor hired from across the Euphrates, he would shave the land of Judah, cutting off all its pride and glory: orchards, trees and plants, everything they had worked so many years to produce. Only a few men would survive, living on "milk and honey," products of the uncultivated land—for the faithful, gifts of Yahweh (7, 21-22). Those few would be rescued because they sought their strength in Yahweh—that is, they had "believed" (10, 20). Their faith in the nearness of Yahweh found expression in the motto: "God is with us" (8, 10). The "house of David" would be punished with destruction together with the land and people. Only a stump would remain, not bearing the name of the glorious David, but of his unknown father (11, 1). From this stump would spring forth the new David who had been expected from of old.

But Isaiah made him into a sign for Ahaz by predicting that he would feed on milk and honey like the remnant of the "faithful" and as their representative would bear the name "God with us," Emmanuel (7, 14-15). Empty of egoism and selfishness, he could be completely filled with the spirit of Yahweh (11, 1-3). His power would not be taken by force. It would be his from birth; as a child, dominion would be placed upon his shoulders, and he would receive the most august titles that could be found for the vicar of the Holy One (9, 5). However, he would not receive the title of "king," for Isaiah reserved that for Yahweh alone.

The above was an attempt to see Isaiah's words about the Messiah and the faithful "remnant" (that spiritual edifice with the Messiah as cornerstone, according to 28, 16) in their context—namely, his fundamental experience of the Holy One living in Zion. We meet this in all his authentic words: the overwhelming notion of the holy God who transcends everything and yet is so near. His divine majesty cannot endure an attitude which encroaches upon his glory by seeking support in one's own measures, power and achievements. In 2, 12-17 the prophet summarizes a list of human achievements as well as a number of symbols used for them. Yahweh cannot but oppose all of this, and will do so on his "day" which will inevitably come: "Yahweh alone will be exalted on that day!" And so everybody and everything that casts a shadow on God's majesty is doomed to destruction, whether that be the proud "daughters of Zion" (3, 16—4, 1) or the powerful armies of Assyria. The Assyrian kings were only summoned by Yahweh as an instrument of chastisement for Israel. But they carried that order too far. Therefore Yahweh will punish them, too, for their pride (10, 5-19):

> Does the axe claim more credit than the man who wields it,
> or the saw more strength than the man who handles it?
> It would be like the cudgel controlling the man who raises it,
> or the club moving what is not made of wood!

Not only Assyria will be destroyed by Yahweh for its pride (cf. also 10, 24-27; 14, 24-27; 30, 27-33; 31, 8-9). He will likewise punish the Egyptians together with the Judeans who sought military help from their famous chariots instead of looking to the Holy One of Israel (30, 1-5; 31, 1-3). The only correct attitude toward the Holy One who lives on Mount Zion is to renounce all security apart from him and to place complete trust in the silent presence of the heavenly ruler on Zion for whom the tranquil "waters of Shiloah" are a striking symbol (8, 6). Thus spoke Yahweh (30, 15):

> Your salvation lay in conversion and tranquillity,
> your strength, in complete trust.

Perhaps Isaiah already sees the relation between this spiritual attitude and the "poverty of spirit" where he, at the end of his words to the legates of the Philistines, says (14, 32):

> Yahweh has laid the foundations of Zion,
> and there the poor of his people shall find refuge.

Whoever makes such a repeated and urgent appeal to a personal surrender of conscience in a society permeated by self-sufficiency could expect only mockery and opposition (cf. 28, 9. 14; 30, 11). God's call proclaimed by the prophet penetrated but a few hearts.

The mass of the people and their leaders rejected it stubbornly. This effect of Isaiah's preaching is described as follows in 6, 9-10:

> He said: Go, and say to this people,
> "Hear and hear again, but do not understand;
> see and see again, but do not perceive."
> Make the heart of this people gross,
> its ears dull;
> shut its eyes,
> so that it will not see with its eye,
> hear with its ears,
> understand with its heart,
> and be converted and healed.

Here the prophet seems to receive the express task to harden "this people," and therefore the task to render the people of Judah "obdurate." All four evangelists quote something of the last verses of this text in reference to Jesus' life (Mt. 13, 13-15; Mk. 4, 12; Lk. 8, 10; Jn. 12, 40). There, too, they refer to the obscure mystery of the human heart which possesses the terrible possibility to reject the good it sees. That God would send someone to harden men in this choice seems to be a biblical way of conceiving things.

We will try to illustrate this as follows, with our apologies if it all sounds too ordinary. Imagine a group of people who coolly and out of thoughtless routine are doing evil and are not concerned about it. When someone comes along and denounces them, they are confronted with a choice. A *crisis* is created, a parting of the ways. Those who afterward continue doing wrong therefore do so *more consciously,* on the basis of a clear decision. This is apparently the inevitable effect of "prophetic" preaching among us men such as we are with those mysterious possibilities in our heart.

The prophet, unlike the Greeks with their precise distinctions, saw the negative result, so to speak, of his divinely ordered activity as being part of God's intention. He was sent to bring about the above-mentioned crisis and therefore to be the occasion for a number of people to *more consciously* turn away from the good. Of course, no one in that world spoke of "the good" as the Greeks would, but rather of the concrete wishes of Yahweh. That which was rejected, therefore, was not an ideal or a norm; it was the Lord himself.

Isaiah likewise brought others to a more conscious acceptance of Yahweh. His preaching called to life the "remnant" we spoke about above. It consisted of those who, to put it in modern terms, chose faith above "religion." All the prophets, each in his own way, have confronted men with this choice. But in the case of Isaiah, that is clearer than for the others, not only because he acted in situations actually involving a question of existence or non-existence, but also because he was privileged to see the heart of the matter very clearly and to be able to describe it in undying words. For that reason he is called both "the prophet of God's nearness" and "the prophet of faith."

Micah

Even if the book of the Twelve did not include a collection attributed to the prophet Micah of Moresheth, we would still know that he was preaching in Judah as a contemporary of Isaiah. In the book of Jeremiah Baruch relates that his master was once preaching in the temple shortly after 609 B.C. and was arrested. They wanted to put him to death for announcing the destruction of the city and the temple. Then several men from among "the elders of the land"—that is, the highly respected citizens, mostly the heads of older families—brought something forward which had occurred nearly a century previous. They said (Jer. 26, 18-19):

Micah of Moresheth, who prophesied in the days of Hezekiah king of Judah, had this to say to all the people of Judah, "Yahweh says this: 'Zion will become ploughland, Jerusalem a heap of rubble, and the mountain of the temple a wooded height.' " Did Hezekiah king of Judah and all of Judah put him to death for this? Did they not rather, fearing Yahweh, entreat his favor, to make him relent and not bring the disaster on them which he had pronounced against them? Are we now to burden our souls with such a crime?

This Micah was apparently an undaunted man, a fact confirmed by the other words we know to be his, for they have come down to us in the collection bearing his name. He was born and bred in the gently rolling hill country which separates the Philistine coastal plain from the high Judean mountains, called *shephélah* by the inhabitants—that is, the "lowland" or "netherland." In those simple farming surroundings, the old traditions of the Yahwistic religion still lived on, whereas in the large cities they were often crowded out by Canaanitic ideas and customs. There, too, lived the landowners who exploited the farmers of the "lowland," the judges who accepted the bribes of the rich, and the prophets and priests who gave official approbation to all such acts, calling crooked straight and evil good. Micah was far more touched by the social abuses which embittered the lives of so many farmers and country folk than he was interested in the major foreign affairs occupying most of the inhabitants of the two capitals—Samaria, whose destruction he experienced, and especially Jerusalem, the residence of Yahweh. With a straightforward and sharp manner which makes one think of Amos, Micah reproached the leading classes for their crimes, so completely incompatible with the nearness of Yahweh in his temple and with the confessions and prayers uttered there.

In chapters 1—3 those who collected his sayings have put a number of those reproaches and threats together. After his diatribe against the false prophets and his proud witness to his own conviction of having been called (already cited on pp. 161f.), this concluding accusation of the leaders of Judah, addressed here by the ancient sacred names of Jacob and Israel, follows (3, 9-11):

> Now listen to this, you princes of the house of Jacob,
> rulers of the house of Israel,
> you who loathe justice
> and pervert all that is right,
> you who build Zion with blood,
> Jerusalem with crime.
> Her princes pronounce their verdict for bribes,
> her priests take a fee for their rulings,
> her prophets make divinations for money.
> And yet they rely on Yahweh. They say,
> "Is not Yahweh in our midst?
> No evil is going to overtake us."

Micah answered this slogan with that word about Jerusalem's destruction (3, 12) which a century later was still alive in the memory of Jerusalem's elders. It is understandable that those who gathered these sayings together, during or after the exile, attempted to mitigate the effect of that cry of doom by placing an imposing vision of Zion's future immediately after it (4, 1-5). That encouraging text

was dear to other prophets' disciples as well, for it was also incorporated in the book of Isaiah (2, 2-4). All peoples will one day
come to Zion to learn from Yahweh how they are to live together.
Such will be the result of this loyal acceptance of Yahweh's will:

> They will hammer their swords into ploughshares,
> their spears into sickles.
> Nation will not lift sword against nation,
> there will be no more training for war.

That is quite different from a Zion which a small group builds for
itself on broken promises and bloodshed!

Among the promises which follow, mention should be made of
that word to Bethlehem, too small to be reckoned among the clans
of Judah and yet destined by Yahweh to bring forth his ruler
whose origin lay in a mysterious distant past (5, 1-3). Those
verses are already well known from their place in the story about
Herod and the magi from the East (Mt. 2, 6).

Equally famous is the verse from the impressive judicial pro-
ceedings between Yahweh and his people, with which the last part
of the collection opens (6, 1-8). After all of creation has been
summoned as a witness in the lawsuit which Yahweh brings
against his people, he begins his accusation with a plea which has
been incorporated into the liturgy of Good Friday, reflecting our
sublime feeling of relationship with the faithful of the Bible:

> My people, what have I done to you,
> how have I been a burden to you? Answer me.

When Israel then asks repentently whether it can atone for its sinful conduct with certain sacrifices and even manifests its readiness
to sacrifice the most precious of possessions, its first-born sons, to
Yahweh, the prophet answers that their search is misguided:

> What is good has been explained to you, man;
> that is what Yahweh asks of you:
> only this, to act justly,
> to love tenderly (*hèsed*)
> and to walk humbly with your God.

Zephaniah

This humble attitude is one of the major themes in the preaching of Zephaniah, the ninth in the list of the Twelve. According to the title of this short collection of sayings, divided into three chapters, he was active "in the reign of Josiah" (ca. 640-609 B.C.). From the content of the authentic sayings we may infer that the first years of that reign were meant, before the king undertook his reform (in 621—cf. p. 98).

The innumerable merchants who lived together in their own quarter of the city were certainly responsible in part for the introduction of all kinds of foreign customs in Jerusalem. Foreign gods and goddesses were worshiped alongside Yahweh. The leaders of the nation and the regents of the young king likewise took part in those idolatrous practices. They, too, became more and more "open-minded," and they relativized Yahweh. Yahweh will find those who, indifferent, no longer seek him, those (1, 12)

> who are stagnating on their lees,
> those who say in their hearts,
> "Yahweh has no power
> for good or for evil."

He will find them on his day, that "Day of Yahweh" known from of old. This theme, already taken up by Amos (5, 18-20) and Isaiah (2, 12-17), appears again here in Zephaniah (1, 15-16), elaborated in words which many Christians will recognize from the *Dies Irae,* the day of wrath, that grandiose medieval poem which has been set to music by so many composers (Cherubini, Mozart, Berlioz, Verdi and others):

> A day of wrath, that day,
> a day of distress and agony,
> a day of ruin and of devastation,
> a day of darkness and gloom,
> a day of cloud and blackness,
> a day of trumpet blast and battle cry
> against fortified town
> and high corner-tower.

Again it is the "faithful" in Isaiah's sense who will survive that terrible Day of Yahweh. In 2, 3 (the conclusion of this first section), Zephaniah calls them "the humble":

> Seek Yahweh,
> all you, the humble of the earth,
> who obey his commands.
> Seek integrity,
> seek humility:
> you may perhaps find shelter
> on the day of the anger of Yahweh.

After a number of oracles about foreign nations, forming the second of the three parts (following a customary outline: cf. p. 178), words addressed to Jerusalem reappear, culminating in a promise of salvation. That rebellious and polluted city, refusing to listen to any prophetic voice, not trusting Yahweh and unwilling to approach its God, will be chastened in the end. It is addressed as a woman (3, 11-12):

> When that day comes,
> you need feel no shame for all the misdeeds
> you have committed against me,
> for I will remove your proud boasters
> from your midst;
> and you will cease to strut
> on my holy mountain.
> In your midst I will leave
> a humble and lowly people,
> and those who are left in Israel
> will seek refuge in the name of Yahweh.

That purified Jerusalem is then invited to exult and rejoice (3, 14. 16-17):

> Rejoice, exult with all your heart,
> daughter of Jerusalem. . . .
> Zion, have no fear. . . .
> Yahweh your God is in your midst,
> a victorious warrior.

For the evangelist Luke, all of this became reality when Mary gave birth to Jesus. It is interesting to note that the Hebrew word translated here as "midst" can also mean the innermost part of the human body, and thus also the womb, as well as the center of a city or country. Likewise, the word "victorious" in Hebrew is almost identical in sound with the name Jesus. Thus it is easy to understand why Luke allows the angel to address Mary with these words from Zephaniah: "Rejoice, so highly favored!" and "Do not be afraid," when he announced to her that she would conceive in her womb the Savior, identical with Yahweh in the prophetic text (Lk. 1, 28-31).

Jeremiah

The title of the book of Jeremiah gives the thirteenth year of King Josiah's reign as the date of the prophet's calling—i.e., about 627 B.C. Reflecting on the few verses in which Jeremiah describes his calling, a modern reader might wonder what could have been the purpose of such a detailed reference to the year it "occurred." In contrast with the overwhelming experience apparently granted to the great Isaiah one day in the temple of Jerusalem, Jeremiah relates a simple conversation between Yahweh and himself. He gives the impression that the two of them had been the closest of friends for many years. It may be that in this particular year in the reign of King Josiah, it was made clear beyond all doubt to the young man from Anathoth that Yahweh had favored him with such intimacy in order to make him his spokesman before the king and people of Judah. This sensitive and somewhat shy descendant of a priestly family did not feel himself equal to the task. But in that year, 627, Yahweh's insistence made itself unmistakably felt. Understanding for what awaited Jeremiah and a firm promise of assistance accompanied the calling, but Yahweh's decision was not to be changed by entreaty!

> So now brace yourself for action.
> Stand up and tell them
> all I command you.
> Do not be dismayed at their presence,
> or in their presence I will make you dismayed.
> I, for my part, today will make you

into a fortified city,
a pillar of iron,
and a wall of bronze
to confront all this land:
the kings of Judah, its princes,
its priests and the country people.
They will fight against you
but shall not overcome you
for I am with you to deliver you—
it is Yahweh who speaks.

This conclusion to the introductory chapter prepares the reader quite well for what follows. Despite its disorder, a consequence of the complicated history of its origin, the book as a whole gives an exceptionally vivid picture of the prophet's experiences after his calling, especially in the last years (after 609) of the kingdom of Judah. In this regard Jeremiah was quite different from Isaiah. The latter's words which have been handed down betray nothing of what was actually going on in his heart. Jeremiah, on the other hand, has a poetic manner of preaching in which his richly varied inner life finds expression. More than anyone else Jeremiah breathed new life, as it were, into the traditional formulas of prayer. We have a good example of this in his conversations with Yahweh which he evidently revealed to his disciples. Thus we know how unbearable it was for him to preach calamity and destruction to the people whom he loved no less than Yahweh did. What a burden it must have been for one who so much liked sharing at a distance the good cheer of people enjoying themselves to see everyone turn against him. In the end he was avoided and hated by rich and poor in Jerusalem and even by his own towns-people. Yet he never succeeded in resisting the impelling presence of God who wanted to speak through him. Jeremiah therefore experienced, more than any of the other Old Testament personali-ties known to us, what it meant to be mediator between a passion-ately loving God and his recalcitrant people. Thus Jeremiah pre-pared the way for Christ, not through descriptions of the coming Messiah, but by his faithful execution of his task as mediator.

It cannot be a coincidence, therefore, that several situations in Jeremiah's life make one think of Jesus of Nazareth. A few indica-tions should suffice to stimulate the reader to take up this extremely rich prophetic book and to read it for himself. First of all, one should notice the dauntlessness with which Jeremiah made the will of Yahweh known to all, showing no partiality or fear. The collection of statements addressed to the kings of Judah (22, 1—23, 8) shows that the prophet without mincing his words announced to those "anointed of Yahweh" their punishment for no longer "knowing" their God, just as Josiah had failed to do before them (22, 16). Jehoiakim learned from the prophet of the extremely shameful end he was to suffer, without the customary lamentations, and, worst of all, without burial (22, 19):

> He will receive the funeral honors of a donkey
> —dragged away and thrown
> out of the gates of Jerusalem.

Likewise, the king's son Jehoiachin, also called Coniah, heard his fate foretold: together with his mother he would be cast out into a foreign land like a broken pot that is no longer wanted (22, 26-28).

The subsequent collection (23, 9-40) reveals that Jeremiah was just as harsh when preaching against the influential cast of *nabis* (23, 15):

> . . . since from the prophets of Jerusalem
> godlessness has spread throughout the land.

Nor were the scribes and teachers of the Law overlooked (8, 8):

> How dare you say: We are wise,
> and we possess the Law of Yahweh?
> But look how it has been falsified
> by the lying pen of the scribes!

It is easy to understand that the inhabitants of the village of Anathoth began to show less and less sympathy for the prophet who was making himself an object of hatred in the capital and thus also bringing discredit upon his birthplace. After all, Jerusalem on the other side of the Mount of Olives was the only market for their agricultural products. And when buyers came by their stands in the market and said, "You are from Anathoth, the place where that

. . . prophet comes from? No, thank you!" then they experienced what damage this idiot was doing to the village community. Why wasn't he married like all other adult Judeans? Why was he so eccentric? Why did he hold himself aloof from the customary social obligations, such as paying condolence and the village feasts (16, 1-9)? Certain men made plans to murder him, but the prophet was warned in time (11, 18-19; 12, 6). Here the Christian will certainly think of the prophet from Nazareth who was mocked for being a "eunuch" (the only background against which Jesus' use of this term in Matthew 19, 12 can be explained), who was held to be insane by his own townspeople (Mk. 3, 21) and dragged to the brow of a hill where they intended to throw him to his death (Lk. 4, 29).

The charge brought against Jeremiah at court for something he said about the temple is likewise deeply meaningful. The prophet attacked the belief that Yahweh's presence in the temple guaranteed of itself the security of the people. Against this reduction of faith to a kind of magic, Jeremiah proclaimed in the name of Yahweh (7, 9-11):

Steal, would you, murder, commit adultery, perjure yourselves, burn incense to Baal, follow alien gods that you do not know?—and then come presenting yourselves in this temple that bears my name, saying: Now we are safe—safe to go on committing all these abominations! Do you take this temple that bears my name for a robbers' den? I, at any rate, am not blind—it is Yahweh who speaks.

And again (26, 6):

I will treat this temple as I treated Shiloh, and make this city a curse for all the nations of the earth.

When Jeremiah was arrested and accused, he said calmly (26, 14-15):

For myself, I am as you see in your hands. Do whatever you please or think is right with me. But be sure of this, that if you put me to death, you will be bringing innocent blood on yourselves, on this city and on its citizens, since Yahweh has truly sent me to you to say all these words in your hearing.

Some distinguished citizens recalled, as we saw above, that in former times the prophet Micah had not been put to death, although he had spoken along the same lines. But their plea was not enough to save Jeremiah. Baruch, the narrator of this scene, implies as much by telling what pains the royal police took to capture alive a certain Uriah, who had spoken the same prophecy as Jeremiah, so that the king could personally order his execution. (This parenthetical allusion by Baruch is the source of all we know about the existence of that prophet-martyr!) Baruch attributes Jeremiah's rescue to the intervention of an influential friend (26, 24).

More than once, Jeremiah felt that he could no longer bear his thankless burden and tried to throw it off. Some well-known texts bear witness to sentiments such as these, or better, to these struggles with God: 18, 19-23; 20, 7-18, and his complaint in 15, 10-18. In response to this last one, Yahweh answers with a rebuke which is followed by an assurance of help and support, almost identical with the last verses of his original calling (15, 19-21; 1, 18). Very poetically the prophet describes a similar encouragement mixed with mild reproach in his rendering of the conversation he had with Yahweh on the occasion of the plot against his life at Anathoth. In this connection the leader should note that in those days lions and panthers still lived among the tropical undergrowth along the Jordan:

> If you find it exhausting to race against men on foot,
> how will you compete against horses?
> If you are not secure in a peaceful country,
> how will you manage in the thickets along the Jordan?

Yahweh expressed himself here in the poetical language of the prophet. The intention of the questions seems to be the following: Are you afraid already? You will have far worse hardships to endure, for the very reason that I count on you!

Yahweh was not let down in his expectations and trust. Jeremiah persevered until the bitter end; this he was made to suffer in the despised land of Egypt some years after the catastrophe of 587. The Christian will have all the more admiration for this prophet when he realizes that he never had the least suspicion of a life after death, an "eternal happiness." We will discuss this extensively further on. Thus, when Ebed-melech, a sympathetic negro slave, once saved the prophet's life and by this courageous deed proved that he trusted in Yahweh, Jeremiah could "at most" promise as his highest reward that the slave would be rescued at the capital's destruction (38, 7-13; 39, 17-18). This most precious of Yahweh's gifts Baruch, too, would receive for his dedicated service to Jeremiah. The words containing this promise he added as a kind of signature to the end of chapter 45, the original conclusion of the book (45, 5):

> I am now going to bring down disaster on all mankind—it is Yahweh who speaks. As for you, I will let you escape with your own life, wherever you may go.

Jeremiah's only reward consisted in the certainty that he was doing the will of his God. Does this mean that he had no expectations for the future? Not for himself personally, but for the people to which he belonged during his lifetime. But his vision of Israel's future was not, like that of Isaiah and so many others, dominated by the radiant figure of an ideal scion of the house of David, a perfect Messianic sovereign. Jeremiah had seen too much of the perversion of the Davidic kings to entertain such a hope. For him who enjoyed such intimate relations with Yahweh and who devoured his words with such pleasure (15, 16), the salvation promised to Israel could consist only in the direct, cordial and unbreakable union of each and every person with Yahweh. Of course, this could be realized only after a complete renovation and re-creation of men's hearts, for more than anyone else Jeremiah had experienced the total depravity of the human heart. All the reforms of an energetic and pious king, all the harsh warnings and all the terrifying threats could not bring the Judeans to a life of justice—that is, to an attitude of loyalty toward Yahweh and each other. The experience of many years of fruitless toil are condensed in the seven Hebrew words of 17, 9:

> Devious / is the heart / more than any other thing /
> it is / perverse! / Who / can know its secrets?

"Devious" (*'aqob*) calls to mind the meaning of Jacob's name, "he deceives" (cf. p. 66). The word for "perverse" (*anush*) is used

for wounds which are "incurable" (15, 18) as well as for a day of
"disaster" (17, 16), but at the same time the Hebrew would
almost inevitably think of the similar sounding word for "man"
(*enosh*) which so characterizes man in his weakness. (We meet
this word in Job 9, 2 and 33, 12 among other places.) One could
hardly speak more concisely about man's sinfulness. Jeremiah
experienced that evil is so deeply rooted in the human heart that
alone man can do nothing to better his situation. He says this very
picturesquely in 13, 23:

> Can the Ethiopian change his skin,
> or the leopard his spots?
> And you, can you do what is right,
> you so accustomed to wrong?

For him the glorious future toward which God will finally lead his
people can only consist in a new Covenant, a relationship with God
in which his will is no longer made known from outside by means
of a declaration of regulations. No, Yahweh will impress his will
and wishes deep in the heart of every man, that center from which
all actions proceed. In this way a new and everlasting intimacy will
come into being between God and his people (31, 31-34). This
text about "the New Covenant" comes to mind at every celebration of the eucharist, and in Hebrews 8, 8-12 it forms the longest
Old Testament quotation in the New Testament. In it we read:

> There will be no further need for neighbor to try to teach
> neighbor, or brother to say to brother, "Learn to know
> Yahweh!" No, they will all know me, the least no less than
> the greatest—it is Yahweh who speaks—since I will forgive
> their iniquity and never call their sin to mind.

IV
FOOD FOR THOUGHT

This kind of first acquaintance with the prophets often brings
the faithful to the realization that "revelation" did not take place
quite as simply as they once might have thought when attending

catechism lessons, as if God audibly communicated a number of truths from heaven which people heard, passed on and wrote down in God's own words. A closer look at the prophetic books makes one realize that God did not really speak to them from outside at all. Rather, one gets the impression that he irresistibly took hold of their consciousness as the all-sovereign personal reality who could demand nothing less than the total surrender of man to him—first of all, that of the prophet himself, but always with an eye to the surrender of all his people. It seems to be this irresistible conviction which forced the prophets to speak. This we refer to as their "calling."

We see that each prophet expressed this concept in his own individual way, determined by his temperament, education and the situation in which he and his people found themselves. That is why there is such a great difference between the preaching of an Isaiah and a Jeremiah, for example. God therefore used many very different kinds of persons to reveal in as many ways as possible the reality of himself and his wishes to his people.

But despite all their differences, the prophets are nevertheless very much related to each other, and not only those who reveal certain similarities of temperament and view of life. One can discern similarities of this latter kind between Hosea and Jeremiah A reflective reading of Jeremiah 2 (especially verses 2-13, 20-25 and 32-35) and parts of chapter 3 (verses 1-5 and 9-13) gives one the impression that Jeremiah must have even been acquainted with certain utterances of Hosea. A similar suspicion arises when comparing the great Isaiah and his predecessor Amos. More important, however, is the relationship they all share because they all represent the same tradition. Within Israel an experience of the divine could only be an experience of Yahweh, as men knew him from the beginning. In the final analysis, it was this tradition which most fundamentally determined their preaching.

We add the following examples by way of illustration. We saw in Isaiah's statement—a witness of faith but absolute foolishness to the outsider—that it was Yahweh, the God of little Zion, who brought the armies of the mighty Assyrian empire in motion and sent them to Judah. He calls that enormous military force a club in Yahweh's hand (e.g., 10, 5). Jeremiah is clearly thinking along the same lines when he speaks of Nebuchadnezzar, the greatest monarch of the new Babylonian empire, as a "servant of Yahweh" who was simply carrying out his orders (27, 6). A further step in the same direction is to be seen in Deutero-Isaiah (cf. p. 166) who even attributes to Cyrus the honored title "anointed of Yahweh"! In the vision of this prophet it is Yahweh, the God of the insignificant little group of Judean exiles, who raised up the powerful Persian world conqueror *for the sake of his people* (Is. 45, 1-4).

However, this line of thinking did not originate with Isaiah. It began with Moses. "Since the days in the land of Egypt" (Hos. 13, 4), Israel's existence was determined by the belief that Yahweh was not, like other gods, a power of nature bound to the rhythm of the seasons and fertility, but that he had the character of a person who surpassed and ruled over all the powers of nature and could likewise exert initiative free of their influence. For this reason he could enter man's own domain, human history. This he had shown by rescuing Israel from slavery in Egypt. After that, Israel believed that everything which happened to it was a revelation of him. And when other nations came within its horizon, Israel believed itself to be the center of that history which Yahweh governed and guided. The roots of what is called "the prophetical interpretation of history" were already firmly planted at the very beginning. That is why historical works, such as that of the Yahwist and the Davidic "court history," could be written even before the appearance of the great prophets.

When the prophets cry out at injustice, violence, exploitation and suppression, they stand in a direct line with Elijah and Nathan, a line likewise having its beginning with Moses. No one doubts any longer that the original versions of Exodus 20 and Deuteronomy 5 date from Israel's beginning. By appealing to this ancient tradition, the prophets are in agreement with the priests who formulated texts like Leviticus 19 and determined the conditions to be fulfilled for entering the temple, as in Psalm 15. One can even say that the prophets, far from being reformers, defended the original, authentic Yahwistic faith in the paganized society of both kingdoms and thus were traditionalists far more than modernists.

At the same time, they enriched that Yahwistic tradition immeasurably by their incomparably penetrating preaching with its rich variety. Thanks to their faithful disciples, that preaching reached the post-exilic community whence it resounded through the ages. In this way the prophetic experience penetrated the every-day piety of the faithful. They learned to understand their own lives as a dialogue with Yahweh whose word, addressed personally to them, they heard in the writings of tradition as well as in everything that happened to them in daily life. A number of psalms bear witness to this as well. And, finally, our study of the gospels will show us very clearly to what a great extent Jesus stood in the line of the prophets.

VI
The Wisdom of the Nations in Israel

We now turn to the group of writings which are sometimes called "the books of wisdom" or "the sapiential books" and sometimes "the didactic books." To this group belong first of all the three major works which stand at the top of the third part of the Hebrew canon—namely the Psalms, Job and Proverbs. Further, it includes the "Wisdom of Sirach" or Ecclesiasticus, of which only the Greek text is extant, and the book of Wisdom, written in Greek at Alexandria in the century prior to Christ's birth. Finally, "the five rolls" are included as well as the Song of Songs and Ecclesiastes.

These books make up almost one-fourth of the Old Testament. Nevertheless, this section of the canon does not demand as detailed an introduction as did the historical and prophetic books. The reason is that its contents correspond more directly to human experience in general, as will already be clear in the following brief outline of our sketch. We will begin by showing that "sapiential literature" was already a phenomenon with a long history in the ancient East when Israel appeared on that scene. Then a concise analysis of the book of Proverbs will lead us to a consideration of the ways this genre developed within Israel. Finally, we will take up a problem which especially occupied the wisdom teachers; this problem eventually led one of them to write the book of Job.

211

I

AN "INTERNATIONAL" PHENOMENON

In the highly cultured nations of the ancient Near East there existed the custom of putting all kinds of rules for a successful and happy life into concise sayings and passing these along to succeeding generations in written form. In anthologies made from the innumerable texts which have been uncovered and deciphered, we find many examples of this kind of literature. We will begin with several illustrative quotations, making grateful use of J. Pritchard's *Ancient Near Eastern Texts Relating to the Old Testament* (Princeton, 1955).

Texts from Egypt

From the instruction of Ptah-hotep, a minister of the 5th dynasty, ca. 2450 B.C.:

> If thou art one of those sitting at the table of one greater than thyself, take what he may give when it is set before thee. Do not pierce him with many stares, for such an aggression against him is an abomination. . . . Let thy face be cast down until he addresses thee, and thou shouldst speak [only] when he addresses thee. Laugh after he laughs, and it will be very pleasing to his heart. . . . If thou desirest to make friendship last in a home to which thou hast access as master, as a brother or as a friend, into any place where thou mightest enter, beware of approaching the women. It does not go well with the place where that is done. (pp. 412-413)

> How good it is when a son accepts what his father says! Thereby maturity comes to him. (p. 414)

From the instruction for King Meri-ka-re written at the end of the 22nd century B.C.:

> More acceptable to the divinity is the character of one upright of heart than the sacrificed ox of the evildoer. . . . (p. 417)

From the instruction of Ani, a father teaching his son, written before the 12th century B.C.:

Double the food which thou givest to thy mother, and carry her as she carried [thee]. She had a heavy load in thee, but she did not leave it to me. Thou wert born after thy months, [but] she was still yoked [with thee, for] her breast was in thy mouth for three years, continuously. Though thy filth was disgusting, [her] heart was not disgusted, saying: "What can I do?" She put thee into school when thou wert taught to write, and she continued on thy behalf every day, with bread and beer in her house.

When thou art a young man and takest to thyself a wife and art settled in thy house, set thy eye on how thy mother gave birth to thee and all [her] bringing thee up as well. Do not let her blame thee, nor may she [have to] raise her hands to the god, nor may he [have to] hear her cries. (pp. 420-421)

And finally we include several quotations from the sapiential book of Amen-em-opet which must have been written somewhere between the 10th and 6th centuries B.C. It consists of an introduction and thirty short chapters. The Roman numerals correspond to the chapters cited.

The beginning of the teaching of life, the testimony for prosperity, all precepts for intercourse with elders, the rules for courtiers, to know how to return an answer to him who said it, and to direct a report to one who has sent him, in order to direct him to the ways of life, to make him prosper upon earth. . . .

(I)
Give thy ears, hear what is said.
Give thy heart to understand them.
To put them in thy heart is worthwhile,
[But] it is damaging to him who neglects them.
Let them rest in the casket of thy belly. . . .

(II)
Guard thyself against robbing the oppressed
And against overbearing the disabled.

Stretch not forth thy hand
Against the approach of an old man. . . .

(VI)
Do not carry off the landmark
At the boundaries of the arable land,
Nor disturb the position of the measuring-cord;
Be not greedy after a cubit of land,
Nor encroach upon the boundaries of a widow. . . .

(VII)
If riches are brought to thee by robbery,
They will not spend the night with thee. . . .
They have made themselves wings like geese
And are flown away to the heavens.

(IX)
Do not associate to thyself the heated man,
Nor visit him for conversation. . . .
Thou shouldst discuss an answer
[Only] with a man of thy own size,
And guard thyself against plunging headlong into it.
Swifter is speech when the heart is hurt. . . .

(XI)
Be not greedy for the property of a poor man,
Nor hungry for his bread.
As for the property of a poor man,
It [is] a blocking to the throat,
It makes a vomiting to the gullet.

(XXI)
Empty not thy belly to everybody,
Nor damage [thus] the regard for thee. . . .
Nor associate to thyself one [too] outgoing of heart.
Better is a man whose talk [remains] in his belly
Than he who speaks it out injuriously.

(XXV)
Do not laugh at a blind man nor tease a dwarf
Nor injure the affairs of the lame.
Do not tease a man who is in the hand of the god,
Nor be fierce of face against him if he errs.

For man is clay and straw,
And the god is his builder.

(XXX)
See thou these thirty chapters:
They entertain; they instruct;
They are the foremost of all books;
They make the ignorant to know. . . .
Fill thyself with them; put them in thy heart,
And be a man who can interpret them. . . .
As for the scribe who is experienced in his office,
He will find himself worthy [to be] a courtier. (pp. 421-424)

Texts from Mesopotamia

Many collections of proverbs and wise counsels have been found
in Mesopotamia. Here are a few examples:

As long as a man does not exert himself,
He will gain nothing.
Whosoever has neither king nor queen,
Who is then his lord?

Do you strike the face of a walking ox with a strap?
Friendship is of a day, slavery is perpetual.

Where servants are, there is quarrel.
Where cosmeticians are, there is slander.

Hasten not to stand in a public assembly,
Seek not the place of quarrel;
For in a quarrel you must give a decision,
And you will be forced to be their witness.

Give food to eat, give date wine to drink;
The one begging for alms, honor, clothe:
Over this his god rejoices.
This is pleasing unto the god Shamash,
He rewards it with good.

Do not slander, speak what is fine.
Speak no evil, tell what is good.

Whoever slanders [or] speaks evil,
As a retribution to the god,
Shamash will pursue after his head. (pp. 425-427)

A great number of such proverbs and counsels are also to be found in the famous story of Ahikar, chancellor of Sennacherib at the Assyrian court, who relates his own experiences. He had no son of his own and adopted his nephew Nadin. In the story he mentions the many lessons which he gave him in the form of proverbs. Despite these, Nadin betrayed his benefactor in a very cowardly manner; Ahikar could barely escape with his life. According to the story, by giving a sample of his exceptional wisdom, he was restored to honor and thus again had plenty of chance to give instruction. Many versions of this very popular story were already in circulation (cf. p. 153) before excavators found parts of the original Aramaic text in 1906 on the island Elephantine in the Nile near Aswan. Several examples of Ahikar's proverbs follow:

Two things are meet, and the third pleasing to Shamash: one who drinks wine and gives it to drink, one who guards wisdom, and one who hears a word and does not tell. Behold, that is dear to Shamash.

More than all watchfulness watch thy mouth, and over what thou hearest harden thy heart. For a word is a bird; once released, no man can recapture it.

The bear went to the lambs. "Give me one of you and I will be content." The lambs answered and said to him, "Take whichever thou wilt of us. We are thy lambs." Truly, 'tis not in the power of men to lift up their feet or to put them down without the gods. Truly, 'tis not in thy power to lift up thy foot or put it down.

A High Standard of Morality

When reading texts such as those just quoted, it should be remembered first of all that for many centuries this kind of literature was accessible only to relatively small groups of people. Prior to the use of the alphabet in the ancient East, the art of writing was extremely complicated, cuneiform in Mesopotamia and hieroglyph-ics in Egypt. If someone in the Nile region or in Babylon or As-syria wanted to take up a career, he had to train himself for years in the art of reading and writing. That took place at schools which were primarily intended for future government officials. Only those who could read and write were eligible for a priestly function or an administrative position in the national government. In order to give the students some practice in writing, they were obliged to copy those "classical" books of wisdom with all their rules of conduct necessary to achieve honor and respect in society. In this way they killed two birds with one stone! It is only because of the home-work tablets of those students that we are now in possession of many of the extant Egyptian wisdom books and fragments. How-ever, they are sometimes filled with mistakes which give the modern Egyptologist a headache and often obscure the text to such an extent that certain translation is impossible.

This wisdom instruction was orientated, therefore, toward suc-cess in society. How does one gain esteem and influence among one's fellow men? How does one find favor with men of impor-tance? How does one build a successful career? Hence the stress on such virtues as reliability, benevolence and self-control. In Egypt silence was particularly recommended. The "heated one," the hot-tempered person who did not keep his passions and his tongue under control, was bound to fail. Success was only for the "cool man"—that is, the calm, reserved person, often called "the silent one," who never lost his head, who knew how to hide his emotions and never allowed an inconsiderate or rash word to pass his lips. The Christian may be inclined to look with a certain amount of disdain at rules of conduct and counsels which seem only to be concerned with success in society. But he must not forget that man is essentially a social being and that his moral perfection should be measured principally by his conduct toward his fellow men. The reader was surely impressed with the high moral conviction ex-pressed in the quotations above.

To strengthen this impression even more, may I conclude by recalling the famous texts from the so-called "Book of the Dead." Citations from this book were buried with the deceased in Egyp-tian graves. Among them were texts like the following (cf. Prit-chard, p. 34) which the deceased could recite when he stood before the heavenly judge (a sort of "negative confession"):

I have not committed evil against men.
I have not done violence to a poor man.
I have not done that which the gods abominate.
I have not defamed a slave to his superior.
I have not made anyone sick.
I have not made anyone weep.
I have not killed.
I have given no order to a killer.
I have not caused anyone suffering.
I have not had sexual relations with a boy.
I have not defiled myself.
I have not diminished the *aroura* [a measure of land area].
I have not added to the weight of the balance.
I have not taken milk from the mouths of children. . . .

One final observation. Although every Egyptian worshiped various gods, many of the wisdom texts speak of "the god," without mentioning any divine proper name. Some scholars have inferred from this that already in the period of the old kingdom (2850-2050 B.C.) the Egyptian sages were "monotheists in practice." That is to say, in questions of morality and conscience they recognized only one supreme judge who knew all their actions and to whom every person was responsible.

II
THE PRACTICE OF "WISDOM" IN ISRAEL

When treating prophetism we saw how a general ancient Eastern phenomenon gradually took a particular form in Israel. Something similar—though only remotely—took place with the wisdom literature. Before sketching that historical development in broad lines, we will mention several collections which make up the book of Proverbs. This will then be a point of reference for our sketch.

The Nine Sections of Proverbs

In the book of Proverbs nine parts can be distinguished, seven of which begin with a title. In the old Greek translations the sequence is somewhat different, and here and there other proverbs have been added. One can infer from this that the various collections first existed independently; it was only relatively late that their text became so "canonical" that no further changes could be made. In the following outline the titles are printed in italics.

I (1—9): *The proverbs of Solomon, son of David, king of Israel.* The title actually continues until verse 6 and shows that the "learning and wisdom" offered here are particularly concerned with one's conduct in daily life. Then, without any clearly logical order, warnings and counsels follow, some long and some short; they are often addressed to "my son" or "my sons." In several places wisdom is personified as a woman who preaches in public as a kind of prophet and bears witness to her intimacy with the creator in a famous poem (8, 22-31). Her pressing admonition stands in opposition to the shameless temptations of another woman called "Dame Folly."

II (10, 1—22, 16): *The proverbs of Solomon.* Under this title 375 short sayings are brought together, without a clear logical sequence. Each one consists of two complementary or contradictory half-verses. They do not give encouragement or admonitions, but for the most part state quite simply how life is for men and women, parents and children, rich and poor, the lazy and the industrious, kings and slaves, depending whether their conduct is wise or foolish. The background seems to be that of a society of farmers, city folk and merchants who are subject to the authority of a king.

III (22, 17—24, 22): *Sayings of the sages.* This section is clearly a supplement to the previous one, especially when the expression used as a title is seen as part of the first sentence ("Give ear and listen to the sayings of the sages," according to the Hebrew text). One notices the difference between II and III immediately: here nearly all the individual proverbs are longer, and furthermore most of them are in the imperative mood.

IV (24, 23-24): *The following are also taken from the sages.* This is obviously a second supplement, differing little in form from the previous one.

V (25—29): *The following also are proverbs of Solomon transcribed by the men of Hezekiah, king of Judah.* This collection consists of 128 sayings, generally consisting of two half-verses, and is quite similar to II, with which it has several proverbs in common.

VI (30, 1-14): *The sayings of Agur, son of Jakeh.* Following this last proper name there is a word which can be translated by "oracle" or regarded as a reference to the Arabian tribe "Massa" (mentioned in Genesis 25, 14). Besides the sighs, rhetorical questions and prayers, there are a few loose sayings which were the occasion for including this section among a collection of proverbs. The conclusion (11-14) has the nature of a summary and introduces the following appendix.

VII (30, 13-33): No title. Most of these sayings have the form of so-called "numerical proverbs." We already saw this form in Amos (cf. p. 187) and also in the first example from Ahikar's collection. Perhaps it had its origin from the riddle, "Name four things which. . . ."

VIII (31, 1-9): *The sayings of Lemuel, king of Massa, taught him by his mother.* These are some counsels for an oriental prince. Here the reference to the Arabian tribe is without question.

IX (31, 10-31): No title. This poem on the perfect wife is "alphabetical": each of the 22 verses begins with a consecutive letter of the Hebrew alphabet. Monsignor Knox illustrates this very clearly in his version:

> *A* man who has found a vigorous wife. . . .
> *B*ound to her in loving confidence. . . .
> *C*ontent, not sorrow, she will bring him. . . .
> *D*oes she not busy herself with wool and thread?

A complete rendering is of course impossible, the simplest reason being that the Hebrew alphabet only has 22 letters. This form was probably chosen to connect a number of loose sayings. At the same time, it suggests the idea of completeness and facilitates remembering the sayings. One also finds similar alphabetical poems in the book of Psalms (25, 34, 111, 112 and 145; cf. also 119 where each consecutive eight verses begin with the same letter) and in Lamentations (the fifth follows this form only in maintaining the *number* of verses—22!).

"Wisdom" and the Monarchy

In the story of the judge Gideon we are told that he asked a young man from the city of Succoth, in the Jordan valley, to write

down the names of its chief citizens. There were 77. The storyteller takes it for granted, therefore, that in those days, long before
David's time, the ordinary citizen could read and write.

That was not completely improbable. Above we spoke about the
complex character of the writing systems which were developed in
Mesopotamia and Egypt. The inhabitants of "Canaan," the coastal
region joining those two ancient cultures and thought to have had
contacts across the sea in Crete, put an end to the confusion by
their development of alphabetical writing (only one symbol for
each individual sound). The oldest known data on this go back to
about 1500 B.C. Several centuries later we see the Phoenicians
with their alphabet of 22 letters which neighboring nations either
took over in its entirety, as did Israel, or adapted to fit their own
language, as the Greeks did. Among the tremendous results of this
ingenious discovery belongs what we might call the "democratiz-
ing" of the art of writing. This could no longer remain the prerogative of one class.

What the Gideon story relates about the young man is therefore
not historically impossible. Yet, we can hardly expect written literature—or, better, a real literary tradition—in Israel until David
organized the tribes of farmers into a kingdom. An ordered government, the enactment of laws and measures from a central point,
censuses necessary for taxation and recruiting an army, officials'
credentials, negotiations and agreements with other nations—all
this kind of thing supposed exercise of the art of writing by a
growing number of Israelites. Many of those were directly in the
service of the king and came into contact with foreigners and their
literary interests at court.

But legates were not the only foreigners at court. From the lists
of high officials which have come down to us in 2 Samuel 8, 16-18
(cf. 20, 23-26) and in 1 Kings 4, 1-6, as well as from other
details, historians have determined that David modeled his young
kingdom along foreign lines, especially Egyptian, and that important posts were even filled by foreigners. Biblical authors and copyists were apparently at a loss to render the strange name of David's
chief scribe. In the present text he appears as Sheva, Shavsha,
Shisha and Seraiah! His eldest son held a high office under Solomon; his name was Elihoreph, or, according to the Greek text, Eli-
haph. "Eli" means "my god," and the second part of the name
refers to an Egyptian god, probably Apis. In this way, that father

who made his career in Jerusalem gave his son a name showing that he had been entrusted to an Egyptian god: "My god is Apis." Even in Isaiah's day, Shebna, a high official in Jerusalem, thought he had to behave in Egyptian fashion by driving horses and chariots, and he prepared his own tomb with typical Egyptian care (Is. 22, 15-19).

It is no wonder that the first flourishing period of Israelite literature occurs under David and Solomon and in the years immediately following. As we frequently see in history, the first period produced works which were never to be surpassed. We have already spoken about the "court history of David" and mentioned the work of the "Yahwist." In the light of the preceding, one can perhaps better understand the suggestion of some that a remarkable piece of Yahwistic history, the "novel" about Joseph and his brothers (Gn. 37—50), had its origin in the literary circles of Solomon's Jerusalem. It is certain that the "wisdom" which the clever Joseph so clearly exhibits was a matter of practice at the Judean court in the same way as in the official circles of Egypt. That King Solomon himself took a leading role in this certainly has historical roots, although we must admit that the stories of 1 Kings 2—4 reveal many legendary tendencies.

Likewise, in the following centuries, wisdom literature would continue to flourish in official circles. You will recall the patronage attributed to King Hezekiah in section V of Proverbs (25, 1). Jeremiah mentions "sages" in addition to the groups or classes of prophets and priests. They were apparently officials who "gave advice" (18, 18; cf. p. 202). In another place he seems to use the term "wise men" to mean those priests who explain the written "Law of Yahweh" (8, 8).

To a certain extent it is understandable that a tension existed between the real prophets and the teachers of "wisdom." As we have already observed, we are dealing here with an international phenomenon, something that was not specific to Israel. The modern Christian might think of it as "humanistic." Curiously enough, nowhere in the court history of David does a miracle or an explicit confession of faith take place. On this point it agrees with the story of Joseph. Not even something as fundamental as the exodus from Egypt is mentioned anywhere in the entire book of Proverbs, which reflects the oldest wisdom tradition. There is no mention of the Covenant, nor do we find in these innumerable

practical rules of conduct any reference to the laws and commandments as the revealed will of Yahweh. Not one word is devoted to
things which, after all, did belong to the core of the Yahwistic
faith, such as the Promised Land, the temple on Zion, the Davidic
promises, etc.

On the other hand, the older biblical historians took it for
granted that this wisdom was something common to all men. They
speak simply of the wisdom of the Egyptians and of that of the
Arabians, "the sons of the East" (1 Kgs. 5, 10 or 4, 30; cf. the
titles of sections VI and VIII of Proverbs). The book of Jeremiah
mentions the wisdom of the Edomites (e.g., 49, 7). The author of
the book of Job situates both the hero and his friends in a milieu
east of Palestine; they do not belong to the people of Israel.

Evident Relationship with Foreign Works

It is not surprising, therefore, that someone who is well acquainted with the sapiential literature of the Bible will frequently come across more or less close parallels when reading
non-biblical texts of the same genre. There is rarely if ever a question of direct dependence, in the sense of a biblical saying being a
translation of the Egyptian or Babylonian courterpart under consideration. It is rather that both the biblical texts handed down to
us and the foreign texts which excavation has brought to light represent or reflect a very broad and varied common inheritance.

The sapiential instruction of Amen-em-opet is perhaps an exception. We cited this book extensively above in order to give the
reader the opportunity to compare those texts with the first half
of Proverbs, section III (22, 17—23, 11). He will notice that
almost all these biblical sayings have a parallel in the citations
from Amen-em-opet. There are, however, curious variations. In
23, 5 for example the (Egyptian) geese are replaced by the (Palestinian) eagle! Precisely where this relationship lies is another
question and one that has elicited many different answers. The
author of the biblical text may have known the Egyptian book, or
at least a particular version of it, since different versions of the
texts were in circulation. Or, the same original may have served as
a model for both texts. Someone has even proposed that the Egyptian writer was in possession of the text of the book of Proverbs.

Especially striking is the case of Proverbs 22, 20. Until the publication of the book of Amen-em-opet in 1923 (the papyrus had already been in the British Museum for many years!) one word of this verse had remained a puzzle. In the following translation we will transcribe the consonants of the word (there are no vowels in the Hebrew alphabet):

> Have I not written for you *sh-l-sh-m*
> of advice and knowledge?

The root meaning of *sh-l-sh* is "three." There is a word pronounced *shilshom* which means "the day before yesterday." Many modern commentators take this in the wider sense of "earlier," though not without hesitation.

> Have I not written you earlier
> of advice and knowledge?

This could then refer to an instruction given previously to a disciple who was being addressed again here. Yet this does not fit in well in the total context.

That interpretation was at any rate more probable than the one then offered by famous Jewish commentators, who read *shalishim*, the plural of *shalish,* "third." In ancient Hebrew this word, probably via "the third man on a chariot," referred to an "officer," a high position at court held by distinguished citizens and the nobility. In our text it would have to be used figuratively, therefore, in the sense of "noble, excellent sayings." The oldest Greek translators, followed by the Latin, rendered the word as "three times." But they created this possibility themselves by putting the whole sentence in the imperative mood: "Write them three times for yourself!"

The text from Amen-em-opet's book offered a new solution, probably the correct one. *Sh-l-sh-m* can also be pronounced *sheloshim,* a sort of plural of "three" meaning "thirty." The Jewish author apparently knew the number of chapters into which Amen-em-opet had divided his instruction. This number could have been traditional in Egypt. Although there may be different opinions as to how section III (22, 17—23, 11) is to be divided into thirty proverbs, the text meant to say:

> Have I not written for you thirty [instructions]
> of advice and knowledge?

Broad Lines of Development

Of the many works written during the reigns of David and Solomon and in the subsequent years in both kingdoms, almost everything has been forever lost. The Bible preserves only a few fragments of the national literature which in 721 and 586 B.C. perished with the two kingdoms. With it almost all data about the milieu, the social position and the mentality of those involved in literary activity likewise perished. Therefore, not much can be said concretely about the background of the fragments of sapiential literature which have come down to us from the time of the kings. As was explained above, no information at all is available for the life of the Jewish community during the centuries after Ezra and Nehemiah. Thus, when we attempt a sketch of the evolution in the area of sapiential literature, it is obvious that we can only do so in broad lines.

In the highly differentiated society of the period of the monarchy, it was evidently possible that certain circles showed a preference for a "humanistically" orientated experience of faith in Yahweh, while a very different mentality characterized the prophets and their followers, and still other elements of the tradition were cultivated by the priests and all those connected with worship. The destruction of Judah as a nation undoubtedly put an end to this pluriformity of mentalities and their literary expressions. During the exile a deeply religious group came into being. It returned to Jerusalem with the ideal of establishing there a real theocratic community. That ideal, a source of inspiration to all, did not admit much variety in religious experience for quite some time. It could hardly be otherwise for a group of people, all of whom left the same milieu in Babylon with the same goal in mind. It was to be expected that the literary forms of expression would be influenced by the new situation. The old forms of wisdom literature would be used to communicate religious inspiration. It is partly for that reason that they would no longer be distinguished so strictly from the forms which in the past had been more exclusively connected either with prophetic sayings or with liturgical expressions.

The development might be described succinctly as follows: in regard to the *contents,* sapiential literature evolved from what is generally human to something more specifically Israelite and

Jewish; in regard to *form,* it evolved from short and terse sayings to longer explanations of an admonitory or reflective character. In this framework we can situate the most important of the biblical wisdom books.

1. *Proverbs II and V.* The greater part of the short sayings in sections II and V of the book of Proverbs were collected *before the exile.* They reflect something of the variegated society of the monarchy. It is taken for granted that Yahweh sees and knows everything, the false weights on the scales as well as what takes place in the hearts of men. In the end he is the one from whom the just receive their "blessing," prosperity and happiness, and the wicked their punishment in the form of disappointments and an early death.

These sayings are almost all declarative. In section II there are but six or seven in the imperative mood, and only in one of those do we hear the address, "my son" (19, 27). Section V as a whole seems to be of more recent date. There are fourteen sayings in the imperative, one of which is addressed to "my son" (27, 11); furthermore, one notices the tendency to group sayings together according to subject and also to expand them (e.g., 27, 23-27). The mention of "Hezekiah" in the title (25, 1) does not exclude the possibility of later proverbs having been inserted here and there. This kind of collection lent itself better to this than any other text. For example, from its content and especially its choice of words, 28, 13 seems to be a post-exilic saying:

He who conceals his thoughts will not prosper,
he who confesses and renounces them will find mercy.

It goes without saying that translators of the book of Proverbs, especially in these two sections, were sometimes confronted with insoluble difficulties. Both the proverbs written by the "lettered" in the circles of courtiers and officials (or sometimes "discovered," just as a witty play on words "comes" to a person) and the striking words of wisdom circulating among the people contained in their terse style, sometimes resplendent with rhymes and alliterations, all kinds of associations and references which are no longer clear to us, nor will they ever be again. Thus one should not be surprised to see a certain proverb in one translation completely different from its rendering in another version. I recall a French translation which in a few places gives only the verse number and then a series of dots, with a footnote listing the "possible meanings"!

The Bible reader who finds this astonishing should think of the many English words and expressions, whose original meanings few people still remember. A well-known anecdote told of King George I of England and the architect of St. Paul's Cathedral in London, Sir Christopher Wren, provides us with a good illustration of how words change their meanings. Upon the completion of the impressive masterpiece, the king told Sir Christopher that his church was "artificial, amusing and awful." Wren was highly flattered by the compliment, for in the early 18th century *artificial* still meant *artistic, amusing* meant *amazing* and *awful* meant *awe-inspiring*. Likewise, how many of us are still aware that the word "teetotaler" really has nothing at all to do with drinking tea, but had its origin in the emphatic form *T-total,* applied to total abstinence from intoxicating drinks? Projecting this situation into the future, we can imagine the difficulty an archeologist in the year 4000 A.D., for example, might have deciphering the familiar American slogan against leaving rubbish in public places, "Every litter bit hurts."

2. *Proverbs I.* Many scholars believe that the final edition of Proverbs 1—9 dates from *after the exile,* about the *end of the 5th century.* When one reads this section after II and V, the differences are immediately noticeable. Here the short statements have almost entirely given way to longer admonitions and descriptions, although here, too, no clear sequence has been followed. Where they are addressed to "my son" (15 times) or "sons"—i.e., children—(4 times), we imagine a wise and experienced man speaking to his disciples. However, in several of those places it is Wisdom herself personally issuing the admonitions. In 1, 20-33 we already see her delivering a sort of sermon in the streets and squares. She says that she will "pour out her heart" to those who turn to her, but threatens those who mock her. When they are in anxiety,

> ... they shall call to me, but I will not answer,
> they shall seek me eagerly and shall not find me.

In prophetic texts it is God who speaks thus to the people. In her famous address—8, 4-36—Wisdom does indeed seem to be very close to Yahweh; as his first creature, she was by his side when he created the world and was deeply interested even then in the happiness of man.

After the pressing invitations of Lady Wisdom to walk the straight road leading to life, the section ends with several verses summarizing the temptations of "Dame Folly." Whoever follows her, the last verse warns, should know that he is heading directly for the realm of the dead (9, 18). This temptress has much in common with the "alien woman" who was the subject of warnings in previous chapters. Association with her likewise led to death according to 2, 16-19. In chapters 5 and 6 she seems first to be a whore and later an adulterous woman; with piquant details chapter 7 describes how this foreign woman coaxes a young man to her house with her "seductive patter." That house is "the way to Sheol, the descent to the courts of death" (7, 27). Some commentators think that this "alien woman" is *more* than an ordinary whore and that the warnings to avoid her and to seek one's happiness exclusively with one's own wife have a *deeper* meaning than the stimulus to marital fidelity. They point out that, after Hosea, participation in religious practices of other peoples could be characterized as adultery and fornication. Now, after the exile, the Jewish community was a small minority in a land inhabited by large numbers of non-Jews. A Jew who took up with one of their women ran the risk of committing both "ordinary" fornication and that described by Hosea as well, by accepting the ways of a foreign piety. In his fidelity to his wife, "fair as a hind, graceful as a fawn" (5, 18), the sensible Jew would therefore experience his fidelity toward Yahweh who so forcefully spoke to him in the person of Lady Wisdom.

However this may be, it is certain that the sages speaking in section I were thoroughly familiar with the words of the great prophets and the preaching of Deuteronomy (1—11; 28—30). The dilemma in which they place the reader reflects the conclusion of Moses' last sermon: "See, today I set before you life and prosperity, death and disaster. . . . Choose life then. . . ." (Dt. 30, 15. 19). It is also clear that this section was placed at the beginning so that the often "profane" and seemingly ordinary sayings of II and V would be read in the light of this fundamental appeal. This probably occurred before Ezra bound the Jewish community so exclusively to the Law, for nowhere is there mention of Israel or of anything specifically Jewish. Wisdom is universal. Although exegetes are not yet in agreement concerning the meaning of the word with which Wisdom refers to herself in 8, 30 (it can mean "pet," but also "master craftsman" or "architect"), it is clear from the description as a whole that she was with God "from the beginning," created before he made heaven and earth, and that she was delighted even then to be with "the sons of men," desirous of happiness for all without distinction.

3. *Ecclesiasticus or the Wisdom of Sirach. Shortly after 200 B.C.,* a certain Jesus Ben Sirach of Jerusalem published a large book along the lines of Proverbs. Here the reader (often "my son") is urged in long admonitions to fear the Lord, to be patient in times of trial, to have respect for his parents, to be humble, sympathetic and good. The author enlarges on themes such as friendship, relationship with women, hospitality and self-control which one must practice in all his relations with others.

In the first verses Sirach says that Wisdom is something divine, that she is with God as his first creature and given by him to those who seek her in the "fear of the Lord." Between his warnings he continually comes back to that mysterious figure. In 4, 11-19 he paints the man who runs after her, finds her home, stares through the window, listens at the door and there pitches his tent. She then comes to him and nourishes him with her food and drink. In chapter 24 the author lets Wisdom speak about herself, in the manner of Proverbs 8. But here she goes further. She was with God in the beginning and wanted to be with the children of men. She sought an abode with every people and nation, and finally it was granted her among God's people:

> Then the creator of all things instructed me,
> and he who created me fixed a place for my tent.
> He said, "Pitch your tent in Jacob,
> make Israel your inheritance". . . .
> In the beloved city he has given me rest,
> and in Jerusalem I wield my authority.

After she has sung the praises of her own beauty and goodness, the author declares:

All of this is no other than
the book of the Covenant
of the Most High God,
the Law that Moses enjoined on us
as an inheritance for the communities of Jacob.

For the people of the milieu of Jesus Ben Sirach it was an established fact, therefore, that the Wisdom which had existed with God
before all ages had received concrete form in the Law of Moses!
That was their way of standing firm while being washed on all
sides by the waves of Hellenism. Unlike the "progressives" (cf. pp.
127f.) they did not let themselves be blinded by the new insights
and philosophical theories flooding Palestine. These were said to
come from the great philosophers, "lovers (*philoi*) of Wisdom
(*sophia*)." On the contrary, true Wisdom, coming from the creator
himself, had taken up her dwelling in Jerusalem and there held
sway over the faithful people of God by means of the Law.

Unlike Proverbs, where no mention is made of Israel, Jesus Ben
Sirach added a kind of Bible history to his warnings and observations (44—50). It is a long gallery of the great men of the past
portrayed as the Bible depicts them. After Enoch, Noah, Abraham
and Moses, the priests Aaron and Phinehas receive considerable
attention. Then follow the great kings and prophets, Elijah, and
even the Twelve, and then after Nehemiah, the builder of the
walls, the list concludes with a great man whom the author himself
had the privilege of experiencing as a youth, the high priest Simon
II. His term of office had lasted from 220-195 B.C., and Sirach
described his activities with great admiration. This writer was not
only intimately acquainted with all the sacred writings of the Jews
(his ideal was the all-surpassing profession of being a teacher of
the Scriptures: cf. 39, 1-11), but he also frequented the temple
faithfully. He put his whole heart and soul into the prayers sung
there (see those recorded in 36, 1-17 and 50, 1-12).

It is understandable that this rich wisdom book was widely read
by pious Jews. Even several centuries later we see it frequently
quoted by rabbis, sometimes even with the formula used to introduce a scriptural citation: "It is written. . . ." Yet, the Wisdom of
Sirach was never taken into the Hebrew canon, with the result that
the Hebrew text disappeared from circulation. By chance, part

(two-thirds) of a late and not very reliable copy was uncovered in 1896. In addition, several fragments of copies used by the Essenes have come to light among the Dead Sea Scrolls.

The Greek translation made by Jesus Ben Sirach's grandson in Egypt (cf. p. 87) became very popular among the Jews. Christians also had a high opinion of it, judging from allusions and citations in New Testament writings (in particular, the epistle of St. James) and from extensive quotations in the works of the Fathers of the Church. In the Latin Church the book even received the name *Ecclesiasticus* [*liber*], "the ecclesiastical book," possibly because it served as a kind of handbook of instructions for leading a solidly Christian life. Next to the book of Psalms, the Wisdom of Sirach has been the source of more texts for the Latin liturgy than any other book of the Old Testament.

4. *The Book of Wisdom. In the last century before Christ's birth*, a Jew of Alexandria wrote the book which is sometimes simply called "Wisdom" and sometimes "The Wisdom of Solomon." The author addresses himself immediately to the "judges of the earth" (or the "rulers of the earth"), urging them to govern justly. Next he shows them the disasters awaiting sinners after their evil life and how those who have lived here in justice will enjoy a blessed immortality with God forever. In 6—9 he expressly urges princes and kings to seek Wisdom just as he himself had done. He relates in an elevated style how he fell in love with Wisdom,

> ... reflection of the eternal light,
> untarnished mirror of God's active power,
> image of his goodness.

Then he tells them how he prayed for Wisdom to God, who let him build the temple on his holy mountain, and how he asked that he might be a worthy successor to his father as ruler of God's people. Thus the author indicates quite clearly that he has assumed the person of Solomon, although he never mentions the name explicitly.

In the third part of his work (10—19) he first discusses certain personalities from biblical history, just as Jesus Ben Sirach had done, but here too without mentioning one single name. The same

Wisdom was the protector of "the father of the world, the first being to be fashioned, created alone," and the one who "delivered him from his fault"; she, too, led the "virtuous man, fleeing from the anger of his brother" along straight paths.

> She showed him the kingdom of God
> and taught him the knowledge of holy things.

Another virtuous man she did not forsake,

> but she kept him free from sin;
> she went down to the dungeon with him;
> she would not abandon him in his chains,
> but procured for him the scepter of a kingdom.

The author leaves to the reader who knows his Bible the joy of recognizing those well-known personalities. In this passage we first saw Jacob, and then he was talking about Joseph in Egypt. At the exodus and the Egyptian plagues he pauses briefly to consider the mystery of God's justice, and afterward he discusses in some detail the idolatrous religious practices and foolish animal worship of the Egyptians. After these interruptions he develops the theme of how Wisdom manifested herself by using those same natural powers to punish Egypt and to deliver the people of God.

While Jesus Ben Sirach hardly seems to have been influenced by the Hellenism he opposed, this present writer was a product of it. He had an excellent command of the literary language of Alexandria with its wealth of words and rhetorical style; besides the manners, customs and new scientific insights of Ptolemaic Egypt, he also knew the philosophical words of the times which an educated man of the city was expected to use. But in all of this he remained a deeply faithful Jew who above everything else was most acquainted with the Greek translations of the sacred books of his forefathers.

Among the Christians it was mostly the "intellectuals" who read this part of their Greek Bible. Both Paul and John the Evangelist were familiar with it. They borrowed motifs and terms from it when they wanted to express something of the mystery of divine Wisdom which had become recognizable in the person of Jesus Christ.

III
THE MYSTERY OF DEATH AND LIFE

No one can be thoughtfully engaged for any length of time with guidelines for human conduct without encountering two fundamental problems. The first is the question of sanctions, rewarding good deeds and punishing evil ones. Does something of this kind really take place, and if so, how and when? This immediately raises the second question: What is the role of death in all of this? Does man cease completely to exist, or does he go on living? If the latter is true, is the nature of that life after death determined to some extent by what one does before death?

Wise men of the ancient East were accustomed to take human experience as their point of departure. This taught them that quite a lot of good and evil is rewarded or punished in the ordinary course of human events, the result of a kind of law which apparently lies at the base of human society. Whoever deceives his fellow men time and again will eventually lose their confidence, will no longer be able to earn a living, and thus will be reduced to poverty and misery. And so we say that the liar received his "just deserts" without the intervention of a judge. A trustworthy man will climb higher on the social ladder as a matter of course. People like to do business with him and entrust him with responsible duties, and thus his honesty is rewarded with honor and prosperity.

To the extent that a society develops and attempts to bring a greater diversity of human activities into an organic whole, certain norms of conduct are expressly formulated in rules and laws. Together with them an organ is created to guarantee their fulfillment by passing judgment on and punishing transgressions.

But does another operation of justice exist alongside or above this one? For the ancients there was no question about it. They had not the slightest doubt that there were powers above the earth involved in the workings of virtue and wickedness in the world of men. Furthermore, after death each one would have to face the gods who rule over the world of the dead. This was known in Mesopotamia just as well as in Egypt, however different their representation of the deceased's journey to that world and his stay there.

Israelite sages also were obliged to formulate their thoughts about what awaited man in return for his deeds, and they, too, had to face that unavoidable given—death—which snatches man away from his earthly judges. But they could view these things only in the light of their faith in Yahweh. Thus they arrived at different ways of posing the problem and different solutions from those of their foreign colleagues.

Death and the Realm of the Dead

"We must all die," the wise woman of Tekoa told King David in her plea for Absalom's return. "We are like water spilt on the ground that can never be gathered up again. . . ." (2 Sam. 14, 14). Some years previous David had refused to perform the customary fast when his little son died: "But now he is dead; why should I fast? Can I bring him back again? I shall go to him, but he cannot come back to me" (2 Sam. 12, 23). Death is irrevocable. The Israelite hoped that after death he would be "gathered to his fathers," as the expression went—that is, to be buried in the family tomb. He evidently intended in that way to remain in contact with the living entity of which he had been a part. Jeremiah heard Israel's ancestor Rachel lamenting from her grave about the deportation of her children. She lay buried in Ramah, in the territory of Benjamin (Jer. 31, 15). The old Barzillai was not very much in favor of David's generous offer to come to live in his palace at Jerusalem. No, he wanted to die in his own city and be buried with his parents (2 Sam. 19, 37). Perhaps he was also thinking of the care which his children would give their parents. Every excavator in Palestine who uncovers a housing complex hopes to find in the surroundings the corresponding burial site. Along with all kinds of data about the inhabitants, it would yield in any case a large and colorful quantity of unbroken ceramic ware, for people in Canaan buried food and drink with their dead, and, as appears from many such discoveries, the Israelites continued this custom for centuries.

Except for a few disputable allusions, no reference to this charitable attitude toward the dead has been preserved in any of Israel's writings in the Old Testament. Undoubtedly the reason is that this practice was in conflict with the "official" faith, which forbade any contact with a deceased person, for a corpse was thought to be a source of "impurity" rendering the believer unfit for union with Yahweh. Although the deceased was allowed to rest in the family tomb and thus in some way still belonged to his clan, *at the same time* he descended to the underworld, the realm of the dead, and thus had fallen completely outside the sphere of Yahweh's influence.

Many texts, especially in the sapiential literature and the Psalms, speak about that far away domain—in Hebrew usually called *sheol*—but they do so only in passing. However, if one gathers all those scattered statements together, it is possible to sketch at least in rough lines the Israelite's conception of that underworld. Not a single ray of light penetrates that "land of no return." Job 10, 21-22 could not be more vivid:

> . . . the land of murk and deep shadow,
> where dimness and disorder hold sway,
> and light itself is like the dead of night.

There the dead live as shades—"weaklings" is the actual meaning of the Hebrew—in the lowest possible state of existence. They no longer know any feelings: "Their loves, their hates, their jealousies, these have all perished." They can neither do nor devise anything, "for there is neither achievement, nor planning, nor knowledge, nor wisdom in Sheol" (Eccl. 9, 5-6. 10). This "land of oblivion" is sometimes simply called "silence" (Ps. 94, 17): no sound is ever heard there, and the shades sleep on, never to be wakened (Job 14, 12). The great poet of Isaiah 14 does allow some commotion when the king of Babylon arrives. At that the princely victims of his conquest stand up and say: "So you, too, have been brought to nothing, like ourselves" (Is. 14, 10). That is but a poetic way of saying that all men are the same there. One would have to be in extreme torment and unbearably miserable to be able to desire, as Job did, the complete rest of such an existence:

> Down there bad men bustle no more,
> there the weary rest.
> Prisoners, all left in peace,
> hear no more the shouts of the jailer.
> Down there, high and low are all one,
> and the slave is free of his master.

Job wanted to lie down there and sleep, free of all disturbance (Job 3, 13. 17-19).

The essential characteristics of Israel's conception of Sheol can thus be condensed within the limits of one paragraph. It is quite meager when compared to the very detailed descriptions found in Mesopotamian and Egyptian texts. In some of these the realm of the dead seems to have been charted on a map, with city wall and gates, and with the various stages through which the deceased had to pass, among gods and monsters, to reach its center. In Egypt the living took special interest in the "hereafter." People there often dreamed of those western regions where the sun terminates its daily journey. After their earthly journey the dead, too, would arrive there to go on living in a new kind of existence. If they succeeded in getting by the judges with no ill consequences (cf. pp. 217f.), they would enjoy there all the beautiful things which were present in their tomb, their "house of eternity," whether in reality or symbolically (that made no difference). Many Egyptians spent a great deal of their energy and wealth in furnishing their tombs. Thanks to their desire to have everything in which they took pleasure during life represented there, the tombs of kings and great men have yielded countless art treasures, providing us with an exceptionally accurate picture of the customs and utensils—in short, of the daily life of the ancient Egyptians.

It is remarkable that Israel, despite the immediate proximity and strong influence of Egypt (especially during the creative period of the first kings: cf. pp. 221f.), borrowed nothing from the major Egyptian opinions concerning life after death. Instead, it continued to maintain its meager *sheol*. The tenacity of their nomadic past possibly made itself felt here as well. Characteristic of the attitude of sedentary peoples to the world of the dead is that they bury their dead in the ground from which they live. They maintain a bond with them and experience that bond in the form of religiously colored practices. Some of their divinities rule over that realm of the dead. Nomads, on the other hand, move on continually and thus have no bonds with their deceased. The one god who leads them, their invisible shepherd, is by nature, therefore, "a god of the living." Israel's abhorrence of images of men and animals, probably not entirely independent of that nomadic origin, implied an abhorrence of the most striking expressions of Egyptian involvement with the world of the dead. Their exceptionally strong convictions about the divine mystery probably also preserved the Israelites from speculations and dreams about realities which completely fell outside human experience. Their God asked fidelity and obedience and the exercise of justice and love in their ordinary daily life with each other. The world of the dead does not interest him at all and thus falls outside his sphere of influence.

No, Yahweh no longer "remembers" the dead. They are, as we read in Psalm 88, 6, "deprived of your protecting hand"—i.e., of God's loving care. Nevertheless, we sometimes read of Yahweh raising someone up from the underworld and restoring him to life—for example, in Psalm 30:

> Yahweh, you have brought my soul up from Sheol,
> of all those who go down to the pit you have revived me.

Here one should keep two things in mind. For the Israelite the underworld was *both* a place *and* a power—the place under the earth where the dead had their abode, but also the power which snatched them out of the land of the living. They sometimes referred to this power as a gluttonous monster, never to be satisfied. In the book of Proverbs, Sheol heads the list of things which can never say, "Enough!" (30, 16). To say that the eyes of man are never satisfied is to compare them to insatiable death (Prov. 27, 20).

Secondly, one should remember that, when speaking of "life," the Israelites do not mean the same thing we do. For them life was what we call "a happy life." A man who is healthy, who has a large family, who enjoys prosperity and is respected by his fellow men—such a man, they would say, possessed life. If essential parts of this picture began to fall away, then his existence began to approach that of the shades. Whoever fell sick—i.e., became a "weakling"—or was reduced to poverty because of setbacks on the farm or in business or lost the respect of men through slander and accusations believed himself to be in the grip of death, in the power of Sheol. But although he was already counted among the shades, there was still hope for him as long as he could still call upon Yahweh, the hope of the drowning man who can still hold his hand above water, for Yahweh could still "save" him, restore him to a state worthy of the name "life."

When a sick man recovered, or a defamed man was restored to

honor, or a poor man gained prosperity, he went to the temple to thank Yahweh for saving him from the grip of the underworld. Several psalms of thanksgiving reflect something of the rites and prayers observed at such a time. Elihu very strikingly describes such a thanksgiving ceremony in the book of Job (33, 26-30). The man who had recovered from sickness goes "in happiness to see his face"—i.e., to visit God in his house, the temple. There he tells the bystanders how he had sinned and turned from the just path, but how God was still merciful to him in the end. God preserved him from the descent to the underworld and granted him the joy of living again. And then Elihu says to Job:

> All this God does twice, thrice with a man,
> rescuing his soul from the pit,
> and letting the light of life shine bright on him.

This was written in a spirit of authentic gratitude. The creator who bestows life is for Israel the merciful one, patient, ready to pardon and full of pity. It is no joy for him to take away the gift of life. Thus he wishes to restore health to the man who is sick through his own fault. He wants to rescue him from the power of death. He sometimes does this twice in a man's life and—the writer adds enthusiastically—even three times! But of course every man eventually ends up in Sheol. This is his irrevocable destination. As a shade he will meet all those who went before him, "the virtuous and the wicked, the clean and unclean, him who sacrifices and him who does not. . . . That one fate comes to all" (Eccl. 9, 2).

The Problem of Retribution

With this outlook many Israelites were able to live happy lives as true believers. They knew that death would separate them for good from their people and their God, and therefore in gratitude they enjoyed the years he gave them. It was, after all, a privilege to be allowed to have some little part in that wonderful relationship between Yahweh and his people, and in one's own life to contribute something to Israel's answer to his inviting personality. To live seventy or eighty years in that way and then to pass out of life "sated with days"—that is, having enjoyed it to the full—could indeed be called a privilege.

In addition, two other things were certain. The Israelites believed that Yahweh saw everything that happened on earth and that he knew what was going on in the heart of each person. Furthermore, they were certain that he, the highest Lord and judge, would not let any good deeds go unrewarded or allow evil to be unpunished. This he did, of course, during the person's lifetime, for the underworld lay outside his sphere of activity, and retribution could no longer reach the shades.

From the information provided by the Bible, the Israelites experienced no difficulties with this belief until sometime in the 7th century B.C. They evidently thought that God's justice indeed functioned in that way, within the limits of earthly life. They probably believed it to be at work in the ways in which virtue and vice were rewarded or punished in the natural course of human society, and also in the activities of Israel's courts which passed judgments in the name of Yahweh. The oldest collections in the book of Proverbs leave no room for doubt. The just—i.e., the clever, the honest, the diligent and the self-controlled—would live out their lives to the full, while the evil—i.e., the foolish, the deceivers, the lazy and the licentious—would die before their time. Furthermore, perhaps also in circles other than those of the "sages," God's justice was seen to be at work in the lot of Israel as a whole. In that case more attention was paid to the collective entity than to the individual. National disasters were punishments for national faults. In this regard, think only of the preaching of the pre-exilic prophets.

However this may be, it is with Jeremiah that we first meet an expression of doubt about the justice of God's rule. Imagine that I would go to court against you, Jeremiah says to Yahweh (12, 1); you would, of course, appear to be right and win the case. But, all the same, I would like to have a word with you sometime concerning a point of justice:

Why is it that the wicked live so prosperously?
Why do scoundrels enjoy peace?

Put in modern terms, this complaint asserts that the people's ancient belief is contradicted by the facts. Jeremiah had dedicated himself entirely to the service of Yahweh, and because of that his life was often unbearable. The chiefs of Anathoth wanted to put him to death, as we saw in chapter 5, probably because he was a threat to the village's good name and thus to its prosperity. It was in connection with that threat to his life that he posed the above question (11, 18—12, 6). Jeremiah deserved better treatment! But there were also quite a few other facts which did not jibe with their faith. King Josiah gave himself heart and soul to the affairs of Yahweh. Such a person certainly deserved a long and happy life. Why then was he mortally wounded on the battlefield of Meggido, still far from being "sated of days"?

One could of course say that Josiah had to do penance for the sins of his ancestors—his father Amon, and his grandfather Manasseh, who was even more impious. Had not Israel confessed through the centuries that Yahweh is a jealous God, who punished "the father's fault in the sons and in the grandsons to the third and fourth generations" (Ex. 20, 5; 34, 7; Num. 14, 18)? After the catastrophic destruction of Jerusalem in 587, the young people of Palestine complained about this before Yahweh (Lam. 5, 7):

> Our fathers have sinned; they are no more,
> and we ourselves bear the weight of their crimes!

Almost cynically the same thing was repeated in figurative language.

> The fathers have eaten unripe grapes,
> and the children's teeth are set on edge.

In the spirit of prophetic preaching, which appealed to each one's personal decision (cf. pp. 194f.), it was especially Jeremiah and Ezekiel and their disciples who protested against this reproach of God by which those complaining deprived themselves of every prospect of salvation. You abuse that old saying, said Ezekiel in a famous discussion (chapter 18), for I assure you in Yahweh's name that the son will not be punished for the injustice of his father, nor the father because of his son. Each one is personally responsible for what he does. However hopeless your situation may seem to be, the path to life is open to everyone, because everyone is capable of turning to God. Jeremiah's disciples spoke in this same way (31, 29-30), and under the influence of their preaching the Deuteronomists "corrected" the above text about the third and fourth generation: "Yahweh is ... the faithful God ... who punished *in their own persons* those who hate him. He is not slow to destroy the man who hates him; he makes him work out his punishment *in person*" (Dt. 7, 10).

After the exile this very certainty (namely, that man was responsible to God alone for his own deeds), combined with that other certainty about the lot of all being absolutely the same in Sheol, was the source of a serious crisis of faith for many Jews. It was in those years after the exile that the facts—and they, too, were Yahweh's "doing"!—began more and more to conflict with their beliefs about his absolute justice. The Jewish community in Jerusalem remained under foreign domination. It was one thing to be allowed to have their own theocratic form of government, but it was clear that the Jews who had some influence with the foreign authorities and did business with their merchants could not very well be strictly observing the Law of God. And they were precisely the ones who had the best chances to become prosperous and attain honor. They were being blessed with the good things of the earth, and, of course, by God, for where else did good things come from? Those who held strictly to the Law had much less chance of getting ahead. Their fidelity to the express will of God often resulted in an extremely low standard of living, if not poverty and destitution. A punishment from God? What for? If he could not reward or punish man's deeds after death, then the least he could do was show his beneficence to his faithful servants through tangible blessings, the fullness of "life." And those who paid no attention to his wishes should feel this punishment in poverty, suffering and an early death.

When a pious Jew suffered misfortune, then he could only suspect that he had committed some fault against God. From sympathetic visitors he could expect no other consolation than the serious advice, "Look back over your past life. You must have done something to deserve this!" Likewise, the prosperity of the Jews who openly and shamelessly transgressed the Law could be a serious temptation for the pious.

One solution was to declare the facts invalid, as it were, regarding them as too volatile for one to allow his faith and his expectations to be destroyed by them. There is a striking example of this in Psalm 37, a sapiential psalm in alphabetical form (cf. p. 220) which begins with these lines:

> Don't worry about the wicked,
> do not envy those who do wrong.

According to this psalm, the faithful Jew should try to maintain his conviction about two things: the happiness of the wicked lasts but a day, and your fidelity will soon be rewarded. Believe me, the old wise man says, I speak from experience:

> Now I am old, but ever since my youth
> I never saw a virtuous man deserted,
> or his descendants forced to beg their bread. . . .
> I have seen the wicked in his triumph
> towering like a cedar of Lebanon,
> but when next I passed, he was not there.
> I looked for him and he was nowhere to be found.

But many Jews had too great a feeling for reality to be able to retain this attitude much longer. It was too simplistic to survive in a life filled with deprivations. Many continued to wrestle with the problem. Some did so in writing—hence the origin of the book of Job and the reflections of Qoheleth (Ecclesiastes).

The Book of Job

Tennyson called the book of Job "the greatest poem of ancient and modern times," and Carlyle wrote, "It is one of the grandest things ever written with the pen. . . . There is nothing written, I think, in the Bible or out of it of equal literary merit." These opinions may be partially determined by the scriptural formation of these men of letters and the taste of their times, but nevertheless it is generally accepted that the book of Job belongs to the great literature of the world. In recent years, similar works from the ancient cultures of Egypt and Mesopotamia (most of which are only fragments) have come to light. They represent those peoples' treatment of the problem of the just man weighed down with suffering. Not one of them approaches the literary qualities and depth attained in the book of Job. Here we must limit ourselves to a few introductory remarks which may facilitate a first acquaintance with this book.

The work was probably produced in the course of the 4th century B.C. It is not certain that one author wrote the whole book as it is found in our Bible today. Of the numerous suppositions which have been made concerning the origin of the book, we will mention only the opinion, embraced by many scholars, that the speeches of Elihu (chapters 32-37) did not belong to the original and were inserted at a later date.

The use of language and the style in Job make it certain that the author(s) obviously intended to produce a piece of "literature." Many words and expressions are extremely rare or entirely unique in the Hebrew literature which has come down to us in the Bible, often because they were indeed "foreign words," borrowed from related languages. This is what St. Jerome meant when he wrote in the Foreword to his Latin version that he "had translated the text from Hebrew and Arabic, and sometimes from Syriac [i.e., Aramaic]." But even for modern biblical scholars, who know more ancient Semitic languages than Jerome, a number of details revealing concise poetic language remain obscure. Even more often than in Proverbs, the reader who uses several translations of Job will find surprising variants. I sometimes give Job 38, 36 in four different translations as an example:

From *The Revised Version,* 1913:

Who hath put wisdom in the inward parts?
Or who hath given understanding to the mind?

From *The Revised Standard Version,* 1952:

Who has put wisdom in the clouds,
or given understanding to the mists?

From *The Confraternity Edition,* 1955:

Who puts wisdom in the heart,
and gives the cock its understanding?

From *The Jerusalem Bible,* 1966:

Who gave the ibis wisdom
and endowed the cock with foreknowledge?

Despite the obscurities in details, the book's purpose and train of thought are very clear. The writer treats the problem which is bothering him, not in the manner of the Greeks, by rational analysis, but in the Hebrew way, by allowing a concrete man to wrestle with it. This he does *a la* Bible, for the author is thoroughly acquainted with the sacred books, especially the prophetic literature, Proverbs and a number of Psalms. Likewise, he must have traveled extensively, perhaps even in Egypt, and been very observant. He had undoubtedly suffered and prayed very much.

The book can be divided into seven parts:

1. In the *prologue* (chapters 1—2) the author immediately introduces his hero. He portrays this oriental "sheik" in the most complimentary terms in the Hebrew language to denote a good man: "a sound and honest man who feared God and shunned evil." And as expected, God had blessed him in everything. Although Job did not belong to Israel, he is pictured as a biblical patriarch with his rich herds and large family. He had seven sons and three daughters. When they had held a banquet for each other, Job would offer a holocaust for the sins which they might have committed during the festivities. Such a man was the irreproachable Job!

In the period when our author was writing, the Jews had given considerable thought (in their concrete, figurative manner of course) to the "messengers" or "angels" who, according to so many ancient texts, represented Yahweh when he wanted to do something in the world of men. They had come to the conclusion that there were also malicious ones among them; they were thought to be man's accusers before God and to work against him in all kinds of ways. To express this they used the word *satan,* "adversary" or "accuser." When considering a text from Chronicles, we saw how this supra-worldly figure provided the Jews with a way to avoid attributing evil motives and foul purposes to God, whom they knew to be involved in all that happened (p. 117).

After Job the author introduces this figure of Satan, who makes his entrance on a sort of elevated stage. He allows Satan to appear there in God's council chamber, where he receives permission to test Job's attitude toward God. On the lower stage we see how bands of robbers and natural catastrophes destroy everything Job possesses. When all the bad news is brought to him, he says with deep faith, "Yahweh gave, Yahweh has taken back. Blessed be the name of Yahweh!" After that Satan gets permission to attack Job's very person. Despite the mockery from his wife, Job is still resigned to accept his sickness. Then he is visited by three of his friends who are also inhabitants of lands east of Palestine. As if struck with dumbness they sit before him in silence for seven days and seven nights.

2. *The conversations between Job and his three friends* comprise the largest part of the book (3—27). After those seven days Job bursts forth in a woeful lament. He curses the day he was born. It would have been better to go immediately from the darkness of the womb to the pitch-black underworld. It is better not to live at all than to live in misery. Each of his three friends has his say, one after the other, and each time they receive an answer from Job. This happens three times; however, in the last series the text seems to be confused.

The friends were just as ignorant as Job of what the author had shown his readers on that raised stage, the permission given to Satan being the actual cause of Job's suffering. Repeatedly and always more insistently they try to convince Job that he must have done something to deserve all his misery. After all, God is just! One who has done nothing wrong would not be made to suffer. Job should confess his sins and contritely turn back to God. Then he would again be blessed with honor and good health. Job passionately protests against these insinuations. Time and again he turns from speaking to his friends to address God, sometimes with harsh reproaches and strong accusations. Why does God not tell him what crime he has committed? Did the Almighty make that little man only to spy continually into his doings and at his smallest fault to punish him, making him a target for the arrows of his wrath? A closer look reveals that even these blasphemous words come forth from Job's desire for God. He may take everything away from him, everything which people look upon as a blessing from God, as a sign of his favor. Let him take all these things, but then show himself to Job, if necessary at his descent to the underworld, as his defender before the other three, as his protector and his friend. Then Job will be happy.

These conversations provide a magnificent piece of literature, but in the manner of biblical poetry, with many repetitions and much recasting of the same themes in different words. For our

Western taste they may be rather tiring sometimes. Therefore, one should at first limit his reading to several small sections.

The reader will notice that the proper name of Israel's God, Yahweh, is not used anywhere in the entire dialogue (its use in 12, 9 must be attributed to the work of a copyist). Job and his friends refer to God with general Semitic terms; they also use the ancient name *Shaddai,* usually rendered as "the Almighty." Did the author intend this only as an indication that Job belonged to the era of the patriarchs who used this name (Ex. 6, 3)? Or did he wish to emphasize that Job and his friends were not of the people of Israel, as another way of saying, "The problem of the suffering just man is common to all of humanity"?

3. Chapter 28 is a *hymn in praise of Wisdom,* more precious than all treasures, but beyond the reach of searching man. God alone knows the way to her abode and called her to his side at creation. For man "wisdom" is the fear of the Lord and the avoidance of evil. This beautiful poem seems to be out of place here. The author possibly wrote it as an independent piece of poetry, and it may have been given this place in his book on Job later on.

4. *Job's monologue* (29—31) seems to have been designed as a conclusion to the conversation with his friends and as an introduction to the speeches of Yahweh. First, Job describes his past prosperity and his present misery in order to finally make a kind of examination of conscience, something that resembles the "negative confession" of the Egyptians (cf. pp. 217f.). One who still thinks that Old Testament morality falls short of that of the New Testament should read this chapter 31 immediately. Job concludes with something like a "dare." He has had his say; now let the Almighty come forward with his accusation!

5. *The speeches of Elihu* (32—37) form an independent unit with their own style and usage. This fourth friend, not mentioned among the visitors of 2, 11, is said to have been silent all that time because he was younger than the others. He expressly takes up things which Job and his friends asserted, and he points out that suffering can be a chastisement for faults which one hardly noticed, or a means used by God to lead man to the good and to protect him from pride. One gets the impression that the pedantic Elihu has already studied the speeches of Yahweh which are still

to come (cf. below)—hence the opinion that these chapters were written by one or more later disciples with the intention of completing their master's work with later insights.

6. *The two speeches of Yahweh* (38—41), each ending with a perplexed word from Job, describe in a grandiose style several of the miracles which Yahweh has worked and continues to work in his awe-inspiring creation. Job has the last word (42, 5-6):

> I knew you only by hearsay;
> but now, having seen you with my own eyes,
> I retract all that I have said,
> and in dust and ashes I repent.

In a flash Yahweh gave Job an overwhelming insight into the mysterious way in which he creates, regulates and directs all things. Job suddenly realizes how foolish it is for tiny man, with his simple notions about good and evil, reward and punishment, to criticize God's guidance of his life and that of others.

7. In the same prose style as the prologue, *the epilogue* relates how Job at God's command offers a holocaust for his three friends. Then he receives twice as much as he ever possessed in the past. His flocks are increased twofold, and an old translation even doubles his sons: he received 14 sons and 3 daughters. Daughters evidently did not count for the Aramaic translator. Such was not the case with the author. He gives them cute names and says that they were extremely beautiful. Job even gave them the same inheritance rights as their brothers. With this closing scene, presenting a Job who "lived happily ever after," the author seems to give his book with all its tremendous dimensions a place in the midst of ordinary men. Although we sometimes must go on through misery and doubt, and although the mystery encircling us surpasses all understanding, with the author of Job we believe that that mystery is well-disposed toward us. Such a faith enjoys a "happy end."

Ecclesiastes or The Preacher

A treatise in twelve chapters, with quite a different purpose, content and style, comes down to us from the man who called himself *Qoheleth,* presumably referring to the function of one who speaks in the assembly (*qahal, ecclesia*)—hence the name Ecclesiastes or the Preacher. This wise man, too, is dissatisfied with the simplistic view of the causes of happiness and unhappiness in the life of man as expressed in Psalm 37 and by Job's friends. The hard facts are quite different (7, 15; 8, 14):

> In this fleeting life of mine I have seen so much:
> the virtuous man perishing for all his virtue,
> for all his godlessness the godless living on. . . .
> The good . . . receive the treatment the wicked deserve;
> and the wicked the treatment the good deserve.

Like the author of Job, the Preacher, too, is firmly convinced that the wide world around him is full of secrets which remain hidden for man with his short life. However, his "wide world" is not that of Job with its starry heavens and clouds, oceans and plains and all the marvelous animals inhabiting it. His world is rather that of endless time in which generations of men come and go, and just keep on coming and going. To look for any continuity in what happens to man during the few years of his existence is utter nonsense. In our circles of sages it has been said from of old that wisdom leads to life and foolishness to death. But it is not so, for just as men and animals both die, so too the fool and the wise man. And do not say that the wise will at least live on in the memory of men, for everything will soon be forgotten; the sage and his wisdom will be no exception.

To drive this home the author presents himself as King Solomon, without however mentioning his name expressly. In the person of that legendary wise monarch, at the same time both the most powerful and the richest ever to rule in Jerusalem, he could say that he had truly tried out all the possibilities life has to offer, achieved everything which could be achieved, and taken the utmost pleasure in the world's delights, and all of this with a wisdom never surpassed by another. This Solomon came to the conclusion that everything is vanity, everything is fleeting, empty, senseless. The only sensible thing man can do is to take grateful delight in the little bit of happiness within his grasp:

> I know that there is no happiness for man
> except in pleasure and enjoyment while he lives.

> And when man eats and drinks and finds happiness
> in his work, this is a gift from God.

This we read in 3, 12-13, a sort of conclusion to the only part of this book in which we can discern a certain order (1, 2—3, 13). The author previously touched upon this theme in 2, 24, and he repeats it with almost the same words in 5, 17; 8, 15 and 9, 7, in between his unordered and musing reflections which he sometimes interrupts with proverbs and sayings in the traditional strain. At the end he urges young men to enjoy their youth to the full. Likewise, in opposition to the earlier wisdom teachers who saw in the blessings of old age the highest reward for a good life, the Preacher next describes the decline of man as he grows older. This he does for the most part in figurative language, the puzzling character of which is all the more intriguing (11, 9—12, 7).

Qoheleth probably lived in or near Jerusalem in the 3rd century B.C. If that be the case, he was certainly not exceedingly "progressive" or fervently "traditional" (cf. p. 128). He was too skeptical to take sides and too taken up with his thoughts on death as the end of everything. He did write in Hebrew, the sacred language of Jewish tradition, but he obviously did not take the trouble to master that language. His style and use of words reveal the influence of popular Aramaic, which often makes it difficult for us to understand what he meant.

His book just made it into the Hebrew canon under the wire. The rabbis with whom St. Jerome studied recognized that the Preacher held God's creation to be all "vanity" and that he placed passing pleasures above all else. Only because of its closing words, which give primary importance to fearing the Lord and obeying his commandments, and which point to God's judgment (12, 13-14), was the work "counted among the number of divine books," in the words of Jerome's Jewish masters. Some Fathers of the Church and modern exegetes have maintained that the author's intention was to give the various opinions of others, while he himself was only responsible for the "orthodox" statements. But this opinion does not have to be accepted. It seems rather that some of the "orthodox" remarks, which give the impression of being out of context, were added later (this is generally accepted for 3, 17; 8, 12b-13 and 11, 9b). The Preacher undoubtedly knew something of the contemporary thinking about man's life in the circles outside

Judaism. But in all his reflections and musings this Jew held fast to his God, without intense expectations for himself, his nation or the world, and without passionate conversations with him. His way was to accept with gratitude the simple pleasures granted him by that completely unintelligible Reality.

The Prospect of "Eternal Life"

In the last century before the Christian era, many faithful Jews lived in the hope that after death they would go on living with God, a hope in an unimaginably happy "hereafter." Evidently they had abandoned the somber perspective of a Sheol. It is no longer possible to trace precisely the path which this development in their faith followed. The texts are much too scarce for this. However, it is possible to point out several factors which in all probability contributed to the formation of that new perspective. We would like to attempt a brief description of three such factors.

1. *A deep experience of their communion with God in prayer* gave some the certainty that this contact would not be interrupted by their death. God would not break with them and allow them to fall into the bottomless depths of the underworld, far from his reach. He would hold onto them and take them to himself forever.

Psalm 73 puts this certainty into very striking words. The poet describes how he was troubled by the old question of Jeremiah: Why are the godless blessed with such good fortune, while I, after all my devotion to God, am so weighed down with sickness and misery? Although he gives priority to God's goodness (verse 1), the experience that its outward signs are refused him, while given in abundance to godless mockers, brings him almost to the point of despair. During reflective prayer, possibly while visiting the temple, the future of those happily living sinners is suddenly clear to him. In a flash they will be *shammàh,* "utter desolation" (verse 19). With this word Jeremiah had so often pointed to the lot awaiting the land and people of Judah because of their hardness of heart— total destruction which would horrify those who look on (cf. pp. 130f.). Verses 23-24 may be rendered thus:

> As for me, I am always with you;
> you have seized my right hand;

in your counsel you will lead me
and afterward take me into glory.

The wicked man will perish when God passes judgment, but the faithful one will remain with him. God will seize (take hold of) his right hand. Deutero-Isaiah used this term to describe the exceptional privilege of King Cyrus, the "anointed of Yahweh" (45, 1), after he had applied it to Israel: "For I, Yahweh, your God, I am holding you by the right hand; I tell you, 'Do not be afraid, I will help you'" (41, 13). This now was what God would do for the psalmist, "in his counsel," that plan of salvation which surpasses anything man could conceive (cf. Is. 55, 8-9). God will "receive" or "take him"! This term was used for Enoch who on earth walked with God and then vanished "because God took him," and also in the story about Elijah's being "taken up to heaven" (Gn. 5, 24 and 2 Kgs. 2, 1-10). Although the grammatical function of the term "glory" is not entirely clear, in any case the psalmist knows that he will not be separated from his God, who now is everything to him and always will be, even if his flesh and heart fail him.

This same certain expectation is expressed in Psalm 49, a "sapiential poem" on the same theme of the prosperity of sinners. Although the connection between the sometimes almost untranslatable sayings is not always clear, the meaning of verse 16, again with the term "take," seems beyond question:

But God will redeem my life
from the grasp of Sheol,
and will take me.

One who was familiar with this perspective would also understand other prayers in the same light—for example, the charming words with which Psalm 16 describes the precious security of the faithful with God (verses 10-11):

You will not abandon my soul to Sheol,
nor allow the one you love to see the pit;
you will reveal the path of life to me,
give me unbounded joy in your presence,
and at your right hand everlasting pleasures.

2. *Yahweh had restored his people and would do the same for each believer.* The exile was experienced by many at that time as a kind of collective death. "Our bones are dried up, our hope has gone; we are as good as dead" was the lamentation of the deported Judeans in the words of Ezekiel. This formulation of their despair came to him from the parable which he told in the form of a vision. He saw a wide valley covered with human skeletons. At Yahweh's command he was to prophesy over those piles of bones. He heard the noise of the bones as they came together and saw how they took on muscles and flesh which were covered with skin, how life entered into them when he ordered the "wind" from the four corners of the earth to blow over them. (The word used here can be rendered as "breath," "wind" or "spirit.") Then Ezekiel was to answer the doubting cry of the exiles: "The Lord Yahweh says this, I am now going to open your graves; I mean to raise you from your graves, my people, and lead you back to the soil of Israel" (37, 1-14).

After the exile, too, the restoration of the community in Jerusalem was spoken of in terms of being raised from the dead. Yahweh himself will give the land new inhabitants, says the poet of Isaiah 26, 19:

> Your dead will come to life,
> their [my] corpses will rise;
> awake, exult,
> all you who lie in the dust.

As appears from many of the Psalms, individuals were accustomed to regard their personal lot in the light of what Yahweh had done for Israel as a whole, especially in the exodus event. Thus it is possible that after the exile the believers saw that "awakening from death" of the whole nation as an image of what they could expect for themselves personally from their almighty and faithful Lord.

In that way Sheol probably lost its "neutral" character in their eyes. As a place the underworld was now reserved only for the godless, and as a power it stood in opposition to God and his plans for salvation. Thus Sheol could then become the domain of Satan; the old underworld became hell.

3. *The death of the young men who fought at the side of the*

Maccabees for the cause of Yahweh rendered the traditional teaching about retribution and Sheol forever untenable. The premature death of those brave believers could not possibly be explained as a punishment. If anyone ever deserved to share in Yahweh's ultimate victory over the powers of evil, they certainly did! And in fact we meet the first clear expression of belief in a future resurrection to life in the book of Daniel, which was written in those years.

This expectation was quick to take possession of the Jews in the Diaspora. We have already seen that the author of 2 Maccabees firmly believed in the resurrection of those who had died for God's will (cf. p. 137). Another Egyptian Jew of that same century, the writer of the book of Wisdom, strikingly proclaimed that same hope, especially in the first five chapters which describe the different lot awaiting the godless and the faithful. The sinners think that after this life there is nothing; they live licentiously and attack the believer who so terribly irritates them. He says that God is his father; therefore, we'll put him to the test and torture him. If he is truly the son of God, as he says, then God will come to help him (2, 16-20):

> Let us condemn him to a shameful death
> since he will be looked after—
> we have his word for it.

The writer then explains how foolish those people are, for the souls of the just are in God's hands, and no torment can tear them loose. Later on, at the judgment, he puts words of regret in the mouths of the sinners (5, 4-5):

> This is the man we used to laugh at once,
> a butt for our sarcasm, fools that we were!
> His life we regarded as madness,
> his ending as without honor.
> How has he come to be counted as one of the sons of God?
> How does he come to be assigned a place among the saints?

In a series of beautiful images the sinners describe the transitoriness of their life (verses 9-13). Thus, says the writer, their hope, too, is like chaff that has blown away, like smoke driven by the wind, as fleeting as the memory of a one-day guest (5, 14-16):

> But the virtuous live forever,
> their recompense lies with the Lord,
> the Most High takes care of them.
> So they shall receive the royal crown of splendor.

VII
Daniel

Although it is not our intention to treat the Bible in its entirety, the book of Daniel is in various respects so important for the Bible reader that we cannot pass over it in silence. It possesses something of all three different kinds of literature treated in the previous chapters. It resembles in part the later narrative writings, it has some relationship with the prophetic books, and, finally, the author clearly belongs to the class of wisdom teachers represented by Jesus Ben Sirach, who devoted himself primarily to the knowledge and explanation of Holy Scripture. Thus the book of Daniel is in a "category all its own," so to speak. First, we will treat the content and form, and then the date of origin and intentions of the book, with the final section being devoted to the genre which it represents.

I
CONTENT AND FORM

The English text which we find in Catholic Bibles is translated from three different languages. One part of the book was written by the author in Hebrew, and another in Aramaic. Finally, still other sections were added in a Greek version. Most Protestant editions of the Bible do not include these last additions.

If we leave the Greek additions aside for the moment, we will notice that the book consists of two very different parts. Chapters 1—6 contain six very simple stories which could easily be retold. They relate incidents from Daniel's life during his stay at court in Babylon. In chapters 7—12 we find visions, described and explained by Daniel himself. These are for the most part so complicated that it would take a great deal of effort to retell them from memory.

After the exile, as we have already seen a number of times, Aramaic became the ordinary language of the Jews, whereas Hebrew was reserved more and more for the liturgy and theological treatises. One would therefore expect that the six simple stories about Daniel would have been written in Aramaic and the more "intellectual" visions in Hebrew. But that is not quite the case, for the first of the six stories is in the Hebrew of the learned, and the first of the visions in popular Aramaic.

Furthermore, we should note that most of the stories and visions begin with a precise date, a particular year in the reign of the respective monarch. If we convert those into our system of dating, the book presents us with what Daniel did and saw in the years between his deportation from Jerusalem in 607 B.C. and his final appearance under Cyrus in 536—hence a career of 70 years.

To give the reader something to go by during our further treatment, a short outline of the book's contents, including the dates as given and the language in which the various parts are written, is printed on the opposite page.

II

TIME OF COMPOSITION

The reader already knows what is coming. Until the 19th century Christians regarded the whole book of Daniel as a strictly reliable historical account of the following facts. In the 6th century B.C. God allowed the great rulers of Babylon to feel his power by continually rescuing Daniel from their grasp and by granting this strict follower of the Law a wisdom which put all Babylonian learning and knowledge of the hidden to shame. Enlightened by the true God, Daniel had foretold what would happen centuries later. According to the convictions of many Christian exegetes, he had described the advent of Christ in mysterious terms and, just as precisely, foretold the year of his crucifixion, which in fact did "put an end to sacrifice and oblation" by replacing them with the perfect sacrifice. This they read in the chapter about the seventy weeks, evidently weeks of seven years each, the beginning of which

STORIES

1 (HEBREW) *In the third year of the reign of Jehoiakim* Daniel is brought by *Nebuchadnezzar* to his court in Babylon. Together with other Jewish youths he remains faithful to the Law. He remains there until *the first year of King Cyrus.* **2** *In the second (twelfth?) year of the reign of Nebuchadnezzar* the king has a dream. His magicians are summoned and answer in

ARAMAIC. The explanation of the statue made of four metals is given by Daniel, who then receives a high position at court.

3 *Once Nebuchadnezzar* had a golden statue made. The three young men refused to worship it and were thrown into the furnace.

(GREEK) Azariah's prayer in the furnace and the song of the three young men.

Nebuchadnezzar pays homage to the God of the three youths.

4 *Nebuchadnezzar* personally relates his madness, praises Daniel's wisdom and extols his God.

5 Feast given by *Belshazzar, son of Nebuchadnezzar;* "Mene, Tekel, Persin." Daniel is honored; Belshazzar is murdered.

6 *Darius the Mede* becomes king; Daniel in the lion pit; Daniel flourishes during the reigns of Darius and *Cyrus the Persian.*

VISIONS

7 *In the first year of Belshazzar* Daniel describes the vision of the four beasts and the Son of Man, with an explanation by an angel.

8 (HEBREW) *In the third year of Belshazzar* Daniel sees the vision of the ram and the he-goat, again with an explanation by an angel.

9 *In the first year of Darius, son of Ahasuerus, the Mede,* Daniel receives the explanation of the seventy weeks.

10-12 *In the third year of Cyrus king of Persia* Daniel sees visions of the future in which the angel Michael appears as Israel's champion.

STORIES

13 (GREEK) Daniel and the chaste Susanna.

14 When *Astyages* is succeeded by *Cyrus the Persian* Daniel unmasks the priests of Bel and is miraculously rescued from the lion pit.

they situated in such a way that the death of "the anointed one" did in fact fall in 30 A.D.

When an historical approach to the book was undertaken, it became evident that Daniel had to have been written in the period of the Maccabees. That Hebrew-Aramaic book even had to have been completed before the spring of 165 B.C. We will mention three of the reasons leading to this insight.

1. We saw in the last chapter that the "classical" prophets addressed themselves to their contemporaries, even when they spoke about the future. What they had to say about the future was vague, and always determined both by their character and formation and by the situation in which they and their audience found themselves. They did not speak from a precise foreknowledge of later events. In Daniel, however, we see just the opposite. The narrations about the situation in Babylon, which Daniel is said to have experienced, are inaccurate and sometimes incorrect; this is also true for what Daniel himself says about it. In the visions *he describes the future more accurately, the further it is away from his own time.*

We notice this already in chapter 2. The huge statue with its head of gold and lower members of metals continually diminishing in value emerges in the explanation to symbolize a series of four successive world empires. The golden head is the rule of Nebuchadnezzar himself. While the second and third empires receive only one sentence (verse 39), the fourth and furthest from Daniel in time is given extensive attention (40-43).

Likewise, in the first of the actual visions (chapter 7) about the four monsters which emerged from the sea, the first three receive far less attention than the fourth. The angel who explains that they symbolize four successive empires devotes the most time to the "little horn" which sprouted from the head of the fourth beast. That is a powerful king who will "speak words against the Most High, and harass the saints of the Most High. He will consider changing seasons and the Law. . . ." It is clear that Daniel and the angel are speaking about Antiochus IV and his attack on Judaism. That situation lies behind the meaning of chapter 8 as well. Again it is the "little horn" that attacks God's dwelling place and there puts an end to the daily sacrifice for 2,300 days and nights. In chapter 9 the prophecy of the seventy weeks of years also culminates in the days of the Maccabees. By the "anointed one" to be put to death the author probably meant the high priest Onias III, murdered in 171 B.C. (cf. the story in 2 Maccabees 4, 34-38).

2. If one reads further with the situation of the Maccabees in mind, then it is quickly evident that "Daniel" *does not see the distant future, but the very recent past.* The covert allusions of chapter 11 give a rather accurate outline of the history of Palestine after Alexander the Great, the "mighty king" of verse 3. The "land of splendor" will become an apple of contention between the "kings of the north" and the "kings of the south"—i.e., the Seleucids and the Ptolemies. Just as in chapters 2, 7, 8 and 9, this historical outline culminates in an extensive description of Antiochus IV (verses 21-39), who abolished the daily sacrifice and installed the "disastrous abomination" in the temple (cf. pp. 130f.). All of this corresponds with the historical events known from other sources. But the angel's proclamation in verses 40-45 concerning Antiochus' death no longer jibes with the historical facts. This seems to be an indication that the book, at least the last chapters 10—12, was written before the death of Antiochus in 163 B.C. And since the author was evidently not aware of Antiochus' campaign to the east in the spring of 165 B.C., the book was probably already completed at that time.

3. Finally, from his treatment of "Darius the Mede," whom he places before Cyrus in Babylon (5, 30—6, 1; 9, 1), it appears that the author *completed his defective knowledge of ancient history with data from the prophetic books of the Bible.* He was acquainted with the four-successive-empire schema used by some Hellenistic historians. In it Alexander's empire was preceded by that of the Assyrians, the Medes and the Persians. Our Jewish author took over this schema, but in the place of the Assyrian empire he put Nebuchadnezzar's Babylonian empire. That monarch had deported his hero Daniel to Babylon. For the rest he kept strictly to the schema. But it was difficult for those later generations to distinguish between the Medes and the Persians. Cyrus' mother was indeed a Median princess, and soon the precise course of events in the power struggle between the Medes and Persians· was no longer clear. The author of the book of Daniel did not know one single Median monarch by name. This is why he allowed the second of his four empires, the Medes, to be ruled from Babylon by a monarch to whom he gave the famous royal Persian name

Darius. In reality, however, the power in Mesopotamia passed directly from the Babylonians to the Persians. In history there was no Darius the Mede who ruled in Babylon.

The following list of rulers and dates (some approximate) may help to clarify this:

Babylonians		Medes	
Nebuchadnezzar	605-562	Cyaxares	625-585
Weak successors	562-556	Astyages	585-553
Nabonidus	556-539		

Persians

Cyrus rules over Media	553-529
and also over Babylonia	539-529
Cambyses	529-522
Darius I	522-486
Xerxes I	486-465

But according to Isaiah, Yahweh had nevertheless said that he turned the Medes against Babylon (13, 17; 21, 2). That also was clearly recorded in Jeremiah (51, 11. 28). Therefore, the Medes ruled in Babylon before the Persians took over, and thus Cyrus the Persian was preceded by a Mede, of course a Darius!

III

THE AUTHOR'S INTENTION

Those who were involved in the Maccabean revolt had good reason to be somber about the future. As we have already seen, Alexander the Great did his utmost to stimulate a further penetration of Hellenistic culture. In the course of the 3rd century B.C. many members of the Jewish community gradually adopted the "modern" way of life.

Without a doubt, the Greek language, Greek clothes and customs and Greek thought would dominate in the coming generations. Whoever clung to the Jewish traditions could only see himself as someone standing in the way of human progress.

Antiochus IV who deliberately attempted to annihilate Judaism completely was an extraordinarily powerful monarch ruling a vast empire. Not only did he have strong armies at his disposal, but he found his most reliable allies among the Jews themselves, the upper class which proved itself very open to modern opinions and "adaptation."

The members of the "resistance" had all the more reason to think that they were fighting for a lost cause. They had always believed that the one God determined the course of events and that the community of the Jews was his chosen people, representing him on earth and the beginning of his universal rule, as it were. But now it seemed that he had abandoned his original plans and would let his faithful perish in the flood of the new godlessness.

At that time our writer took the bold decision to strengthen his brothers in their faith by means of a book, the book of Daniel. Let us try to say in our own words what he intended to express in his stories about Daniel (A) and in the visions he let him see (B).

A. "My brothers, you surely know some of the popular stories about the hero of our history whose name was Daniel (God, *el,* is judge, *dan,* or my judge, *dani*). Now, I am going to help you recall him. I picture him as one of the group which Nebuchadnezzar, that infamous enemy of our people, deported in the third year of King Jehoiakim. I make him remain among the courtiers of the mighty kings who succeeded Nebuchadnezzar as rulers over the whole world. In my version of these stories you see Daniel in a situation which greatly resembles the one you are in at present. Those influential pagan kings did everything in their power to make Daniel deny his Jewish faith and customs, just as Antiochus is trying to do now with your small minority. But look! Time and again Israel's God proved himself more powerful than the rulers of this world. He foiled their impious plans, he saved Daniel from certain death, and the divinely inspired wisdom of this Jew confounded everything the pagan magicians could bring forward. So, too, will the Almighty, our God, assist us in our struggle against the impious oppressor. When confronted with all the wisdom God has given us in the Law and the prophets, the Greek philosophies and oriental paganism with all their appealing attraction for the modern mind will become completely pale. Be assured, God will soon rescue us from the fiery furnace into which Antiochus has thrown us and from the jaws of the hungry lion. . . ."

B. "Because you have been struggling so long and the end

seems beyond reach, you may sometimes tend to think that Yahweh is no longer the Lord of history. In your heart you are sometimes afraid that he had to abandon you to the chaotic powers of this world. But try to remember that such thoughts and such a fear are tantamount to rejecting the core of your faith. This faith tells you: no single event escapes Israel's God. He also foresaw this attack by Antiochus. I will make this very clear by portraying in my book how the crisis you are now experiencing was revealed centuries ago to Daniel. It was shown to him not just as one event among many others, but as a prelude to the end of history, as the last struggle between divine and human powers. It will not be long now before Yahweh will destroy this last and most terrible enemy of his "heritage" on earth. Then he will establish his dominion over all peoples and nations, and his eternal kingship will be revealed and given to us. Therefore, my beloved brothers, do not be discouraged; continue to persevere a while longer. That establishment of Yahweh's eternal kingship for which our fathers hoped from the very beginning, when he sealed his Covenant with them and which was foretold time and again by the prophets, is at hand. Do not worry about the lot of your brothers who died on the battlefield, and do not be afraid for yourselves. Yahweh will raise from the dead all those who gave their lives for his cause and will give them a place in his kingdom."

When one tries to make the intention of the author his own in this way, he probably experiences two reactions. On the one hand, he will appreciate the impressive character of this manner of "preaching." The book is a tremendous witness of an unconditional reliance on the sovereign power of Yahweh, and likewise of the firm faith that he directs the course of history inevitably toward a climax—namely, the establishment of his majesty in which all creation will recognize him as its God. The author stresses God's sovereignty by pointing out that his kingdom will not be the result of the work of man. For example, in the dream of Nebuchadnezzar where a stone smashes the statue (the symbol of earthly powers), the author relates that it broke loose from the mountain "untouched by any hand." That stone then "grew into a great mountain, filling the whole earth." In chapter 7 the powers of this world are depicted as huge monsters which emerge from the sea—i.e., the underworld. The kingdom of God, on the contrary, is as "one like a son of man, coming on the clouds of heaven" (7, 13).

On the other hand, the modern reader might wonder whether the very form in which the author presented this "preaching" did not render it ineffective. How can one rouse others to confidence in God's help by means of a *fictitious story* about divine rescue? If those three young Israelites had never really been thrown into a fiery furnace in Babylon, if a certain Daniel had never really been saved from a lion pit, how could the author's *imagination* convince the people that they would be rescued from their *real* distress? And if Daniel's prediction of Antiochus' death was but an expression of the author's wishful thinking, how could it be a source of encouragement for his contemporaries? A satisfying answer to these questions could only be given by the author himself and his first readers. We can no longer reconstruct their feelings or enter into their mentality. All we can try to do is to make an attempt at an answer. To do so we must say something about apocalyptic literature.

IV
AN "APOCALYPTIC" BOOK

In chapter 5 we saw that the prophets were primarily speakers who confronted their contemporaries with Yahweh's demands and promises. In the disasters which overcame the nation, they saw the hand of Yahweh who chastised his people for its sins. Sometimes they foretold that the faithful remnant would enjoy a future which, after the purifying judgment, would bring to fulfillment what Yahweh had said of old. That fulfillment was for them *an extension of the situation as they knew it*. The city of Jerusalem and the temple would remain the center of God's kingdom where peace and justice would reign forever; under an ideal sovereign from the house of David, all of mankind, Israel together with all other nations, would fulfill God's will and thus live in perfect peace.

After the exile the idea developed that this world was much too corrupted by sin to be able to be transformed into God's kingdom. *That would require a total re-creation*. From then on the main prophetic theme became "the Day of Yahweh," which, extended to the whole cosmos, would put an end to all corruption. The faithful therefore lived in the expectation that the present world would first have to disappear. Then Yahweh would call an entirely new cosmos into being, the perfection of which would meet the expectations of his sovereign majesty.

In the third part of the book of Isaiah, which consists for the most part of post-exilic works (cf. p. 179), we meet this expectation of "new heavens and a new earth" (Is. 65, 17; 66, 22). From the 2nd century B.C. onward, people began more and more to speculate about the new situation which would have to be preceded by the disappearance of the old world; these speculations took the form of what we call the "apocalyptic genre." It differs in many respects from the ancient prophetic literature. Let us look at a few of these differences.

1. The authors of the apocalypses are not primarily speakers, but writers and learned men. They thoroughly know the letter of the Sacred Books, especially the Law and the prophets; they often use them as a point of departure and borrow figurative material from them for their speculations.

2. The concise, pregnant sayings, so characteristic of the prophets of the classical period, give way in this genre to elaborate descriptions and cryptic suggestions.

3. Their speculations about the end of the world and the structure of the cosmos usually take the form of visions which they attribute to great figures from the past. Thus we have writings which describe visions of Enoch, Noah, Abraham, Moses, Ezra and others. Hence the name "apocalyptic," from the Greek verb *apokaluptein* meaning "to reveal, to disclose" and the substantive *apokalupsis*, "revelation, disclosure." The secrets of the world and its future were revealed to those great men of God.

4. In many works of this genre angels play an important role. One of them usually acts as the interpreter of the visions and sometimes also as the seer's guide on his journeys through heaven and the underworld.

Of the unusually rich apocalyptic literature which flourished from the 2nd century B.C. until the 1st century of the Christian era, the book of Daniel is the only work which secured a place in the Hebrew canon. In the Christian canon, too, there is but one—the "Apocalypse" or "Revelation" which is attributed to St. John.

Returning to our question about the effect of the book of Daniel on its first readers, we must keep in mind that *the book belonged to a very definite literary genre and that its readers were well acquainted with that genre.* They could not even conceive of the authors of such books trying to deceive their readers. If we buy a novel about Napoleon, we do not feel cheated if the book is not an historical account based on the latest critical research. And when we read Shakespeare's *Hamlet,* we know very well that it is not an exact reproduction of what actually took place in the Danish palace. We all know what to expect from a book and what not, almost as a matter of course; people living in the 2nd century did too. We expect a serious novel to be a fascinating description of human experiences and situations, and a detective story to be captivating and relaxing. In the same way the author of Daniel wanted to instruct his readers in a fascinating way about their faith and to strengthen them in it; there can be no doubt that he succeeded. For many his book apparently answered a need.

It may be that a certain amount of success is partly responsible for the present form of the book as well. Let us suppose that the author first published a work in Aramaic, beginning with the dream of Nebuchadnezzar (chapter 2, where "apocalyptic" features are already visible) and ending with the vision of chapter 7. The success of this work, which made Daniel a very popular figure, might have encouraged the author to expand his work by adding an introductory story about Daniel's arrival at the Babylonian court (chapter 1) and a few more apocalyptic visions— both of these in Hebrew. But all of this is of course pure hypothesis.

It is certain, however, that many variants of the Daniel stories were in circulation among the Jews. This is clear from fragments found among the Dead Sea Scrolls and also from the additions made to the book in the Greek version, as found in Catholic editions of the Bible. We met similar additions in Esther, but in the case of Daniel the Hebrew-Aramaic book was already explicitly religious. Daniel is a pious man who prays often and fervently. The writer puts a beautiful hymn of praise on his lips (2, 20-23) after the secret of the king's dream was revealed to him, and a long penitential prayer when he tries to understand the seventy weeks of the text of Jeremiah (9, 4-19). He also lets the kings of Babylon use formulas from the Jewish liturgy when they confess the transcendence of Israel's God (e.g., Nebuchadnezzar in 3, 29 and 4, 31-32 and Darius in 6, 27-28).

In this case the Egyptian Jews continued in the line of the author when they incorporated other prayers. In chapter 3 they let one of the three Jewish youths in the furnace utter a prayer of supplication which was apparently a part of their liturgical usage. That it did not fit very well in the story's context (the young men in Babylon had been very strict in their observance of the Law and could hardly confess that they had "not listened to the precepts of your Law . . . not observed them") disturbed neither the redactors nor the readers. Why not? The reader knows the answer already, but it is worth repeating. For those people the *meaning* of a story was primary. For them the young men in the fiery furnace were all believers-in-distress. After several lines of narrative in which the furnace was being stoked even hotter and the "angel of the Lord" (from 3, 25 in the Aramaic text) made the inside as cool as a morning breeze for the young men, the three of them begin the hymn of praise known to us as the *Benedicite,* "May you be blessed, Lord. . . ." In it, just as in Psalm 148, all of creation is called upon to praise God and finally Ananiah, Azariah and Mishael as well; these God had "snatched from the underworld, saved from the hand of death, and from the burning fiery furnace."

Besides these prayers within the text, two stories were added at the end. The first (chapter 13) about Susanna, the chaste woman who was falsely accused by two sensuous old men, and the young man who came to her rescue during the trial probably circulated first as a separate work, without any connection with the book of Daniel and its hero. The young man's skill in securing a just decision was expressed in his name, Daniel (cf. p. 261). This may also be the reason for its incorporation into our book. In the second story (chapter 14) other ancient narrative motifs seem to have played a role. There Daniel again appears as a favorite at Cyrus' court. After he exposed the deception of the pagan priests and subsequently played the role of dragon killer, the Babylonians accused the king himself of "turning Jew." He orders Daniel to be thrown into the lion pit, with the same result as in chapter 6. The only difference is that here Daniel also miraculously receives something to eat. The prophet Habakkuk with his basket of food is carried away by an angel from Judah to Babylon, just as Ezekiel was "carried away" by the hair in the opposite direction (Ezek. 8, 3).

Part II
The Four Gospels

VIII
History, Origin
and Nature

The twenty-seven "books" of the New Testament constitute less than one-fourth of the Bible, and the first four, the gospels, hardly one-tenth. Yet these four works are the best known by far, and of all the books of the Bible, even of all human literature, they are read the most. Likewise, no other single work has undergone such scrutiny, been studied so critically and discussed so passionately as these four little books. As to their length they are more like pamphlets which could easily be printed together in the Sunday supplement of a large city newspaper. But their content is dominated by the mysterious person of Jesus who never ceases speaking to mankind through those texts.

Because of their exceptional interest, the gospels might well take up most of the pages in an introduction to the Bible. That we devote only these short chapters to them here is not solely due to the schematic character of this book. We believe that the preceding chapters have already provided an introduction to the gospels in a certain sense, for the people involved in their making belonged to the same milieu as the biblical historians at work in the Old Testament. The literary work of the evangelists, through which that specific event from the recent past, which so captivated their lives, was made to live in the present, could not but correspond to that of their Old Testament predecessors. Therefore, they did not share our modern interest in a precise sequence of events (cf. chapter 2, pp. 62-84). The evangelists' work of collecting and passing on Jesus' words likewise bore the hallmark of age-old traditions, some of which we saw in chapters 6 and 7. Hence our conviction that to become acquainted with the "historical" and other books of the

Old Testament is at the same time a first, indirect acquaintance with the disciples who passed on their recollections about Jesus and with the authors of the four gospels.

We will begin this chapter with the historical framework within which the four books came about. Then we will give a short summary of what people have thought about their origin and character in the course of history. The final section will briefly introduce our approach to the genesis of the gospels according to modern insights.

I

The Historical Framework

Jesus lived in Palestine at the beginning of the 1st century A.D.; toward the end of that century the four gospels made their appearance. The chart on the opposite page listing the names of those who were ruling or trying to rule the restless national groups in Palestine should help us recall something of the historical situation of that time. On the far left are the Roman emperors, the supreme rulers. Among them we inserted several legates who in their name governed the province of Syria, which also meant that they had to keep an eye on Palestine.

At the top of the wide column in the middle is Herod the Great. After his death in 4 B.C., Emperor Augustus divided the territory among three of Herod's sons who had not been murdered by their father. Archelaus was given dominion over Judea and Samaria. He ruled very poorly and was exiled in 6 A.D. His territory then came under the Roman procurators or governors who in turn were responsible to the legate in Syria. The fifth in a series of seven was Pontius Pilate. Galilee and Perea across the Jordan fell to Herod Antipas who bore the title of tetrarch—i.e., one ruling over a fourth of the whole. At that time this was a common title for rulers of small territories. He ruled much longer than his brother, but in 39 A.D. he, too, came under Roman suspicion and was exiled to Lyons. To his right on our chart is Philip, the most competent governor of them all. He died childless in 34 and his tetrarchate first went to Syria. However, the cunning Julius Agrippa, grandson of Herod the Great and a product of Roman education, was soon able to obtain that territory for himself from Emperor Caligula. In

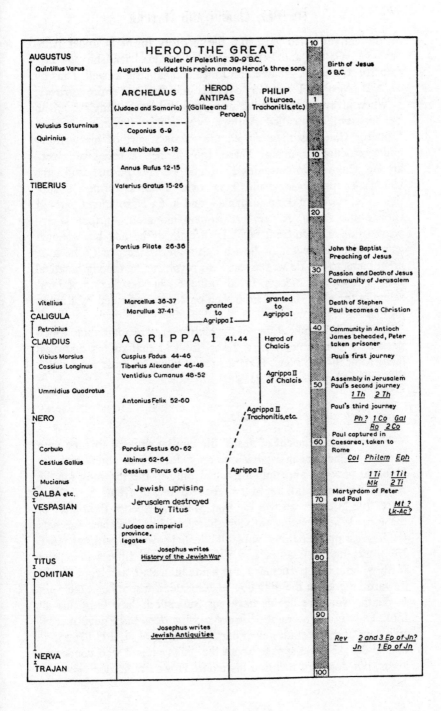

39 the emperor also gave him the territory formerly under Anti-pas—i.e., Galilee and Perea. In return for his friendship the new emperor, Claudius, granted him Judea and Samaria as well. Thus by 41 A.D. Agrippa I was king over his grandfather's entire territory.

When a severe abdominal illness resulted in the king's death in 44, his son, also called Agrippa, was still too young to reign. Emperor Claudius then placed the greatest part of his territory under procurators again. These, too, formed a series of seven, among whom were Antonius Felix and Porcius Festus. In 53 the young Agrippa was made king over Philip's former territo-ries—i.e., northern Transjordania—and in 64 Nero added parts of Galilee and Perea. A very pro-Roman monarch, Agrippa II ap-pears to have ruled until 90 A.D. Previously he had been named as a kind of inspector of Jewish cult in Jerusalem. In 66 he took great pains to put down the senseless revolt raging among fanatical Jews, but without success. It led to the terrible destruction of Jeru-salem in the year 70, and from then on Judea was ruled by Roman legates.

In the right-hand column of the chart there are some facts which pertain to our subject: first, Jesus' lot and that of his disciples; then, some of the New Testament writings. We must now say a word about both series of data.

Exact Chronology Is Impossible

Not one single event of Jesus' life can be situated in time with certainty. The reason is that our only documents about him are "biblical history" and thus interested only in the meaning for the reader of what is said, not in the precise dating of events.

A little later on we will see that Mark's gospel is the oldest of the four. When reading through that gospel as a whole, one gets the impression that Jesus' public life lasted several months at most. He works first in Galilee and its surroundings, travels back and forth without any particular route being indicated, and from 10, 32 onward he goes in the direction of Jerusalem, where he is then put to death. Nowhere do we have any indications how long this all took. Only in the account of Jesus' passion does Mark give succes-sive days and sometimes even parts of a day (14, 1. 12. 17; 15, 1. 25. 33-34. 42). He speaks about the "high priest" who condemns Jesus, but does not mention his name. However, he does give the name of the Roman governor, Pilate (his second name). From non-biblical sources we know that Pontius Pilate governed Judea from 26 to 36 A.D. But Mark does not tell us precisely when during those ten or eleven years Pilate sentenced Jesus.

Luke is the only evangelist who expressly places an event in the framework of what we might call "general history." Like all other Christians, he considers John the Baptist to be the last of the prophets. Now, in some books of the Bible the appearance of a prophet is dated as follows: "In such and such a year of King . . . the word of the Lord came to. . . ." (see, for example, Jer. 1, 1; 26, 1; 27, 1; Ezek. 29, 1). In that same way Luke begins his account of John the Baptist's ministry (3, 1-2):

> In the fifteenth year of Tiberius Caesar's reign, when Pontius Pilate was governor of Judea, Herod tetrarch of Galilee, his brother Philip tetrarch of the lands of Ituraea and Trachonitis, Lysanias tetrarch of Abilene, during the pontificate of Annas and Caiaphas, the word of God came to John son of Zechariah, in the wilderness.

We know that Tiberius' predecessor and stepfather Augustus died on August 19, 14 A.D. The fifteenth year of Tiberius' reign ran, therefore, from August 19, 28 until August 18 of the following year. But in the East it was the custom to count the year during which a monarch came to power as the first of his reign. Did Luke do this too? If so, that fifteenth year would have been from October 1, 27 until September 30, 28 A.D.

Even if we knew exactly how Luke counted in such cases, we would indeed have the precise year John the Baptist began to preach, but we would not yet know anything with certainty about Jesus. Luke does not tell us how long John was baptizing before Jesus came to him. He does say that "Jesus was about thirty years old" (3, 23), but it is not at all certain that the evangelist intended to provide an historical fact in the strict sense. Rather, he was probably thinking of great figures in Scripture who began their careers at thirty. Jesus' baptism was for Luke an "anointing with the Holy Spirit" (cf. Acts 10, 38). After David was "anointed king of Israel," he too was said to have been "thirty years old" (2 Sam. 5, 4; see also Gn. 41, 46 for Joseph and Ezek. 1, 1 for Ezekiel). That little word "about" can be an indication that Luke was more concerned with the biblical parallel than with providing historical information.

Those thirty years should not be used, therefore, to determine the year of Jesus' birth. Matthew and Luke situate that event in the reign of Herod the Great, who died in the year 4 B.C. Here we must remember that Christians in the Roman Empire continued for several centuries the practice of dating events *ab urbe condita,* "from the founding of the city (Rome)." Pope John I, who died in 526, introduced the custom of dating things *a Christo nato,* "from the birth of Christ." The man to whom he entrusted the calculations, a certain Dionysius, made several mistakes (or copied them from another person). The result was the incorrect situation of Jesus' birth in the year 753 *ab urbe condita*—i.e., four years after Herod's death. Due to insufficient data it is now no longer possible to determine just how many years before Herod's death Jesus was born.

Likewise, the gospels do not provide sufficient data with which we can determine with any accuracy the length of Jesus' public life. Whereas Mark gives the impression that it only lasted several months, mostly in Galilee, and ended with Jesus' one single journey to Jerusalem, John mentions several visits to the capital, twice on the occasion of the Passover (2, 13; 6, 4) and once for another feast (5, 1). That suggests more than two full years of activity before the Passover which provided the occasion for his death. However, here, too, we can question whether such data were intended to be historical information.

The years 27, 30, 31 and 33 have all been defended by scholars as the year of Jesus' death. There is much to be said for the year 30. Those who opt for the year 33 cannot, of course, agree with one of the dates suggested as the year of Paul's conversion— namely, 31!

Biblical people were simply not interested in data which our modern Western sense considers indispensable. To our way of thinking, an event hangs in the air as something vague and undetermined unless it is connected with a specific day and year.

It is not only because of our way of thinking, however, that modern biblical scholars continue searching for certainty on this point, hoping for new data, for there are cases where a date can be very important for the meaning of a fact. For example, whether Jesus was crucified on the 14th of the month of Nisan according to

John, or on the 15th according to the other evangelists, is related to another question: Was Jesus' last supper with his disciples the Passover supper or not? And this question is indeed important.

With regard to the chronology of Paul's ministry, Acts provides some information which makes it possible to pinpoint a few dates more or less accurately. The clearest of these is Gallio's stay in Corinth as proconsul while Paul was working there (Acts 18, 12). According to an inscription found in Delphi, Gallio came there in 51/52 or 52/53. Some of Paul's letters can also be dated accurately within a few years. However, it is no longer possible to determine how long and where Paul worked after his release from house arrest in Rome, with which Acts concludes (28, 30-31), or to attain certainty about the year of his martyrdom there.

The Growth of the New Testament

The facts in the right-hand column of our chart should therefore be movable, capable of sliding up and down a bit. Their order, however, *is* certain. This is very important for the "facts" which we printed there in italics—namely, the sequence in which the New Testament writings came into being. The reader will notice that Paul's letters to the Thessalonians are the oldest among them. Further, he will see that most of his letters were already written, and Paul himself was already dead, when the four gospels made their appearance. Thus many Christian communities already existed in remote parts of the then known world *before* the four gospels were written. All those churches had to make their way during those early years without these books.

Many of the faithful are still very surprised to hear this. Until now they had often spoken about "the gospels" as something written: "The gospel says. . . ." This idea probably became ingrained partly as a result of their church attendance, for there they listen to readings from "the holy gospel." If they ever thought about Paul going out to preach the gospel, they no doubt pictured a man reading passages from a book and explaining them. In addition, they imagined those passages to have been written down by eyewitnesses, who had made notes of what Jesus said to his disciples "at that time" and written an account of his deeds.

But that is not the way it was. The Church had already existed for several decades when the written word was first put to use as an aid to the transmission of the apostles' preaching. And it was not until the 2nd century that those writings were collected in a canon, just as we saw the Jews doing with their Bible, the Old Testament. A comparison between these two formative processes may help clarify the matter.

There is a certain *similarity*. During Israel's earliest years traditions were passed on by word of mouth. After David, the written word began to play a role in this, but not a dominating role. People lived and experienced their religion in the cult, in the preaching and instructions of priests and prophets. In that many-sided experience, written texts also acquired certain functions—for example, as aids to the memory, documentation and the like. It was only after the exile that certain texts began to fulfill the role of "Holy Scripture." The reason for this is clear to a certain extent. Everything that once held the people of Judah together, such as political independence, the monarchy and the national cult in the royal temple with its innumerable attendants, was destroyed by the Babylonians in 587. After that disaster, the returning Judeans and their brethren in Babylon and elsewhere were united only by their blood relationship and their faith. To put it briefly: from a nation Israel became a church. That faith found expression in texts, in "holy" books which were likewise norms for their actions and thoughts. Outside the temple of Jerusalem, in the synagogues of Palestine and of the worldwide Diaspora, reading from "the Law, the prophets and the psalms" was the high point of the gatherings in which Jews met each other as Jews. When the temple of Jerusalem was destroyed by the Romans in 70 A.D., one of the first concerns of the Jewish leaders was to establish a definitive canon. It was clearer than ever that only Holy Scripture could keep Judaism from falling apart.

In a much shorter period of time, a similar process took place in the early Church. At the very beginning there was nothing but the proclamation of the word. Later on, preachers sometimes took up the pen, but their writings still played a subservient role in the life of Christians. Paul kept in contact with the communities he founded, but even this tireless traveler could not go everywhere his presence was desired. Hence he took to writing letters, but only as something temporary. Sometimes they served to recall what he had said or to set certain things straight, and frequently they were designed to announce a visit from him personally in the near future. Now and then he added that his letter should also be read in the neighboring communities. It is understandable that later on people would also read those letters once in a while, especially after Paul's death, and that other communities would also want copies of them. Hence the origin, in the course of the 2nd century, of the *corpus Paulinum,* the collection of letters which Paul was believed to have written, whether with his own hand or not.

Recollections about Jesus' words, deeds and final lot were also passed on orally at the beginning. Sometimes a disciple would write out a series of miracle stories or a number of sayings to assist his memory. Notations of this kind probably circulated in some communities as an aid in the instruction of new members. It was only when the generation of eyewitnesses began to pass away that such writings also began to have documentary value. At that time the different gospels known to us also came into being, first of all for the sake of a particular community or group of communities or perhaps even for a particular person and his circle of friends (Theophilus in the case of Luke; cf. Lk. 1, 3 and Acts 1, 1). After that it took several decades before copies of those writings reached other parts of the Church and there began to acquire the same kind of authority which was accorded to St. Paul's letters. But then we are already well into the 2nd century. At that time all kinds of new practices and serious differences of opinion began to threaten the solidarity of the Christian communities. Many writings of suspect origin were making the rounds. The need for adherence to the primitive traditions was felt. Hence the formation of a Christian canon, the canon of the New Testament.

A major difference between this and the origin of the Jewish canon is that from the very beginning Christians had their Holy Scripture, their Bible. That was the Jewish book which only later would come to be called the Old Testament, after the Church had established her own canon. Jesus and his disciples regarded those Scriptures as God's word set down by Moses and David and so many of the prophets "in the Holy Spirit." Paul's letters show in many different ways how that book constituted part of the basis of the new communities which were founded on his apostolic message. Of course, Christians of Jewish origin were already well acquainted with it. They had heard the Scriptures read and explained in their synagogues. What made them into a new community was the entirely new note they heard in those Scriptures, a completely new explanation of them. Since they had accepted Jesus as the Messiah and the Son of God, they saw allusions to him everywhere in that holy book. It provided them with manifold images and terms with which to reflect upon and to express what God had bestowed on mankind in this last and greatest of his beneficent gifts, the crowning of what he had done for Israel in former centuries.

In that "biblical atmosphere" the twenty-seven writings of the New Testament came into being. This fact alone makes it sufficiently clear that a good understanding of it is hardly possible without a certain familiarity with the Old Testament.

II
ORIGIN AND NATURE OF THE GOSPELS: THEORIES

What we have just written about the growth of the New Testament is of course based on the modern historical approach to the question. Before we take up a detailed study of the gospels in the light of this approach, we will first sketch briefly the various ways in which men of the past described their origin and character.

Biographies of Christ

In the course of the 2nd century more and more gospels began to make the rounds, often bearing the name of an apostle—e.g., the gospel according to Thomas, or Peter, or James, etc. They related all sorts of fantastic things about Jesus which obscured the actual meaning of his person. Their childish representations were partly responsible for furthering the recognition of the four gospels which went back to the oldest witnesses and were sealed with the authority of the apostles. All four enjoyed that authority to the same degree. Since they had a number of passages in common, some thought it a good idea to reproduce the contents of the four books in one work. That seemed less cumbersome.

About the year 170 a certain Tatian, who lived in Syria, published just such a work. Greek-speaking Christians gave it the title *to dia tessaron euangelion,* "the gospel [compiled] from the four." Unfortunately the original Syrian version of that "harmonized gospel," as such books are sometimes called, has been lost. Only fragments of commentaries and versions in various ancient languages remain; there is even one in 13th-century Dutch.

It seems that Tatian used the fourth gospel as a framework. As if creating a mosaic he artistically placed in it passages from the other gospels, insofar as they differed from one another. However, he also included details from "unauthentic" gospels, which could partly have been the reason why his book never attained more or less official recognition.

The tendency to combine the four gospels in this fashion persisted through the centuries. It became even stronger after the 16th century. At that time many Christians thought that "divine inspiration" ensured the historical exactness of every detail (*inspiratio,* "breathing in" by the *spiritus,* "wind" or "spirit"). In this way everything contained in the four gospels was accorded the same value. When two stories about Christ or two of his sayings differed in some small detail, they were therefore thought to relate two completely different facts or sayings.

Thus when Jesus visited Jericho during his last journey to Jerusalem, he was believed to have cured four blind men there. According to Luke he cured one as he approached Jericho (18, 35-43). Mark writes that a certain Bartimaeus, a blind beggar, called out to Jesus as he was leaving the city; without Jesus even touching him, the man's sight returned (10, 46-52). And then Matthew relates that Jesus cured two more blind men who were also sitting along the road when he was leaving Jericho. Jesus touched their eyes, and they regained their sight (20, 29-34).

Luke's passage about the "Our Father" is shorter than Matthew's version, which we all know, and furthermore Luke says that Jesus prayed that prayer in response to the question: "Lord, teach us to pray. . . ." (11, 1-4; cf. Mt. 6, 9-13). Therefore, Jesus taught his disciples two versions, a long one and a short one.

Many pious descriptions of Christ's passion and death consist in or are based on a combination of details from the four accounts of the passion. To these we owe the well-known "Seven Last Words" uttered by Jesus on the cross:

From *Luke*	"Father, forgive them; they do not know what they are doing."
From *Luke*	"Today you will be with me in paradise."

From *John*	"Woman, this is your son. . . . Son, this is your mother."
From *Matthew/Mark*	"Eli, Eli, lama sabachtani."
From *John*	"I am thirsty."
From *John*	"It is accomplished."
From *Luke*	"Father, into your hands I commit my spirit."

Shortly after World War II, a high school student in France sent me a small textbook, published in 1937, which they were using at school. It furnished precise dates for all the events in Jesus' life and fifteen maps showing all Jesus' journeys besides. Here are a few points from that book as a sample:

The end of 6 B.C.	The birth of John the Baptist announced.
March 25, 5 B.C.	The announcement of Jesus' birth.
The end of March	Mary's visit to Elizabeth.
The end of June	Birth of John the Baptist
December 25	Birth of Jesus.
October 18-20, 29 A.D.	The man born blind. The Good Shepherd (Jn. 9—10)
The end of October	The three callings (Mt. 8, 18-22; Lk. 9, 57-60). Mission of the 72 (Mt. 10, 40; Lk. 10, 1-12).
November, 29 A.D.	Return of the disciples. The yoke of Christ (Mt. 11, 25-30; 13, 16-17). Parable of the Good Samaritan (Lk. 10, 25-37).

The writer based his chronology, as he himself explained, on that of John's gospel, weaving the material of the other texts into it. Tatian's principle was still at work!

The Gospels Side by Side

Tatian and his modern followers considered each of the four gospels separately without paying any attention to their prehistory. One of the first to do that was the famous Father of the

Church, St. Augustine (354-430). Being a great writer himself, he gave some thought to the reasons why three other people would write a gospel when one already existed. He supposed that their sequence in the canon, Matthew-Mark-Luke-John, was also that of their origin. Mark, he thought, wrote after Matthew to give the people a shorter version of that long gospel. And so Mark got the name "abbreviator of Matthew." After those two attempts to "draw up accounts of the events that have taken place among us," Luke decided to write a new book for his friend Theophilus. In it he made use of Matthew and Mark. Finally the profound John thought it necessary to complete these three concrete historical accounts with a fourth gospel which would shed more light on the supernatural character of Jesus' personality.

In this way Augustine opened the door to the study of the mutual relationship of the four gospels. For a good understanding of the modern theories on this, we still have two points to consider.

The "Synoptic" Question

The first three gospels have quite a few stories about Jesus as well as sayings of his in common, and they are often reproduced in the same order. Luke's gospel with its 1,150 verses and Matthew's with its 1,079 are much longer than that of Mark which has only 661 verses. Moreover, 600 of these 661 are also found in Matthew and more than half in Luke.

These similarities have led to an edition of the three gospels in the form of a "synopsis," in which the respective texts are printed in parallel columns. This has the advantage that all of them can be seen at a glance (*syn,* "together" and *opsis,* "seeing"). When such a synopsis gives the complete text of the three gospels, the column for Mark is often completely blank. This is to be expected, of course, since Matthew and Luke have so much more material. However, a large number of texts besides those common to the three gospels are common only to Matthew and Mark: 235 verses, mostly consisting of Jesus' words.

By way of illustration the following page gives a sample of what a synopsis looks like. The order of the columns is Mark-Matthew-Luke. This page begins with the concluding words of Matthew's "Sermon on the Mount" (Mt. 5—7). The version of the "Sermon" in Luke (Lk. 6, 20-49) ends with the same parable.

SAMPLE PAGE OF A SYNOPSIS

Matthew 7	*Luke 6*
25. Rain came down, floods rose, gales blew and hurled themselves against that house, and it did not fall: it was founded on rock. 26. But everyone who listens to these words of mine and does not act on them will be like a stupid man who built his house on sand. 27. Rain came down, floods rose, gales blew and struck that house, and it fell; and what a fall it had!	48. *. . . when the river was in flood* *it bore down on that house, but could not shake it, it was built so well. 49. But the one who listens* *and does nothing is like the man who built his house on soil, with no foundations: as soon as the river bore down on it,* *it collapsed; and what a ruin that house became!*

The Amazement of the Crowds

Matthew 7, 28-29

Jesus had now finished what he wanted to say, and his teaching made a deep impression on the people because he taught them with authority, and not like their own scribes.

Cure of a Leper

Mark 1, 40ff.	*Matthew 8, 1ff.*	*Luke 5, 12ff.*
	1. After he had come down from the mountain large crowds followed him.	12. Now Jesus was in one of the towns when a man appeared, covered with leprosy. Seeing Jesus he fell on his face and implored him.
40. A leper came up to him and pleaded on his knees: "If you want to," he said, "you can cure me." 41. Feeling sorry for him, Jesus stretched out his hand and touched him. "Of course I want to!" he said. "Be cured!" 42. And the leprosy left him at once, and he was cured. 43. Jesus immediately sent him away and sternly ordered him, "Mind you say nothing to anyone, but go and show yourself to the priest and make the offering for your healing prescribed by Moses as evidence of your recovery."	2. A leper came up and bowed low in front of him. "Sir," he said, "if you want to, you can cure me." 3. Jesus stretched out his hand, touched him and said, "Of course I want to! Be cured!" And his leprosy was cured at once. 4. Then Jesus said to him, "Mind you do not tell anyone, but go and show yourself to the priest and make the offering prescribed by Moses as evidence for them."	"Sir," he said, "if you want to, you can cure me." 13. Jesus stretched out his hand, touched him and said, "Of course I want to! Be cured!" And the leprosy left him at once. 14. He ordered him to tell no one, "But go and show yourself to the priest and make the offering for your healing as Moses prescribed it, as evidence for them."

But Luke gives it a different place in his gospel; hence the parallel text is printed in italics. Mark does not include any of these words, and so his column is blank. Matthew is the only one to make the observation after the "Sermon." Then all three of these so-called synoptic evangelists include the subsequent cure of a leper. One can see at a glance that the same scene is introduced in different ways.

When browsing through a synopsis of this kind, one quickly observes that Augustine's theory could be entirely correct. According to him, as we saw, Mark had written an abbreviated version of Matthew. That sometimes seems in fact to be the case. Mark seems to summarize the well-known story of Jesus' triple temptation by Satan (Mt. 4, 1-11) as follows (1, 12-13):

Immediately afterward the Spirit drove him out into the wilderness and he remained there for forty days, and was tempted by Satan. He was with the wild beasts, and the angels looked after him.

But further on Mark has stories which are much longer than the version found in Matthew. For example, he tells the story which culminates in the return to life of Jairus' daughter in twenty-two verses, whereas Matthew only needs nine verses to relate the same incident. Where Matthew recounts the healing of the epileptic boy in eight verses, Mark does it in sixteen. In these and similar cases Matthew seems rather to be the abbreviator of Mark.

Augustine noticed these things too. However, it is not necessary to take up his reasoning here, for the great Father of the Church could not possibly have developed accurate theories in this matter since he did not have access to copies of the gospels which were reliable enough to be able to furnish an accurate view of their mutual relationship. This became possible only after the study of textual criticism was sufficiently developed.

Textual Criticism

The scrolls or sheets of "papyrus" (a writing material made from strips of pith from a reed called *papyros*) on which Paul wrote his letters and the evangelists their gospels were soon lost. That material is very sensitive to dampness, and since such scrolls were passed on from hand to hand, it is easy to understand that they took quite a beating. But then copies of them were made, and when they too were worn out, still other copies replaced them. In the 4th century many Christians could afford parchment. It was more expensive, but much more durable. The continuous expansion of the Church, however, made it necessary to reproduce these too, and copying by hand was again the method used.

With all that copying, changes in the text, conscious and unconscious, were inevitable. One copyist made spelling corrections here and there, for in the course of time the spelling rules had changed too. Another replaced old-fashioned terms with more modern expressions, or corrected awkward sentences. Still another added a word of clarification. In a milieu where Mary's virginity was disputed, someone replaced "his [Jesus] parents" in Luke 2, 41 with "Joseph and Mary." If one of Christ's sayings in Mark was a bit different from the rendering in Luke, it often happened that someone would adapt Mark's text to that of Luke: after all the Master could have said it only in *one* way. An adaptation of this kind could also happen unconsciously. When copying Luke's gospel, a Christian who knew the official "Our Father" by heart automatically wrote "your will be done" after "your kingdom come." Likewise, a tired copyist sometimes skipped from one line to another one further on which began with the same word. And so on. . . .

When a bishop wanted a new lectionary of the gospels, it could happen that he would ask a learned deacon to put together a new text from three existing copies, which possibly differed considerably from each other. The new one would then be a kind of common denominator, and it was the copyist's task to prepare a smooth and easily readable text. If the bishop was rich enough, then he might take the new text to a "scriptorium," a copying firm (the "printing shops" of those days), and order thirty copies for the parishes in the country. In such a scriptorium the text was dictated to thirty people who wrote out the whole thing. Sometimes the reader would pronounce a word indistinctly, with the result that the error might be reproduced in all thirty copies. Or perhaps one of the official copyists went to bed too late the night before and himself was responsible for mistakes in one of the copies, which years later might have to serve as a model for another twenty books. And so on. . . .

Of course the same kind of things also happened in the reproduction of Latin translations. These versions had been made according to a Greek manuscript, which itself already differed in many places from the original text. Augustine worked with copies of Latin translations!

The many differences between those Latin versions were already an object of intense study at the medieval universities. However, it was not until the 16th century that the search for the real underlying text began. This came as a result of the desire to multiply the "original" Greek text by means of the newly discovered art of printing. In preparing the first printed text of the Greek New Testament (1516), Erasmus used six manuscripts. Two centuries later Professor John Mill of Oxford worked through seventy manuscripts for his edition. He printed the text of the manuscript which he considered the best, and in footnotes he listed the sixty-nine "different readings," *variae lectiones* or "variants" of the other manuscripts. He counted some 30,000 such variants.

"Textual criticism" as an independent branch of science first began to flourish in the 19th century. Investigators traveled all over Europe, Asia Minor, Palestine and Egypt to track down old Greek manuscripts of the Bible in libraries of patriarchates and cloisters. By the turn of the century they had located about 4,000 containing the New Testament, either in its entirety or in part. All these texts were carefully compared with each other. If in a number of copies the same variants were observed, this was an indication that they had a common "ancestor." If this version (whether an actual copy of it existed or not) manifested a certain resemblance with the "ancestor" of another group, then both were said to go back to an even earlier version. By establishing the "family trees" of manuscripts in this way, scholars were able to approach the biblical authors' phraseology very closely. On this point, too, the search continued. The dry Egyptian sand in places where it never rains yielded some very welcome surprises in the form of pieces of papyrus with fragments of the New Testament. These are much older than the oldest manuscripts in our possession. Further surprises of this kind may turn up. But there has already been an enormous amount accomplished. Of all the works of antiquity which have come down to us through the hands of copyists, the New Testament is the only one whose original text we can approach so closely. This comes from the enormous number of manuscripts we possess. People are sometimes shocked to hear that the number of variants in the texts exceeds 150,000, but they should realize that this is due to the vast number of manuscripts. We have all of these now, thanks to the countless believers for whom the New Testament was the most precious book they knew and which they copied endlessly. Of course, they were human, and thus they made many mistakes. Hence the variants, but also our certitude. There are famous works by classical authors, philosophers and historians of which there are but a few late manuscripts extant. Therefore, we are much less certain about their text than we are about that of the New Testament. In other words, when we cite Plato or Cicero from a modern critical edition and when we do the same with Mark or Paul, we can say "Mark or Paul wrote as follows. . . ." with much more scientific certitude than we have when we state "Plato or Cicero spoke as follows. . . ."

The "Double Source Theory"

The new and better editions of the New Testament contributed to the insight, arrived at after 1860, that Mark's book had to be the oldest of the three gospels. The other two would have then borrowed details from Mark, since it was much more a collection of loose incidents without a clear logical or temporal sequence than a thought-out story. Most of the evidently loose episodes (certainly before the journey to Jerusalem—10, 32—but also afterward until the actual beginning of the passion narration—14, 1) could be arranged in a completely different order without changing the book very noticeably. But where Luke treats the same material as Mark, he does so in the same arbitrary sequence. From this it follows that for the most part Luke must have used Mark's gospel as his source, or at least a book corresponding to it. Something similar also applies to Matthew. Where that evangelist presents material from Mark in a different sequence, it can sometimes be shown why he made the changes.

Now, Matthew and Luke must have used another common source besides Mark, for they often render Christ's words in exactly the same way, sometimes literally in the same Greek words. Therefore, there must have been a document written in Greek from which both Matthew and Luke derived sayings of Jesus. German scholars often call that supposed document the "Logien-Quelle," the source (*Quelle*) with sayings (*logia*—i.e., the

plural of the word *logion,* "saying"), which they abbreviate with Q
for the sake of convenience.

This theory about the two sources, Mark and Q, which both
Matthew and Luke were thought to have used, did not, of course,
solve all the questions regarding the mutual relationship of the first
three gospels. But, accepted or not, it continued for a long time to
be the point of departure for many studies about the synoptic texts.
The outline on the following page may help to clarify this point.
The meaning of the various arrows which join the w's (Jesus'
words) and d's (deeds) above the cross to the gospel documents
will become apparent in the following paragraphs.

"Formgeschichte" or Form Criticism

World War I gave a new impulse to biblical scholarship. In chapter I we saw that students of the Pentateuch turned away from a
strictly literary analysis—determining documents and sources,
etc.—*in order to go in search of the real life behind the dead texts*
(cf. p. 25). This same thing happened in the study of the gospels.
Suppositions about still other documents, a primitive form of
Mark, further sources for Matthew and Luke, etc., led in many
different ways to an expansion of the double source theory. This
path became more and more tiring. It seemed to be a dead end.
Partly influenced by new approaches in other areas of the history
of literature and by various factors already at work in the study of
the books of the Old Testament, immediately after the war some
German scholars set a new course. Their method is usually
referred to in German as the "Formgeschichtliche Methode" or
simply as "Formgeschichte"—i.e., the study of the history of literary forms, in this case those found in the gospels.

The first and most fundamental books on this method appeared
in 1919 (K. L. Schmidt and M. Dibelius) and 1921 (R. Bult-
mann) independently of each other. This is indeed an indication of
how much the new approach was prepared by previous developments, "ripe for the picking," so to speak.

These learned scholars took as their point of departure that
remarkable characteristic of Mark's gospel which attracted our
attention above. It seemed to consist for the most part in a number
of short, well-unified episodes describing one of Jesus' miracles or
presenting a conversation complete with conclusion, a parable or a

THE GENESIS OF THE GOSPELS
a schematic view

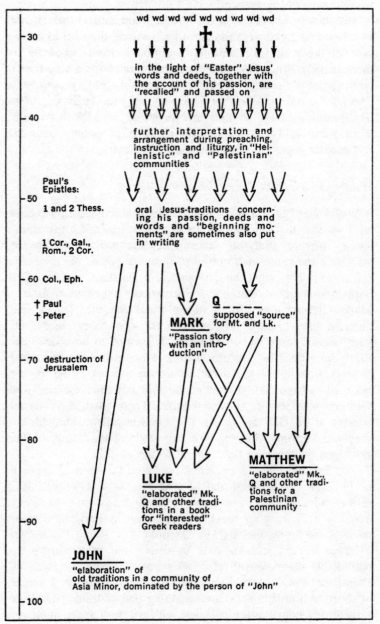

wd wd wd wd wd wd wd wd wd

-30

in the light of "Easter" Jesus'
words and deeds, together with
the account of his passion, are
"recalled" and passed on

-40

further interpretation and
arrangement during preaching,
instruction and liturgy, in "Hellenistic" and "Palestinian"
communities

Paul's
Epistles:

-50

1 and 2 Thess.

oral Jesus-traditions concerning his passion, deeds and
words and "beginning mo-
ments" are sometimes also put
in writing

1 Cor., Gal.,
Rom., 2 Cor.

-60 Col., Eph.

Q _ _ _ _
supposed "source"
for Mt. and Lk.

† Paul
† Peter

MARK
"Passion story
with an intro-
duction"

-70 destruction of
Jerusalem

-80

MATTHEW
"elaborated" Mk.,
Q and other tradi-
tions for a
Palestinian
community

LUKE
"elaborated" Mk.,
Q and other tradi-
tions in a book
for "interested"
Greek readers

-90

JOHN
"elaboration" of
old traditions in a community of
Asia Minor, dominated by the person of "John"

-100

once compared the gospel of Mark with a handful of pearls left over from a broken necklace. In the terms of that same image, one could now say that the evangelists strung those loose pearls on a new string by means of introductory words, which often indicate the time, place, audience and circumstances ("Then Jesus said. . . ." "In the evening of that day. . . ." "Then he went on further. . . ." "Once the Pharisees came to him. . . ." and so on).

These observations formed the point of departure for the new approach. Described roughly, it took place in two phases. First, each individual section of the synoptic gospels was *classified according to its literary form.* If we draw out the image used above a bit further, the pearls were taken off the three strings and similar ones were put in separate piles. Jesus' words and stories about him formed the first major division. His words were further separated according to types: sayings in the style of the old wisdom books, beatitudes, prophetic utterances about the future, parables, rules of conduct, "Ich-Worte"—i.e., sayings about his mission and about his person. In a similar way the narratives, too, were divided into miracle stories (which took on different forms according to their subject matter: exorcisms, healings, raising the dead or exercising power over nature) and narratives about Jesus' lot and activities or those of others, sometimes called *"novelle"* and sometimes "legends." The latter were also further subdivided according to form. A separate group consisted in a combination of sayings and narratives where a concise saying of Jesus is introduced by narrative sentences. Thus the disciples pick ears of corn on the sabbath and evoke the criticism of the Pharisees, which is then the occasion for Jesus' saying about the sabbath, clearly the high point of the pericope (Mk. 2, 23-28). In such cases the narrative element forms the setting, so to speak, in which the jewel of Jesus' saying is placed.

In the second phase scholars tried to clarify the origin and development—thus *the history*—of the forms. They did this, on the one hand, by calling into play all kinds of material from outside the Bible, inasmuch as the first Christians were simple people. Now, the study of the literature of a people shows that stories develop in such surroundings according to specific laws. When retelling a story, one makes it more lively by letting the hero himself speak in direct address, details are added to make the story more fascinating and the hero's activity more gripping, names are

given to the supporting characters, etc. The adherents of the new
method naturally sought material for comparison, especially in the
immediate surroundings of the early Christian community. Jewish
literature, in which sayings and details about famous rabbis from
the first centuries were passed on, and popular Hellenistic literature, containing miracle stories, provided some of their material.

On the other hand, scholars tried to determine the "Sitz im
Leben" of the various forms—i.e., the particular function which
they had fulfilled in Christian society. By means of data from Acts
and the apostolic epistles, they tried to determine which forms
grew up as a part of the Church's preaching. Some may have been
designed to teach the faithful about their conduct and their future
lot, or to illustrate and confirm their faith in Jesus as Son of God,
the Messiah of the Jews and Lord of all men. Other forms seem to
have developed within the framework of their liturgical celebrations, and still others in their discussions with the Jews before
whom they had to justify their convictions and practices, which
they did by appealing to their Master.

After nearly half a century this approach is so taken for granted
that we hardly think anymore how excitingly new it was in those
first years. Many gospel texts suddenly began to live. Instead of
just being purely objective reports about what happened at a given
moment, many of those texts were also seen to reflect something of
the colorful life and deep faith of the first Christians. People suddenly began to catch sight of details which were hardly noticed
before. And above all, each little unit appeared in one way or another to bear witness to the faith. It was no longer necessary, so to
speak, to preach about those texts, for by their very nature they
themselves were already a proclamation of the gospel. With a glance
at the chart illustrating the previous section, we might say that the
space between the life of Jesus and the oldest gospel—in the past a
completely obscure void—now suddenly began to clear up. Something of the life process of the tradition, elements of which lay
hidden in the texts of the gospels, became visible.

Unfortunately the pacemakers of the "Formgeschichte" and
some of their followers quickly aroused a deep distrust of the new
method among faithful Christians. In youthful enthusiasm about
their discovery (Karl Schmidt was 28 years old when he published
his pioneering study in 1919!) the conclusions they drew were too
far-reaching.

Thanks to the "Formgeschichtliche Methode," as it was called, we can now go back to the period before the gospels and penetrate the life of the oldest Christian communities as it was lived in the first decades after Jesus' death. But what lies prior to that period we can no longer reach. The Christians' every word about Jesus was permeated by their faith in him as the Messiah—that is, "the Christ"—and as the Son of God, their Lord. It is possible that a few stories and sayings in the synoptic gospels go back to an event which actually happened or to one of Jesus' utterances during his earthly existence, but this can seldom be proved. All that we can say with certainty is that everything which the gospels tell us had its origin in the milieu of those who worshiped Jesus, whether that be the ascended Messiah who would soon come again (some thought that this aspect was prominent in the Christian communities of Palestine), or the Son of God and Lord who is mystically present in the midst of those who believe in him (according to the Hellenistic communities). Even in their earliest shape the "forms" were at the service of the *kerygma,* the proclamation about Jesus. For this reason the actual history is forever lost to us. A previously posited contrast was stated again all the more forcefully: *an unbridgeable gulf exists between the historical Jesus and the kerygmatic Christ.*

Outside Germany, and especially in England, where realism plays a greater role in people's thinking and historical facts are not so easily compressed into a system of thought, the new method was applied only after some time, and then very critically. Thus irresponsible conclusions were also avoided. The investigation was always subservient to human, matter-of-fact considerations, along the lines of what C. Moule once wrote: "When one comes to think about it, it is obvious enough that once someone had accepted the *kerygma,* he would need a filling out of it and (as it were) an 'embodiment' of Jesus who had been thus briefly proclaimed as Lord. The evangelistic message of Paul, as we deduce it from references in his epistles, would have lacked the power to hold the affections and loyalty of the believer if it had never been reinforced by a portrait of the Lord in his words and deeds; and, what is more, it would have been virtually impossible to explain Christianity to an inquirer or defend it against an antagonist without some circumstantial account of 'how it all happened.' It is all very well to say to the Jerusalem crowd very soon after the crucifixion that

the Jesus whom they crucified has been made Lord and Christ
(Acts 2, 36); but hearers remoter in time or place would neces-
sarily ask, 'Who is this Jesus, and how came he to be crucified by
his own people?' And even the already converted would very soon
ask, 'What is known about his story? What sort of words and
deeds are connected with him? Why did his own people turn
against him?' It is in the context of such inquiry that the gospels
seem most likely to have taken shape" (C. F. Moule, *The Birth of
the New Testament,* pp. 86-87). This consideration is indeed more
realistic than the usual assertions that the first believers did not
have any interest at all in historical events.

After World War II, reactions likewise appeared in Germany
against certain suppositions and assertions of the first "Form Critics." They had attributed the origin of the rich evangelical tradition
to the anonymous group of first Christians. But this was difficult to
prove. A mass of people is never creative. That is the prerogative
of gifted individuals. Furthermore, new studies on the Jewish
milieu of the early Church drew attention to the way authoritative
statements of teachers in that milieu were usually imprinted in the
memory and passed on orally. Thus a new confidence in the purity
of the synoptic rendering of Jesus' words took shape. This was
especially true for the parables or elements of them. In this way
the verbal tradition appeared more and more to be a solid bridge
from the Christ of the gospels to the historical Jesus. Finally, more
recent analyses of the individual gospels showed that the evangelists were not mere collectors, but authors in the strict sense of the
word. Of course, they worked with material that had been handed
down to them, but in their choice of the material to be incorporated, in ordering it and especially in their presentation of it they
let themselves be guided by very specific intentions.

III
OUR APPROACH

We would now like to sketch the genesis of the four gospels as it
is conceived at present, thanks to the "Formgeschichte" and the
criticism of its questionable suppositions and conclusions.

At the beginning of a talk on the four gospels I once used four
portraits of the same man as a visual aid. They were of the famous

Dutch art critic H. P. Bremmer (1871-1955) who was often sketched and painted by artists, such as Jan Toorop and Albert Servaes. It was immediately obvious that the four very different portraits all rendered the same man. The Bremmer of Jan Toorop was *at the same time* Bremmer and completely Toorop, and the one by Servaes was unmistakably "a Servaes."

The audience understood the comparison immediately: thus the four gospels all render the same person Jesus Christ, but in very different ways. The first one completely bears the stamp of the writer Matthew, the second of Mark, and so on. However, I remarked immediately that they drew that conclusion too quickly, and with that the discussion got under way. A written portrait is obviously different from one that has been painted, but there are much more important differences besides. While Toorop, Servaes and the others had Bremmer before them as a model and rendered the *direct impression* he made on them, the evangelists described their hero *as he lived forth in their faith*. Even more important is another difference, related to a certain extent with the previous one. For those who painted a portrait of Bremmer, he was only one of their many subjects. Perhaps they did that portrait out of admiration for his work or in recognition of him personally, but those feelings were of a temporary nature, and in any case they did not have a penetrating influence on their personalities. The evangelists, on the other hand, described a man who had come to dominate their lives completely and who continued to exert influence on all their thinking, their feelings and everything they did. Hence their portrait could be nothing else than *a witness,* both a kind of declaration of their personal dependence and an attempt to instill or strengthen that attitude in their readers. One of them actually expressed the purpose of his portrait, stating that he had written his gospel "so that you may believe that Jesus is the Christ, the Son of God, and that believing this you may have life through his name" (Jn. 20, 31).

It is for this reason that the four gospels form a *kind of literature all their own,* essentially different from descriptions of any other person who ever lived. No other person can have the all-important meaning for others which Christ has for Christians.

We would like to clarify this exceptional meaning of the gospels to some extent by a short description of the way in which they originated. To do so we divide that history into four moments or phases. The first is, of course, the phase in which it all began, the public life of Jesus. We will take as the second phase the repercussions which Jesus' reappearance after his death caused among his faithful followers, with the result that all their impressions of him were seen in a new light. Then they put those impressions, those "memories," into words. By writing them down and passing them on, their accounts took on certain forms. We will treat that process of transmission as the third phase. That was still going strong when the fourth phase began. From the treasury of traditional stories and sayings, the evangelists drew the material which they elaborated in their "portraits" of Jesus, each in his own way, with his own motives and from his own personal points of view.

After the above exposition of modern research in the area of the gospels, it goes without saying that our sketch can only be *the global reproduction of a reconstruction*. By a careful analysis of the gospels and an extremely precise comparison of their various texts, sometimes using data from other parts of the Bible and from contemporary non-biblical documents by way of explanation, Scripture scholars have drawn up a description of how the process of the gospels' origin more or less must have taken place. We say "more or less," for quite a few details still remain to be clarified. Some of them will always remain encased in darkness because of a lack of sufficient data. Others will become clearer in the future, thanks to the ever greater precision in analyzing the available data and perhaps also to the unearthing of still unknown material from antiquity or to new research methods.

A sketch of this kind "according to the present-day level of knowledge" also serves a very practical purpose. Often those who know the Bible speak about certain gospel texts in the supposition that everyone listening to them or reading their works are just as familiar with the pre-history of those texts as they themselves are. In general, that is not the case, and misunderstandings or "short circuits" easily arise. Even more expressly than the previous chapters, the pages to follow hope to do their part in eradicating all such "evils." In order to help the reader remember that the first three phases are concerned with the pre-history of the gospels, no references will be made to their chapters and verses. The gospels simply did not yet exist.

IX
Jesus' Public Life: The First Phase

The stage on which Jesus Christ first appeared was dominated by John the Baptist. Later, the course of events was simplified somewhat by allowing Jesus to begin his preaching only after his "predecessor" was removed from the scene. Mark seems to do this where he writes: "After John had been arrested, Jesus went into Galilee. There he proclaimed the Good News from God. 'The time has come,' he said, 'and the kingdom of God is close at hand. Repent, and believe the Good News.'" Nevertheless, this provides us with a good point of departure for our sketch of the first phase.

In the Footsteps of the Baptist

In chapter 6 we saw that Israel's great prophets entered the scene at times of national crisis. At the beginning of the Christian era the Jewish community was in the grips of just such a crisis, and the situation became even worse as time went on. In short, it consisted in the growing resistance on the part of the Jewish citizens against their rulers. Herod the Great, the non-Jew who owed his royal power to the Romans, had in many different ways exploited the working class. His son and successor Archelaus had gone so far in ten years that his chaotic rule was even too much for Rome to put up with. Caesar Augustus replaced him with Roman "procurators." All those changes were coupled with endless intriguing in the higher circles and with many bloodbaths. Under the rule of the procurators it became even clearer for the common man that the Romans' only concern was the profit they could extort from Palestine. Hence the growing resistance and the reason for speaking of a crisis, for Rome was unconquerable. Persevering in resistance against that power could only lead to the destruction of the Jewish nation.

It is extremely important for the modern reader of the gospels to realize that in the Jewish community it was self-evident that such a national resistance would have a religious tint. The nation as a whole believed in a God who was always at hand, always actively involved in the lot of his people, the center of mankind. When speaking about the book of Daniel, we saw how an untenable situation brought the age-old expectation of salvation to new life and caused it to take a definite form. In the face of that crisis they looked for God to intervene and make his superior power felt once and for all. Something similar also happened in the crisis under the Romans. Then, too, expectations were high, especially among the Jews who were suffering the most from the corrupt government. Of course each of them shaped his expectation of what God was about to do in a mold all his own, according to his character and milieu. Some hoped, along the lines of the book of Daniel, for a sudden intervention which would be like a universal explosion of his blinding majesty, at the same time destructive for the sinners and beneficial to the pious. It would leave Israel, "a nation of saints," as the sole survivors in a totally re-created world of unimaginable happiness. Many pious Jews prayed daily for that final intervention which would make Yahweh's eternal kingship visible in that of his chastened people. Others thought that God's majesty was already being revealed in those who faithfully observed his will. In such persons God's reign was already visible. And thus faithful observance of the Law brought God's kingdom closer; the disobedient impeded it. One who was dedicated to God's cause was to avoid sinners with their contagious misbehavior. Many of the Pharisees thought in this way.

Other pious people isolated themselves entirely from society in order to prepare in complete concentration for the coming event, far from everything that could render them impure. This is what some of the Essenes did, in a settlement on the rough coast of the Dead Sea. Not long ago remains of that settlement were discovered.

On the basis of many different prophetic texts from the Bible, the "Messiah" was given a major role in many of those salvific expectations, and again in very diverse ways. For countless ordinary people God would send him as a national leader, a hero just as Gideon and David, who in the vanguard of his unconquerable troops would save Israel from its suppressors, both the Romans and their Jewish collaborators. He would then usher in a peace and prosperity of unimaginable and fairytale-like proportions.

Jews for whom the cult in the temple was the actual heart of their national life expected, besides the "political" Messiah from the tribe of Judah, another "priestly" Messiah from the tribe of Levi who would lead Israel in an absolutely perfect life of the Covenant.

A very different "Messianic movement" was launched in the third decade of the 1st century under the leadership of a man named John. He wandered about in the desert east of Jerusalem and farther away in the barren countryside flanking the Jordan riverbed. He called to the people who passed by, crossing at the forge, that God was in fact about to intervene, but in this sense: the fire of his wrath would soon burst into flames over Israel and destroy all wicked and faithless Jews. Only those who would "be converted," just as the prophets of old had demanded, would escape that terrible judgment. That meant choosing a way of life that was centered on God. Whoever was prepared to undertake this total conversion allowed himself to be immersed in the Jordan by John as a sign of that decision. Thus that prophet was called "the Baptist."

That immersion was especially meaningful for the Jews. Long before, they became God's people when he had led them safely through the waters of the Red Sea into the desert and there bound himself to them forever. The promise of a land all their own, made at that time, Yahweh fulfilled when he once again led them through water, this time that of the Jordan River. All those old themes—desert, salvation, a new future by passing through water—were very deeply anchored in Israel's experience, and the people recognized them in the rite which John performed on the banks of the Jordan.

But with his baptism John also pointed to something else—or, better, to someone else. God would let his judgment on Israel be effected by the one whom so many Jews expected: the Messiah. The Baptist portrayed him as a man of violence; he, too, would baptize Israel, but with fire, at once destructive and chastening. This he would soon come to do, on a day that was imminent, the

"Day of Yahweh," which an old prophet had said would be as fiery as an oven. Another image which John used was that of the harvest: "the one to come" stood on the threshing floor ready to separate the chaf from the wheat. In the past those words were used to describe Yahweh himself, when he would come in judgment. For John it was the Messiah who would do that. No Jew was apt to think of that person in such terms.

People of every class and position in society came out in large numbers to hear John. He had to take on helpers to make his message heard by the pressing crowds and to perform the baptism ritual for them. The crowds' excitement mounted continually—especially when he said that the "one to come," "the stronger one," who was so superior to him, already stood in their midst.

One day in 1960 in that same Jordan valley, just a little to the north, I could not help but think of that tremendous excitement. King Hussein was about to pass that way. People flocked by the thousands from the villages to the main road. You could feel the emotion mount when a dispatch-rider arrived from the direction of the capital and shouted, "The king has just passed Salt!"—a town about halfway between us and the capital. But to get a feeling for what the Baptist evoked, we should rather think of the population of a city about to be bombed. Those who believed the radio announcement about the oncoming bombers have left everything behind and fled to the shelters; there they tensely await the crucial moment when the violence—now so imminent—will break loose in the heavens.

The movement around the figure of the Baptist expanded. Among his disciples and helpers there was someone from Nazareth, a carpenter by trade, who attracted quite a number of listeners. John noticed this and could only rejoice at his "success." Could that Jesus be the "one who was to come?"

Galilee: The Gospel of God's Coming as King

The territory east of the Jordan, "Perea," fell with Galilee under the rule of Herod Antipas. This prince could not put up with any "Messianic" and thus popular nationalistic movement among his subjects. When the Baptist, in an authentically prophetic way, criticized Antipas' married life, the latter seized the opportunity to arrest him, thinking that the movement would then quickly fall apart. Indeed Jesus did return to the region of his birth, Galilee, but there he continued the work he had begun in the Baptist's circle.

That fertile territory, with an enchanting lake forming its eastern border, was open both to the trade centers on the coast (Phoenicia) and to the heavily populated cities of Syria. From ancient times it had a very mixed population. That was already apparent in its name, derived from the complete Hebrew phrase *geliel ha-goyim,* "province of the Gentiles" (Is. 8, 23). In 104 B.C. Aristobulus I, grandson of Simon Maccabaeus, had made the territory of Galilee part of his dominion and forced the people there to be circumcised and live according to the Jewish Law. Remarkably enough, this coercive measure had had a lasting effect in several parts of the territory, especially among the common people in the villages. Partly because families from Judah came to live there and the spiritual leaders promoted the religious life in their synagogues, in the 1st century A.D. Galilee was a center of an enthusiastic, living Judaism, with a strongly nationalistic strain. More than was true of most Jews in Judah, especially those of the upper classes, the "converts" of Galilee were opposed to all non-Jewish influence, especially that of the Romans. Hence the famous Galilean resistance movement of the Zealots, those who were "zealous" for the national cause. And that is also the reason why calling someone a "Galilean" came to mean something like: "He belongs to the resistance movement," or at least, "He sympathizes with the resistance movement." Thus one can understand that Herod, who was after all only a puppet of the emperor, continually had to try to maintain order among his subjects and in that way to stay on the good side of the Romans.

There, in Galilee, Jesus continued what he had begun in the footsteps of the Baptist. He announced the imminent appearance of God and urged the people to prepare for it by a true conversion. But even more clearly than before, in Galilee it became evident how much Jesus' preaching differed from that of the Baptist.

In the first place, this was to be seen in the different manner in which they made contact with the people. John stayed in the desert and spoke to those who came out to him. *Jesus went out to the people* in their villages and homes. Of course, like all pious Jews, he avoided the cities which Herod had built or remodeled in Hellenistic style, such as Tiberias on the lake, which was thus named to flatter the emperor. In general, however, he did preach in those cities on the lake which were inhabited chiefly by Jews. Among these were Capernaum, Chorazin and Bethsaida and the many other villages and hamlets of Galilee.

Another difference is also related to their contact with the people. John had emphasized in particular the terrifying character of the imminent "Day of Yahweh." At that time God would definitively put an end to all evil and sin. Jesus announced that same definitive intervention by God as "gospel" (*euangelion*). That Greek word, "good news" or "good tidings," is the translation of a Hebrew term which had received a specific meaning from its use in the Jewish Scriptures. In ancient times, bringing good tidings was usually connected with the report of a military victory (e.g., 2 Sam. 18, 19; 1 Sam. 31, 9). But since the preaching of Deutero-Isaiah, the word was definitively associated with God's victory as described by the prophet. In highly poetic terms he had announced to the deported Jews in Babylon that he already saw Yahweh rescuing them. On a freshly cut path through the desert he was returning to Zion as victor, and what he had taken from the enemy he brought with him: his people! He led them into his land as a careful shepherd does his flock (Is. 40, 11). The prophet could already hear the bearers of the good news proclaiming to the cities and villages of the Judean hill country, "Behold, here comes your God!" In 52, 7-10 he poetically paints such a bearer of good tidings by calling his feet "beautiful." From afar this messenger calls to Zion, "Your God is king. . . . Yahweh is consoling his people, redeeming Jerusalem. . . ." And using a very ancient image for Yahweh's salvific work, the prophet has this messenger cry out:

> Yahweh bears this holy arm
> in the sight of all the nations,
> and all the ends of the earth shall see
> the salvation of our God.

Although we do not know for certain if Jesus ever used the word "gospel" himself, we are sure that he announced God's coming in the spirit of those prophetic texts, and thus with a different emphasis from that of John. This leads us to an even greater difference. The Baptist had said to the people that God's violent appearance was imminent; yes, the one who would carry out his judgment was

already present. Whoever decided to make *that coming event* the
guide of his life was immersed by John in the Jordan. Everything
the prophet said and did bore the mark of an immediate preparation. Jesus proclaimed that the tensely awaited event *was already
at work in what he himself said and did.* That is why Jesus no
longer made demands on the people by calling them to be baptized. Instead he bestowed something on them, in the form of healing and driving out evil spirits. John was not known to have
worked any miracles; it was his baptism that "signified" what he
preached. Jesus immediately attracted attention by healing all
kinds of sickness and by freeing possessed persons from the power
of their evil spirits. Those miracles "signified" what he preached.
In this connection one should realize that in Jesus' audience both
the sick and possessed were equally thought to be victims of Satan,
God's great opponent, who held them in his grasp. Since Jesus proclaimed that God revealed himself as king in his words and deeds,
he had to verify that by actually driving Satan from the domains
he occupied. And he did this so simply, often with one word, and
at the same time with such authority, that the bystanders should
have been able to recognize "God's finger" at work.

Yet, it was not granted to everyone to see those deeds as
"signs." Those who objected to Jesus' announcement of God's
majesty could explain them in another way. Many wonder-workers
were known in the wide world of antiquity. In little Palestine there
were rabbis who drove devils out of possessed persons by the
laying on of hands and prayer. Egypt was still well known for its
specialists in the magical arts. Jesus could have been one of their
disciples. More educated Jews were familiar enough with the phenomena, which we moderns speak of as suggestion, hypnosis, shock
and the like, to be able to give quite acceptable "explanations" for
Jesus' miracles. Only for those who accepted Jesus' word were his
miracles signs of that something in him which made such an
authoritative impression on the people.

Mysterious Authority

We can get some idea of how they felt when we listen to Jesus'
words which have come down to us. A German scripture scholar,
Heinz Schürmann, once lifted them out of the familiar texts of the
synoptic gospels and ordered them according to themes (in the

paperback *Worte des Hern*). In this "anthology" he listed all the sayings which could stand alone—both the very short sayings (such as "Do not judge, and you will not be judged") and the longer parables (such as that of the Good Samaritan). He limited his list, therefore, to sayings which were not woven integrally into a story (such as the words over the bread and wine at the Last Supper).

Whoever reflects on these 245 sayings and parables is first of all struck by the simplicity and directness of Jesus' imagery. The whole of Galilee's colorful life is reflected in his words. The characters of his parables were all familiar figures there: the landlords and the tenant farmers, the fishermen and the merchants, the shepherds and the young men who went out looking for adventure, the pious Pharisees and the doctor, the poor widow and the whining children. Everything Jesus said was absolutely familiar to his listeners. They were the ordinary things of human life, coming and going, good and bad: the lamp on a stand in the parlor, the sparrows on the roof, the flowers along the road, the ox that falls into a pit, the friend who drops in unexpectedly, the farmer who foretells the weather, the steward who deceives his master, those out of work who hang around the marketplace, etc.

People are astonished to hear the "founder of a religion" always speaking common everyday language and expressing himself in such a "worldly" way. But *what* Jesus said in that everyday language was at the same time surprising, often shocking, and actually very "unworldly."

That is very clear in the parables, of which about thirty-five have come down to us. They are too different to put into any one category. But they must have surprised those who heard them because they portray something very unordinary. Sometimes they give a great deal of attention to things which people rarely notice. More often, Jesus lets ordinary things take an unexpected turn. It is always different from what people are used to. It goes without saying that corn germinates in the earth and grows into stalks and ears while the farmer sleeps and works and again goes to sleep without doing anything more to it. Growth takes place simply as a matter of course! Jesus describes such a scene and then goes on to pay considerable attention to the seeds that "fall by the wayside" and never produce ripe ears. Why all the emphasis? That was only the normal loss expected by every farmer. Likewise, no Palestinian would ever hope for a harvest of thirtyfold or sixtyfold, much less one hundredfold. That was sheer foolishness. Again, it was quite normal for a landlord to hire extra workers at the time of the grape harvest, but that he would do so late in the afternoon—and, what is more, under the same working conditions as in the early morning—was nonsense. Of course a shepherd would try to get lost sheep back into his fold. But to leave ninety-nine of them behind unprotected in order to go in search of one is irresponsible. Jesus told a story about a man who was entrusted with a sum of money; rather than doing business with it, he buried the money. Then he lets that man be severely punished, whereas those who exposed their money to all the risks of commercial investment are praised. That is rather strange, to say the least. And what were they to think of the rich master who, upon returning from a journey, rewards his watchful servants by himself serving them at table like a slave!

Many of his short sayings, too, must have astonished the people. The words used are familiar enough, but their combination often makes for drastic, piquant or exaggerated sentences. The largest animal Jesus knows, the camel, he places before the smallest hole, the eye of a needle. Those who work the soil in Palestine are familiar with the ever-present fear of two animal bites, which meant almost certain death for children. Jesus says, "What father among you would hand his son a snake instead of a fish? Or a scorpion if he asked for an egg?" On windy days in the dry season a tiny piece of straw can easily blow into one's eye. Jesus says of the companion who wants to take it out: "He himself has a whole plank in his eye and doesn't see it!" Sometimes his sayings even sound harsh. A man who lost his father and wants to bury him before coming to follow Jesus is told, "Let the dead bury their dead!" And then there are impossible demands such as: "Love those who hate you" or "If your hand is a source of scandal to you, cut it off. . . ."

One is also struck by the tone of authority which characterizes so many of Jesus' sayings. That impression must have been much stronger for his listeners than it can be for us, for it did not become Jesus to speak so authoritatively. We should remember that in Jesus' surroundings God was not "dead." On the contrary, he was very evident, the only self-evident being. And he still spoke to them. What he had to say to his people they could read in the Scriptures, set in writing by his mouthpieces, Moses and the prophets. What God demanded of every Jew in daily life was explained by the *competent authorities,* the official doctors of the Law. They determined what was and what was not permitted in certain circumstances, and in so doing they appealed to former teachers of the Law. Great masters who formed a school around them not only knew the whole Torah by heart, but also all the authoritative explanations of it. Essential to their teaching was that Rabbi X had said this and Rabbi Y had said that. They communicated this vast knowledge to their disciples, and these passed it on in their turn, enriched by the interpretations added to the treasure by their master. *Jesus never appealed to any authority.* He, too, spoke about God's will and intentions and about man's attitude toward God, but he never cited texts or statements of others. He spoke only on his own authority: "I tell you. . . ." He knew the Scriptures and sometimes cited them, but in such a way as to clarify God's full intention in a specific passage. Sometimes he went so far as to seem to call Moses' authority into question. Concerning divorce, for example, that "lawgiver" had indeed permitted a man to write out a writ of dismissal and divorce his wife. But, according to Jesus, that was a dispensation which Moses had granted "because of the hardness of their hearts," and it was contrary to God's original intention.

For the truly pious a statement of this kind was appalling. In a sense, their familiar world was being shaken at its very foundations. How dare someone speak about Moses in that way! Where did he derive those unheard-of pretensions? Admittedly, in earlier times there were prophets who acted in this way. Jeremiah had leveled sharp criticism at the priests and those who explained the Law. The common people regarded Jesus as such a prophet, a sort of new Jeremiah. People even spoke of "the" prophet, the one Moses seemed to have announced in Deuteronomy 18. But Jesus was surely not a real prophet, for Isaiah, Jeremiah and the others were expressly called by Yahweh to fulfill that office. They themselves had related how that happened, complete with the date: "In the year . . . in the reign of King. . . ." Or they would record the year of a certain monarch's death, as in the case of Isaiah, who then was allowed to gaze upon the immortal king and from him

received his task. Those stories of their calling were their credentials. Evidently Jesus did not have any.

Furthermore, the real prophets always referred to him who had
taken them into his service. They generally introduced their sayings with the formula: "Thus says Yahweh. . . ." This expression
is used 435 times in the Hebrew Bible. Or they used the term
"oracle of Yahweh," which we find 361 times, as prophetic quotation marks, so to speak. *Jesus never spoke in such a way, on
behalf of God.* He, too, sometimes used an introductory formula to
strengthen his "I say to you. . . ."—namely, the liturgical exclamation "Amen!" sometimes rendered as "I tell you *solemnly"* in
modern English translations. No prophet had ever confirmed *his
own words* in that solemn way, as if by an oath.

Once someone became attuned, so to speak, to Jesus'
"unheard-of claim," he saw it manifest itself in many different ways.
Thus that village carpenter—what more could he be!—once told
bystanders very solemnly, "How privileged you are to be allowed
to experience all of this! Prophets and kings had longed to see and
hear what you are seeing and hearing, but it was not granted to
them!" That was certainly nothing less than regarding his own
preaching and miracles as the fulfillment of Israel's history for
which the great and privileged men of the past had so fervently
longed.

He seemed to arrogate something similar to himself when he
spoke about the Baptist. No admirer could have a higher estimate
of John than the one Jesus had. He proclaimed him greater than
all the men of God who preceded him. But Jesus said these things
about John precisely because he had prepared the way for him,
and had introduced him to his task, so to speak. When John sent
messengers to Jesus from his prison cell to ask if he was indeed the
"one to come," they were told, "Go back and tell John what you
hear and see; the blind see again, and the lame walk, lepers are
cleansed, and the deaf hear, and the dead are raised to life and the
good news is proclaimed to the poor." According to the prophet
Isaiah, that would all take place when he would finally reveal himself as king. Thus God was doing this in Jesus' words and deeds.

That great "Day of Yahweh" would be preceded by the return
of the prophet Elijah. That was written in so many words in the
last sentence of the book of the twelve prophets. Likewise, all
kinds of expectations about Elijah's appearance were in circula-

tion. Jesus put it quite simply: Elijah had already come, in the person of John the Baptist. He could just as well have said that God was "at hand" in his own life and work.

One might also see a similar claim in the attitude Jesus took toward Israel. Although himself a Jew by birth, he spoke about his people as if he himself did not belong to that "flock without a shepherd." That was apparent from his choice of a select group of twelve from among his disciples—clearly an unmistakable allusion to that creative moment in Israel's history when Yahweh himself chose twelve tribes in order to make them his people. This was one more indication that Jesus put himself in a place, or attributed to himself a function, which belonged to the God of Israel.

For the pious Jew who followed all of this reflectively from a distance, Jesus seemed to be obsessed with that claim; this annoyed them greatly, for it was blasphemy in the full sense of the word. But those who were closely associated with him could hardly get that idea, for despite his authoritative way of speaking and acting, Jesus never made any demands for himself. He always had time for everyone and took interest in them. One who thinks himself important does not act that way. People dragged him from one sick person to another; quietly and patiently he accepted it. He gave himself fully to people and to what he saw as his task: to bring them the message of God's kingdom. Sometimes there was not even time to eat in peace, but usually that much time was granted him at least. What he ate he received from others, for he himself had nothing. Later on the disciples recalled how his relatives in Nazareth were perturbed at this, so much so that they even tried to get him to return to a normal life. "Everyone says it's a shame," they had said. "Why, rumor even has it that he is out of his mind."

In the eyes of many he was a lunatic perhaps, but not presumptuous. If crazy, then he was crazy about God, but in such a way that one could hardly think of blasphemy. He always gave all the glory to God, as the phrase goes. A man who had addressed him as "Good master," in the sense of "You are a good teacher," got the sharp reply, "Don't call me good. God alone is good!" In all his words there resounded the consciousness of what we would call God's incomparable majesty and holiness. But at the same time his manner of praying revealed what a familiar relationship he enjoyed with God. Even when he turned to him in the usual formulas of the Psalms and other prayers, he brought something very personal to them by addressing God as "Abba." That was a word children would use, something like "daddy" or "papa." Until the present time no indication has been found that a Jew ever addressed God in this way. There is *one* text, however, from which one could conclude that little children ("not yet having reached the age of reason") spoke to God in this way in their baby prayers. Thus the adult Jesus would have clung to a form of prayer dating from his earliest years. In any case, his use of "Abba" at prayer was entirely unique, and therefore characteristic of him. Equally characteristic was his effort to involve the people in that intimate relationship with God; tirelessly he never stopped speaking about their Father in heaven.

Although his faithful friends had a greater appreciation of him than the Jew who observed it all from a distance, he nevertheless remained a mystery to them, a mystery at once attractive and frightening. Who was he? He preferred not to answer that question. Was there perhaps no term or title with which to express it? Sometimes he spoke about the "Son of Man" in the third person, but it was usually clear that he was referring to himself. However, that term could just as well be a reference to figures from the Bible, meaning simply "man." He had refused to be called a "good teacher." Once he did say that people should accept his words because he was "meek and humble of heart," but that was no title or indication of an office. Perhaps he was the Messiah of their dreams after all. Then his glory would one day burst forth and they, the twelve, would sit next to him on thrones and together with him rule over an independent and chastened Israel. Who could know? He was so bewildering. He himself was just like the world he called forth in his parables, where the ending was always different than what they expected.

Conflict and Downfall

More and more criticism was brought against Jesus in official circles. He worked within the Jewish community and gave instructions there as a rabbi, but he had received no *recognized education* or an assignment to do so. The common people regarded him as a prophet, but he could not be that either, for he continued to *refuse to present his credentials*. When the authorities demanded that he work a miracle as a sign that he was sent by God, he refused indignantly. But he was also saddened. They simply did not want to understand that such a sign was impossible—even for God. The disciple who later told of his visit to Nazareth understood that perfectly: "He could not work any miracles there because of their lack of faith." When he was expressly asked on one occasion by what authority he acted so independently, he responded with a further question, "You first tell me where John the Baptist derived his authority." For the Jewish leaders all of this was both irritating and a challenge.

Furthermore, Jesus irritated many right-thinking Jews by his way of life. He had such great respect for the Baptist. All well and good, but he at least lived soberly. This successor of John accepted invitations to banquets in cities and villages alike and took part in everything just like everybody else. They called him a "glutton and a wine-bibber," but undoubtedly in less dignified terms than in this translation. If he wanted to be like everybody else, why then didn't he get married like every other normal Jewish man? Wasn't bringing forth children a command from the creator? And wasn't childlessness a curse? He should certainly have known that. Wicked tongues were quick to mock him with the term "eunuch"—a mean word not only in the Roman world of those days, but, if possible, even more so in the Jewish community. At the same time many were annoyed at Jesus' candid attitude toward women. He not only healed sick women, but even instructed them, as the equals of men. For the Jewish feeling, that was quite out of the ordinary, to put it mildly. It was even said of him that he accepted the caresses of a prostitute without blushing or batting an eye!

These things revealed something in his behavior that was more than just remarkable and irritating. He was quite simply a "heretic." Jesus addressed his message about God's kingdom *to all Jews without exception,* men and women, the educated and the simple, rich and poor, but also, cutting across all those distinctions, to the good and the bad, to the "just" and the "sinners." With that he touched something which in the eyes of those in authority belonged to the foundations of their faith. It directly concerned Israel's existence and the way God worked in the world of men. Jesus held fast to his point of view and his way of acting—hence the conflict in which he found himself. That conflict was quickly coming to a head and would lead to his downfall. One can safely say that he risked his life for sinners.

The reason for this was that the presiding figures and leaders of the community of the faithful were Pharisees. The reader is already acquainted with the period in which that group had its origin. In chapter 6 we described the effort exerted by the Jewish community in order to survive in the whirlpool of Hellenistic culture. At that time this boundless worship of "the Law" evolved. We saw how the wise Jesus Ben Sirach glorified that holy book as the concrete form of God's wisdom in this world. The Maccabees and their supporters had fought for Jewish freedom so that they could live according to that Law and, in so doing, give as clear an expression as possible to their religious "apartheid," for themselves and others.

The result had been the salvation of the Jewish faith. But already under the last of the Maccabees a group or party had sprung up within the community, whose members called themselves the "separated" (*perushim,* from which the name Pharisees is derived). These people felt that most of the Jews were not concerned enough about the Law. They "separated" themselves chiefly for the purpose of living as purely as possible according to authentic Jewish piety, not only by strictly observing all the commandments of the Law, but also all the many further stipulations which had been added, "the traditions of the ancients." Most of them did that with deep sincerity and with the dedication of their whole person—hence the great respect which the common people had for them. Seeing that politics and religion were so closely woven together in that milieu, their "party" could exert a great influence on the course of events.

The Pharisees thus made obedience to God their first and most important duty in life. They were, so to speak, the just by profession, "professionals" at religion, the only true Israelites. For us moderns, religion is primarily a question of inner conviction, something very personal. That was not the case with the Jews. They were formed in the school of Moses, the prophets and sages. There everything depended on one's actions. Even the well-known appeal to Israel, repeated daily by every Jew, "to love God with his whole heart," was understood in a practical way. He alone loved God who was guided in everything he did by God's will. For the Pharisee that will was expressed completely in the Law and all the traditional commandments and prohibitions which had been added to complete it. These he observed as strictly as one possibly could. Of course he failed now and then, but the extra good work he did, above and beyond his obligations, would certainly outweigh his faults in God's judgment.

Thus in the life of the Pharisees one could see what actually happens when God is in fact recognized as Lord and king. They realized in their lives, so to speak, what Israel as a whole should be: the domain of God's majesty in this world. Although his kingship would not be revealed until the end of time, when all the disobedient would be destroyed for good, something of it was already visible in "the just." On that last day God would raise up to life all those dedicated to him, and they would enjoy an eternal reward in his kingdom—they alone. They had chosen to stand with God. They were on God's side. The others were not. All those who scarcely paid any attention to God's prescriptions in their daily lives stood on the wrong side. Each day the price which they would have to pay for their sins increased, while their chances of surviving the judgment and being admitted into God's kingdom diminished. Conversion to a life of justice was perhaps possible, theoretically, but then only an excess of good works could swing the balance of God's judgment in their favor. Who among them could possibly manage that? Unfortunately this was the fate of the great majority of the Jewish people. They stood completely outside the circle of the just, outside the true Israel which alone was acceptable to God. That was obviously even more true for those who worked at dishonest and disreputable professions. Those who had leased the right to collect one of the many taxes could not but commit injustices by exercising that right. Suppose that such a "tax collector" wanted to be converted. To do so he would have to live quite a few lives to be able to make up for the injustice he had committed. And God, the just judge, *had* to demand this of him. "Tax collectors" therefore had absolutely no chance, not to mention prostitutes and all others who associated with corrupt people.

Since God's commandments pertain to every detail of daily life—food and clothing, living and working—a conscientious Pharisee had to carefully avoid every form of association with those sinners. Hence the clear distinction, noticeable in every aspect of social life, between "the just" and "the sinners."

This sketch is obviously a simplification, but it is not a carica-

ture. Of course, those principles were not practiced by all Pharisees to the same degree and in the same way. This can be seen in
the gospels as well as in Jewish literature dating from the time of
Jesus. It is certain, however, that they were universally accepted by
the Pharisees with whom Jesus came in contact.

Those principles were totally incomprehensible to Jesus. In his
eyes no man, however good, could presume to be "just" before the
holy God. If any man were to come face to face with that God,
he would see his need for "conversion." For Jesus, being converted
meant that man must abandon all his presumptuous claims and
look for his salvation and future from the merciful Father alone.
We have already seen how Jesus announced the coming of that
God as "gospel," the good news of salvation.

It is possible that the more the Pharisees protested his public
activity, the clearer his different "point of view" became. However
that may be, Jesus tried to reach all without exception, common
people as well as more conspicuous "sinners." He accepted their
invitations to dinner, and in so doing he could hardly have been
observing all the prescriptions pertaining to ritual purification and
pure food. He also proclaimed his message on the sabbath, and
thus it happened that he cured the sick on that day as well. That is
to say, he "worked" on the sabbath and sometimes ordered the
person cured to carry the bed on which he was brought to Jesus.
That was not allowed. Thus Jesus was leading others into sin. But
what was worse, he even called the "just" to conversion and faith.

Many of Jesus' sayings in the gospels had their origin in his disputes with the Pharisees. His criticism of their way of life might be
summarized as follows. According to Jesus they misjudged God's
holy majesty by fancying that they enjoyed certain rights before
him. They reduced him to a severe master who never overlooked
anything. Therefore he had to take all their good works into
account. *Just as* blasphemous in Jesus' eyes was the way the Pharisees excluded others from community with God on those same
grounds. Thus they arrogated to themselves a judgment which
belonged to God alone. Likewise, they misjudged what he out of
pure love had revealed to Israel from the very beginning: that he
was first and foremost a "Savior." To cause distress to one's fellow
men was always branded by the spokesmen of Israel's God as a sin
against him personally. The Pharisees committed that sin by using
their official authority to declare that so many of their fellow Isra-

elites had no chance before God, that they were "accursed," excluded from his kingdom, and thus had no future. In this way they led the mass of "sinners" to despair.

Jesus must have reprehended them often. Calling them "flea strainers" was a severe rebuke indeed. According to the Law, contact with a corpse rendered a person unclean. Now, a dead flea is also a corpse, and a flea corpse can now and then turn up in a glass of milk. For safety's sake, to avoid every risk of becoming impure, the Pharisees carefully strained everything they drank. Furthermore, if we recall that in Moses' Law the camel was listed among impure animals, and thus not to be eaten, we can feel the drastic sharpness of Jesus' rebuke, "You strain out the flea, but swallow the camel!"

In their zeal to fulfill God's will down to the smallest detail, the Pharisees failed to see what he actually wanted of them. Jesus once rebuked them for this in the conversation which follows—a conversation, we should remember, with people who from their earliest years had performed "God's will" with the utmost care. He proposed this situation: "A man had two sons. He went and said to the first, 'My boy, you go and work in the vineyard today.' He answered, 'I will not go,' but afterward thought better of it and went. The man then went and said the same thing to the second who answered, 'Certainly, sir,' but he did not go. Which of the two did the father's will?" The Pharisees had to answer, "The first, of course." Then Jesus continued, in that familiar authoritative tone, "I tell you solemnly, tax collectors and prostitutes are making their way into the kingdom of God before you." The emotional value of that "before you" may very well have been "instead of you," and thus "not you."

This is even more evident from another encounter with them, known as the "parable of the Pharisee and the publican." Jesus told them of the words used by a Pharisee to address God in the temple. With his head held high and full of self-confidence, he thanked God for allowing him to belong to the group of the just and not having anything to do with the publican standing some distance behind him in the temple. The latter just stood there looking at the ground and mumbling a prayer for mercy while he struck his breast. The Pharisees possibly felt that this description was a bit exaggerated, but all the same basically correct. After all, the sinner really had no chance. But Jesus' closing words were a direct contradiction of their view of the two types described: "I tell you, at that very moment God accepted the publican and not the other."

Jesus declared God accessible to every person who humbly turned to him, no matter what sin he had committed. That turning with one's whole heart to the mercy of God was the demand which the holy God made to each one, and indeed had to make. But that was precisely what the Pharisees found unacceptable, basically for two reasons. First of all, with that theory Jesus was undermining, so to speak, the whole morale. Expressed in the thought of the Pharisees, this meant that he was actually destroying Israel's "apartheid," the task given this people to be a living expression of God's kingdom by the faithful fulfillment of his Law. The second was perhaps worse yet in the minds of the leaders. Jesus was making it too easy for the sinners. It seemed that the Pharisees' lifelong struggle to be and remain "just" had been in vain. This objection against Jesus they likewise made known. He tried to paint for them God's true nature, and in the light of that to unmask their own attitude as selfish and jealous. Thus he once told them another story in which "the just" and "the sinners" were symbolized by two sons of one and the same father. That became the famous "parable of the prodigal son." The one son abandoned his father's home and squandered his inheritance in a foreign country. When he was almost dying of hunger and misery, he returned repentently to his father. Apparently the father had been waiting for him all the while and gave a great feast in his honor. There was to be no more talk about the past; that was all forgotten. This was too much for the other son, who had always faithfully served his father, and he refused to take part in the banquet, even when his father pressingly urged him to do so. This then was the way Jesus saw the attitude of the Pharisees. He did not go on to tell how the story ended. Did the older son remain oustide sulking, or did he let himself be persuaded to go in and take part in the festivities? Thus he left it to his listeners to decide what they were going to do: go on protesting or rejoice at God's loving concern for sinners which Jesus preached and himself put into practice.

The well-known story of the vineyard owner who paid the laborers hired last just as much as those who had worked through the heat of the day was also intended for the Pharisees. The master's answer to the protest of the laborers who felt cheated contains the whole meaning. The Pharisees could not agree with the conduct of God as Jesus expressed it in his speech and actions; they refused to grant him the freedom to be good, for because of his goodness they themselves felt cheated: "I choose to pay the last-comer as much as I pay you. Have I no right to do what I like with my own? Why be envious because I am generous?"

It was all in vain. Jesus could not get through to them, and every day the gulf between them widened. When he went to Jerusalem to celebrate the Passover, his disciples were apprehensive about going with him. They had the feeling that the decision was at hand. He had already spoken vaguely about what the "Son of Man" would have to endure in the capital.

There in Jerusalem he would continue preaching, unafraid. Even his opponents had now and then noticed what his disciples already knew for a long time: Jesus took no one into account; he was no "respecter of persons." There was no one he feared, for he did not take himself into consideration, and therefore he could put that complete sincerity into practice which according to him was characteristic of the spirit of God's kingdom. Its dominating aspect was what he called "purity of heart," that undivided dedication which knows no ambiguity in thinking and acting. Even in Jerusalem he would not mince his words; he would honestly say what he thought about the recognized "pious," who liked so much to be honored outwardly by those same common people whom they so despised and excluded from the kingdom of God. On every occasion Jesus would continue to bear witness to the true nature of Israel's God and fearlessly stand up for the chances open to the sinners, the masses who were officially written off as "accursed" —and all of this in the framework of his appeal to all Israel to be converted, from his evident conviction that his appearance had ushered in the "Day of Yahweh," the climax of God's history with his people. His life and works belonged to the "last things": he was offering Israel one last chance.

This he did in Jerusalem when the feast of the Passover was at hand. In those circumstances, that could only lead to his downfall. The reader will recall how critical the situation was. Each year at the Passover the political leaders in Jerusalem feared the worst. These men, the high priest and his council, were more "liberal" in their opinions than the Pharisees, more realistic. The salvation of "Israel" in their day consisted chiefly in maintaining good relations with the occupying power. It was a politics of give and take, of negotiation and intrigue, directly with the procurator, and, at the same time, behind his back, with Rome; this was the only kind of politics that could save Israel from extinction. That is why each Passover was so terribly dangerous. On that feast Jews came to Jerusalem from every corner of the country and even from abroad, tens of thousands. The city swarmed with Galileans. It was bursting at the seams with pilgrims, and the hillsides all around were dotted with tents, where great numbers spent the chilly spring nights.

Especially dangerous was the enthusiastic mood felt everywhere, for the Passover was actually a kind of national independence day. The Jews commemorated on that day the exodus from Egypt, their liberation from the power of Pharaoh. Part of that commemoration was a festive banquet, the ritual of which suggested that those taking part were actually present on that great day of salvation, personally involved in it. At the same time, that celebration pointed to the future: at the end of time Yahweh would free his people forever from all present and future suppressors. Those expectations, too, were expressed, again by way of suggestion: a place at table was left free for the Messiah, for he was sure to make his appearance during one of their Passovers. Perhaps it would be this one. Who could know?

It is understandable that the Roman procurator left his beautiful villa on the sea to come personally to Jerusalem during those festive days. He took over the leadership of the garrison, strongly reinforced for the occasion, so that he could intervene immediately. The least spark could cause the smoldering coals of the Jewish resistance to burst into flames.

Jesus could be just such a spark. He rode into the city on a donkey, people were saying, and a number of his admirers gave him a royal welcome. Now, it was not unusual for popular rabbis to be received in such a fashion. But with so many Galileans involved, this manifestation was still alarming. Besides, Jesus had carried on insolently in the temple court, when he drove out a number of merchants as if he had something to say about the affairs of the priests. And with all of this there was that illimitably irritating "I tell you solemnly. . . ." The plan was quickly made and executed. The procurator would only be too happy to exhibit a crucified resistance leader at the entrance of the city's busiest gate as a warning to others. Then the grubby masses could see what happens to one who poses as "king of the Jews." Thanks to a tip from one of his twelve intimate disciples, they were able to arrest Jesus in the dark of night. After a short hearing the Jewish leaders turned Jesus over to the procurator. He passed sentence without delay, and Jesus was scourged in the customary way. Tied to a pillar he was beaten with a whip which had pieces of bone and metal fastened to the thongs. Such a beating left a healthy and sound man mortally wounded, a total wreck, within half an hour. The Roman soldiers could give rein to their hatred of the Jews in the person of this victim. After this scourging Jesus was made to carry his cross to the place of execution. When he collapsed under the weight, the soldiers forced a passer-by to help him. Several hours after the cross was raised, Jesus died. A pious Jew, a kind of contemporary Tobit, buried him before the beginning of the sabbath.

When the feast days had passed and life in the city was back to normal, the responsible leaders gave a sigh of relief. Pilate returned content to Caesarea; there were no riots to be reported to his superior in Rome. The leaders of the Phaisees had eliminated their irritating opponent, that dangerous deceiver of the people. They had also been able to provide the high council with an occasion to do the procurator a favor and to support him in the maintenance of order. The more humane members of that council naturally thought it a shame that this had meant the life of still another Jew. But such things cannot be avoided in politics. Thus it sometimes seems better for one man to die than for the whole nation to perish.

X

In the Light of Easter: The Second Phase

Jesus was dead. He belonged forever to the past. It was taken for granted that the group of his followers would fall apart and the whole affair would soon be forgotten.

But that did not happen. After his death this Galilean was able to inspire his followers anew, and in so doing he launched a movement which within a few decades began to spread across the whole world. He himself remained the source of its inspiration. Thus he likewise called into being a unique kind of literature, the genesis of which we are trying to describe here. It was only then that his disciples began to see the full meaning of all those experiences they had shared with him. Their recollections of his words and deeds, his passion and his death, received in that way an irreplaceable character: for all future members of the movement, nothing told or listened to can match them in importance. As such they became the material for the writing which came to be called the "gospels."

Hence the consideration of the way Jesus began anew to inspire his disciples after his death is a separate phase of the origin of those gospels. This phase, however, cannot be described in the same fashion as the previous one. The principal reason for this lies in the nature of the documentation available to us. The well-known stories about the empty tomb and about Jesus' apparitions did not intend to give an account of facts. That is likewise true for the descriptions of the first days and weeks after Easter, which Luke gives at the beginning of Acts.

A deeper reason might be found in the nature of those first experiences themselves. By way of illustration, I sometimes refer to the origin of a masterpiece, such as a novel, a painting or a piece

319

of music. The artist can generally speak about the time it first began to take shape in his hands. But he can say little or nothing about the first brain wave, the first captivation by a mysterious creative power, that something we call inspiration and in which the actual origin of the work lies. That moment was too mysteriously pregnant to permit even an approximate description.

Here we are confronted with something similar. Therefore, we can only hope to indicate some elements which in all probability were present in the disciples' experiences. In so doing we cannot avoid dividing up what in reality was a unified experience. Furthermore, we are concerned here with a group experience. Undoubtedly the various disciples will have given prominence to different elements, according to their characters, their abilities to express themselves and their personal relationships to Jesus. But there will likewise have been a very intense exchange of experiences and insights within the group.

A New Beginning for All

Although the relationship between Jesus and his most loyal followers was of a very special kind, it included in any case the element of friendship. No man gives up his home, his work and his family to follow another unless he loves him very much. For his part Jesus let his followers participate intimately in his work, and, in more than one sense, he gave them the very best he had to give.

If only for these reasons, his death must have shocked them very deeply. One who has never had the bitter experience of losing his dearest friend or his "better half," in the strict sense of the word, can perhaps try to feel something of what that means by reflecting upon a good poetic expression of it or upon the famous pages which St. Augustine devotes to the death of his friend in the Confessions (Book VI). That experience includes the feeling that one's own life, too, seems to end. To live on no longer has any meaning. The future is completely black.

What made the dismay of Jesus' friends especially unbearable was the realization that they were partly responsible for his death. They had not defended him. They did not do anything to rescue him. Peter was the only one who mustered enough courage to go unnoticed to the courtyard of the high priest to see what the outcome of Jesus' trial would be. And then a scornful remark of a servant girl was enough to make him solemnly swear that he had nothing to do with Jesus. They had left him to carry his own cross; they had left him to die alone, and even the final sign of friendship they had left to an outsider.

Their religious despair was perhaps the worst of all. In Israel pain and suffering and especially an untimely death were always regarded as punishments from God. What Jesus had undergone was the lot of the worst of sinners, of those who despised the Law, the lot of the proud. He could certainly not have deserved that. Or perhaps he did, on account of his unparalleled presumption. But then they would have been in error, misled; they would have given up everything for an illusion! That did not seem possible—and yet there was the hard fact of Jesus' execution. Was Israel's God not accustomed to speak through events? Hence the disciples' severe torment; all was dismay, sorrow and despair.

Then he appeared to them. We will never know precisely when, precisely where and precisely how. But that they bore witness to his appearance is certain. Paul successively names Peter, the whole group (the twelve, though there were only eleven then), a group of more than five hundred disciples (most of whom were still alive when Paul wrote, some twenty years later), James and finally himself. We can say with certainty that all these people experienced something which they described as "seeing Jesus." He was seen by them or let himself be seen; he "appeared" to them, as the classical term expresses it (1 Cor. 15, 3-8).

If they experienced his death as the end of everything their own lives had become, then this seeing him again must have evoked an overwhelming sense of newness. The great judge of men referred to above, St. Augustine, once uttered a beautiful sentence in a sermon: *Nihil homini amicum sine homine amico.* Rendered freely it seems to say, "Nothing smiles upon a man without a friend." The presence of their friend again in their midst must have caused the whole world and everything in it to smile upon them, to take on an unprecedented light. But what is more, his appearing to them likewise meant that he had forgiven them. They had abandoned him; they shared in the guilt of his death. But now he came to them again. Their guilt thus belonged with his death, with that evil past he had overcome.

Here, too, we might refer to a universal human experience: the feeling of a person who has just been forgiven a heavy debt. If that debt involved a sum of money, then he already experiences the happy feeling of being able to begin anew, "with a clean slate." Much deeper still is the feeling of one who has been forgiven a personal debt, an offense against one's fellow man. By his forgiveness the other gives himself, as it were. We can hardly think of anything in which one experiences more clearly that the past is really behind him and the future completely open.

But then Jesus' forgiveness was also meant for all the others who were guilty of his death, and first of all, his own people. Better than anyone else, his disciples knew how much effort he had put forth to prepare Israel for God's coming. He had called them to make his appeal heard in the land of Galilee. In so doing they were not to go to the pagan inhabitants of that region and surrounding territories, but they were to limit themselves to the Jews, to "Israel," just as Jesus himself also did. Finally, he had risked his life by calling all, even "the just," to conversion, and this he did even in the capital. Then the leaders of the Jewish people let him be put to death. But now God had raised him up. In this way God had also proclaimed his forgiveness to all Jews, his will to create a new "Israel."

However, that Israel would no longer consist only of Jews. More immediately and more deeply than Jesus' first disciples, Paul was made aware of what it meant for the crucified to appear to him. Prior to that moment, he, the zealous Pharisee, had had his own opinions about those who adhered to Jesus. They belonged to the "sinners," the people who failed to live according to the Law and thus would have no place in the future world. Their situation was precisely the same as that of the pagans who did not know the true God. That these accursed "sinners" now proclaimed their former master as the one sent by God—yes, the Messiah—and even went about spreading propaganda about him could not be tolerated in Israel. Paul was also aware that this Jesus had denied the distinction between sinners and the just, and thus also the essential role of the Law as the norm of Jewish life and as the foundation of the chosen community. He had likewise actually violated the prescriptions of that community, desecrated the sabbath and preached against the temple. Therefore, he was justly put to death—and on

a cross. It was written in so many words in the Law (Dt. 21, 23):
"One who has been hanged on a tree is accursed of God." God
had spoken thus. All the words of men would pass away, but the
words of the Law would not pass away. Paul believed this passionately. However, that inner conviction alone was not enough for
him, and he quickly became the most active among the Pharisees
of Jerusalem. His colleagues had eliminated Jesus himself, and
Paul could help them to wipe out all traces of that Galilean and
destroy the movement which he had started.

Then Jesus also appeared to him. At that moment, the God of
Israel, the living God, the only one who can give life, made it clear
to Paul that he had taken the part of that man who was accursed
by the Law. Thus the Law was no longer his last word. That word
which he now proclaimed in Jesus, his Messiah, was a word of
pure forgiveness. He had sent his Messiah to those in Israel who
did not deserve it, to those who were "written off," to those whom
even conversion could not render capable of the merits which
would dispose God to accept them into his kingdom. That was
bewildering. The Messiah had taken upon himself the lot of sinners; yes, he had shared their lot by becoming an "accursed one"
himself. And now, raised up by God, he remained with the sinners
who called upon his name. Later Paul related what he had heard
Jesus saying at that moment, when he was pursuing the disciples:
"Why are you persecuting *me?*"

The way of the Law was no longer the way to God. All that
counted now was his forgiveness, that re-creating gift of self which
posited no conditions. This also meant that *every distinction disappeared,* the distinction between the just and sinners, all sinners,
and thus also the distinction between Israel and other nations, the
"pagans." Paul remained the zealot for God that he had always
been. But from then on he no longer worked to win the Jews
for him through fidelity to his written Law, but to win all men for
him through faith in Jesus, his redeeming word. Later on, looking
back to that moment when his work for God took a new turn, Paul
says, "Then God . . . called me through his grace and chose to
reveal his Son in me, so that I might preach the good news about
him to the pagans."

All of this has possibly raised the question for some readers
about what precisely were the apparitions of Jesus, with their uni-

versal historical effects. If he recalls what we tried to explain in chapter 2 about the "dimension" which can become visible to the believer in certain events, and furthermore what we said in this chapter about the "meaning" of Jesus' miracles, the reader may suspect how we would undertake to answer this question. In the world of Jesus and Paul it was not as unusual as it is in our modern, Western culture for someone to have visions or hear mysterious voices. That belonged to certain forms of religious experience (just as was also the case in the Middle Ages). Now, we saw something similar in the cures which Jesus performed and in his driving out of devils. These were likewise not regarded as abnormal, certainly not in the presence of personalities who were considered to possess divine powers. That is also the reason why they did not have to be "proofs" for the message of the miracle worker. Only those who accepted Jesus as God's representative saw his miracles as signs of God's kingdom coming in him.

The same thing seems to be true in the case of the apparitions. Outsiders could think of hallucinations, mental disturbance and phantoms, and could give all kinds of other qualifications for them. "Seeing Jesus" meant that God has raised him from death to life only to those who knew that God was at work in those experiences. In speaking above about the reactions to the apparitions, we therefore attributed them sometimes to Jesus and sometimes to God, for the disciples and Paul saw God at work in the Jesus who let himself be seen by them. Put in another way, the "apparitions" of Jesus took on that far-reaching meaning because of the broader framework in which they were placed by those who saw them in the light of faith. That framework was determined by the "Scriptures."

The Scriptures: Explaining and Explained

In the preceding paragraphs we had to separate what in reality forms a whole. Those reactions of the disciples to what they called "seeing Jesus" are unthinkable without the background and penetrating action of the Scriptures. For the very reason that they belonged to the people of Israel, Jesus and his disciples were part of a tradition. That tradition had brought forth the Law, the prophets and the writings and was itself nourished by them. Even if they had never seen a written text of the Bible with their own eyes, their thought and faith would still have been entirely determined by that tradition.

This is a "given" which, in short, contains two things: form and content. In chapter 2 we attempted to formulate the ways in which biblical people conceive and express things. That also applies to Jesus and the disciples. Likewise, their experiences and speech show no traces of the sharp boundary line we modern Westerners draw between symbol and reality, between the individual and the community of which he is a member, between a person and his actions, between past and future.

Furthermore, it is certain that the content of the biblical traditions also contributed to their formation. No other competing "world view" or "way of life" existed for them. The reality they experienced was determined by God's great deeds in the past: the creation of the world, the promise to Abraham, liberation from Egypt, and the entire biblical history with its great figures, the kings and prophets. The future, too, they could see only in the light of the Bible; its culmination would be that last great "Day of Yahweh," when the divine majesty would finally and forever reveal itself. He was the God of Israel, and therefore at that great climax of history his people would stand in the center of humanity, the place it had held in everything since Abraham. Even those who gave some positive thought to the role and the future of the people outside Israel could not conceive any other possibility than that God would grant them happiness and peace by means of Israel. Thus the milieu in which Jesus and his disciples lived bore the hallmark of authority along the lines of the promise to Abraham: "In you will I bless all the tribes of the earth" (Gn. 12, 3).

If we grant that Jesus and his disciples were entirely formed in their thinking and acting by the biblical tradition, one might ask to what extent they knew the literal text of the Bible from personal reading and study. In all probability they knew certain parts of the Scriptures almost literally, since they were regularly read aloud to them at school and in the synagogue as well as translated and explained in the vernacular (Aramaic). We can no longer determine what those texts were. The legislative parts of the Pentateuch were probably left to the teachers of the Law. Ordinary people certainly knew many of the narratives by heart and were familiar with sections of the late prophets and the Psalms as well. Of the former, Isaiah and Jeremiah were no doubt their favorites, whereas Ezekiel was regarded as very difficult. An indication of this choice also came to light in the fragments of the library of the Essenes, those pious contemporaries of Jesus, who in their isolated settlement on the Dead Sea prepared for the revelation of God's kingship.

One thing is certain. Everything the disciples knew about the Scriptures, globally and in details, began to receive a new meaning when Jesus appeared to them. He had often given them to understand that his ministry ushered in the "Day of Yahweh," that climax of history which kings and prophets had anxiously awaited. That was all very puzzling to his disciples. What could possibly be the connection between a homeless wanderer who lived on alms and their idea of that marvelous climax of history which would literally be world-shaking and accompanied by explosions of divine wrath and blinding glory? Likewise, Jesus' preaching had become completely unintelligible when God's official representatives delivered him over to the Romans to be crucified.

Now that God had raised him from the dead, they suddenly understood the connection to which he himself had alluded in his mysterious way. This was indeed the climax of that long history in which God's actions were always seen to follow a certain "pattern." It had begun with the exodus from Egypt when he revealed himself as Savior by rescuing an insignificant people from destruction and creating them anew as a people existing for him alone—the "people of God." Centuries later the great world powers had executed God's judgment upon his people and led them away to exile in Babylon, a kind of non-existence. Again he had rescued them. He had given them a new start, and that was experienced as a resurrection from death. Many psalmists and the countless men and women who prayed the Psalms had born witness to how they themselves had personally experienced God's way of working in accordance with that "pattern." By curing them of deadly diseases, Yahweh had rescued them from the clutches of the underworld and given them new life, to be spent in praise of him.

That same pattern would characterize his way of working at the anxiously awaited climax of history. Through the chastening fire of his judgment, God would create a holy people, made up of all the just whom he would raise up from death to live and reign eternally with him. This he had now begun by raising Jesus to life.

This awareness, coming in the wake of Jesus' apparitions, must have overwhelmed the disciples like an unexpected, crushing wave. When we think that the biblical world view and way of life were the only ones conceivable, then it must have seemed that the very roots of existence were being laid bare and that they were being initiated into the deepest meaning of everything that was or would be. Together they no doubt immediately recalled everything they had once learned and quickly went to the written scrolls themselves for an exciting voyage of discovery through "the Scriptures."

If the reader might like to take up his Bible in order to make his own, as it were, something of what the disciples' discovered, we would be happy to point out a few of those "surprising" texts. But then he must try to read them as the disciples did, forgetting for a moment everything we said in the previous chapters about the modern approach to the Old Testament. The need to know the historical background and original intentions of those texts did not exist in Jesus' milieu. The written word was read as God's word just as it stood. Texts which they regarded as "prophetic" could refer immediately to their own situation. Furthermore, no one objected to "citing a passage out of context," so to speak. Therefore, the reader who wishes to place himself among the disciples as they go about referring all those divergent texts to Jesus, to his humiliation and his glorification, will have to "think" as they did, with a deep feeling for images and symbols, for "global" connections, leaving aside his need for sharp distinctions and logical contexts.

We can begin with the book of Psalms, for the belief among the Jews that some of its texts referred to the coming Messiah was already quite ancient. Jesus himself probably once used the opening verse of Psalm 110 to illustrate the supra-human character of that Messianic figure. Everyone could read in the title that it was a psalm "of David." Now, many believed that the Messiah would stem from the house of David and thus be "David's son." If this is now the last word on the matter, Jesus asked, how then can David here address that son of his, the Messiah, as "my Lord"? He must therefore be superior to his ancestor David. In any case, the disciples saw now, after God had raised Jesus from the dead, that this was clearly a description of their master's glorification, not only because the great David calls him "Lord," but because God had said to him: "Sit at my right hand." Thus in this psalm verse they found the terms for their confession of faith, terms which will always live on in the Christian Credo: "He . . . sits at the right hand of the Father."

Likewise, in Psalm 2 the Jews saw a description of their coming Messiah. What the disciples had noticed of Jesus' exceptionally intimate relationship with his Father they recognized in the divine decree of verse 7: "You are my son; today I have become your father." Therefore, that was not just a personal feeling of his; God himself had called Jesus his son.

Both of these psalms speak of a Messiah who will rule by force of arms. In the eyes of the disciples, this was obviously not a reference to Jesus; that did not constitute a necessary conclusion in their way of reading the Bible. Yet, attributing to the Messiah the role of high priest "according to the order of Meschizedek" (Ps. 110, 4) provided them with a way to characterize Jesus as the only mediator between God and man.

Just as the triumphant Messiah who was to be given dominion over all the nations of the earth came to life in these texts, so too the persecuted and tortured soul praying Psalm 22 was a foreshadowing of Jesus. He begins his prayer with a cry of desolation directed to the only one who can save him: "My God, my God, why have you deserted me?" In forceful images he describes his distress, caused by men who do him wrong. His tormentors jeer at him and even divide his garments among themselves and cast lots for his clothes (verse 19). But then his prayer suddenly changes to a description of his gratitude to God for rescuing him (verse 22). He celebrates that rescue by calling together the humble of the world, even from the very ends of the earth, for a kind of thanksgiving feast, a banquet which would culminate in praising the God who frees men from death.

The disciples also saw Jesus prefigured in the "David" of Psalm 69—that man so loaded with contempt. Zeal for God's house devours him (verse 9), and for this he is severely persecuted. Yes, they even give him poison to eat and vinegar to drink in his thirst (verse 21). Here, too, the lament changes to a song of thanksgiving (*eucharistia*), and the psalmist calls all who seek God to join in (verses 30-34). The disciples recognized in this what they themselves were doing when they gathered for the eucharistic celebrations, the center of their common life.

One might also read Psalm 80, especially in order to get used to the line of thought in which the people of Israel is at once the vine which God planted, the son raised by God and the son of man. This last term takes us back to the seventh chapter of Daniel. There, as the reader will remember (cf. pp. 261f.), the author offered the community of faithful Jews, that group so severely persecuted, the prospect of God's kingship being revealed in the near future. In that chapter he describes Daniel watching what was to happen at the end of time (i.e., very soon, in the author's mind). The earthly powers who had so horribly mistreated the people of the Most High would be sentenced, and then God would give everlasting dominion over all nations to "the people of the saints," represented here as being "one like a son of man." We also saw (cf. p. 252) that further on in Daniel the salvation of the group included the raising up of the deceased faithful to eternal life. All these things now became clear, their connection suddenly visible. Jesus was at once the first of the just whom God had now, at the new end of time, raised from death and the Son of Man who in his own person was the expression of the people of the saints, tortured and rescued by God. Thus it was to him, Jesus, that God had granted everlasting sovereignty over all peoples, nations and languages.

In the Old Testament there are many more descriptions of that "end of time," which the disciples now saw in a new light because Jesus had "fulfilled" them. For example, in the seemingly unconnected unit formed by chapters 9—14 of the book of Zechariah, we read something about the future king who comes to Zion "riding on a donkey." That was clearly Jesus, the just one, the Savior, but likewise the humble king who would proclaim peace to all the peoples of the world (9, 9-10). The following verse speaks of liberation "because of the blood of your Covenant." A bit further on Israel is referred to as a flock without a shepherd (10, 2), and in 11, 12-13 there is mention of a shepherd who receives his wages in the form of "thirty shekels of silver." At God's command he throws that money, the ordinary price of a slave, "into the temple of Yahweh." The next chapter refers to the inhabitants of Jerusalem who "will look on the one whom they have pierced" and "mourn for him as for an only son" (12, 10). Finally, we read of the shepherd whom Yahweh "will strike . . . so that the sheep may be scattered," and the concluding sentence of this remarkable prophecy consists in the prediction that "there will be no more traders in the temple of Yahweh, when that day comes" (13, 7 and 14, 21).

The book of Isaiah appeared to be the most complete in its descriptions of Jesus' person and lot. This great prophet had already proclaimed him to King Ahaz as *Emmanuel,* "God-with-us." He would spring from David's stock; he would be a divine hero, a prince of peace who would rule over all nations, completely filled with the spirit of Yahweh. He would take no notice of outward appearances; he would take the part of the desolate and strike the wicked with the scourge of his words. That was Jesus from head to toe in the way he took the part of the rejected, in direct opposition to the Pharisees (Is. 7, 14; 9, 5-6; 11, 1-5).

Later in his book Isaiah announces to the people in exile that their God would soon appear as king; this was to be proclaimed as the good tidings of salvation. Among all those enchanting words about Yahweh's coming to Jerusalem, often directed to "Israel, my servant" and "Jacob, my chosen one," there are several places where that chosen servant does not seem to be the people. Rather, he is described as an individual, and sometimes he even speaks himself. In those texts the disciples saw the figure of Jesus described with surprising clarity. First of all, he was the beloved and totally dedicated servant of Yahweh who both modestly and frankly exemplified what true piety was (42, 1-4). A little later on he himself tells how he sees the work as his reason for existing, his task in life. When he encounters sharp opposition from his people and feels that he is laboring in vain, God makes it clear to him that his task is greater still, even worldwide. He is to be a light for all other peoples as well, and to bring God's salvation to the very ends of the earth (49, 1-6). Thus he goes on preaching, even when the people attack him, beat and mock him. He does not cower in the face of the suffering they inflict upon him; in some way, he is certain, his God will justify him (50, 4-10). Finally, Isaiah relates how that servant met his end, a story which sounds unbelievable. He is so mistreated that no human form can be recognized in him.

Then the prophet lets nameless masses of people confess that their iniquities caused the innocent servant to suffer so. After he is put to death as a criminal, God will enlighten him and through him carry out his resolution to make "just men" of the countless masses of humanity—that is, to bring them to live in such a way that all their possibilities will come to perfect fruition (52, 13—53, 12).

Like the other texts about the servant, this last one is also found among descriptions of the joy and exultation which will burst forth when God comes to Zion as king and Savior. That is likewise the case further on in Isaiah where a figure similar to the servant declares that Yahweh has anointed him and sent him "to bring good news to the poor. . . ." Those words too (61, 1), uttered by an anointed one (i.e., "Messiah" or "Christ," following the Greek), are preceded and followed by descriptions of the happiness and glory which will radiate from Zion when God reveals his majesty to her (60 and 62).

When the disciples read those texts, they remembered that Jesus had alluded to them a number of times. They thought back to the very beginning when Jesus answered John's question from his prison cell by referring to what was taking place: "The good news is proclaimed to the poor" (cf. p. 307). They also thought of their last supper together before his passion. During that meal, as a kind of prophetic action, he had passed bread and wine around to them and said that in so doing he was giving himself, his body broken by suffering and the blood he would shed. But this gift of himself was not only for them; it was also "for many." That infrequent term had also been used for the countless masses of mankind in the description of Isaiah 53.

The reader will now see the reason for the somewhat unusual title at the beginning of this section. The disciples had come to know Jesus and had been very close to him; he was put to death and afterward appeared to them. Now they saw that all of this had been described in many scriptural texts. For the first time it became clear to them that those texts referred to him. But at the same time, in the light of those texts, they saw who he really was. What had always been a puzzle before his death was now clear. He was the Messiah, but in a manner they had never dreamed of. That was the surprising thing about those texts of the Scriptures: *he explained the texts and the texts explained him.*

Action of "The Holy Spirit"

All of us have experienced that very special feeling which present-day psychologists refer to as the "Aha experience." This happens, for example, when one suddenly discovers the solution to a problem he has been working at for a long time. It can happen to one working a difficult puzzle. First there is that maze of possibilities which seems to become more complicated with every new combination he tries. Then in a flash the solution is as clear as crystal. "Of course, that's it!" It seemed to come from somewhere outside: "It hit me all of a sudden." Furthermore, it brings with it an enchanting feeling which one can hardly keep from sharing. Besides artificial problems, such as puzzles, one might think of a complicated problem in mathematics, the solution of which may have important consequences for the future. Or the problem might involve human relationships where the solution may consist in one's suddenly revealing his true intentions in all honesty. Likewise, it may concern things which touch the very meaning of one's life. It goes without saying that the sudden solution of such serious problems gives rise to an "Aha experience" which is much deeper, with more permanent effects, than that experienced by one who solves a crossword puzzle.

From what we have seen above, it will be clear that this kind of experience was part of what overcame the disciples after Jesus' apparitions. He had been a mystery to them. He had indeed said that with his preaching and work the "Messianic era" had dawned, but that did not at all correspond with what people expected of the Messiah to come. In making the surprising discovery which we sketched in the preceding section, they suddenly saw how everything was connected. And that was literally "everything." We already indicated that they were granted a new look at everything which ever was and ever would be. Jesus cast new light, so to speak, on everything past, because at its very roots it was directed toward him, and at the same time he determined the future of humanity and the world.

That God had allowed them to be so intimately involved in that great event, toward which he had directed all of history, especially contributed to their feeling of enchantment. In their relationship with Jesus they had indeed sensed that God was active in him in a

very special way and that he spoke to them through Jesus. Now
that inkling had become the certainty that God was now also at
work in them because of their relationship to Jesus, and that he
was speaking to all mankind through them.

They noticed how this certainty was the source of their untiring
strength. Fearlessly they went out to all men, to the highest authorities as well as to the beggars in the streets. They could do this, for
with the coming of the great "Day of Yahweh," what was important once now fell by the wayside: rank and class, respect and possessions. They felt that all those things belonged to the past; they
no longer meant anything to them. They experienced a tremendous
sense of freedom. It was not difficult for them to gather their possessions together and to share them with others.

But that was not all. Another very remarkable experience was
theirs besides. That same enchantment and that same feeling of
freedom also took hold of those who accepted the disciples' witness. As soon as they heard the story about Jesus and called upon
him as their Lord, at once they too seemed to become new men,
caught up in that same overwhelming new look at everything and
that feeling of being free. That happened to Jews, for whom the
old Scriptures began to take on a new meaning, as well as to
pagans. From this it was evident that association with Jesus was
not a condition for that experience. Others also shared in it. It was
something contagious. It spread like wildfire.

It goes without saying that the disciples regarded the way their
movement quickly spread also as God's work. It was an extension
of the work he had begun by allowing Jesus to preach his kingdom
and by raising him from the dead. Yet they had reasons for not
speaking simply of "God," but of "the Spirit of God." We would
like to explain those reasons briefly.

The English word "spirit" does not call to mind the same thing
as the Hebrew word which it renders and which sounds the same
as the Aramaic word in the everyday language used by Jesus and
his disciples. That word actually meant "wind" and "breath." The
wind, especially the storm wind, was one of the most striking symbols of God's activity in the world, for it can come up quickly,
from any direction, and then exert unbelievable force, stir up
water, move sand dunes and root out trees, *without ever being visible itself.*

That word likewise referred to the mysterious wind issuing from the mouths of men and animals, breath, the unmistakable sign of that other mysterious something we call "life." In their figurative language, ancient biblical people sometimes called the storm wind the powerful breath which the living God exhaled from his mouth or nose. He, too, was the one who breathed the breath of life into man and the animals—and continues to do so. If he were to cease that life-giving breathing even for a moment, everything would die. Should he send forth that wind again, everything would be created anew.

Biblical people liked to say that "Yahweh's storm wind" or "his spirit" has taken hold of the great figures of Israel's history, enabling them to perform supra-human tasks, for that creating breath of God could make someone into a new man. After the exile, when people had become so deeply aware of the individual's impotence and sinfulness, some prayed to God that he would make them new men through his "breath of holiness" of "sanctifying wind," rendered in our translations as "Holy Spirit." Granting this prayer meant that he would wipe out—forgive—their sinful past and give them a new heart which would be directed entirely toward him.

All these things came to mind when people heard the term "spirit of Yahweh" and other formulations such as "the spirit of [his] holiness" or simply "the Holy Spirit." The same was true for those who spoke Greek and were accustomed to the Greek Bible, for there the term was usually translated by *pneuma,* which can also mean both "wind" and "breath."

However, the Scriptures did not only speak about "the spirit of Yahweh" in connection with God's activity in nature or in Israel's history. There were also descriptions of the future "Day of Yahweh" in which God was said to act upon men through his Holy Spirit. We read the following in the book of Joel (3, 1-2; in some Bibles, 2, 28-29):

> After this I will pour out my spirit on all mankind.
> Your sons and daughters shall prophesy,
> your old men shall dream dreams,
> and your young men see visions.
> Even on the slaves, men and women,
> will I pour out my spirit in those days.

This was precisely what the disciples were experiencing, that feeling of newness, accompanied by a surprising new view of things and an enchantment which forced them to speak out—that is, to prophesy. And furthermore the contagious nature of those experiences and the way they took possession of all who accepted Jesus as their Lord and called upon "the name of the Lord," whether they were young or old, men or women, slaves or free men, could be nothing else but the result of the unequaled action of Yahweh's spirit foretold by Joel.

One could say that it was Jesus who brought about this "explosion" of the Holy Spirit and unleashed that mysterious power which proved itself capable of renewing so many people in ever growing numbers and of making them into new creatures from within, so to speak. But one could also say, and perhaps more in line with the Scriptures, that Jesus' activity itself had been the work of that Holy Spirit. Indeed, according to Isaiah, the spirit of Yahweh would rest upon the Messiah who was to come forth from the stock of David (11, 1-3). Yahweh would let his spirit rest upon his chosen servant (42, 1), and he, too, would bear witness to the presence of Yahweh's spirit resting upon him (61, 1). In his case, however, it was not necessary that the spirit make him into a new man, for already in his mother's womb God had set him apart for the task he was to perform (49, 1).

The Structure of the Message

About fifty years after Jesus' death, the evangelist Luke published the book which later would come to be called the "Acts of the Apostles." Under this title it took its place in the New Testament after the four gospels. After a thorough Hellenistic education in a non-Jewish milieu, probably in Syria, Luke devoted himself in particular to the study of the Jewish Scriptures. He preferred the narrative parts, and through them he became thoroughly acquainted with what we have called "the biblical ways of conceiving and expressing things." In writing Acts he clearly intended to instruct and encourage his readers by showing them how the Christian message, beginning at Jerusalem, spread with irresistible force across the world and penetrated even the heart of the Roman Empire.

In an authentically biblical way Luke summarized the experiences, which we attempted to describe in the preceding paragraphs, by means of an "origin story" (cf. pp. 73-78) known to us as "the descent of the Holy Spirit" (Acts 2, 1-13). The reader will understand why the author let a powerful wind blow through the house. Likewise, the appearance of "tongues of fire" will no longer seem strange to him, for the disciples' enchantment indeed made them fiery witnesses of Jesus.

Here we can prescind from treating the other experiences which Luke elaborated in meaningful details in his story (such as the knowledge that in his own day Christ was already confessed as Lord in so many different languages—for example, by Parthians, Medes, Elamites, etc.). We are concerned with what he describes as taking place after that scene which marked the magnificent beginning of the triumphal expansion of the message. Some of the bystanders look for the meaning of that sudden explosion of enthusiasm, whereas others are ready with an explanation: "Those men are simply drunk." Peter then addresses the men of Judea and inhabitants of Jerusalem; he is evidently the spokesman of the group of twelve (the empty place having been filled in the meantime), and perhaps, too, of the larger group of the "120 brethren." According to Peter, that excited proclamation of the greatest thing God had done in Jesus and its being understood in so many different languages meant that "the Day of the Lord" had dawned. It was just as the prophet Joel had described. After that introduction the actual speech begins as follows:

Men of Israel, listen to what I am going to say: Jesus the Nazarene was a man commended to you by God by the miracles and portents and signs that God worked through him when he was among you, as you all know. This man, who was put into your power by the deliberate intention and foreknowledge of God, you took and had crucified by men outside the Law. You killed him, but God raised him to life. . . .

That last point Peter explains by means of Psalm 16, and he then continues, making use of Psalm 110:

God raised this man Jesus to life, and all of us are witnesses to that. Now raised to the heights by God's right hand, he has received from the Father the Holy Spirit, who was promised, and what you see and hear is the outpouring of that Spirit.

For David himself never went up to heaven; and yet these words are his: "The Lord said to my Lord: Sit at my right hand until I make your enemies a footstool for you." For this reason the whole house of Israel can be certain that God has made this Jesus whom you crucified both Lord and Christ.

Those listening were deeply moved. When they asked what they must do, Peter answered, "You must repent, and every one of you must be baptized in the name of Jesus Christ for the forgiveness of your sins, and you will receive the gift of the Holy Spirit."

Reading further in Acts, one will notice that other "speeches" also reveal the same structure which is so clearly visible in Peter's sermon. The argument generally follows this pattern: (a) Jesus, clearly sent by God, was put to death at the instigation of the Jews; (b) that took place according to God's plan just as he had revealed it in the Scriptures; (c) God raised him from the dead and (d) gave him a new name or function; (e) all of this was likewise foretold in the Scriptures; (f) we, his disciples, are witnesses of all those facts, and (g) therefore we call you to penance and conversion that you may share in the future which God has unveiled in Jesus.

The points listed here recur in their entirety or in part in Peter's next sermon to the people (3, 12-26), in his speeches before the high council (4, 7-8. 12; 5, 29-32; cf. the prayer in 4, 24-30), and in his sermon to Cornelius and his circle of family and friends (10, 34-43). Likewise, the speech which the writer puts on the lips of Paul in the synagogue of Antioch during his first missionary journey reveals the same structure, at least in the second half (13, 23-39).

Although Luke lets his heroes make use of the Christian vocabulary, which was beginning to take form in the meantime, there can be no doubt that the basic theme of their speeches corresponds with that of the earliest preaching. We have already seen how their deep conviction that God had entrusted them with a very special task had been part of the first disciples' experience. Even back in Galilee Jesus had involved them intimately in his work. He had instructed them and sent them out to make his message heard in wider circles. In the light of Easter they understood what God had intended when he had bound their lives so closely to that of Jesus. As eyewitnesses of his life, passion and glorification, they were the obvious ones to bring the good news to the people. God had indeed revealed his kingship, for the long awaited Messiah had come so that God's dominion might be exercised in the world of men. This filled them with a very strong sense of responsibility, as if God had placed the lot of mankind in their hands.

On the one hand, "the twelve," and perhaps other intimate disciples of Jesus as well, already had some experience in preaching God's kingdom. After the apparitions of their crucified master, on the other hand, that activity took on new and wider dimensions. This was not only a question of the overwhelming insights, certainties and feelings which they attributed to the action of the "Holy Spirit." The content of the message was also involved. They no longer only preached that God was at work as king in the words and actions of Jesus. Now they went much further. The message of their witness was that the events and the Scriptures made it clear that God had constituted Jesus as the Messiah, or the Christ, and thus as Lord and judge of all men. He was therefore the one who reigned over the newly dawning "Day of Yahweh." The future of mankind lay in his hands. Whoever accepted that and, so to speak, let his own future depend on him could summarize that new view of life in the confession: "Jesus is the Christ" or "Jesus is the Lord."

That profound difference between the preaching before Easter and that after Easter has sometimes been pinpointed as follows: preaching *of Jesus* became, after Easter, preaching *about Jesus.* Put somewhat differently, one might say: *Jesus the preacher* became, after Easter, *the preached Christ.* Despite their clearness, abridged definitions of this kind can be misleading, for after Easter the disciples most certainly took up again what they had seen, heard and preached in Jesus' name before his death. Of course, everything they remembered about him was seen in the light of Easter and thus became the material from which the gospels would one day be written. The following chapter will attempt to indicate how this took place.

XI
Formation of the Traditions: The Third Phase

A man involved in an automobile accident relates his experience one way to his wife, who is always so worried about him, another way to his friends, who drop in for a drink and always enjoy a tall tale, and still another way to the judge, whose duty it is to decide who was at fault. Ten years later he will tell the story differently still, perhaps because the accident in question turned out to be the first of a whole series.

Completely honest people also relate one and the same experience in different ways. The reason for this is that our memory is not some kind of electrical apparatus which faultlessly registers all our impressions. "Recalling" a memory is therefore completely different from looking up a snapshot in an album or playing back a tape recording. Our impressions are absorbed into the living entity that we are. When recalling such memories, we also express what we are at the moment we tell them. And that is further determined by our relationship with those to whom we are relating the impressions. Sharing memories is often a way of expressing mutual friendship. How often we hear old friends say, "Remember when the two of us. . . ."! Or, recalling memories can sometimes stem from the desire to get another person's attention: "You should hear what happened to me. . . ." Again, one might feel that it is very important for another person to know something that has taken place so that he can do what is necessary in that situation: "I can't keep you in the dark; you must know that. . . ."

This last example brings us close to our actual subject. What Jesus' disciples had experienced, everyone should hear about as quickly as possible in order to take whatever measures were necessary. Humanity had reached the critical hour, and the disciples were called to announce that to every man. In Jesus God had ushered in the climax of history and had established him as Lord and judge of all men. The disciples, therefore, had to speak out. Silence was impossible. Every man simply had to be told how things stood.

We might define that as the core of the message. But, of course, it immediately met with opposition and questions, both from Jews and pagans. People said that Jesus had trespassed against the Law; how then could he be the Messiah? How could someone sentenced to death on a cross by the unsurpassed Roman courts be regarded as innocent and even as judge over the whole world?

If those who heard the news saw the light and accepted the disciples' message as an appeal made to them personally, they became part of the group of disciples. Then they wanted to know more about Jesus. They had heard that already in Galilee God had sealed his words with "power and signs." Could his companions of those days tell them more about these things? And how did the Jewish leaders come to be his bitter enemies? Had he really broken the Law? What had he himself said about the approaching end of history? Newcomers to the group asked questions like these all the more so because they felt compelled to share with outsiders what they themselves had experienced as a tremendous freedom.

Thus the disciples came to "recall" what they had experienced when they were with Jesus. And of course the memory played its usual role, as we indicated above. At the time they related those memories, they had become "new men," so to speak, because of the Easter experience. That renewal had left its irremovable mark on their earlier impressions of Jesus. Thus they could no longer speak about Jesus as if they had never experienced Easter.

Likewise, the people to whom they spoke were always a determining factor for the form which their recollections took. Of course, everything Jesus said and did was of the greatest importance for all. But if the one being addressed was an educated Jew who posed questions, then the disciples gave their "report" a different form from the one used when speaking to simple village people or non-Jews who were not familiar with Jewish concepts and customs.

We must not forget that both the first disciples themselves and those who passed on their stories to others had been formed in the biblical traditions. In the preceding chapters we have seen something of the ways in which stories were used to communicate convictions and "religious views" to others. Instead of wanting to know precisely what happened in the past, as we do, the approach best suited to them was to "actualize" those past events and thus to relate them in such a way as to render them present and real for the listener (cf. pp. 82f. and 113). When treating the prophetic books, we saw that short, concise statements of one of God's spokesmen could be repeated literally years later by his disciples. But we also observed that those followers sometimes believed themselves empowered to add their own explanations to those authoritative words or even to alter them in light of changing circumstances (cf. pp. 178f.).

The movement which Jesus and his disciples had launched spread quickly to the various parts of Palestine and further—to Syria, Asia Minor and Egypt. Wherever the message of the preacher led to the formation of a group of disciples, a "Jesus-tradition" took root. The stories told by the preacher and the explanations he himself gave were repeated again and again and thus came to be preserved. The *stories* introduced Jesus to the believers, and he continued to speak to them in his *words*. Thus the "Jesus-tradition" went its own way in each of the many communities or churches. Partly because of the close contact between the leaders of the churches, that tradition remained the same in essentials. But, at the same time, the variety resulting from the great expansion was unbelievably rich. Hence the origin of the treasure from which the evangelists could draw when they set about composing the gospels.

To give the reader some idea of how vast that wealth was, we would like to treat several points a bit more in detail. It goes without saying that we will again be separating things artificially which were very closely connected in the actual and highly colorful historical situation.

Surroundings and Circumstances

We have just mentioned, by way of example, the difference between the various forms their preaching took, depending on whether it was addressed to an educated Jew, to an illiterate Jew or to a non-Jew. That was, of course, a simplification. Within Judaism there were many different groups or "sects," such as the Pharisees and the Essenes whom we have already had the occasion to mention several times. There were still others whom we have not mentioned. Each of those groups had its own way of living according to Israel's faith and its expectations, with particular emphasis on certain elements. When the disciples were speaking to members of these sects, it was only natural that they would make use of their favorite words: "The justice for which you are striving is bestowed by God on those who accept Jesus as the Messiah," or "You divide mankind into the children of light and the children of darkness. By believing in Jesus one can pass from the one group to the other and become a child of the light." With the entry into the Church by Jews from so many different groups, we can understand how the wording of stories about Jesus as well as that of his statements took on nuances which further enriched them.

Furthermore, many Jews were influenced by Hellenistic customs and ideas. Even the Maccabees, as we have seen, could not completely hold themselves aloof from that influence any more than the admirer who wrote of their heroic deeds (cf. pp. 133f.). Opposite these Hellenized Jews on the stage of 1st-century Judaism, both in Palestine and abroad, were the "proselytes"—that is, "those who came over." They were pagans who accepted both circumcision and the entire Law as their rule of life, thus sharing to some extent in the rights of the chosen people. Outside Palestine especially, there were also the "God-fearing" or "worshipers of God" who gathered around the Jewish communities. These pagans, too, were deeply impressed by the purity of the Jews' notion of God and by the high moral norms governing their lives, evidently a consequence of their faith in God. Although they did not let themselves be circumcised or take up the whole yoke of the Law, they did observe the ten commandments and follow certain Jewish customs. It is understandable that an enchanting message which proclaimed not the Law as the last word but the person of Jesus easily found a response among these God-fearing people. They both understood Jewish expressions of faith and were sufficiently familiar with the thought-world and religious needs of the "pagan" outsiders to be able to bring them the new message in a language they would understand.

When a new group of disciples formed around a certain preacher, there were three occasions in particular when he could tell them stories about Jesus or share Jesus' words with them.

There was first of all *instruction* in the broad sense about the message which the newcomers had accepted and the radical consequences that had for their whole way of life. From Paul's letters to the communities he "founded," we know how much time and care he devoted to that instruction. The accounts in the Acts of the Apostles confirm this. During the time he was in Corinth Paul regularly preached on each sabbath in the Jewish synagogue. When he found no response there, he moved to the home of a certain Titius Justus, a God-fearing man, and remained there a year and a half instructing the new converts in God's word (18, 11). A similar thing occurred some time later in another port city, Ephesus. There Paul "took his disciples apart to hold daily discussions in the lecture room of Tyrannus. This went on for two years. . . ." (19, 9-10). From his letters to the Corinthians it appears that in his instructions Paul distinguished between Jesus' sayings and what he himself determined (e.g., 1 Cor. 7, 10). He clearly intended to pass on first what he had received, and in doing so he maintained close contact with the community in Jerusalem. One of its leading figures, Silas (also called Silvanus), accompanied him on his missionary journeys. This Silas represented in the flesh, so to speak, the tradition of Jerusalem.

Second, there was *the celebration of the Last Supper* or "the breaking of bread," a weekly occasion to recall the great events of Jesus' passion, death and resurrection and to explain them by means of stories about what he had done and said. It seems that Paul spoke about all these things that last night at Troas when a young man got sleepy and fell from the window-sill on which he was sitting (Acts 20, 9).

Finally, there were *the discussions* with hesitating newcomers as well as with stubborn outsiders who compelled the followers of Jesus to tell them everything they knew about him.

When treating the historical and prophetic books of the Old Testament, we had the occasion to observe with what ease biblical people were able to combine two qualities when passing on data from the past—fidelity and liberty (cf. pp. 104 and 177). The biblically formed men to whom we owe the material of the four gospels combined these same qualities. Because they stemmed from so many different milieux and continually had to adapt their presentation to changing circumstances, their "contributions" gave the Jesus-tradition its rich variety. We would like to illustrate this with several examples, first from stories about Jesus and then from his words.

The Narration of the Passion

We will begin with the story of Jesus' suffering and death. This is a good example to begin with, chiefly because it is the only instance where the "given" of the story is a continuous series of events rather than one single event. It began with Jesus' arrest and led via his hearing before the high council to the sentence which Pilate handed down and immediately ordered to be executed. Another reason is that these events belong to the core of the apostolic message and were continually meditated upon, discussed and related, in the light of the Scriptures as well as under the influence of new experiences.

We modern Christians are used to the cross; for us it is a distinctive sign and symbol. We are no longer shocked when we hear that "the Lord Jesus was crucified." Therefore we must make an effort to realize how absurd the wording of that sentence must have sounded to those who first heard it. Likewise, such a realization is necessary to understand something of the development which the account of the passion has undergone.

The death sentence to which Pilate condemned Jesus was in that world the greatest humiliation one could be made to bear. Well-mannered Romans never spoke about it; cross and crucifixion were dirty words. When the great orator Cicero once had to refer to it, he used the superlative degree: *crudelissimum taeterrimumque supplicium,* "the cruelest and most hideous of all penalties." It was reserved for the most despised criminals.

Thus the witness of the first disciples must have terribly shocked and scandalized all who heard it. Their assertion that God had elevated a crucified man to be the Christ—that is, the Messiah—and established him as judge over all men was blasphemy to the ears of the faithful Jews, while to the pagans it was complete nonsense. Some twenty years after Jesus' death Paul admitted frankly in a letter to the disciples at Corinth, "And so . . . here are we preaching a crucified Christ; to the Jews an obstacle that they cannot get over, to the pagans madness. . . ." (1 Cor. 1, 23).

Paul's letters show that he never stopped reflecting on the obscure mystery of the cross. Sometimes he thought about it in terms of Israel's ancient liturgy, the sacrifice, where the peace offering played such a great role. The one making the offering provided the best animal in his possession and hoped that the bloody ritual would restore the living relationship between him and God. What Paul had in mind, therefore, was a kind of renewal of what had once taken place at Sinai with "the blood of the Covenant." Sometimes Paul also meditated on the meaning of such heavily laden scriptural words as "redemption" and "liberation," which of course implied freedom from all oppressive and enslaving powers, of which Pharaoh had become the undying symbol. At such times "the Law," which for him had so long been God's last word, kept coming to mind; he tirelessly tried to understand the role God could have intended for that Law in his former relationship with man, before he had brought it to its climax in the death and resurrection of Jesus. All that was but a searching, now in this direction, now in that. Perhaps what Paul saw most often as the actual meaning of God's work in Jesus was his definitive, total turning to men, in which he did not spare his only Son, but rather offered him up for them. And that Son had made the intention of the Father so much his own that he himself became a total surrender —to God in his "obedience" and to men in his "love." Paul then saw his own existence completely penetrated by the certitude that the Son of God had an unlimited love for him personally (Gal. 2, 20).

In the framework of such reflections, not only was the fact of Jesus' passion recalled, but the story of that event was narrated. Not all disciples felt the same need as Paul for deep reflection. But all were struck that Jesus' suffering was so clearly foretold in the Scriptures. That not only strengthened their certitude that everything had happened "according to God's design and foreknowledge," but also gave them the occasion to relate certain details in their story according to those ancient "prophetic" texts. To their way of thinking, data from those books were every bit as reliable a source of information as the account of eyewitnesses.

At the time, Jesus had spoken in mysterious words about the peril awaiting him in Jerusalem. Now that they understood in the light of Easter who he really was, it became clear to them that he had seen his own lot foretold in the biblical descriptions of the suffering just man, the servant of the Lord. Thus he knew about it all beforehand, even that Judas would betray him and Peter deny him and likewise that all the other disciples would desert him. He knew perfectly what he was doing when he accepted all those horrible things, and despite all his fears and sorrows he obediently fulfilled the will of his Father to the very end.

Besides data from the Scriptures, there were also other facts which began to influence those details of the passion narration. Two things came to light quickly. The Jewish authorities who had eliminated Jesus now began to take measures against his disciples. Outside Palestine, too, Jesus' followers were always encountering the staunchest opposition from dedicated Jews. Another fact contrasted all the more sharply against this background. Among the "God-fearing," those pagans who felt attracted to the doctrine and moral teaching of the Jews, the good news about Jesus usually found eager listeners. They joined the new movement by the thousands, and through them countless other pagans also discovered the way to Christ the Lord.

In addition, it must be observed that the attitude of the Roman authorities in the places where the messengers of Christ came was usually favorable, in contrast with that of the leaders of the often powerful Jewish groups.

The first disciples, all of them Jews, were surprised and overjoyed at the flow of Gentiles to Christ. But at the same time they were troubled that their own nation as a whole refused to accept its Messiah. Thanks to the central chapters of his letter to the Christians at Rome, it is Paul once again whose wrestling with this mysterious fact is best known to us (Rom. 9—11).

In the light of these experiences, the narration of Jesus' hearing before the high council became more and more dramatic. When Jesus asserted there that he was the Messiah, the Son of God, the Jewish nation rejected him through the words of its highest authority.

That dramatization was continued in what followed. It was the "crowds," and thus the mass of the Jewish people, who demanded Jesus' condemnation. They, too, were the ones who forced the Roman procurator to concede, after he, the highest judicial authority, had expressly declared Jesus to be innocent.

When the drama reaches its climax, as Jesus is dying on the cross, there is darkness everywhere—in the middle of the day. This was according to God's prediction for that day of "mourning for an only son," uttered by the prophet Amos: "That day . . . I will make the sun go down at noon, and darken the earth in broad daylight" (8, 9-10). Whenever God gave a decisive turn to human history, Israel usually made nature share in that event. Just as the mountains leaped like rams and the earth quaked at his intervention to rescue his people (Ps. 114), so here too the sun no longer gave its light, and the earth quaked at its very foundations. The first narrators had already added a very meaningful detail to the account. At that moment the "veil of the temple" split in two from top to bottom. What they had in mind was the heavy curtain which completely closed off the innermost part of the temple, the Holy of Holies, where God himself dwelt. That veil was now split asunder, for in the life of Jesus, completed at that moment, God had revealed himself fully and was open to all; from then on there would no longer be any privileged men. In the person of the Roman centurion the whole Gentile world now confesses that Jesus is truly the Son of God.

Miracle Stories

Jesus' miracles were characteristic of his preaching; put biblically, they were the powerful deeds, the awe-inspiring signs which he worked. His faithful disciples had experienced so many of these that they usually only remembered the characteristic details of a few incidents and then went on to speak globally about them.

Those details seldom included the time and place of a specific miracle. No one was interested in data of that kind, and thus they were hardly ever remembered, much less "recalled." They were concerned with the good works Jesus had done for the people. In them he manifested the kingly power of God at work in him. The eyewitness himself might be a lively storyteller who could bring the whole situation to life by his striking details. But he might also be someone who only paid attention to the essentials; his account of the fact would thus be quite sober. It could also happen that later on someone would take that same sober account and, after livening it up a bit with captivating details, would pass it on further.

Likewise, it was not at all unusual for certain details to move from one miracle story to another and even to be combined in different ways. Once a blind man, who heard that Jesus was nearby, shouted loudly, "Son of David, have mercy on me!" It is understandable that people also placed that moving cry on the lips of other unfortunates, such as the pagan woman who entreated Jesus to cure her daughter.

Sometimes Jesus was rather severe when people he cured wanted to glorify his person and spread "sensational stories" about him. He ordered them not to speak about it. This kind of reprimand was characteristic enough of him to relate it in other stories as well. This was also true of that other way he tried to direct attention away from himself. He would say, "Not I, but your faith has healed you."

In connection with this, there is another factor which influenced the formation of the miracle stories in the gospels. Jesus' miracles which accompanied his announcement of God's intervention as king were, no less than his words, an appeal to conversion and faith. He himself once made that clear in a kind of prophetic threat directed to the Jewish cities on the lake of Galilee: "Alas for you, Chorazin! Alas for you, Bethsaida! For if the miracles done in you had been done in Tyre and Sidon, they would have repented long ago in sackcloth and ashes. . . . And as for you, Capernaum, did you want to be exalted as high as heaven? You shall be thrown down to hell." In the prophetic tradition, the pagan cities Tyre and Sidon passed for places which called the most horrible punishments down upon themselves because of their pride (see, for example, Is. 23 and Ezek. 28). Capernaum was sometimes called Jesus' own town, so many were the people he had helped there!

For the first Christians, Jesus' miracles could no longer fulfill their original function of calling them to conversion, for they were already converted and believed in Jesus. Nevertheless, the stories of those miracles were still meaningful for all who told and circulated them. By his gift of faith in Jesus, God "has taken us out of the power of darkness and created a place for us in the kingdom of the Son whom he loves," as Paul once wrote to the Colossians (1, 13). When those first believers heard how Jesus had once freed a possessed person from his tormentor, and in that way snatched him from the power of Satan, they recognized at the same time their own story. There were many other ways, too, in which to describe how their life had taken a new turn through faith and baptism, and how they had been given a new look at everything, a new task in life and a new future. Thus they had formerly been blind to all of that and now were made to see; they had been deaf to God's word, which they could now understand completely; once not able to thank God with all their heart, they were now cured of that dumbness; formerly they were impure because of a contagious sinfulness, and now they were freed of that kind of leprosy; once they lay deathly sick, and now they were full of health to serve others. When the first Christians related how Jesus had relieved people of their impure spirits and cured them of all kinds of illness, they were at the same time describing what he had done for them personally and what he continued to do for each one who joined their ranks by accepting Jesus as his Lord. That "immediate" meaning of the miracle stories surely influenced their formation. The seemingly simple statement that Jesus "raised" Peter's mother-in-law from her sickbed, with the result that she went about "serving" them, was at once a description of what Christians had experienced and what they should recognize as their task. That Jesus had first led a blind man outside his Jewish village before healing him and then had forbidden him to return to it took on a very immediate meaning where Jewish milieux very expressly and sharply opposed the Christians.

Their liturgical life also influenced the formation of some stories. Quite soon the story of the miraculous multiplication of loaves made the rounds in two versions. According to the first, Jesus had fed 5,000 people, who had followed him into the desert, with five loaves of bread. There was such an abundance that the remaining scraps filled twelve baskets. In the other version there were 4,000 people whom he fed with seven loaves; then the leftovers filled seven baskets.

Both versions described in an almost liturgical manner how Jesus took the bread which they had, looked up to heaven, gave thanks and passed it out to his disciples. When hearing those words one could hardly help but think of the eucharistic meal which was celebrated weekly in so many places across the world. There Jesus made it possible to pass out that miraculous bread, again and again, without the supply ever running out. At the time, Jesus had thus fed the people who followed him into the desert.

That piece of data also had an immediate meaning. In those early days being a follower of Jesus usually meant that one had to give up his family and friends, whether they were Jews who continued to regard Jesus as an accursed rebel, or pagans for whom the worship of a crucified man could be nothing but absurd. Whoever accepted Jesus as his Lord took the risk of finding himself "in the desert." But there he found the others who had also been disowned, and together they formed a new community around the table of the Lord. The twelve baskets of the one version clearly referred to the group of the twelve to whom Jesus had entrusted the care of his followers, the new Israel. In the other version, in which so many people had come "from afar," seven baskets remained; they could be seen as symbolizing the fullness of the pagan world.

In both versions they likewise experienced the "fulfillment" of what ancient Israel once went through. That people, too, had followed its God into the desert and there was miraculously fed with manna. Then Israel was led by Moses who enjoyed such an intimate relationship with God and spoke to the people in his name. Jesus was more than Moses. He had spoken to his disciples in his own name and on his own authority; by a simple command, he freed countless people from diabolical powers.

Water—or better, the great masses of water in the seas—was a very ancient biblical symbol for those powers. People sang the praises of Yahweh's absolute majesty as creator and Savior by confessing his sovereign power over the waters. He had subdued the vast waters of the chaos when he created the world; his power over the sea was again manifest when he rescued Israel from Egypt. In connection with this, one might also think of other signs of the "chaos," such as the restless masses of pagan peoples, or the devouring underworld and ever threatening death. That is why people who turn to Yahweh in their desolation sometimes cry out that they see boiling waves threatening to swallow them.

Thus miracle stories which took place on the sea of Galilee embraced a confession that Yahweh's saving power was at work in Jesus. He had walked on the water to his disciples who were wearily rowing against the wind; he had moved across the raging waves, just as it is said of Yahweh in Job (9, 8). More meaningful still was another story in which the disciples' little boat was almost

sinking in a storm while Jesus lay asleep in the stern. They awak-
ened him with a rebuking cry, and then he ordered the storm to be
calm. That story was especially meaningful to the faithful who
were suffering severe persecution. In their trials they did not doubt
that Jesus was near, but yet they rebuked him for sleeping and not
being concerned about their need. "Why are you so afraid? Are
you still without faith?" The storyteller who put these words on
Jesus' lips after the calming of the storm thus made the story into
an authoritative as well as immediate lesson for his listeners.

The reader of this book is no doubt familiar with the observation that precisely in deeply meaningful stories, like the one just
mentioned, the original impressions of the factual event are
scarcely if ever discovered. The *meaning* of the narration was
always primary (cf. pp. 83f.). We think in particular of what we saw
when treating the "symbolic actions" of the prophets. There it did
not make much difference for the meaning if the prophet expressed
the comparison simply in words or acted it out dramatically (cf. p.
172). The way biblical people took it for granted that symbol
and reality overlapped each other can offer an explanation for a
remarkable miracle story about Jesus. On his way from Bethany to
Jerusalem he is said to have looked in vain for fruit of a fig tree
along the road. At that he is supposed to have uttered a curse upon
that tree which immediately took place: the tree dried up instantly.
Now, it is not impossible that this story had its origin in a parable.
For centuries it was customary among the Jews to compare the
good deeds of a man or of a people with the good fruit of a tree.
Jesus, too, had often used that image; one of his parables was even
completely based on it. It was the story of a landowner who had a
barren fig tree in his vineyard. Finally he ordered the caretaker of
the vineyard to cut down that worthless tree. The man asked if the
tree might not be spared one year more. He would then loosen up
the ground around it and fertilize it; perhaps the tree would yet
bring forth fruit. If not, then the master should cut it down. With
this story Jesus not only made Israel's position quite clear but also
indicated how he saw his task. The people of Israel, and perhaps
Jerusalem in particular, were that tree in God's vineyard. They had
not reacted to his call to bring forth the "real fruit of conversion"
any more than they had responded to the Baptist's appeal. Thanks
to a postponement granted him by God, Jesus could preach in

Jerusalem; he had obtained one last chance for Israel. Jesus would still do all he could to bring his people to conversion, but so far he had failed. He had looked for fruit on that fig tree in vain. Perhaps there was indeed a dried-up tree along the road from Bethany to Jerusalem which later provided the occasion to relate the central detail of the parable as an actual fact. Hence our story, which is in point of fact the only "penalizing miracle" attributed to Jesus.

It would lead us too far afield here to give an anthology of the many miracle stories which circulated in the Hellenistic world in which Jesus' disciples preached their message. Many of them are thought to have taken place in temples of Asclepius, the god of healing (whose symbolic serpent we can see every day on doctors' cars). Other miracles seem to have been performed by a contemporary of Jesus, Apollonius of Tyana, who became so famous that later on divine honors were paid to him. One who is thoroughly acquainted with those narrations will quickly understand that the miracle stories about Jesus undoubtedly made a deep impression indeed. The audience must have been immediately struck that the Jesus-stories had nothing of the spectacular, the magical or the fantastic, and especially nothing of the selfishness which characterized the miracle stories so familiar to them.

"Origin Stories"

Before Jesus had chosen the twelve as his collaborators—those men who were to become "official witnesses" of his public life and his resurrection—a number of events had taken place which only later could be seen in their full meaning, in the light of Easter. The stories which we attempted to describe in chapter 2 dealt with facts of this kind. There we saw how biblical people liked to anchor a custom or insight, which was developed later on, at the beginning of that development, usually a creative moment in the life of the group or person in question (cf. pp. 73-78).

The moment when Jesus had responded to John's appeal and went to the Jordan to be baptized by him was this kind of creative moment in Jesus' life. In the light of Easter, Jesus' disciples brought the meaning of that event into sharp focus by relating that Jesus had received a vision confirming his vocation. He saw the heavens open and the Spirit descend upon him in the form of a dove while the voice of God spoke, "You are my Son, the beloved; my favor rests on you." In this way the disciples confessed their belief in Jesus as the Son of God, at once his Messiah (Ps. 2, 7) and his chosen servant (Is. 42, 1). For them there was no question of this being a vocation vision like those received by the prophets of old. In those visions they were called to take up their task and were sent forth to their people. Jesus was never "called" in that sense. He was by nature, so to speak, the "one sent"; he did not become such at the moment of his baptism. Thus God's voice asserted only who he was.

The oldest version of that story seems to have described a personal experience of Jesus. Later forms reveal the tendency to present that inner experience as an event which bystanders could also observe. In the same way a tradition sprung up which showed the Baptist protesting against Jesus' resolution to undergo a rite which was intended to be a sign of true conversion, for Jesus was the only man who had no need of such a conversion. From the very first moment of his existence he was already completely dedicated to God.

John's baptism was full of meaning for the Jews. As we have already seen (p. 299), that rite reminded them of the crossing through the Red Sea, by which God had rescued "his son" (Ex. 4, 22) from the power of Pharaoh. After sealing the Covenant he let his people wander for forty years in the desert. It seems probable that the story about Jesus' forty-day retreat in the desert after his baptism had its origin in the realization that in his own life he "fulfilled" the lot of Israel, that servant and son of Yahweh.

Shortly before his death "Moses" had explained that journey through the desert in terms of an ordeal or temptation (Dt. 8, 2–20):

Remember how Yahweh your God led you for forty years in the wilderness, to humble you, to test you and know your inmost heart. . . . He made you feel hunger; he fed you with manna which neither you nor your fathers had known, to make you understand that man does not live on bread alone but that man lives on everything that comes from the mouth of Yahweh. . . . Learn from this that Yahweh your God was training you as a man trains his child. . . . Be sure that if you forget Yahweh your God, if you follow other gods, if you serve them and bow down before them—I warn you today —you will certainly perish.

Just prior to that, Moses had said to his people, "You must fear Yahweh your God, You must serve him. . . ." and also, "Do not put Yahweh your God to the test. . . ." (Dt. 6, 13. 16).

The story of Jesus' retreat in the wilderness, at the end of which he met Satan face to face and was put to the test by him, took its inspiration, on the one hand, from the texts just cited, read with the conviction that Jesus fulfilled that earlier history. On the other hand, it was a real "origin story." The storyteller summarized in three points the temptations which Jesus had encountered during his public life and which he had overcome in perfect obedience to his task. He had never wished to work a miracle for his own sake (changing stones into bread to assuage his hunger). All requests, even those from men in authority, to confirm his mission by means of a spectacular sign he had always refused (throwing himself from the pinnacle of the temple). He was indignant when people, even Peter, wanted to make a worldly monarch of him, for he regarded their compelling suggestions as satanical temptations (kneeling in worship of the devil in order to obtain dominion over all the kingdoms of the earth).

Both stories not only illustrated who Jesus was and how he carried out his task in obedience to the will of the Father, as expressed in the Scriptures, but they likewise had an immediate meaning for the listeners and readers. Put in another way, they were also intended to be directives for them, for when they had sealed their acceptance of Jesus as their Lord by being baptized, they too had become children of God and had received a share in his Holy Spirit. Their lives would now also be characterized by peirasmoi, "temptations," of all kinds. The story of Jesus' temptation in the desert was a short and concise summary of the exemplary way in which their Lord had overcome his temptations.

Even further back than these events which preceded Jesus' public life, there was another creative moment, the actual beginning of his life. That event lay entirely outside Jesus' public ministry, of which the twelve were the official witnesses. For the men of that time, birth, as well as death, belonged to the great mysteries surrounding the life of every man. Because Jesus was such an exceptional person, some circles of the quickly expanding Christian movement began to express their faith in his person in the form of stories about the beginning of his life. Partly because these "Christmas stories" are so familiar, most people do not know which ones stem from the evangelist Matthew and which from Luke. Since we will treat the work of the evangelists as the fourth phase in the genesis of the gospels, here we would prefer to speak only globally about the "motives" of the nativity stories. This word seems appropriate here, because it can indicate both the reasons which lay behind the stories and the themes which the storytellers incorporated in their narrations.

Instead of referring again to what was said in chapter 2, here it might perhaps be better to take as our point of departure a way of speaking familiar to all of us. When someone consistently excels in a particular form of endeavor, we say, "He was born for it." By that we do not mean that he attained his proficiency in that skill by education and practice, but that he was born with it. He is a "gifted" person. Another related expression is, for example, "He is a born conductor." When the great Toscanini died, I remembered something which his admirers used to say of him. While still a boy, he was attending an opera when the conductor suddenly took sick. He is said to have saved the performance from failure by himself conducting the entire work by heart. In the meantime my memory has probably been at work; the actual story is no doubt different. But if it were told this way in the circles of Toscanini's admirers, people would know that it did not happen exactly that way, and yet at the same time they would accept it as "true," for it illustrates the indisputable fact that the hero was "a born conductor."

In the Middle Ages it was quite common to describe the talents of great men, especially saints, by means of legends about their youth and birth. It is told of several very ascetical saints, for example, that as babies they refused to take their mothers' breast on days of penance and fasting. When the quickly expanding group of preachers around St. Dominic received the name Dominicans, people saw in that name the Latin words *Domini canes,* "the hounds of the Lord," protecting the flock of the faithful. The result was that during her pregnancy Dominic's mother was said to have had a dream in which she saw a dog with a torch in its mouth setting the whole world on fire.

Further back in history and in other cultures it was customary to attribute divine ancestry to famous monarchs and generals. In Egyptian temples one can see paintings of the meeting between the divinity and the queen to whom the Pharaoh, that son of the divinity, owed his life. It was also told of great rulers that soon after their birth they were rescued from death in a miraculous way. That was the case with Sargon, the great king of Akkad (ca. 2500 B.C.). His mother had given birth to him in secret and set him adrift on the Euphrates River in a reed basket smeared with pitch; he was found there by a water carrier. For many years he lived as a gardener before he became the famous king.

This legend was known all over the East and even in Egypt. Many Scripture scholars suppose that it had been the model for the story of Moses' rescue in the papyrus basket (Ex. 2, 1-10). According to the commentator cited earlier (Te Stroete: cf. pp. 81f.), the story of Moses' rescue was a later addition to the Exodus narrative, when people became more clearly aware of Moses' unique greatness.

Besides this legend, which found its way into the Bible, still others about the great figures of Israel's history sprung up when the biblical text had already become unalterable. Thus the birth of Moses is said to have been announced to Pharaoh by astrologers. Jewish tales about Abraham included a similar story. On the day of his birth the astrologers of King Nimrod saw a star rise in the heavens which devoured four other stars, a clear indication that the newborn child would one day take possession of all four corners of the earth.

Biblical tradition had still another way to express the belief that someone in Israel's history "had fulfilled a providential role," as Christians today might put it. The person was said to have been born of a woman who was barren. That was the case with Samson who was to "begin to rescue Israel." His mother apparently became pregnant through the word which an angel of the Lord had spoken to her (Judges 13). Likewise, the mother of the great Samuel had been granted her son because of her unceasing supplication (1 Sam. 1). Or, people told how such a person was born of a woman who, according to human calculations, was too old to have children. In this way Isaac, the "son of the promise," was clearly marked as a creation of the God who remained faithful to his word. These were ways to express the belief that God had taken the initiative in bringing forth such an "historical" human life.

Furthermore, we should remember that in the religious views of the Jews every person was a being whom God had miraculously formed in his mother's womb. The learned writer of the book of Job lets his hero remind God that he had made him as one molds clay (10, 9) and then lets him go on to say:

> Did you not pour me out like milk,
> and curdle me then like cheese,
> clothe me with skin and flesh,
> and weave me of bone and sinew?

With milk the writer seems to mean the male seed, which was thought to congeal in the mother's womb. Note carefully: it is God who made that seed to flow and to congeal, so that he might then work the miracle of the human body, which the author sees God weaving from bones and muscles. The poet of Psalm 139 had this same image in mind where he describes the miracle of his origin in the womb of his mother, that secret place, known only to the creator. There he formed the psalmist's "kidney"—that is, his "self" —and there he weaved him together from a formless beginning. It was a "wonder" which the poet could find no further words to describe.

Thus one sees that our modern knowledge of and interest in the "biology" of birth was completely foreign to biblical people. God's creative work which takes place in the womb of the mother receives all the emphasis. This is also clear in the words which the mother of the Maccabean martyrs spoke to encourage her children: "I do not know how you appeared in my womb; it was not I who endowed you with breath and life; I had not the shaping of your every part. It is the creator of the world, ordaining the process of man's birth and presiding over the origin of all things. . . ." (2 Macc. 7, 22-23).

If one gives sufficient consideration to both of these aspects— namely, the manner in which biblical storytellers attribute to God the initiative for the birth of great figures and the descriptions in admiration of God's creative activity in the womb of the mother—then the real meaning of certain texts and stories will become clearer. First of all, mention should be made of the Greek translation of Isaiah's famous prophecy about *Emmanuel,* "God-with-us," that figure from David's lineage who was at once the personification and the representative of those who placed all their hope for salvation in God alone, "the faithful" (cf. pp. 191-195). Isaiah referred to the mother of that hero with a Hebrew word meaning "young girl," "young woman of marriage-able age," or "a young, recently married woman," whereas the Greek Jews called her *parthenos*—that is, "virgin." In this way they gave a more concrete expression to Isaiah's intention, not only in that passage about Emmanuel, but also in those other ones about the child with the wonderful names (9, 6) and about the ruler from the stock of Jesse who would be filled completely with God's Holy Spirit (11, 1). That final Savior, in the prophet's intention, would be entirely a gift of God, the fruit of his initiative, or—in Isaiah's own word—of his "zeal."

Secondly, that consideration will throw light on one of the pri-mary motives of the stories about Jesus' birth and its announce-ment. In the light of Easter the disciples had seen that he was the long-awaited Savior, the Messiah and the Son of God, who had fulfilled the name Emmanuel in its most literal sense. If ever God alone had been entirely responsible for a human birth, then the origin of this man in the womb of his mother, Mary, was that time.

Many other motives were also woven into the stories which sprung up around this principal one. They originated chiefly from two sources: on the one hand, the disciples' voyage of discovery through the Scriptures which Jesus had fulfilled in such an aston-ishing manner (and sometimes even the Jewish stories about great biblical figures); on the other, the events which the Christians saw taking place, in particular the painful experience of seeing official Judaism reject its Messiah, while those Jews who had been written off were the very ones to accept him, along with the ever growing masses of pagans. Thus the "good news" is first announced to shepherds, those typical representatives of the "outcast" in Jewish society, and to the wise men from the East. The motive which regarded Jesus as the "new Moses" was the occasion for the story about the murder of the Holy Innocents which he escaped. As the "fulfillment" of ancient Israel, which had been called the "son of Yahweh," he had to spend some time in Egypt. The instruction for those journeys to and from Egypt were given to Joseph in dreams, just as in the case of that Joseph of old, the son of Jacob. Zepha-niah had already pictured Jesus' mother as the daughter of Jerusalem who would be privileged to conceive the saving God in her womb (cf. p. 200). She was the new Ark of the Covenant, overshadowed by the cloud of God's presence.

But I should resist the temptation to illustrate here all the details of well-known Christmas stories. One reason is that an explanation of this kind actually belongs to the fourth phase, the work of the evangelists, but above all because our intention is simply to offer the reader a global sketch. Most important for the reader is the insight that the stories about Jesus' birth reflect *a specific form of confessing the faith.* That was their way of expressing their faith in Jesus which had brought them to worship him as the redeemer of humanity, the Messiah and the Son of God, as well as strengthening that of their listeners and readers. They did not intend to give an account of "historical facts." It would be doing the evangelists an injustice if one should use their stories to reconstruct the historical course of events.

The reader will perhaps ask whether such narrative traditions concerning Jesus were formed and spread under the watchful eye of "those who from the outset were eyewitnesses . . ." as Luke writes in the prologue to his gospel (1, 2). Yes, that is in fact the case, except that in those "origin stories" they were not concerned about checking whether or not everything actually happened as written. And that was not so much because they were only eyewitnesses of Jesus' public life and knew nothing of what took place before, but because they were simply not interested in "historical truth" when dealing with that kind of story. They judged the stories according to the intention for which they were written. When the person of Jesus was not distorted—or, in other words, when they were a pure expression of the apostolic faith—such stories were gratefully accepted. Otherwise they were rejected. At this point it would be helpful to take a look at some of the descriptions found in the many gospels which circulated among the Christians after the beginning of the 2nd century. They often had impressive names, such as "the gospel of Peter," or "the gospel of James," as we saw at the beginning of this chapter. Especially where the texts deal with the mysteries of Jesus' life, his birth and resurrection, these stories and all their fantastic details—which are often in bad taste—obscure the figure of Jesus rather than clarify it. That is why they did not "make" the Bible, despite their impressive names.

The Parables

It is one thing to repeat what one has heard another person in authority saying emphatically and in well-chosen words, and quite another to relate what one has seen such a person doing. In the latter case much more of the speaker himself comes out in the telling. He makes a choice of his impressions, which are already the result of an unconscious choice; the arrangement of his impressions into an orderly story is creative work on his part, an expression of who he is. In repeating someone's words, on the contrary, the speaker can be perfectly faithful to the original without contributing anything of himself, except, of course, the tone and the inflection of his voice. That is the reason why we clearly distinguish between the transmission of stories about Jesus and that of his sayings.

To give the reader some idea of the manner in which *logia*—"words" or "sayings"—were repeated and passed on by the disciples, we shall make a rough distinction between longer and shorter ones. Let us begin with some examples of longer sayings, because it is easier to indicate the different ways these were passed on.

Unfortunately, we must make a preliminary observation which may be disappointing. Although we know precisely what Isaiah (8th century B.C.) said, word for word, letter for letter, in certain situations, we are not privileged to say the same in the case of Jesus. He usually spoke in his mother tongue, the Aramaic of the Palestinian inhabitants of that time, but with few exceptions his words have come down to us in another language, Greek. The well-known proverb *traduttore traditore* knows no exceptions: every translator is a traitor. Anyone who has ever been engaged in the art of translating will readily admit this. One may also put it negatively, as did the great biblical scholars who wrote the Foreword of the New English Bible: "No one who has not tried it can know how impossible an art translation is."

Two further observations may lessen this disappointment somewhat. First of all, one should not exaggerate the difficulty by pointing out the profound differences between Semitic languages (Hebrew and, in our case, Aramaic) and classical Greek. In Jesus' day the Greek used as the universal language in the eastern part of the Roman Empire in particular was called *koine*—i.e., the language which all nations had "in common," or the "ordinary" Greek. The precise rules of the classical dialects had not been observed for quite some time in that *koine,* which served people of so many different cultural backgrounds. In the Jewish communities the use of that world language was strongly influenced by the Greek translations of the Scriptures, large parts of which were a more or less slavish rendering of the original Hebrew or Aramaic texts. Thus that Jewish *koine* Greek provided the possibility of rendering everything which Jesus had said without doing serious injustice to the meaning of those words.

Secondly, we should note that among Jesus' companions there were probably some who were more or less fluent in that Greek. But it is quite certain that the earliest Christian community in Jerusalem and Palestine was bilingual from the very beginning. One might compare the Jerusalem of Jesus' day with Brussels under the German occupation, where three languages were in use: Flemish, French and German. In Jerusalem the Roman functionaries spoke Latin, the language of the occupying power. The population spoke Aramaic and Greek. Christians who translated Jesus' sayings into Greek were usually also acquainted with their original Aramaic wording, either because Aramaic was their mother tongue or because they associated daily with Aramaic-speaking Christians. Thus it is safe to assume that the bilingual character of the earliest Palestinian communities provides a guarantee for the reliability of the Greek rendering of Jesus' words.

But when we speak of that reliable rendering, we do not mean a slavish, mechanically pure transmission, for we are dealing here with what scholars prefer to call a "living" tradition. What Jesus had said was passed on and repeated by people who had come to know and respect each other in their mutual acknowledgment of Jesus as their Lord. They believed that he was always speaking to them anew in those words and with that same absolute authority which they had recognized fully after Easter. Therefore, on the grounds of their belief in Jesus' *lordship,* his immediate authority over them, his faithful and intimate followers felt themselves authorized to give a clearer expression to the meaning of his words when they judged that necessary.

Sometimes that was in fact necessary, for not only had the situation of Jesus himself become different after Easter, but also that of his listeners. During his earthly life those were, besides his faithful disciples and "sympathizers," sometimes the people of Galilee who had attached themselves to the wonder-worker, sometimes the faithful in the synagogue where Jesus had preached and sometimes haughty Pharisees and ingenious doctors of the Law. But after Easter, Jesus' audience consisted of those people we like to call the "first Christians." When Jesus had spoken with someone about "following" him, he meant journeying with him through the territories of Palestine and to the capital. That precise meaning could no longer be repeated word for word now that Jesus had been taken up into glory. "Following him" therefore had to be understood in a somewhat different sense.

But I am afraid we are getting ahead of ourselves; we were going to limit this section to a consideration of the transmission of his "longer" sayings. By that we meant the "parables," a name which comes to us from the Greek. As we have already seen, there are roughly thirty-five of Jesus' parables which have been handed down to us. With regard to the process which they underwent from the moment the disciples first heard Jesus tell them until they were set in writing in the gospels, we can separate them into three groups. Some underwent *no change* of any importance, not even when they were translated into Greek; others were likewise passed on virtually unchanged, but *with an accompanying explanation;* with an eye to the new circumstances, both the meaning and wording of the parables in the third group were *changed* to a certain extent during the process of transmission.

In the first group there are several parables in which Jesus depicts God's feeling toward the person who turns to him with a contrite heart. God is then extremely happy, like the shepherd who found his lost sheep after a long search, or like the poor woman who in her excitement goes to tell her friends and neighbors how she swept her house and finally found the coin that was lost.

Such instructions about God's feelings toward those who were supposed to be lost were not only intended as a source of new hope for the people listening, but at the same time were directed against the teaching and practice of the Pharisees. That is why Jesus also gave the father of "the prodigal son" another, dutiful son who had never failed him. In our sketch of Jesus' public life we mentioned several other "polemical" parables (cf. pp. 313-316); they retained their full strength after Easter as well. On the one hand, Jesus had substantiated his preaching of God's love for sinners in his own person; he had thrown himself into the thick of the fight for them and paid for it with his life. On the other hand, the controversy continued, now between Jesus' disciples and the spiritual leaders of the Jews, within as well as outside Palestine.

Other parables in which Jesus had depicted God's attitude toward the person who turns to him also remained just as meaningful after Easter as before. A friend will at first complain if someone awakens him in the middle of the night to borrow some bread for an unexpected guest, but eventually he will grant the favor. In the same way an unscrupulous judge will finally bend for the poor widow who endlessly pesters him in order to obtain a hearing for her case. So, too, the man who asks something of God should persevere in his request and never lose courage.

Let us now look at the second group, the parables-plus-explanation. We begin with a few preliminary remarks. First of all, there was the observable fact that Jesus and his message were more easily accepted by simple people than by the better educated. The latter apparently had their set ideas about God, man and the world; there was no longer any room for the unusual things Jesus proclaimed. Even very drastic words and striking parables evidently were not able to find a chink in the armor of their old familiar ideas.

A second fact is related to this. After Easter when the circle of the disciples enjoyed rapid expansion, it became continually clearer that not only the leaders of the Pharisees but also the Jewish community as a whole refused to accept the message that Jesus was the Messiah. Thus, slowly but surely the community of Christians was being cut off from its origin. For many that process was a painful experience. One of the questions it raised was this: Why had most of the Jews not understood what Jesus really wanted?

In some of the Christian circles the answer to this question was sought in Jesus' manner of preaching. He had spoken "in parables." In Jewish Greek, that word did not have the limited meaning which we immediately associate with it. It called to mind other manners of speaking as well, such as the proverb, didactic poem, satire, epigram and riddle, as well as another kind of comparison which the Greeks called "allegory." That was a figurative description in which each part metaphorically represented an element of some real, though undefined, situation. Hence, a detailed allegory could also be a riddle. One had to discover the "key," as it were, in order to understand what it was all about. This way of thinking provided a certain explanation for the Jews' failure to understand the message of Jesus. He had spoken in allegories; the key to understanding them he gave only to his intimate disciples and not to the Jews outside that circle.

Finally, we should point out another important fact. The twelve disciples, chosen by Jesus himself, as well as those whom they in their turn appointed as representatives of the Lord, believed themselves authorized to speak in his name when addressing the faithful, whether that be a word of encouragement, a rebuke or an explanation. Filled with the spirit of Jesus, they did not hesitate to speak in the first person, for it was Jesus himself who spoke through them to the faithful. The reader can find a good example of this in the last book of the New Testament—Revelation or the Apocalypse—where the writer in the spirit of the Lord addresses seven letters to seven different Christian communities (2, 1—3, 22).

As our first example we will take the familiar parable-plus-explanation in which Jesus describes the work of the "sower going out to sow." Some of the seed was lost—on the path, on rocky ground and among thorns—but yet the man reaped an abundant harvest. That harvest was indeed abundant, for the Palestinian farmer was content with the usual seven or eight sacks of grain he harvested from each sack of seed. Jesus speaks of thirty, sixty and even a hundred sacks!

This parable was evidently an answer to a difficulty raised by the disciples. All of Jesus' work put together seemed so insignificant, and in addition it met with a great deal of opposition and misunderstanding. How could that be the beginning of "the kingdom of God," as Jesus maintained? For everyone who heard it, that term meant something very great and marvelous, something that would be glorious and worldwide. The surprise ending of this parable was probably Jesus' way of saying: indeed, the start is insignificant and there is a certain amount of loss, but you can be sure that this simple beginning will be crowned with success beyond all expectations. Just as in several other parables, Jesus wanted to communicate in this way something of his own trust in the future, a confidence rooted in his relationship with the Father.

But later on one of his disciples made use of this parable in his instruction. *Remaining* a Christian had even then proved more difficult than *becoming* a Christian. If someone was struck by the new message, then he excitedly attached himself to that attractive group of like-minded individuals. That was not so very difficult. But a tiring and painful process followed upon that single moment of conversion. All his thinking, feeling, and acting likewise had to be reformed according to the spirit of Christ. Sooner or later that proved too much for many a newcomer. Confronted with this situation, that disciple, speaking on Christ's authority, drew a new lesson from the parable of the sower by giving it an allegorical explanation. Each detail of the description should therefore refer to some element in the real situation. By sowing, Jesus had meant the preaching of the gospel. The seed would then be "the word," as Jesus' message was often called by the first Christians. With those three references to seed which "failed," Jesus had meant three kinds of listeners in whom the word produced no lasting fruit.

Thus the story told by Jesus to encourage his disciples was "actualized" by the one explaining it and made into a lesson of warning, likewise from the Lord himself, for he was always with his faithful followers and never ceased to speak to them in his words which were being passed on.

Our second illustration is also a story taken from farming, and Jesus could have intended this one too as an answer to a difficulty posed by his companions. They heard and saw that the power of the kingdom was at work in him. But why didn't that power manifest itself more radically? Why drive out devils from possessed persons, why make cripples walk and the blind see, and not obtain justice for the oppressed and smash once and for all the yoke of the godless, both that of the Romans and that of all the exploiters and oppressors among the Jews themselves? That was the same old question of so many of the faithful: How long, O God, how long will you allow the wicked to have their way? That question became very acute for people who with their own eyes saw God accomplishing so many victories over evil.

It was then that Jesus told the story of the farmer who had sown good seed in his field. At night an enemy came and sowed darnel among the wheat. Both came up together. His servants were astonished and asked that farmer whether he had sown only good seed. Yes, he said, but an enemy has sown darnel there too. Shall we weed it out right away? No, said the farmer, for you might pull up the wheat with the darnel. Let both grow up together until the harvest. Then I will say to the reapers, "First collect the darnel and tie it in bundles to be burnt, then gather the wheat into my barn."

The answer of the farmer was clearly meant to emphasize that we should not be too quick at making separations, but should let everything go quietly its own way; the separation will come in time. This lesson becomes even more striking when we recall how the Pharisees, "the separated ones," had clearly separated the just from the wicked, something which those other pious Jews, the Essenes, did even more radically. Jesus himself had not set his disciples apart in a "sect" with their own rule of life and the like, but he always addressed his appeal to all Jews without exception. He forbade judging others, and he refrained from doing so himself. That was something for God to take care of, later on.

In the circles of the disciples, an "explanation" made the rounds, which again treated the story as an allegory. Each of the seven (!) elements in the story represented some aspect of the real situation:

the farmer	= the Son of Man
the field	= the world
the good seed	= the sons of the kingdom
the darnel	= the sons of the Evil One
the enemy	= the devil
the harvest	= the end of the world
the reapers	= the angels

For Jesus the emphasis was on the counsel to be patient and not yet to make separations, but the explanation made the conclusion the center of attention. "Just as the darnel is gathered up and burnt in the fire, so it will be at the end of time. The Son of Man will send his angels and they will gather out of his kingdom all things that provoke offenses and all who do evil, and throw them into the blazing furnace. . . ."

It seems probable that this shift of emphasis was a result of the entirely new situation which Easter had ushered in. Before Easter, when Jesus told them parables about a master who did this or that with his field, his vineyard or his money, or about the way a father acted toward his sons, then he always intended that figure to represent God. By such stories he wanted to unveil for his listeners God's true "character," which was often disfigured in their minds.

But with Easter Jesus himself had become Lord and master. God has raised him from death, seated him at his right hand and given him all power. Jesus dominated the climax of history which had thus been begun; he would also bring that climax to a close at his return as judge over all men, living and dead. For many Christians that return of Christ was at the center of their expectations, as so many texts of the New Testament show, the last sentences included.

Thus it happened that the central figure of the parable just discussed was identified with Jesus, the Son of Man, and that the emphasis was shifted from the order of the master that everything should be left to grow quietly to the coming separation of the good from the bad which Jesus would execute at the end of the world.

Finally, we will give several examples of the third group of parables. In their transmission the situation which Easter had ushered in did not result in an added explanation, but influenced the very wording of the parables. With the passing of time, "Israel's" refusal to accept Jesus as Messiah became more and more apparent. This aspect, too, belonged to that new situation, as well as their awareness that at the same time Jesus was being hailed as Savior by ever growing numbers of pagans. For many Christians, that Jewish rejection of Jesus was sealed in the year 70 when the Romans destroyed Jerusalem and the temple. That was the definitive end of a "world" which in the meantime had been replaced by another. In that old order of things only one nation had access to the true God, and there was only one place on earth where one could worship him, in the usual sense of sacrifice at that time. Now he was accessible to all men, everywhere in the world, and the temple in which he dwelt was formed by Jesus and his faithful, a living entity, built up from "living stones," as it was figuratively described.

The familiar "parable of the unwilling wedding guests" underwent the effects of that new situation. We saw that Jesus addressed himself to all Jews, but also only to Jews. Except for incidental contacts with pagans, the Gentile world remained outside the horizon of his preaching. They were sometimes spoken of indirectly, particularly at the time Jesus made his last appeal to the Jews, in the form of a threat: If you do not repent and be converted now, you for whom the kingdom of God was first intended, then "many will come from the east and west to take their places with Abraham and Isaac and Jacob at the feast in the kingdom of heaven; but the sons of the kingdom will be turned out into the dark." The happy union of all in eternal bliss was depicted here in the usual Jewish way as a banquet. This was one of the reasons why Jesus could give his threat the form of a story.

Someone had once invited many guests to a banquet. When everything was ready, he sent his servants out to the homes of those invited, as was customary in those days, to announce that the tables were spread and ask them to come. But suddenly it appeared that not a single one could make it. One said that he had just bought a field and had to inspect it, another had to try his new oxen, and still another had just been married. At that the host was furious and ordered his servant to go out into the road and try to force people into the banquet hall, for he was determined to hold the feast. The conclusion went as follows (in the familiar authoritative tone!): "I tell you, not one of those who were invited shall have a taste of my banquet."

Looking back, we see that even before Easter the Jews who were officially excluded from the kingdom of God, the "sinners," were invited by Jesus to take part in that very community with God. After Easter the pagans, too, were included. Maybe that was the reason why the servant in the older version is sent out twice—the first time into the city (Jerusalem and the Jewish nation), and the second time outside the city (the Gentile world).

The story took on many more such "allegorical" elements (cf. p. 363) when passed on in another milieu. In that version the host became a king (God) who held a wedding banquet for his son (the Messiah). After his first invitation failed, the servants (the prophets and apostles) whom he sent out a second time with an even more urgent appeal were mistreated and even murdered by those invited (Israel). The king was furious and sent his armies to kill the murderers and destroy their city (Jerusalem). Then his servants bring in all the people they can find at the crossroads and thus the banquet hall (the Christian Church) is filled.

We will take as our second example a parable which is the source of a term used in our everyday speech. When we say that someone is gifted with "many talents," we are using a word and an image which has come down to us from the gospels. We have seen that Jesus' conflict with the Pharisees had its roots in his totally different experience of God. To his way of thinking they defiled the divine majesty by asserting their rights before God and by excluding others from community with God. They lowered him to a kind of strict taskmaster and thus became themselves scrupulous servants who held themselves strictly within the limits of commandments and prohibitions and carefully avoided every risk of transgression. To impress upon them how seriously mistaken they were in their idea about the God of Israel, Jesus told them the following story, hoping that the unexpected ending would make them think.

A rich man once took a long journey, entrusting his capital to his servants. They put the money to good use, just as they had always seen their master doing. They invested it and thus made more besides—that is, all but one; instead of doing business with the sum entrusted to him, he buried it in the ground. In those days that was thought to be the best "safe." After some time their master returned and the servants had to render an account. He was very pleased with those who had successfully invested his money and allowed them to keep the money as well as their additional earnings. One would expect that the man who had safely buried his money, the most prudent one who had taken no risks, would receive the highest praise. But that was not the case at all. When the master asked him about the money, he said, "I had heard you were a hard man, reaping where you have not sown and gathering where you have not scattered; so I was afraid, and I went off and hid your money in the ground. Here it is; it was yours; you have it back." His master retorted, "You wicked and lazy servant! So you knew that I reap where I have not sown and gather where I have not scattered? Well then, you should have deposited my money with the bankers, and on my return I would have recovered my capital with interest." To everyone's surprise the master took the money from him and gave it to the man who had made the greatest profit.

The conscientious servant had totally misjudged his master. He had considered him to be a hard man instead of what he really was, a "dynamic" businessman who knows that one only succeeds in life by taking risks. This was the lesson: the Lord had entrusted the treasure of the Law to the leaders of Israel as "capital" and expected them to do something with it. They were to make the entire nation into a devoted "son" of God, a convincing witness of the living God in the world of men. Instead, those leaders had projected the petty feelings of their narrow hearts into their Lord and therefore selfishly buried the treasure of the Law in their own little group.

For the Christians, that situation belonged to the past; it was part of that world which was now gone forever. But this parable had something to say to them as well. They, too, were servants of a master who had left them for a while and entrusted them with a great treasure. They, too, lived in the expectation of his return, and they knew that they had to make the most of that treasure, for the benefit of all nations. At the same time they saw that in the various communities there was a great diversity in the gifts which Jesus had left them for that purpose.

Thus the parable was reshaped in the course of its transmission. In one of the traditions the parable describes the departing master (Jesus) as giving rather large sums of money to his servants (one talent was equivalent to about seventy-five pounds of gold), but still in different quantities. One servant received five talents, another was given two, and a third only one. But when compared to eternal happiness, even those large sums were of little value. Thus in that version the master (God) said to the two industrious servants on the day of reckoning (the last judgment), "Well done, good and faithful servant; you have shown you can be faithful in *small things*. I will trust you with greater; come and join in your master's happiness" (his heavenly company). The adapted version did not change anything in the conversation of the master with the third servant—the climax of Jesus' parable. Likewise, the Christian who regards his religion only as a system of laws and prohibitions, given in view of his own personal eternal salvation, has misjudged his Lord. Next, this version added one of Jesus' short sayings which has come down to us in other contexts as well: "Anyone who has will be given more; from anyone who has not, even what he thinks he has will be taken away." And finally, the third servant is thrown "out into the dark" (hell).

In another milieu, a slightly different version of the parable made the rounds. It was combined with a story which circulated among the people and perhaps was even used by Jesus himself. This story had its roots in an historical fact. When the tyrannical Herod the Great died in 4 B.C., the remainder of his family immediately went to Rome to negotiate with Emperor Augustus concerning his successor. A Jewish delegation also went to Rome with a petition for the emperor, asking to be freed of the Herodian family and especially Archelaus, whom Herod had indicated as successor in his last will and testament. The Jews preferred to be governed directly by the Roman emperor. Nevertheless, Archelaus won the case; upon his return as monarch to Judea, he took bloody revenge on those who had opposed his succession.

Thus we have the version of the parable in which a man of noble birth goes to a distant country to be appointed king and afterward returns (Jesus who had gone to heaven will return as king). To each of his ten servants he gives one pound (one-sixtieth of a talent, or 1¼ pounds of gold) with the explicit injunction to do business with it until his return. Then a delegation of his fellow citizens is sent on his heels with the message: "We do not want this man to be our king." Nevertheless, he returns as king. One servant has made ten pounds with the one entrusted to him, and he is rewarded with the government of ten cities. The second servant's pound has earned five pounds; he is put in charge of five cities. Next the conversation with the third servant follows, the climax of Jesus' story. It is almost identical with the other version, the only difference being that the servant did not bury his money in the ground, but put it away in a handkerchief. His pound is given to the first servant, the man who had been given the government of ten cities. Just as in the other version, the saying about the man who has being given even more is incorporated here as well. The conclusion resumes the theme with which the parable began. The nobleman who has been made king then orders the execution of all those citizens who opposed his succession to the throne. This last detail was very probably an allusion to the punishment the Jews would suffer for their opposition to Christ. That would take place at the last judgment, but it is quite possible that they regarded the destruction of Jerusalem by the Romans as an anticipation of that judgment.

Short Sayings

No less characteristic of Jesus' teaching are his short sayings. Like the prophets and the wisdom teachers of old, he used to condense his teaching in short concise sentences, often in rhythmic form and sometimes including striking contrasts and challenging images. The authority with which they were uttered had the effect of imprinting such sayings deep in the memory of attentive listeners, much more so than the circumstances in which Jesus spoke. These blurred very quickly. When Jesus prepared his followers for their mission to the towns and villages of Galilee, he certainly provided them with many such short sayings about the kingdom of God. Later, too, he no doubt expressed the conclusion of some teaching or discussion with the Jewish leaders in similar short pregnant sayings. Thus after Easter the disciples realized that they were in possession of a great treasure of short sayings. They could repeat them as the teaching of their master whom they now recognized as their Lord in a much more definite way. Thus the *logia* could serve as an expression of what the Lord wanted them to do in the new situation. They repeated them, therefore, sometimes without any alteration, sometimes clarified or complemented in view of the new circumstances. But in this respect the approach is different from that used for the parables. A parable, as we saw, could be handed down as an isolated unit, but this could not be done with a very short saying. Therefore, in the transmission of these sayings we can discern the following three methods used by the disciples: a saying was linked up with other short sayings, it was connected with a parable, or it was inserted in a narrative.

Let us begin with some illustrations of these three methods. In connecting short sayings with one another—i.e., making groups—the disciples followed the example of their forerunners who in former centuries had collected the sayings of a venerated prophet or wisdom teacher. Those disciples often combined two or more sayings because the same word occurred in all of them. This was an old and proven aid to memory. There was a saying of Jesus about punishment in hell which ended with the expression: ". . . where the *fire* does not go out." Three other sayings were connected with this one, namely: "For everyone will be *salted* with *fire*"; "*Salt* is a good thing, but if *salt* becomes insipid, how can you season it again?"; "Have *salt* in yourselves and be at peace with one another."

More often the connection was made on the basis of the sayings' similar content or of a related theme. Here is an example of such a combination: "Would you bring in a lamp to put it under a bushel or under the bed? Surely you will put it on the lampstand? For there is nothing hidden but it must be disclosed, nothing kept secret except to be brought to light." Another example: "The amount you measure is the amount you will be given—and more besides; for the man who has will be given more; from the man who had not, even what he has will be taken away." Since both of these examples start with the idea of "measure," they could easily be combined to form a quartet.

The second method of passing on Jesus' short sayings was to connect them with a parable. We have already seen an example of this in the preceding section. The saying about the man who has been given even more was handed down in close connection with the parable of the talents or pounds. On one occasion Jesus had given expression to his disappointment that most of the Jews had not accepted his message, "Many are called, but few are chosen." This was passed on in connection with the parable about the wedding guests which treated the same theme (cf. p. 367). On another occasion he illustrated how the coming of God's kingdom reverses all the norms governing class and status in human society by saying, "The last will be first and the first last." This seemed to be well expressed in the parable of the laborers in the vineyard (cf. pp. 315f.).

A third way of remembering an isolated saying was to introduce it by means of a short story. Thus the disciples remembered two sayings in which Jesus justified his attitude toward sinners: "It is not the healthy who need the doctor, but the sick" and "I did not come to call the virtuous, but sinners." Since Jesus had expressed God's love for outcasts by eating with tax collectors and sinners, the disciples described such a meal, reproducing at the same time the criticism of the Pharisees: "Why does he eat with tax collectors and sinners?" Then they included the two sayings just quoted as Jesus' answer on that occasion.

It goes without saying that these three methods of transmitting Jesus' short sayings were also often combined. This is the way the disciples related the accusation of the Pharisees that Jesus drove out devils by the power of Beelzebul, the figure which Jewish tradition regarded as the leader of the well-organized army of devils. They recalled how Jesus had pointed out the stupidity of such an accusation: "How can Satan cast out Satan? If a kingdom is divided against itself, that kingdom cannot last." This answer together with the accusation could of course be passed on without any concrete occasion. But it was also possible to attach it to a particular deed of Jesus—for example, his healing of a possessed man who was likewise blind and dumb. In that way they provided the saying with a narrative introduction. Likewise, that saying of Jesus could also serve as a point of departure for other statements on the theme of "Satan"—for example, his saying about the strong man, the wording of which may have been borrowed from Isaiah (49, 24-25): "No one can make his way into a strong man's house and burgle his property unless he has tied up the strong man first. Only then can he burgle his house." By combining this with the saying just quoted, it became quite clear that by the "strong man" Jesus meant Satan. And since that Satan was in fact Jesus' chief opponent, another saying of his could conveniently be added as well: "He who is not with me is against me; and he who does not gather with me scatters."

If we carry this process one step further, we can see that some of Jesus' longer "sermons" could also have come about in this way, and thus we are not surprised that they sometimes seem to be an illogical hodgepodge of loose statements. But the example above brings us to another point. We touched upon it at the beginning of this section. Like the parables, Jesus' short sayings were often handed down unchanged, but some of them were clarified or complemented with an eye to new circumstances. First of all, sayings which were remembered apart from the concrete situation and context in which they were originally spoken could naturally be understood in different senses. Without a word being changed, they could take on a certain meaning just from the statement or story to which they were attached. The saying quoted above, "There is nothing hidden but it must be disclosed, nothing kept secret except to be brought to light," could be passed on in connection with the mystery of the kingdom of God, which Jesus withheld *for the time being* from the masses, to whom it was to be announced later on. But that saying could also function as a warning against hypocrisy, something like this: "Be on your guard against the yeast of the Pharisees—that is, their hypocrisy. Everything that is now covered will be uncovered, and everything now hidden will be made clear [at the last judgment]."

We saw how the somewhat puzzling saying about the "strong man" became clearer simply by connecting it with Jesus' statement about Satan. But an explicit clarification could also be added to a saying. An example of this approach is Jesus' saying about the way a person becomes "unclean." The Pharisees conscientiously avoided all foods which according to the Law would make them impure. We have already seen how Jesus condemned this misplaced obedience (cf. p. 314). Short and to the point, he once said, "Nothing that goes into a man from outside can make him unclean; it is the things that come out of a man that make him unclean." It is quite probable that a disciple was responsible for the subsequent explanation: "Can you not see that whatever goes into a man from outside cannot make him unclean, because it does not go into his heart but through his stomach and passes out into the sewer?" However, there is no doubt that it was a disciple who attached the further explanation: "It is what comes out of a man that makes him unclean. For it is from within, from men's hearts, that evil intentions emerge: fornication, theft, murder, adultery, avarice, malice, deceit, indecency, envy, slander, pride, folly. All these evil things come from within and make a man unclean."

When Jesus announced the coming of God as the good news, he had made it a point to stress what a privilege it was to be allowed to experience that climax of history, "Happy the eyes to see what you see. . . ." Because, according to the prophets, God took special interest in the poor, the sorrowful and the hungry, Jesus, too, called them "blessed." This was his way of saying that the Messianic times had dawned. When in the light of Easter the disciples had recognized him as their Messiah, there was no longer any need for this specific meaning of the beatitudes. Thus the disciples adapted them to their new situation. For example, it could be a consolation for the poor and the sad to hear that later, in the world to come, they would be rich and happy: "Happy you who weep now. . . ." But it was also possible to interpret the beatitudes as the attitude of the real disciples of Christ, poor in spirit—that is, without any pretensions, and hungry and thirsty for real justice.

Jesus had referred to himself with the Aramaic word which was rendered in Greek as "Son of Man." For Jesus and his contemporaries, that term could mean quite simply "man." We have seen that after Easter the disciples saw a description of Jesus in the mysterious figure of the "Son of Man" who was to come "on the clouds" in the book of Daniel. That was partly the foundation for their expectation of the Lord's "second coming." It seems probable that some of the texts where Jesus speaks about himself as "Son of Man" were colored by that expectation.

It is quite clear, however, that the historical course of events influenced the formulation of certain of Jesus' sayings. This is especially true for the words with which he announced his coming passion and resurrection. He himself made only vague allusions to them and certainly did not go into detail. He spoke of the chalice he was to drink and the baptism with which he was to be baptized: "There is a baptism I must still receive, and how great is my distress till it is over!" Baptism is always an initiation into a new life, into a new communion with God. That which the leaders in Jerusalem would do to him Jesus saw as a baptism. He knew that it would be the "door" to a new life with God. As the opposition against him increased, Jesus began to speak more openly in this way about what was awaiting him. For him that death was the fulfillment of the task his Father had given him. Nevertheless, he certainly never spoke about it in the clear details we find in some of the "predictions of the passion" which Christians incorporated in the coherent narrations of his life. Those narrations were actually passion-stories-with-an-introduction, a kind of framework into which separate traditions containing Jesus' miracles and sayings were brought together. But with this observation we have already made the transition to the fourth and last phase of our sketch of how the four gospels came about.

XII

The Evangelists at Work: The Fourth Phase

We modern Westerners are known for our weak memories. Now and then we have perhaps learned a text of some length by heart for an examination or the like, but for the rest we leave that to people who do it professionally, such as actors and reciters of poetry. We no longer have the need to memorize things. What we want to remember we write down, and more extensive knowledge we can always look up in books and encyclopedias.

In regions where there are not yet any printing presses, books and magazines, people have to know many more things by heart. Furthermore, there is a greater demand in those regions for people who must know long texts by heart, especially with an eye to entertaining and engaging their fellow men. We often spend long winter evenings watching television or listening to the radio or recorded music, reading or just browsing through illustrated magazines. In all those ways something which others—people with literary, musical, technical and many other talents—have created (or are creating) comes to us mechanically and holds our attention, as well as that of thousands of other men at the same time. Where that mechanical transmission of human experience is lacking, not only is the human memory better developed than in our society, but there are also relatively more people who can recite texts from memory—for hours on end.

This rather long introductory observation is not without its purpose. Earlier in these pages we indicated the important role which oral tradition had in the formation of many scriptural texts (pp. 175f.). Now that we are treating the origin of the gospels, this point deserves very special attention. This is true, first of all, because the

377

common people who followed Jesus read no books and seldom wrote things down. Their memories, therefore, were much better exercised than ours. Furthermore, it was characteristic of their milieu that the religious leaders knew by heart not only the Law but also all the sacred traditions. Those who felt called to become a rabbi and later take the places of those spiritual leaders had to spend years doing little else than listening, memorizing and reciting. They were possibly even forbidden to take notes to help their memory. Now, it was in that Jewish society that the Jesus-tradition had its origin. It goes without saying that it was handed on orally, at first in Aramaic of course, but quite soon in the colloquial Greek (*koine*) which was spoken by so many Jews in and around Palestine. Only when those traditions about Jesus had become the inheritance of Christians in the great cities of the Roman Empire were they sometimes put in writing. City people did not have such a good memory; they were used to writing down what they wanted to remember. But yet, as long as the eyewitnesses and their close associates were alive, such written presentations of the tradition remained of secondary importance. The accounts of Jesus' words and deeds, his passion and resurrection, given by living people with apostolic authority, continued to set the tone. That situation changed when the first generation began to die out. Then more and more attention began to be given to the written accounts of what had been passed on about Jesus, and they were collected in "gospels." Four such documents received unquestioned authority in the whole Church and eventually took their place in the Bible. We would like to conclude this sketch of how they came into being with some remarks about the personalities, motivations and work of those who wrote them.

Mark and the Persecuted

There are some indications that the oldest gospel, later called "according to Mark," was written at Rome between 65 and 70. Thus it might possibly be read against the background of the burning capital and the atrocious measures taken afterward against the young Christian community. On July 19 in the year 64 the fire broke out; it raged for ten days and destroyed almost the whole center of Rome. Emperor Nero (54-68), to whom Paul had appealed so confidently several years previous (Acts 25, 11), had begun more and more to behave as an insane despot. Immediately after the fire he indeed took measures to have the debris removed and the city rebuilt, and he opened his royal parks near the Vatican hill for the masses of homeless victims. But his enemies spread the rumor that the emperor, who imagined himself to be a divine artist (Apollo!), had himself started the fire for the sake of artistic pleasure. To direct the people's wrath away from the emperor, the Christians were singled out as the guilty ones and were made to endure their punishment at rough and boistrous spectacles organized for the people. Apparently they were already known in the eyes of the ordinary Roman cityfolk as a separate group, distinct from the Jews, and not enjoying the official protection granted to the synagogue. The historian Tacitus, who was born in 55 and thus still a boy at that time, later wrote how the Christians, wrapped in the skins of animals, were torn to bits by dogs, or fastened to crosses and burnt as torches. According to another Roman, their women were made to take part in dramatic presentations during which they were actually murdered.

Both Peter and Paul were probably among the victims of that persecution or of the explosions of popular violence which followed in its wake. It is easy to understand that the Christians who survived wondered about many things. Would their brothers elsewhere in the empire also be persecuted in this way? And how was their community to go on living? Or was this perhaps the prelude to Jesus' coming in glory? In the near future they would probably only be able to come together in the utmost secrecy, or perhaps not at all. Who among the faithful helpers of the apostles were still left to organize such gatherings and to preside at them? It does not take a very vivid imagination to see that there were plenty of reasons for setting the apostolic preaching about Jesus in writing. Then they would have an authoritative text which could be read at their gatherings and given to those in hiding.

As we said, it was only later that this gospel was given the title "according to Mark." Other texts of the New Testament sometimes mention a certain Mark, and in such a way that he could very well have been the writer of this gospel. In Jerusalem, according to Acts 12, 12, Peter went "to the house of Mary, the mother of John Mark, where a number of people had assembled and were praying." Only a widow was referred to as the mother of a son who enjoyed a certain reputation. That was apparently the case in the milieu in which the author of Acts lived. According to his story, that same Mark was evidently not up to the difficulties of a missionary journey in the service of his cousin Barnabas and the inexperienced Paul (see Acts 12, 25; 13, 5 and especially 15, 36-39). But as appears from other data, he later belonged to the highly respected collaborators of Paul. He stayed with him as a faithful companion during Paul's house arrest (Col. 4, 10; Phm. 24) and probably also during the imprisonment at Rome which preceded his execution (2 Tm. 4, 11). In addition it should be noted that in his first letter written from "Babylon" (i.e., Rome) Peter calls Mark "my son" (5, 13), an expression of intimacy which might well have its roots in the common memories of those early days in Jerusalem when the disciples gathered at the home of Mark's mother.

After the death of Peter and Paul, Mark may have been the man needed by that troubled community to put in writing what until then had been passed on orally about Jesus' ministry, about his words and miracles, his passion, death and resurrection. That would be even more probable if Mark's "ministering" (cf. 2 Tim. 4, 11) should indeed have consisted in the faithful repetition of the traditions circulating about Jesus and of what he had so often heard Peter preaching.

The connections suggested here between the oldest gospel on the one hand and the burning of Rome with its subsequent persecution, the death of Peter and Paul and the person of Mark on the other cannot all be irrefutably demonstrated. However, they can help the reader recognize some of the peculiarities of that gospel.

It gives the impression of having been written in a hurry, as if the author could not allow himself much time to weave the great variety of material at his disposal into a single unified tapestry, so to speak. Some of his stories are so true to life that we almost see Jesus standing before us and hear him speaking. But others, mostly short episodes, are rather schematic, as if the details got worn off in the telling and only the most essential things remained. There are also several series in which sayings follow one right after the other. These Mark seems to have taken over directly from the tradition. Certain "compositions" in which stories and sayings are ordered in a particular sequence likewise give the impression of having been found by Mark in that form.

Even his narration of the passion, clearly the climax of his work, seems to have been composed from a sober account which the Roman community had perhaps been reciting for some years, and from some lively episodes which Peter used to relate. But the entire gospel works up to that climax, so to speak, and especially after Peter's famous confession of Jesus as the Messiah. Then Jesus begins to speak more and more openly about the suffering which is awaiting both him and his faithful followers. Thus this theme of suffering provides a certain unity.

But, apart from Mark's own style of writing, it seems to be his deep reverence for the central character which makes his gospel, despite all its literary "fragmentation," into a finished entity. Something of that deep reverence can be felt in all its details; we are given a taste of that astonishment which has never ceased to captivate the dedicated followers of Jesus. They had lived with the Son of God and understood nothing about him, nothing. No one understood him. His family did not; neither did the people of Nazareth nor the Jewish leaders, not even themselves. It was as if a thick crust had encased their hearts. Only the devils had grasped it all, but Jesus ordered them to be silent. Yes, they, too, were commanded to tell no one when they began to have suspicions. His task as Messiah and Son of God was to serve and to perfect that servile existence by giving his life. Only then would those Messianic titles be fitting.

The reader who might like to experience something of the effect of the gospel as a whole may find the following brief outline helpful. The prologue (1, 1-13) introduces the central character. The prophets had announced a herald of God's coming; that was John the Baptist. As precursor he bore witness in advance to Jesus' power. When he baptized him, the Holy Spirit descended upon Jesus, and God himself called him his beloved Son. Then in a mosaic of short episodes Mark presents a general view, preceded by a summary (verses 14-15), of Jesus' first activities in Galilee (1, 16-45; note the command not to speak about them in verses 25, 34 and 44). Five short stories in which the scribes and Pharisees criticize Jesus (probably already forming a unit in the tradition) conclude with the remark that they "at once began to make plans . . . discussing how to destroy him" (3, 6). Jesus' ministry is already cast in the light of his passion and death. The summary description of his activities on the lake seem to be from Mark himself (3, 7-12; note the boat and the order to keep silent) as well as the introduction to the names of the twelve apostles (3, 13-19). Among the episodes immediately following we see the saying discussed above about Satan and the strong man (p. 373), here without a concrete introduction. Then Mark reproduces a bit of catechesis about the parables (4, 3-32) in the framework of his remarks about the prepared boat (verses 1-2) which likewise has a place in the first of the four detailed miracle stories (4, 35—5, 43). With short transitional sentences Mark joins the episode about the lack of faith in Nazareth and the instructions given to the twelve before their first missionary journey; then follows the striking narration of the Baptist's execution—even in his way of dying John is a precursor (6, 7-13).

Mark then resumes his story about Jesus. In his own words he introduces the story of the miraculous feeding of the five thousand, which he joins with that of Jesus' walking on the water, and again closes with a summary (6, 30-56). Completely independent of the lake scene, a long discussion with the Pharisees and teachers of the Law about ritual purity follows (7, 1-23; verses 15-23 were discussed on pp. 374f.). Then we see Jesus performing two good deeds for believing pagans (7, 24-37); this is clearly a kind of conclusion, for there follows a second series which likewise begins with a miraculous feeding, this time of the four thousand (8, 1-9). Again we have a discussion with the Pharisees, followed by a conversation, perhaps composed by Mark himself, between Jesus and his disciples who do not understand him (8, 14-21). This series likewise closes with a good deed, here the healing of a blind man (8, 22-26).

The second part of the gospel begins with Peter's profession of faith at Caesarea Philippi which is followed by the command to keep strict silence (8, 27-30). From that moment on, the story seems to pick up speed, perhaps because Mark twice more repeats Jesus' prediction of his passion which traditionally followed Peter's confession and, after each of those three prophecies, allows Jesus to speak about what his followers are to do and what is awaiting them. The first series of such sayings (8, 34-39) is followed by the story of Jesus' transfiguration on the high mountain (9, 1-8), to which Mark himself adds a word about Elijah (9, 9-12). A very colorful and instructive miracle story concludes this section (9, 14-28).

After the second prediction of the passion, Mark has the disciples quarreling about which of them would be the greatest. Then *logia* follow on the theme of becoming like a little child plus several others as well, obviously grouped together on the basis of their related use of words (9, 32-49); the last member of the series was given as an example on p. 372). Jesus now leaves Galilee and along the way gives further instruction: on marriage, on accepting the kingdom of God as a child and on being detached from material goods. Here Mark again clearly seems to be bringing together traditions circulating in the young Church (10, 1-31; the saying about the first and the last—cf. p. 373—takes on a new meaning at the end of this section).

Mark lets Jesus predict his passion for the third time at the moment he sets out, full of determination, on the road to Jerusalem. Jesus' words here are the most detailed of all (10, 32-34). After a moving conversation about the lot awaiting him and his followers and about true greatness which is to be found in serving others, Mark concludes the entire preparatory narrative again, as we would expect, with a good deed, this time the healing of the blind Bartimaeus of Jericho (10, 46-52). The last section begins with Jesus' entry into Jerusalem which is followed—rather awkwardly—by the episodes of the barren fig tree cursed by Jesus and his expulsion of the money changers and merchants from the temple. A series of sayings about faith and prayer is then added (11, 1-25). Next we find an impressive group which Mark also seems to have found in the tradition—namely, Jesus' last disputes with his enemies. To this group belongs the breathtaking parable of the wicked husbandmen who so ruthlessly reveal exactly what they are planning to do. After the disputes there follows a short word against the scribes (12, 38-40) in which the word "widow" is used. That was probably the reason for inserting the episode about "the widow's mite" at this point (12, 41-44). The famous "discourse" about the destruction of Jerusalem and the world and about the Son of Man coming on the clouds of heaven, which Mark may have found already completed in the tradition as well, he introduces with several narrative verses (13, 1-4). Then the gospel reaches its climax, the narration of the passion. As we have said, it is a composition of data from various sources, but at the same time it possesses great dramatic power (14—15).

The conclusion of Mark's gospel is still an unsolved riddle. The narrative seems to break off suddenly right in the middle of the story about the experiences of the women at Jesus' sepulcher (16, 1-8). After the apparition of the angel, they ran away from the tomb and did not dare to tell anyone, "for they were afraid." Perhaps the rest of Mark's text has been lost. But there are also scholars who believe that Mark himself gave his gospel that astonishing conclusion, because for him the concept of "fear" meant the awe and reverence for the mystery of God's appearance, a concept which fills his entire work.

Matthew and the Church

The tyrannical misgovernment of the insane Nero was anything but conducive to peace in the worldwide empire. In many regions, smoldering ashes of opposition and resistance threatened to burst into flames. Two years before the emperor poisoned himself, the long-prepared rebellion broke out in Palestine (66 A.D.). The hard and embittered fight of the Jewish nationalists led to the destruction of Jerusalem in the year 70. By that time the spiritual leaders of the Jews had already convened in the little town of Jamnia, west of Jerusalem and not far from the sea; there they set about the work of reorganizing Jewish life according to the principles of the Pharisees. Only with explicit norms governing worship and life could Judaism go on existing in the new situation. Characteristic of that new picture was the absence of the capital and the temple, but that was not all. It had also become necessary to draw up clear boundaries between themselves and the fast-growing movement of the Christians which in the preceding three decades had broken more and more with its original milieu. The work of the leaders in Jamnia was one of the factors contributing to the attitude which regarded Jews who became Christians after the fall of Jerusalem even more as apostates than previously. The converts themselves looked upon their acceptance of Jesus as the Messiah not as apostasy, a break with their past, but as the perfection of that past intended by God himself. Together with the believers from among the pagans, they formed the one universal people of God, the new Israel, for which the history of the old nation was a prelude.

Thus we find ourselves in the environment which was the birth-place of the gospel "according to Matthew," for that gospel seems to reflect the religious views and experiences of a community of Christians in Palestine or its surroundings, in the ninth decade of the 1st century. That would be the very same period when the Jamnia resolutions were being carried out, and our gospel perhaps reflects a confrontation with them. The reasons why that gospel was written there and at that time are likewise somewhat clear. For years people had been reading the gospel of Mark which under-standably enjoyed the respect of a highly authoritative document. It was likewise its authority that induced them to publish an aug-mented edition, for it was not complete. Mark said often enough that Jesus "preached the word" and "gave instructions," but his coverage of what the Master had said on those occasions was far from exhaustive. This they knew from a document, circulating in many churches, which contained quite a few of Jesus' sayings not included in Mark (i.e., the source we call "Q": cf. pp. 286f.). Fur-thermore, in their own community there were living traditions which deserved to be incorporated in a larger unified work. Cat-echetical instructions were usually given by teachers who were dedicated and industrious students of the Scriptures. In order to gather that enormous wealth of data about Jesus into one scroll, someone wrote the gospel "according to Matthew." It is no longer possible to determine with certainty whether that was really the author's name, or whether the community enjoyed a special rela-tionship with the Matthew who belonged to the twelve. But this question is much less important than how the writer went about his work and the picture of Jesus and his Church which he left us.

The introduction begins with the genealogy of Jesus, son of Abraham through David. The consonants in the latter's name form the number 14 (d is 4 and v is 6). Thus, after a prehistory of 3 times 14 generations, God made a new beginning. Jesus was con-ceived of the Holy Spirit; according to the prophecy of Isaiah, his name is the Messianic "God-with-us." In the person of the wise men from the East, we see the Gentile world coming immediately to worship him, just as it was foretold in Psalm 72 and Isaiah 60. They are given directions by old King Herod on the basis of the clearly prophetic information about the Messiah which the priests and scribes of Jerusalem had in their possession. Just as Pharaoh before him, Herod now orders the massacre of the Jewish babes, but Jesus, like Moses, escapes in accordance with God's plan. He follows ancient Israel's footsteps further by spending some time in Egypt. Then, according to his plans which had been announced previously, God lets him live in Nazareth, in "Galilee of the Gentiles." Matthew chose that same region for the closing scene of his work. There on "the mountain" the disciples worship their master who now possesses all authority in heaven and on earth. After he solemnly commissions them to make disciples of all nations, the God-with-us utters his last word, "And know that I am with you always; yes, to the end of time."

Within this very meaningful framework Matthew places his augmented edition of Mark's gospel. He shortens Mark's detailed miracle stories quite a bit, but he adds many other traditional episodes and especially a number of sayings. Many of these he arranges in large contextual units, which give the impression of being longer "discourses." As soon as Jesus, already at work preaching and healing, attracts large crowds of people, he climbs the mountain, as the new Moses, and proclaims the "constitution" of the new people of God. This is "the evangelical discourse" or "the Sermon on the Mount" (5—7). After several miracles illustrating the power of his word, Jesus sends forth the twelve with another sermon, "the apostolic discourse" (10, 5-42). Moreover, he adds four more parables to the three which Mark gives (although replacing one of them), thus arriving at the seven in "the parabolic discourse" (13). Beginning with the scene where Jesus calls a little child into the group of the disciples, Matthew gives some practical instructions for the community life of the disciples, "the discourse on the Church" (18). Mark's short confrontation with the scribes is expanded by means of other sayings to become what we might call "the penal discourse" against the scribes and Pharisees (23), followed immediately by "the eschatalogical discourse" or "the sermon on the last things." To Jesus' words about the fall of Jerusalem and the end of the world, Matthew joins three parables on watchfulness (the third being that of the talents: cf. p. 370) and, before turning to the gospel's climax, he concludes his introduction with that grandiose scene of the last judgment to be executed by the royal Son of Man (24—25).

In all of this Matthew paints a different portrait of Christ from that of Mark. The spontaneous awe and reverence for the mystery of God's Son, who dauntlessly performed his ministry until the very end and only then caused the splitting of the veil separating men from God, made room in Matthew for reflective worship. The reason for this was that in his community people had been reflecting for years on Jesus and his work in the light of the Scriptures. In them they discovered all kinds of figures and words with which to express the fullness of that mystery. Jesus was "the fulfillment" of their whole pre-history: the promised Son of David, the God-with-us who would have dominion over all nations, and the Son of Man who was to appear in glory to judge all men. And that would be a judgment according to his own Law, the "fulfillment" of the old, for he was likewise the new Moses, the lawgiver of the true Israel. Thus in Matthew the Jesus of Mark has become more exalted, solemn and majestic. Among the details which Matthew leaves out are those concerning Jesus' intense emotional life. Also omitted are his harsh rebukes of the disciples. Those disbelieving men who did not understand him become "men of little faith" whom Jesus mildly and patiently instructs for their later task as responsible leaders of God's new people, the Church.

Behind all of this lay the conviction that Jesus is the Lord of the Church. Matthew is the only one to relate Jesus' famous words about building his community on the rock, Peter, the disciple who receives very special attention in his gospel (16, 18-19; likewise proper to Matthew are 14, 28-31 and 17, 24-27). The privileges of ancient Israel passed over to that new community. Jesus had preached exclusively to Israel, but that people as a whole stood behind its leaders who rejected him (10, 5-6; 15, 24; 21, 43; 27, 19; 27, 24-25, all of which are proper to Matthew). But despite that clear insight there are still tensions in Matthew's community. They are still deeply enough involved in Jewish life to wonder about the extent to which certain commandments of the Law, although "fulfilled" by Jesus, were still to be observed (see the awkward composition of sayings in 5, 17-20 and also the remarkable formulation of the rule of conduct in 18, 17). Obviously an "organization" is taking shape, and that creates a tension because of the seeming contradiction with the expectation of Jesus' second coming and with the watchfulness which he had so emphatically recommended (24, 42—25, 13). But perhaps that tension will

always be characteristic of a Church to whom the last two verses
of this gospel are addressed—and with them the entire work, the
most "ecclesiastical" of the four.

Luke and Mankind

Whereas that work of Matthew bore the hallmark of the community in which it was born and for which it was written, the
gospel "according to Luke" is the work of one individual writer,
someone who "published" a book, and in so doing could in principle count on an unlimited public. He does dedicate his work to a
certain Theophilus (the name means "friend of God"), presumably an important Roman official in a large city, perhaps Antioch.
But Luke's intention was undoubtedly that Theophilus, who had
already had some instruction in the Christian teaching, would see
that a large number of copies of the book were made. Luke says in
his prologue that after so many attempts on the part of others, he
in his turn has decided to give an ordered account of the events on
which the Christian faith is based and thus has gone in search of
authoritative traditions. Fortunately for us, Mark's gospel was
among them; also probably included was a version of the document containing for the most part sayings which Matthew, too, had
used (the source Q). In addition Luke worked in many other traditional elements. That "Lucan material" makes up more than one-
third of his book and to a great extent determines its character and
"atmosphere." Before attempting to characterize that, we would
like to say a few words about Luke's method.

After writing his "origin stories" (1—2, which we will take up
shortly), Luke obviously uses the gospel of Mark as the basis for his
story. He rewrites neatly all of its contents in his own style and
seldom changes anything of Mark's sequence. Most of what he
adds he puts together in larger units and inserts them in fitting
places. Besides the section 6, 20—8, 3 there is the larger insertion
9, 51—18, 14. Only one complex of Mark's gospel is omitted
completely. He leaves the latter's story in 6, 45, only to pick up
the thread again in 8, 25. Perhaps he thought that those pieces
were not very important for his public and found them distractive
for his purpose. And in fact that section of Mark contains the long
discussion on the laws of ritual purity (what could Theophilus possibly do with those!), a second multiplication of loaves (unneces-

sary repetition) and two healings where Jesus used spittle (Luke prefers to emphasize the power which went directly out from Jesus). Furthermore, Mark lists there the journeys of Jesus outside Galilee which Luke seems to have found particularly disturbing for the clarity of his gospel. He lets Jesus work first in Galilee (thus he does not mention that Peter's profession of faith took place in Caesarea Philippi which lay outside Galilee) and then go to Jerusalem to die there. He inserts his largest addition where Mark relates that Jesus left Galilee and resolutely took the road for Jerusalem. Thus he places all that additional material in the framework of the journey to Jerusalem, that destination which he let Jesus speak about on the mountain with Moses and Elijah (9, 31) and which he recalls at set times (13, 22. 33; 17, 11; 18, 31; the village of 10, 38 must therefore remain nameless). When we notice, too, that Luke does not abbreviate Mark's detailed miracle stories, as Matthew did, but that he relates them more skillfully, and, further, that he eliminates the awkwardness of Mark's gospel by a better combination of the latter's fragmentary "bits and pieces," then we can understand that Theophilus enjoyed Luke's book likewise from a literary point of view—just as we still do.

The following short remarks may perhaps help the reader appreciate something of the "atmosphere" or "spirit" of Luke's gospel. Words which indicate his favorite themes are italicized. We have already mentioned (p. 273) that Luke is the only evangelist to give John's ministry a particular date—namely, the year in the reign of the emperor who ruled *the whole world* from Rome (3, 1-2). He also brings that world within the horizon of "the one crying in the wilderness" by extending the traditional citation from Isaiah until the verse: "And all *mankind* shall see the salvation of God" (3, 4-6). Luke derives part of John's preaching from the source Q and part from a source of his own, this last being in *dialogue form* (3, 10-14). At Jesus' baptism the Holy Spirit descends upon him "in bodily shape, like a dove." Also characteristic of Luke is that the voice from heaven speaks to Jesus personally, "You are my Son. . . ." The genealogy of Jesus' supposed father then follows, working back from son to father: ". . . the son, as it was thought, of Joseph son of Heli, son of. . . ." It is interesting to note that after Abraham it works back to the father of *all mankind*, "Adam, son of God" (3, 23-38). In the story of the temptations which follows immediately, taken from Q, Luke reverses the order of the last two, with the result that his version reaches its climax in *Jerusalem* (4, 1-13).

In the subsequent description of Jesus' first ministry in Galilee, Luke inserts two scenes which describe in anticipation the opposition of the Jews against Jesus and against his taking pagans into his company. Jesus' appearance in the synagogue at Nazareth is the occasion for his first public statement, a prophetic utterance from the servant of Yahweh, which Jesus proclaims fulfilled: "*The spirit of the Lord* has been given to me, for he has anointed me (for the Greek reader, "made a Christ of me"). He has sent me to bring the good news to the *poor*." Very dramatically the original sympathy of the synagogue turns to rage when Jesus speaks of God's benefices to *people outside Israel*. The other scene (5, 1-11) describes Peter's calling after he has made a large catch of fish out from the shore in the "deep water"—for Luke's readers an unmistakable symbol for *the world of the Gentiles*.

Luke places his first large insertion (6, 20—8, 3) after the choice of the twelve. Jesus holds a type of "sermon on the mount," likewise beginning with beatitudes and ending with the simile of the two house builders (who use different methods of construction than Matthew's Palestinians!), but the content of Luke's sermon is limited to an encouragement to love even our enemies and to be compassionate and generous to each one (6, 20-49). Luke's own contribution continues with the raising of the young man in Naim out of sympathy for his mother who was a *widow* (7, 11-17), and further with the story of the sinful *woman* who broke all the conventional rules to show her gratitude to him while he was at dinner at the home of a Pharisee. To his host Jesus then addresses the parable of the two debtors (7, 36-50). Then he adds a description characterizing Jesus' ministry by mentioning the *women* who accompanied and ministered to him and his disciples (8, 1-3).

The second insertion, "the journey to Jerusalem," presents in chapter 10 the mission of the 70 (or 72) disciples, the number of nations traditionally representing the whole of *mankind;* further, there is the parable of the good *Samaritan,* followed by the homey scene with Martha and Mary in which Jesus defends the *one who listened to him* against her slaving sister. After his version of the "Our Father," Luke relates the parable of the bothersome friend, an encouragement to *pray* constantly (11, 5-8). Further on come the story of the man who laid up treasures for himself but who was not rich before God (12, 15-21) and that of the barren fig tree (cf. p. 351), followed immediately by the incident in a synagogue when Jesus cured a crippled *woman* on a sabbath (13, 6-17). Luke has Jesus tell the parable of the unwilling wedding guests (cf. pp. 367f.) at a *meal* (14, 1-24). Following the words about the man wanting to build a tower and about the king planning to go to war (14, 28-33) we have that unforgettable chapter 15 with its illustrations of the *joy* God experiences when those who are lost return to him. The parable of the unjust steward (16, 1-9) and the story about the lot of the poor Lazarus and the rich miser, who ends by harshly typifying disbelief, also belong to the material proper to Luke. Of the ten cured lepers, only the *Samaritan* appears to show his gratitude (17, 11-19). The parable of the unscrupulous judge and the importunate widow is again an encouragement to pray without losing courage, and the subsequent story, about the Pharisee and the publican, shows God's preference for the entreating sinner above the pious man who is self-sufficient (18, 9-14).

Here Luke takes up the thread of Mark again. After the healing of the blind man in Jericho, he inserts the story of Zacchaeus, the hated tax collector, at whose house Jesus wants to come to dinner (19, 1-10), and then, when Jesus is near Jerusalem, Luke puts his version of the parable of the talents on the Master's lips (19, 12-27; cf. p. 371). In the narration of the passion we should notice Jesus' conversation with his disciples at their last meal together, composed by Luke from various sources (22, 14-28), and Jesus' glance at Peter (22, 61). Likewise, in chapter 23 we should pay attention to the scene of Jesus before Herod (8-12), his words to the weeping *women* along the way of the cross (27-31), his prayer asking *forgiveness* for his executioners (34) and his conversation with the good thief (39-43).

"My dear friend Luke, the doctor" is the way Paul refers to one of his non-Jewish collaborators (Col. 4, 14). If this Greek doctor, the faithful companion of Paul, even in his tribulations (cf. Phm. 24 and 2 Tim. 4, 11), was indeed the author of the gospel "according to Luke" as tradition tells us, then much of the above becomes somewhat clearer. As an educated man of that time, Luke was likewise a cosmopolite, and, judging from his choice of profession, he had a sense of concern for his fellow men. Then he must have been fascinated immediately and permanently by the stories about Jesus who impressed him as the personification of unlimited human love. That was how Jesus captivated him personally, but a well-written book about him was sure to win over countless readers to that love. That intention apparently determined Luke's choice of material from among the traditions available to him. His book was to show how Jesus had sought contact with all men, even with the Pharisees—Luke is the only one to mention that they warned Jesus about Herod's plot against his life (13, 31). But most of the material "proper" to Luke has a bearing on Jesus' interest in the rejected, the neglected and the outcasts. It was likewise Luke who preserved for posterity the unequaled parables in which Jesus had so colorfully painted that divine preference. From the italicized words the reader has also observed that quite a few meals and conversations are recorded in those sections which occur only in Luke. They help to create the atmosphere or spirit. Contact is being sought, but not only between Jesus and the people. God addresses his Son at his baptism. Likewise, the only parables treating of prayer belong to Luke's own contributions. There is perhaps a connection between this and that spirit which is characterized by an intense joy, despite the mention of tribulations and suffering and of radical demands to be poor and detached (14, 33 is Lucan, as are "wife" and "life" in 14, 26 and "every day" in 9, 23).

Where he retells stories from Mark, a comparison of the two versions reveals that Luke has touched up the sometimes rugged Jesus of Mark according to his own image of that sensitive lover of mankind. He does not mention Jesus' intense emotional side; he softens his harsh rebukes of the disciples, generally describing them more reverently. Likewise, he sometimes leaves out Jesus' more shocking sayings (this also applies to the material he derives from Q). More often than Mark, he shows Jesus in conversation with God, and the holy fear which overcomes those witnessing a miracle becomes enthusiastic admiration in Luke.

The love for mankind which he so admired in Jesus, Luke puts into practice by not confronting his readers with puzzling situations. If he does not see any way to leave out things which are typically Palestinian or Jewish, he explains them; similarly, he indicates in general terms the location of cities and villages which he cannot avoid mentioning. We have already noted how he simplified Jesus' itinerary.

In conclusion, we should say a word about Luke's "stories of Jesus' birth and childhood" (1—2). The reader will have noticed the remarkably large number of italicized words referring to women in our outline of the material peculiar to Luke. Jewish society was dominated by men; the women formed a neglected group with few rights. Therefore Jesus devoted special attention to them. Some women showed their gratitude by coming to the aid of Jesus and his disciples, even on their journeys through Galilee. In Mark we hear of this only after Jesus' death. Some of the women had followed him to Jerusalem and there proved themselves more faithful than his men followers—they did not abandon him when he was crucified (Mk. 15, 40). Careful writer that he is, Luke relates how those women accompanied Jesus when he was in Galilee (8, 1-3). But he mentions two women there who do not occur anywhere else—Joanna, the wife of a high-ranking official, and Susanna. One could have the suspicion that Luke gathered certain traditions about Jesus from the circles where the memories of these women still lived on. Precisely because they always had to stay in the background and were never permitted to take part in conversations and discussions, the women around Jesus perhaps listened better than the men. Could it be due to this that we have so many beautiful parables and moving scenes in Luke's gospel? This is only a suspicion, but it may serve as an aid to the reader's imagination when reading the stories about Jesus' birth and childhood. Whereas Matthew was only alive to Joseph's problem and likewise lets all the angel's instructions for saving Jesus be given to *him*, in Luke the mother of Jesus stands in the limelight. The angel comes to her with his message; at seeing her the Baptist's mother is filled with the Holy Spirit; it is to her that the old Simeon turns; she is the one who speaks to the twelve-year-old Jesus in the temple, and she is *the* woman who stores everything in her heart.

In any event Luke touches upon a number of his characteristic themes in these stories. We notice the frequent mention of the Holy Spirit. Furthermore Luke joins this intimate family event with a world event, an order from the emperor in Rome (2, 1). From the very beginning, Jesus belongs to those who have no place to go, and the news of his birth is announced to shepherds, people who had a very poor name. The Spirit makes Simeon recognize what he is carrying in his arms: the salvation of all nations. Jesus will be a sign of contradiction, and Mary will share his suffering, but at the same time all these stories, with their three hymns of praise, are surrounded by an atmosphere of intense joy.

Theophilus undoubtedly had some difficulty with the style of these first stories, unless he was already familiar with the Greek translation of the Holy Scriptures. Throughout his gospel Luke uses certain ways of speaking in the manner of that translation (after all, he is writing a kind of "Bible history"), but in the stories of Jesus' birth and childhood nearly every line contains a citation or recollection from it or an allusion to it. That is Luke's often subtle manner of expressing his belief that the Old Testament has its fulfillment in the history of Jesus.

He bears witness to that belief more explicitly at the end of his work, in that grandiose narrative of the disciples of Emmaus and in that of Jesus' apparition to the whole group: Jesus himself explains to them how the Scriptures are fulfilled in him (24, 27. 44-47). Also characteristic of his conclusion is the following. In other traditional accounts the angel at the tomb sends the disciples to Galilee where they were to see Jesus. In Luke he appears to them in Jerusalem. There his story began, there Jesus was presented in the temple—likewise the desire of his heart as a twelve-year-old boy; that city was the destination of his journeys; there, too, he took leave of his disciples, and there in Jerusalem they waited, full of joy, for the Holy Spirit who would let them bring the good news of God's love for mankind to the ends of the earth. That Luke will describe in the second part of his work, the Acts of the Apostles.

John and Us

Mark began his gospel with the "origin story" about Jesus' baptism in the Jordan; then God let his Holy Spirit descend upon him and called him his Son. Matthew and Luke went back to an earlier beginning; in the womb of his mother Jesus was conceived by the Holy Spirit, and God announced through his angels that the child was the Messiah of Israel and his only Son. *The fourth evangelist goes back even further*—he opens with that mysterious beginning alluded to in the first verses of Genesis, "In the beginning..." when God created all things by speaking. God gave expression to something of himself in creation. But this was not recognized by the highest of his creatures, man. Then God spoke to a specific people, his people, "his own," but they too failed to accept him.

Finally he revealed himself totally in a living man—Jesus is the intention of God "become flesh."

Even when reading John's profound introduction or "prologue" (1, 1-18) for the first time, one can hardly help but notice his use of all-embracing, almost philosophical terms, such as word (*logos* for the Greeks), becoming, that which became, life, light, darkness, the world (the *kosmos* of the Greeks), truth, knowledge, contemplation, etc. Interwoven with these terms there are also authentically biblical expressions such as faith, witness, flesh and blood, glory, the Law of Moses, and grace.

Perhaps this rich and mysterious Foreword will become somewhat clearer after we are better acquainted with the book as a whole. Even this will be a strange experience. We meet all kinds of things that remind us of the earlier gospels, but here they are presented very differently. Here, too, the actual story begins with John the Baptist. It does not describe Jesus' baptism directly, but through the words of the Baptist, at the end of his words "as witness" (1, 19-34). Then the evangelist relates how several disciples are attracted to Jesus and immediately confess their faith in him. This is also not what we are used to. At the end of that first chapter, however, the reader will recognize the great titles which the Church has given to Jesus: the Lamb of God who takes away the sin of the world, the Messiah about whom Moses had written in his Law and whom the prophets proclaimed, the king of Israel and the Son of God. Finally, there is a title which Jesus gives himself, Son of Man. (1, 35-51).

Chapter 2 begins the account of Jesus' public ministry. It differs so much from that of the earlier evangelists that we get the feeling that we are in another world. John does not seem to take up the familiar thread again until the passion narrative (18—19).

Our first surprise comes with the miracles which the evangelist relates as well as with the way he treats them. There are seven:

1. The first is the changing of water into wine at a marriage feast in Cana of Galilee (2, 1-11). There are no traces of this event in the other gospels.

2. The cure, at a distance, of the son of a nobleman who lived at Capernaum (4, 46-54) may be a version of a story which we find both in Matthew and Luke (Mt. 8, 5-10; Lk. 7, 1-10).

3. On a sabbath in Jerusalem Jesus cures a paralyzed man (5,

1-15), something which other traditions always relate as taking place in Galilee; here, too, his actions are annoying to the Jewish leaders.

4-5. The story of his feeding the five thousand, followed by that of Jesus walking on the water (6, 5-21), rather closely resembles Mark's account (6, 30-52) which Matthew also follows (14, 13-33).

6. It is again in Jerusalem that the cure of the man born blind takes place. The way Jesus treats him makes us think of the blind man of Bethsaida (Mk. 8, 22), but here it happens on a sabbath.

7. The seventh and most spectacular miracle, the calling of Lazarus from his tomb four days after his burial (11, 1-44), forms in this gospel the occasion for the definitive decision on the part of the Jewish leaders to put Jesus to death. Neither the event nor this elaboration of it is found in the other traditions.

The other surprising thing is that the evangelist allows Jesus himself to comment on some of those miracles. After the third, his commentary consists in a kind of sermon to "the Jews," intended as an answer to their protest against his violating the sabbath rest and against the way he made himself equal to God (5, 16-47). Jesus' commentary on the miracle of the multiplication of the loaves is partly in the form of a discussion with the Jews (6, 22-71). A similar mixture of discussion and sayings also follows the sixth miracle. At the resurrection of Lazarus the explanation is woven into the story. Besides these commentaries of Jesus on his miracles, there are also long conversations with people whom he wants to instruct in the meaning of his mission and his person. His conversation at night with Nicodemus about Christian baptism concludes with a solemn monologue (3, 1-21). Further on Jesus stops to rest at Jacob's well and there speaks about the new kind of worship he comes to bring; he addresses those words to a woman, and a Samaritan at that (4, 1-42). Chapters 7—8 give discussions with the Jewish leaders which were occasioned by his teaching in the temple of Jerusalem. Jesus holds his longest discourse during his last meal with the disciples, after Judas has left the room. Actually it consists more in monologues, interrupted now and then by questions from the disciples, and closes with a solemn prayer to his Father. This conclusion of his "farewell discourse" (13—17) seems to be the climax of John's gospel.

In all these passages Jesus speaks very differently from the way we are accustomed to from the gospels treated in earlier chapters. There he spoke mostly in short and striking sayings, and the longer statements were usually in the form of lively, dramatic descriptions. The Jesus of this gospel almost always speaks solemnly and in an exalted manner, in terms which hardly have anything at all to do with the ordinary colorful side of everyday life. It is often difficult to find a line, a "train of thought," in those rather monotonous discourses. Even more surprising is the way Jesus so often speaks about himself. In the other gospels he does that very seldom. There he is constantly announcing that God is coming to them, and that "happens" in what he says and does. But his instructions and appeals do not say what he *is*. It is up to the people themselves to arrive at the solution of their puzzling suspicions. Here in John it is just the other way around. That richly varied preaching on the theme of God's kingdom gives way to Jesus' solemn proclamations about himself: "I am the good shepherd"; "I am the way, the truth and the life." He also speaks very clearly about his unique relationship with God: "I and the Father are one. . . . The Father is in me and I am in the Father." When reading texts such as these, we should remember that the all-holy proper name of Israel's God, which we pronounce as "Yahweh," was explained to Moses by God himself with the words, "I am who I am" (Ex. 3, 14). Thus we understand what the Jesus of this gospel means when he says, "I tell you most solemnly, before Abraham ever was, I am." Not only on that occasion (8, 58), but on others as well, the Jews understood very well that Jesus was thus making himself equal to God (5, 18; 10, 33).

This all seems very far indeed from the historical reality which we attempted to describe as the "first phase" of this sketch (cf. pp. 297-318). Hence the many questions which the fourth gospel raises. How did the writer arrive at this departure from the traditional presentation of Jesus' ministry? Who was he? What was the background against which he wrote and with what intentions? There are not yet universally accepted answers to such questions. However, we can indicate the direction which research on John's gospel is taking. Let us do that in one sentence, the parts of which we will then explain briefly. *The fourth gospel reflects the prolonged elaboration of the Jesus-event by an exceptionally gifted believer, in a milieu that was both Jewish and at the same time subject to Greek influence.*

The word "prolonged" needs very little commentary. The Church has always regarded the fourth gospel as the last one to have been written. Many data indicate the end of the 1st century. That would mean that some sixty-five to seventy years had elapsed since Jesus' death.

However, such a period of time would be of little importance if nothing had happened. In this case, that which happened was a profound "elaboration of the Jesus-event." By elaboration we mean the attempts to understand and to express what an event or series of events *means*—or, in other words, the *interpretation* of them. We have already seen that the experience of Easter was the occasion for the disciples to interpret what they had experienced when they were with Jesus. We also saw that they continued "elaborating" in this way and that the gospels are apparently the result of it *in narrative form*. Let us recall for the moment some of the peculiarities of that form.

In the way a cure was related, the story showed that in a deeper sense Jesus had healed the storyteller himself and his listeners (cf. p. 349). Mark already knew of two versions of the multiplication of the loaves, both bearing specific characteristics of their repeated celebrations of the Last Supper (cf. pp. 349f.). Likewise, in traditions about Jesus already in circulation he found the explanation of a parable he placed on the Master's lips (cf. pp. 364f.). And it was probably Mark himself who formulated the three predictions of the passion in the light of the course of historical events and the preaching of the Church (cf. pp. 375f.). He gave that preaching the form of an event by making the Holy Spirit visible and by making God's voice audible at Jesus' baptism, clearly an "origin story" (cf. pp. 352f.). We also noticed that in a relatively short time the barren fig tree of a parable took form in a concrete tree along the road to Jerusalem (cf. p. 351).

Matthew shows Jesus giving long "sermons." We saw that both his choice of material and the plan of his gospel were influenced by what he himself experienced—namely the opposition between his community and that of the Jews after Jamnia. That is one of the reasons why in his account of the passion Matthew allows the Jewish nation as a whole to reject its Messiah so expressly (cf. p. 346).

In Luke we referred to two scenes which "describe in anticipation" later developments, in the manner of "origin stories."

Already at the very beginning of his public ministry, in Nazareth, Jesus is rejected by the Jews; already at the time of his calling, Peter makes a "large catch" of fish (cf. p. 390). Likewise, we mentioned Jesus' "words of farewell" in Luke's narration of the Last Supper (cf. p. 391).

In the fourth gospel this elaboration-in-narrative-form continues along the same lines, and in this case in the light of circumstances arising first of all from a "Jewish milieu." We have observed in some detail how the disciples' experiences with Jesus became clear for them in the light of the Scriptures (cf. pp. 324ff.). The Christians retained these as their Holy Book, the deepest secrets of which were now unveiled for the first time. But those Scriptures continued to be the Holy Book of the Jews as well. As the two communities grew farther apart, their respective explanations of the Scriptures also came to oppose each other. We can sense this opposition very well in the fourth gospel. Here, too, we find ouselves in the period after Jamnia, but later than in Matthew. The very fact of confessing Jesus as the Messiah meant expulsion from the synagogue. It is with that same punishment that the evangelist lets the Jews threaten Jesus (9, 22; 12, 42). That is to say, he places the intensely hostile opposition involving him personally back in the situation from which it sprung, the life of Jesus. Nicodemus, the "teacher in Israel" with whom Jesus spoke in the dark of night, seems to represent a group of Jewish theologians to whom the Christian community is saying, ". . . we speak only about what we know and witness only to what we have seen and yet you people reject our evidence" (3, 10-11).

The writer must have been very well versed in Jewish piety, scriptural study and theology. He knows what the rites of the great feasts meant to the pious and also the ways in which they gave expression to their reverence for the Law. In our treatment of Jesus Ben Sirach we saw how that writer reverenced the Law of Moses as the personification of eternal wisdom (p. 200). Thus all kinds of figures of wisdom could also be applied to the Law, such as that of the hostess who invites men to eat of her food and drink of her wine (Prov. 9, 1-6). Sirach himself does this where he says that it is the Law which will give man ". . . the bread of understanding to eat, and the water of wisdom to drink" (15, 3). The Law was the light shining on man's path through life (Ps. 119, 105). As a matter of course, people attached a hymn in praise of the Law to the praises of the glorious sun (Ps. 19). To the extent that pious Jews more and more centered their existence on the Law, all the more did they use those figures derived from the most elementary of life's activities. For the evangelist, all those figures apply to Jesus in a deeper sense. He is the true light, the true bread, the true vine, and likewise the true shepherd, for Jesus is the Messiah. The evangelist is also acquainted with the many Jewish speculations about that future figure, "he who is to come." For the Jews his coming was connected with God's judgment, the resurrection and eternal life. Without denying his belief in a future consummation, the evangelist very strongly insists that the one to come has already appeared, and with him those ultimate realities such as judgment, resurrection and eternal life: "No one who believes in Jesus will be condemned; but whoever refuses to believe is condemned already. . . . Everybody who believes in me has eternal life. . . . I am the resurrection and the life" (3, 18; 6, 47; 11, 25).

The milieu in which the evangelist lived was also subject to "Greek influence." He speaks both the language of the Jews and that of the educated men in the Hellenistic world. One of their favorite concepts was the *Logos,* the divine understanding which penetrates everything and which was sometimes regarded as a kind of intermediate being between the absolute immaterial divine reality and the world of matter. Many people hoped to gain contact with that *Logos* and thus to receive a share of his purely spiritual and immortal life by means of *gnosis*—i.e., knowledge—a secret knowledge which was handed down from primitive times and into which one could be initiated. Only those to whom that truth was granted could rise above the uncertainty and the corruption of this material world without perspective in order to enter into the light and life of the *Logos.* On the one hand, the gospel must have shocked these people with its message that "the Logos had become flesh," in an historical—i.e., material—form of flesh and blood, a man who died on a cross. But at the same time they must have recognized the evangelist as someone who spoke to them in their own language about that which they so intensely sought and longed for.

Finally, the fourth gospel is the work of "an exceptionally gifted believer." In the first place he was granted a very close contact with what we called the "Jesus-event." It consisted in daily

association with Jesus as he preached—provided that the evangelist was in fact John, the son of Zebedee, who belonged to the
group of the twelve and who was one of the three apostles closest to Jesus, the other two being his brother James and Peter. In
that case John was a very old man when he wrote his gospel, probably at Ephesus in Asia Minor, the cosmopolitan city where Paul
had worked for years and the residence of an influential Jewish
community. Then that process of "elaboration" would have taken
place in this one gifted man, who seems to refer to himself in his
story as "the beloved disciple" (19, 26 to mention but one place).
Martinus Nijhoff alluded to this in the last verses of his sonnet
"Johannes." The following free translation is an attempt to communicate something of its depth:

> Me he had loved in life,
> But when he died
> He gave so much that years past ere
> I dared to speak of the abundance.

But there are important specialists in Johannine studies who find
this supposition very difficult to correlate with all the data. Some of
them propose a second, later John as the writer. It seems that no
satisfactory answer to this question is possible unless new data can
be uncovered. The proponents of that second John must concede,
however, that he was in possession of first-hand information. This
is evident from his accurate knowledge of the situation in the Jerusalem of Jesus' day which comes out in many incidental references
to details. Furthermore, he must have known and felt something of
the manner in which a faithful disciple went on experiencing
through the years the privilege of that intimacy.

It is certain that the writer (let us call him John from now on)
had received a second gift, even more important than his direct or
indirect knowledge of the facts. We mean the gift which enabled
him more deeply than any other disciple to penetrate the *meaning*
of the person and work of Jesus and to express that in words and
figures which will never become old-fashioned, for they are both
Jewish and Greek, both biblical and universally human. If believing means that one perceives in certain events a "dimension" in
light of which they make an appeal to his innermost "self," we are

certainly justified in calling John an exceptionally gifted believer. Through the centuries, Christians, the learned as well as the simple faithful, have admired him as such.

In our day John fascinates biblical scholars whose historical studies have given them some insight into the endless complications arising both from the Jewish theology and from the Greek speculations with which he was confronted. They especially admire the simplicity, both profound and exalted, with which he gives expression to his vision of Jesus. When compared to the faithful of past generations, some modern believers are at a disadvantage because of their less highly developed *feeling for poetic symbolism.* This is certainly the case in "matters of faith," where they ask whether a given event really took place rather than search for its meaning. One of the reasons is that they are *poorly acquainted* with the great symbols in which the faithful of the *Old Testament* were accustomed to express themselves and celebrate what they experienced. Therefore, it seems useful to conclude this sketch with a bit more detailed treatment of what we called John's *elaboration of the Jesus-event.*

Let us begin with the best known of his seven miracle stories—the first, the changing of water into wine at the marriage feast of Cana, and the last, the raising of Lazarus. But first let us make a preliminary observation. The transfiguration on the mountain, which the other three evangelists narrate, does not appear in John. In Mark that scene is connected with Jesus' passion simply by its position, for it immediately follows Peter's profession of faith and Jesus' first prediction of his passion and death (Mk. 8, 27—9, 6). Luke makes that connection even clearer by letting the glorified Jesus speak with Moses and Elijah on the mountain about "his *exodus* which he was to accomplish in Jerusalem" (9, 31). John seems to have carried that line of thought further. He omits the transfiguration, because for him the divine glory of Jesus is first revealed in his passion and death. Through these Jesus gave himself completely. That was love in its most perfect form and thus the perfect revelation of God. "Lifted up" on his cross, Jesus draws the whole of mankind to himself in order to form a community of love. His death is "the hour" of fulfillment, at once the crowning of Jesus' life and the climax of history for which Israel and mankind had longed.

Though omitting the story of the transfiguration, John nevertheless does include moments before the passion in which he gives a glimpse of Jesus' final glory. For him Jesus' miracles are "signs," not only in the sense of the credentials of his mission, but also anticipations of what would be fully revealed at his death. This is one of the motives behind the story of the "wedding at Cana." The reader should remember that ever since Hosea it was traditional to live and sing of Israel's relationship with God—the Covenant—in terms of betrothal and marriage. They liked to describe the climax of God's history with Israel, the "Messianic age," as a *wedding feast:* in the person of the Messiah God would bind himself forever to his people who would never again be unfaithful. And at that feast there would be an abundance of *wine,* the drink which rejoices men's hearts and thus always has a place in descriptions of Messianic salvation. When we add to this the religious insight that Jesus had replaced the Jewish cult and its many purification rites with a new worship, which John in his own way calls "worship in spirit and truth" (4, 23: that "hour" has now dawned), then we get some idea of what he wished to express in that story about Jesus at the wedding of Cana (2, 1-11).

In the preceding verses we heard the disciples confess that Jesus is the awaited Messiah (1, 35-49). The Messianic age has dawned; thus there must be a wedding. And so there is, at Cana. But there the wine runs out. Jesus cannot follow the suggestion of the faithful, in the person of Mary, for he knows that the Messianic age will not come until "his hour," the moment of his death. Nevertheless, he gives them wine as a "sign" of what will take place then. He replaces the water of the Jewish cult, which only purifies the outside and is not a source of joy, with an enormous quantity of wine. Then he seems to be identified with the figure of the bridegroom who saved this real wine until last, until now. Thus at the very beginning Jesus reveals his glory in the first work he performs, a "sign."

Quite a lot more could be said about the rich symbolism condensed in the eleven verses making up this story. It is of course more than just a story; it is the fruit of deep intuitions and continuous meditation on the Christian mystery. Therefore, people do the evangelist an injustice when they ask whether he is describing everything just as it happened that day in Cana. John is indeed concerned with a fact, but that fact is Jesus, and, in particular, Jesus as a manifestation of the divine mystery through his self-giving love, that inexhaustible spring of new life for mankind. Perhaps John got the idea for this narrative form from stories circulating among his Greek friends in Asia Minor. There it was said that the god Dionysus sometimes delighted his devotees by making pure wine flow from a spring dedicated to him instead of water. But such a supposition is not strictly necessary, for we saw that in Jewish tradition both wine and the wedding feast belonged to the usual symbolism of the Messianic era. Furthermore, Jesus himself had used those figures. In response to the question why the disciples did not fast, Jesus had asked a question in return: "Can the friends of the bridegroom fast while the bridegroom is with them?" In his own mysterious manner he was telling them who he was. John the Baptist had not drunk any wine because he was to announce, in the manner of his many predecessors, that Israel was unfaithful and thus not ready for the Messianic wedding feast. However, John did call himself "the friend of the bridegroom," by whom he meant Jesus (Jn. 3, 29). Furthermore, there was Jesus' statement about "the new wine in new wineskins" (Mk. 2, 22) and other sayings and parables in which Jesus had used the well-known image of the wedding feast. At the Last Supper with his disciples he had given them wine to drink with the words, "This is my blood." In so doing he gave them his own life.

That central theme of the gospel is expressed very dramatically in the seventh "sign," the raising of Lazarus. Most of chapter 11 is devoted to this narrative (1-44), but in order to see its function in the whole composition one should read the account of its consequences (45-53) and the allusions to it in the following chapter (12, 9-11. 18-19). The evangelist explicitly presents this raising of a corpse already in a state of decay as the direct occasion for the Jewish authorities' decision to put Jesus to death. With this John reaches a dramatic climax. Here life and death are involved, so to speak, in a decisive duel: Jesus, life itself, brings a man back from death, and for that reason men decide to put him to death. In this way John unveils the deepest dimension of that first Good Friday. It was the experience of the first disciples and of all who came after them that this Jesus, raised on a cross by men, granted a new and eternal life to all who believe in him.

When one has once become familiar with the "dramatic intentions" of this evangelist (see likewise the dramatic movements or details woven into the Lazarus story itself and those in many others as well—e.g., the cure of the blind man in chapter 9), he will no longer be shocked by a comparison of John with the synoptic gospels. Although they relate more facts from Jesus' last days, they do not devote one word to the spectacular raising of Lazarus, nor do they even seem to know anything about this direct occasion leading to Jesus' death. This would be understandable if the story were a creation of John himself. But it is not a *creatio ex nihilo,* "a creation from nothing," for a further comparison reveals that John seems to reproduce the same evangelical traditions as they do. All three of them know stories about Jesus' power to raise the dead (cf. Mt. 11, 5 and the stories about the daughter of Jairus, Mk. 5, 22-43, and the youth of Naim, Lk. 7, 11-17). They, too, know that Jesus was condemned to death because of Messianic expectations and thus the spirit of rebellion which could result from his preaching and miracles (cf. Lk. 19, 37: as Jesus entered Jerusalem, "people spread their cloaks in the road, and . . . they joyfully began to praise God at the top of their voices for all the miracles they had seen"). John only presented these traditions in a more concrete and, above all, more dramatic form by making the raising of Lazarus, who had already been dead three days, the decisive climax of his ministry (cf. the "climactic" role played by a Lazarus returning to life in the parable of Lk. 16, 19-31). In John's composition, this last miracle seems to be the most "meaningful" of the seven "signs" symbolizing what Jesus does for men and what he is. Raising a corpse is something which only the living God himself can do. Therefore, in this last of the signs, Jesus' glory shines through most clearly. This chapter on Lazarus is thus an appropriate preparation for the conclusion of the first part of the gospel (1—12), sometimes called "the book of signs," serving at the same time as a transition to the second part, "the book of glory" (13—20).

That second part contains the narrative of what happened when Jesus' "hour" had come. It gives the stories of the passion and of the appearances of the risen Lord (18—20). These stories are preceded by a commentary on, or rather a revelation of, their meaning given by Jesus himself during the Last Supper (13—17). These inexhaustibly rich chapters are a splendid illustration of what we called in the above definition an elaboration of the Jesus-event. The following remarks may perhaps guide the reader in his meditation.

He might begin with a saying of Jesus on the nature of his mission among men, recorded by Mark. This evangelist gave it a place after the third prediction of the passion, introducing it with the request by Zebedee's sons for the highest places in the kingdom: "When the other ten heard this, they began to feel indignant with James and John, so Jesus called them to him and said to them, 'You know that among the pagans their so-called rulers lord it over them, and their great men make their authority felt. This is not to happen among you. No; anyone who wants to become great among you must be your servant, and anyone who wants to be first among you must be slave to all. For the Son of Man himself did not come to be served but to serve and to give his life as a ransom for many' " (10, 42-45).

Luke had already "elaborated" these words somewhat by letting them be spoken during the Last Supper. Jesus has already expressed the meaning of his death as a gift of himself by giving the disciples his body and blood in the bread and wine. Besides describing the secular authorities in a bit more friendly manner and giving the impression that a Church community already exists with a semblance of rank and precedence, Luke's formulation also suggests that Jesus served his disciples at table: "Among pagans it is the kings who lord it over them, and those who have authority over them are given the title Benefactor. This must not happen with you. No; the greatest among you must behave as if he were the youngest, the leader as if he were the one who serves. For who is the greater: the one at the table or the one who serves? The one at table, surely? Yet here am I among you as one who serves" (22, 25-27).

That connection between the eucharistic meal and Jesus' intention to serve his disciples, only suggested by Luke, is given a dramatic form by John. At the Last Supper "Jesus knew that the hour had come for him to pass from this world to the Father. He had always loved those who were his in the world, but now he showed how perfect his love was." At this point the Christian reader expects the institution of the eucharist to follow—"institution" because the disciples were to repeat that symbolic representation of Jesus' death. But here John describes another gesture that is likewise to be repeated: "Jesus knew that the Father had put everything into his hands, and that he had come from God and was returning to God, and he got up from table, removed his outer garment . . . and began to wash the disciples' feet." We should remember that this was a humiliating task, so much so that it could not be demanded of free citizens. It was something only slaves were made to do. Introducing it by the words "He showed them how perfect his love was," John clearly regards this as the most moving expression of the meaning of Jesus' death. And as a commemoration of that death, "you should wash each other's feet" and do as "I have done to you."

After Judas departs into the night, Jesus begins to speak confidentially with his disciples. We should think here of the meaning which the Passover had for the Jews. At that intimate celebration the father could go on until deep in the night speaking with his family and the members of his household about the ancient story, about the meaning of all its details and about the expectations it evoked. This is the way John imagines the Last Supper. Jesus explains what his own "passing" means for those who believe in him. The conversation concludes with an unforgettable prayer in which Jesus proclaims his dedication to his Father and to mankind.

For that reason this prayer is appropriately called "the priestly prayer." It may have received its present form during the many years John meditated on the mystery of Jesus while celebrating it with his fellow Christians. The prayer seems to express in Johannine terms what Jesus felt during the moments of the Last Supper when, after a thanksgiving prayer to his Father, he gave himself to his disciples. The simple words and gestures which the synoptic gospels record appear here in the form of a solemn prayer. Asking his Father to sanctify his disciples who are to be sent into the world, Jesus says, "And for their sake I consecrate myself, so that they too may be consecrated in truth." This was Jesus' intention when he gave his very self, flesh and blood, to the disciples. In the synoptic texts this was done both "for the many" and "for you"; here Jesus consecrates himself "for the sake of" his disciples, both present and future, left in the world. According to Matthew, Jesus' self-giving was "for the remission of sins." This intention is reflected in the words "that they too may be consecrated in truth." The last part of the prayer seems to reflect Jesus' desire for union with his disciples. In the other gospels this was expressed in his invitation, "Take and eat. . . . Drink all of you from this. . . ." Elsewhere, in a directly eucharistic text (6, 56-57), John used the verbs "abide" and "live": "He who eats my flesh and drinks my blood abides in me and I in him. As the living Father sent me, and I live because of the Father, so he who eats me will live because of me." His priestly prayer seems to express this desire for consummate communion even more strongly, particularly in the elliptic "I in them" (verse 23), repeated at the end as a final refrain.

Even more clearly than elsewhere in John's gospel, in these chapters Jesus addresses all who believe in him. To put it in modern terms, here "the Christ of faith" is speaking. That is why Christendom was so grateful for the fourth gospel, coming after the other three. It shows us how the others are to be read—not as documents which record facts from the past, but as gospels in the real sense of that word. Hence the "us" in the title of this final section.